ROYAL HISTORICAL SOCIETY
STUDIES IN HISTORY
SERIES
No. 48

THE
D'ALIGRES DE LA RIVIÈRE:

Servants of the Bourbon State
in the
Seventeenth Century

Ce Grand Chancellier, marche sur les pas de ses Ayeuix, pour en renouveller, tous les jours la Memoire, et comme sa Vertu se voit aussi grandqieuse, On peut en le voyant aprendre leurs Hystoires

Etienne d'Aligre III

THE
D'ALIGRES DE LA RIVIÈRE:
Servants of the Bourbon State
in the
Seventeenth Century

D.J. Sturdy

ROYAL HISTORICAL SOCIETY
THE BOYDELL PRESS · WOODBRIDGE
ST MARTIN'S PRESS · NEW YORK

© D. J. Sturdy 1986

First published 1986

Published by
The Boydell Press
an imprint of Boydell & Brewer Ltd
PO Box 9 Woodbridge Suffolk IP12 3DF
and St Martin's Press Inc
175 Fifth Avenue New York NY10010
for
The Royal Historical Society
University College London WC1

UK ISBN 0 86193 205 6
US ISBN 0-312-18079-9

Printed in Great Britain by Short Run Press Ltd, Exeter

CONTENTS

	Page
List of Illustrations	vi
Preface	vii
Abbreviations	ix
Introduction	1
1 The Early History of the Aligre Family	6
2 Etienne d'Aligre II: His Life and Career	20
3 The Property and Family of Etienne d'Aligre II	46
4 Etienne d'Aligre III and the Valtelline Crisis	77
5 Etienne d'Aligre III in Normandie and Languedoc, 1634-1646	94
6 Etienne d'Aligre III and the 'Frondes': Problems of a Royalist	120
7 Etienne d'Aligre III: His Career to the Chancellorship	143
8 The Family and Fortune of Etienne d'Aligre III: before and after the 'Frondes'	165
9 The Family and Fortune of Etienne d'Aligre III in the Last Phase of his Life	187
10 The Family after Etienne d'Aligre III	205
Conclusion	219
Genealogical Appendices	228
Bibliography	231
Index	244

LIST OF ILLUSTRATIONS

MAP   Page
Principal Land Holdings of Etienne d'Aligre
II, 1635   54

GRAPHS
Fig 1 Etienne d'Aligre III: Investment in 'Rentes',
1626-49   183
   2 Etienne d'Aligre III: Rentes Constituées,
1648-70   195

PLATES
Etienne d'Aligre III   *Frontispiece*
Etienne d'Aligre II   *facing* p. 20

The Plates appear by permission of the Bibliothèque Nationale, Paris

PREFACE

My thanks are due to many people, but to none more than Professor R. Pillorget and Madame S. Pillorget, who have given wholeheartedly of their friendship, advice and encouragement over the years. Other scholars assisted me at various stages; in this regard I record my gratitude to Professor R. Mousnier, Mademoiselle M. Foisil, Professor J-M. Constant, and Monsieur G. Dethan. Monsieur G. Fessard of Courville-sur-Eure gave me valuable guidance as to the history of Chartres and its region, and allowed me to consult his private archive which contains material on the d'Aligres. A university teacher based in Northern Ireland must rely heavily on assistance from award-granting bodies if he is to get to France regularly to carry out research. I am grateful to the British Academy, the Twenty-Seven Foundation, the Sir Ernest Cassel Education Trust, and the Research Committee of the New University of Ulster, for their assistance. The New University of Ulster, through its study-leave scheme, provides opportunities for extended periods of research; I have benefited immensely from two such periods. At every stage I have received unstinting support and help from my wife. She now knows as much about the d'Aligres as I do.

D.J. Sturdy
Coleraine

The Society records its gratitude to the following, whose generosity made possible the initiation of this series: The British Academy; The Pilgrim Trust; The Twenty-Seven Foundation; The United States Embassy bicentennial funds; The Wolfson Trust; several private donors.

ABBREVIATIONS

A.A.E., C.P.	Archives du Ministère des Affaires Etrangères: Correspondence Politique
A.A.E., M.D.	Archives du Ministère des Affaires Etrangères: Mémoires et Documents
A.D.	Archives Départementales
A.G.	Archives Historiques du Ministère de la Guerre
A.N.	Archives Nationales
A.N., M.C.	Archives Nationales: Minutier Central
B.N.	Bibliothèque Nationale

INTRODUCTION

In a side chapel of the church of Saint Germain l'Auxerrois in Paris stand two statues of a father and son: Etienne d'Aligre II (1560-1635) and Etienne d'Aligre III (1592-1677), sieurs de la Rivière. They are the outstanding figures in a family that was prominent in French national public life throughout much of the seventeenth and eighteenth centuries. The statues depict their subjects in middle to later years. Etienne II reclines in relaxed but splendid manner and reads from a large tome; he is dressed sumptuously and wears a ruff. By contrast, the costume of his son is austere; he kneels in an attitude of religious devotion, one hand pressed to his breast, the other clasping what is presumably a prayer book or other pious work.[1] The elaborate treatment of the subjects and their presence in one of the most patrician churches of Paris, indicate that they were no ordinary individuals. They issued from a provincial family which even as late as the 1590s was still based in Chartres and as yet had given no hint that within a few decades it would be exercising influence at the highest levels of the state. That such a change occurred, that the Aligres (the 'de' was added in 1624) rose speedily in royal service, was the outcome of the careers of the two Etiennes. By the late 1600s the family was so eminent that the duc de Saint Simon felt obliged to devote several pages of his *Mémoires* to its history and achievements.[2] The father and son are the central figures of this book. It ranges far beyond their lives and careers, but they are the twin points from which so much else radiates.

Why devote a book to this family? Part of the answer has already been suggested: during the 1600s and 1700s they were closely involved in building and shaping the Bourbon state. In a set of introductory remarks it is not possible to do more than indicate some of the areas in which d'Aligres were active, the point being that over a hundred years or so they served the crown in almost every branch of policy: international relations, finance, the armed forces, relations with the catholic church, and so on. It is in this regard that the two Etiennes are so important, for both followed varied careers which took them to one of the most exalted charges, which placed them in innermost, policy-making royal councils and close to the person of the king himself: the chancellorship of France. In their role as servants of

---

[1] The statues are by Laurent Magnier; see M. Baurit et J. Hillairet, *Saint-Germain l'Auxerrois* (Paris, 1955), 71-2, and M. Baurit, *Saint-Germain l'Auxerrois, son Histoire, ses Oeuvres d'Art* (Paris, 1952), 69.

[2] A. de Boislisle (éd.), *Mémoires de Saint Simon,* xxii (Paris, 1910), 252-63.

the Bourbons, agents of their policies, the d'Aligres deserve to be studied. Very little has been published on them. Articles in the standard biographical dictionaries are usually sound on the two Etiennes, but can be unreliable on other members of the family. Most recently, for instance, those by Prévost in the *Dictionnaire de Biographie Française* on Louis and Michel d'Aligre, confuse Louis with an uncle of the same name, running two lives into one, and Michel with a cousin. There exist one or two articles on d'Aligres who were *abbés* of Saint Jacques de Provins. Otherwise, apart from articles by the writer, there is nothing. This wealthy and influential family has been left almost entirely untouched by historians.

The historical significance of the d'Aligres is by no means exhausted by an analysis of their public careers. Several studies exist dealing with individual families and their contribution to the French state; they range from André's great work on the le Telliers (of particular interest in the present context, since they were closely related to the d'Aligres),[3] to more recent publications such as those of Bourgeon on the Colberts[4] and Dethan on the Mazarins.[5] The strength of such works is that in addition to relating the story of their particular subjects, they are able to treat general historical problems by bringing to bear upon them precise examples and concrete evidence drawn from the history of a certain family. Similarly, in this book on the d'Aligres attempts will be made to assess in what degree the material that it contains is of general relevance to our grasp of French society under the *ancien régime*.

One topic upon which the experiences of the d'Aligres can prove helpful concerns the relationship between the state and society in France. As a regime constructs its administrative machinery and appoints the necessary personnel, it can find itself in a paradoxical position: on the one hand the nature of the society over which it rules strongly influences its choice of personnel, especially if the social structure is rigidly hierarchical, supplying well-defined elites; on the other, if the regime selects its agents from less traditional sources, it can help to change the structure of society. In other words, the state machine may be a reflection of the social structure or a source of its modification. In the aftermath of the wars of religion the Bourbons aspired to stabilise society (which would imply a reinforcement of traditional social values and structures), yet needed more and more

[3]L. André, *Michel le Tellier et l'Organisation de l'Armée Monarchique* (Paris, 1906).

[4]J-L. Bourgeon, *Les Colbert avant Colbert* (Paris, 1973).

[5]G. Dethan, *Mazarin et ses Amis* (Paris, 1968); G. Dethan, *Mazarin* (Paris, 1981).

agents with which to do so. Where were they to be found? On what basis should some be advanced and others retarded? What rewards should be given to those who were favoured? What would be the effects upon French society? Many of the social tensions that were to develop in the France of the Bourbons derived from this predicament: was it possible to reconcile an expanding administrative machine and a traditional social structure? The history of the d'Aligres relates very much to this theme. Coming from a solid but unpretentious background in Chartres, they were chosen and promoted by Henri IV, Louis XIII and Louis XIV. The path along which they advanced was far from smooth and uniform; yet they formed one of those dynasties whose success in royal service both illustrated and heightened the problem of the state and society.

Another, but closely related historical problem which can be raised in the context of the d'Aligres, is the nature of social status. Given that the crown could raise a family to the nobility in order to use it in important royal service, were there nevertheless other considerations that could come into play? For example, what role did wealth play in social status? It would be misleading to suggest that social advancement resulted from a simple process: royal service, followed by a title and wealth, followed by higher social status. So straightforward a mechanism might have operated in the early stages of a family's service to the king, but nuances and variations would soon manifest themselves. The wealth of a family could accumulate sufficiently to give them economic independence from the king. To what purpose could that wealth then be put? The question was complicated by the fact that in the seventeenth century the French economy was becoming a cash economy, more and more transactions at every level of society being conducted through the medium of money. Even the government was slowly coming to accept that the range of its policies was severely governed by the availability of cash or credit. There were many implications here for the nobility, especially for those whose access to ready cash was limited, perhaps because their income was largely in the form of goods or services. A further complicating factor sprang from the general shortage of specie in France (as elsewhere in Europe) and from the fluctuations in the value of currency, especially during the middle decades of the seventeenth century when the government manipulated currency to meet military and political needs. As the seventeenth century progressed, so there appeared to develop an ever closer link between social status and wealth. Nobles burdened by heavy debts and lacking wealth either in the form of cash, or in property that could be converted into cash or credit, were apt to find themselves in such dire economic straits as could threaten their status. The problem was accentuated as the royal court became more elaborate, especially under Louix XIV, for attendance at court was exceedingly expensive; yet failure to be present at Versailles or one of the other palaces could severely damage one's reputation and status. Clearly wealth was becoming not only desirable, but necessary to the maintenance of great social status. In itself it could not confer social distinction, but it was becoming an indispensable buttress. The d'Aligres were fortunate to possess a vast fortune by the late seventeenth century, created chiefly by the two Etiennes. Many pages in this book will be devoted to that fortune; to its origins, its expansion, the alterations made in its compositon from time to time, its administration. Equally, attention will be given to the use made of their money and land by the d'Aligres as they reinforced their social status by judicious use of their resources. Whatever their weaknesses in other respects, the d'Aligres never lost their talent for amassing wealth and then putting it to the most effective use.

In recent years family history has passed into vogue among historians. It has proved a fructuous area of study, our understanding of past societies profiting enormously. Among the many techniques that can be brought to the subject is that of the examination of a single family over many decades. Thereby, a great deal of exact information can be acquired and an emphasis placed on the 'human' dimension of the subject. The d'Aligres as much as any of their contemporaries were deeply conscious of belonging to a family and of having responsibilities to future generations as well as to their own. To no less extent were they aware of family history, and conscious that their roots went deep into the past; this is shown, for example, by the care with which they safeguarded family documents, some going back to the 1400s. Each generation of d'Aligres, and especially the head of the family, had to cope with a succession of issues essential to the well-being of all: the education of the children, the preparations for their careers, their marriages, the disposition of the family fortune on the death of the head. Such obligations were foreseeable and were the stuff of the long-term development of any family. But unpredictable crises could arise, and the d'Aligres were to have their fair share of them. Any family could be faced with extinction if the male line failed; this fate confronted the d'Aligres more than once. Infant mortality and other forms of premature death could strike at every level of society; this was to play its part in d'Aligre history. Most families had their 'black sheep' who brought shame and disgrace; so did the d'Aligres. Whether the family is defined in broad or narrow terms, it exercised a powerful influence on its members throughout their lives. As an institution much still remains to be learnt about it. The d'Aligres are one source to be exploited.

A few words on the structure of this book are in order. Chapter 1 covers the fifteenth and sixteenth centuries. It sets the Aligres in their social and economic context in Chartres and traces thair careers and ascension within the limited opportunities provided by the town. The second chapter deals with the career of Etienne II from his earliest days during the wars of religion, through to his rise to the chancellorship. It shows the change of heart which he underwent during the religious wars, moving from the league to the side of Henri IV, thereafter being a successful and effective servant of the first Bourbon king of France. Chapter 3 turns to family matters and the fortune which Etienne II acquired. It will doubtless make heavier reading than preceding chapters for there are technical details spelled out on finance and land; yet it is here that some of the most reliable information on some of the general problems just discussed is to be found. Chapters 4, 5, 6 and 7 together describe and analyse the career of Etienne III. The treatment is chronological, and in chapter 7 there is a general discussion of the significance of Etienne III's career. The next two chapters deal with Etienne III's family and fortune, dividing at about 1660. This is a useful if rough and ready division, because in the late 1640s and 1650s he was both expanding his possessions and having to deal with a number of family matters (mainly marriages and deaths), whereas after 1660, now conscious of his advancing years, he was organising his wealth with a view to its division after his death. The size of his fortune is estimated and its division discussed. Chapter 10 begins with two of Etienne III's sons, Charles (whose life in its earlier stages appears in chapter 9), and François. It proceeds to a survey of the family in the eighteenth century, depicting the principal features of a family now exceedingly wealthy and prestigious, and firmly established among the elite of France.

1
THE EARLY HISTORY OF THE ALIGRE FAMILY

The Background in Chartres

This account begins in Chartres in the fifteenth and sixteenth centuries, for it was there that the Aligres[1] laid the foundations of their later fortunes. The first reference to a member of the family is in the 1440s when a Jean Aligre from Voves, a village twenty miles or so to the south, was a resident of Chartres.[2] Thereafter, he and his descendants worked themselves into positions of influence in the public institutions of the town, creating a local reputation long before they moved onto the national plane.

Chartres owed much of its importance to geographical factors.[3] Situated on the banks of the Eure, it served as the commercial centre for the fertile counties of Le Perche and La Beauce, and supplied grain from that region as well as wine from the vineyards of the Loire, to Rouen and Paris. Boats on their return transported spices and salt to Chartres. Its four chief fairs held on the feast days of Our Lady[4] handled mainly commodities in which local industry specialised: lace, skins, cloth and metal work. Flourishing guilds regulated those industries, especially the *métier de la rivière* which monopolised the production of lace, an activity employing some 2,000 people by the 1620s.[5] Geography likewise imposed military responsibilities on Chartres. Since the town lay within easy reach of Paris, the Loire, the Seine and Normandie, and since it was the key to controlling the great grain resources of Le Perche and La Beauce, the crown often garrisoned troops there, especially in the sixteenth century. The king could not afford to let so strategically important a centre fall into hostile hands. The response of Chartres to the wars of religion will be discussed shortly, but at this point it can be noted that during the wars

---

[1] The name was spelt different ways: Haligre, Halligre, Aligre; the final form will be used throughout this study.

[2] B[ibliothèque] N[ationale, Paris], Dossiers Bleus 11:275, f.21; P. Chasles, 'Mouvement social de Chartres au XVIe siècle', *Revue des Deux Mondes,* xxii (1848), 624.

[3] The following passages are based on Chasles, 'Mouvement social', 607-33 and E. de Lépinois, *Histoire de Chartres* (2 vols., Chartres, 1854-8), *passim.*

[4] Purification 2 February, Annunciation 25 March, Assumption 15 August, Nativity 25 December.

[5] Lépinois, *Histoire de Chartres*, i, 386.

royal troops were often stationed there. Moreover, Henri III stayed in Chartres on numerous occasions: it was distant enough from Paris for him to feel secure when he found the going difficult, but was near enough for him to remain in touch with events in the capital.[6] Henri IV used Chartres as the base of his operations from 1591 until his entry into Paris in 1594, and of course he was crowned in Chartres cathedral instead of the customary Reims which was still in enemy hands.

As a centre for the administration of law Chartres did not merit front-rank status, being overshadowed by Paris, Orléans and Rouen, It nevertheless possessed an array of courts whose rivalries will cause no surprise to a student of early modern France. The complexities, not to say the confusion in the legal direction of the country, where the functions of courts overlapped to an astonishing extent, were a source of bewilderment to contemporaries and historians alike. Until 1552 the senior institution in Chartres was that of the *bailliage* whose personnel, which included the *bailli*, one or more *lieutenants,* and a team of *receveurs*, *auditeurs*, *enquêteurs* and *conseillers*, had responsibilities that were partly judicial in the narrow sense, but also administrative, financial and military.[7] Other courts included those of the *prévôté* and the *prévôté des maréchaux*; the distinction in the competence of these two bodies was hazy in the extreme, for both dealt with civil and criminal justice and possessed certain administrative duties. Then there was the court of the *élection* of Chartres. It was occupied with matters relating to the *taille* and other aspects of taxation. Finally the *grenier à sel* had its court. The *grenier* organised the distribution of salt, collected *gabelle* (a tax on salt), and judged disputes arising from the tax. To this collection of assemblies yet another was added in 1552 when Chartres was selected as the seat of one of the new *présidiaux*, whose formation was promulgated that year.[8] They were conceived as intermediate bodies between the *parlements* and the *bailliages,* one objective being thereby to speed up the process of justice. So many appeals from the *bailliages* to the *parlements* had accumulated, that long delays in the resolution of disputes were commonplace. Henceforth the new institutions could take some of the weight from the *parlements* by settling a proportion of the appeals. As was normally the case in the sixteenth century there was also a financial motive for

---

[6]Between 1581 and 1584 he made eight visits to Chartres.

[7]R. Doucet, *Les Institutions de la France au XVIe Siècle* (Paris, 1948), i, 251-64; M. Marion, *Dictionnaire des Institutions de la France aux XVIIe et XVIIIe Siècles* (Paris, 1923), 32-4.

[8]Doucet, *Les Institutions,* i, 264-7; Marion, *Dictionnaire,* 449-51.

their foundation. To a hard-pressed regime short of funds they provided yet more offices to be put up for sale. The location of a *présidial* in Chartres raised the town in the legal hierarchy, for outside of the *parlements* the new courts were among the topmost levels of provincial judicial assemblies. For instance, any appeals from *présidiaux* went directly to a *parlement*, not to a third body.

If Chartres could lay claim to any special distinction it was in the variety and liveliness of its ecclesiastical life. As the seat of a bishop and the site of one of the great cathedrals of Europe, it dominated ecclesiastical affairs between Paris and the Loire. The architectural splendours of the cathedral should not be allowed to overshadow unduly some of the other churches in the town, especially Saint André and Saint Pierre. Within their parishes lived some of the wealthiest of the citizens, who played an impressive role in charitable work organised by the church. The chief medieval religious orders had their houses in Chartres, as did the Knights Templar before their dissolution, and the Knights of Saint John. During the period of the French counter-reformation yet more religious houses were established, several belonging to orders only recently founded.[9] The impact of protestantism upon the town will be considered later, but at this juncture it can be be noted that the strength of catholicism there was sufficient to keep the community overwhelmingly within the fold. Protestantism made marginal headway, but never threatened the pre-eminence of catholicism.

The survey of Chartres so far has sought to adumbrate its chief corporate activities founded on commerce, industry, law and the church. Beyond this it is difficult to go. Chartres still awaits systematic study by historians equipped with modern techniques of research.[10] The dynamics of life there, the structure of society, the interaction between various groups, their attitudes, their material standing, the rise and fall of the population, the vicissitudes of the economy, are all subjects about which our knowledge remains fragmentary.[11] As we begin to turn away from the environment of

[9]The new foundations included the Capucins 1585, the Minimes 1615, the Carmélites 1619, the Ursulines 1626; later houses included the Visitandines 1647, the Filles de la Providence 1655 and the Soeurs de Sainte Marie 1692 (Lépinois, *Histoire de Chartres*, ii, 528-40).

[10]Since this was written there has appeared the thesis of C. Billot, *Chartres aux XIVe Siècles, une Ville et son Plat Pays* (thesis defended 1980).

[11]Even the size of the population is unknown; between 10,000 and 15,000 is probably about right; other towns in this category were Beauvais (P. Goubert, *Cent Mille Provinciaux au XVIIe Siècle: Beauvais et le Beauvaisis de 1600 à 1730* [Paris, 1968], 29), Arles and Toulon (R. Pillorget, *Les Mouvements Insurrectionnels de Provence entre 1596 et 1715* [Paris, 1975], 14).

Chartres, therefore, and direct attention towards the Aligres themselves, the story as it unfolds has a significance beyond the history of the family alone. It may enable at least one shaft of light to be projected into that darker and lesser-known region, the social and economic history of Chartres.

The Aligre Family

Reference has already been made to Jean Aligre living in Chartres in the 1440s. He held the office of *contrôleur du grenier à sel*.[12] Chartres lay within that area of France known as the *pays de grandes gabelles,* which is to say that its inhabitants were obliged to purchase fixed quantities of salt annually, sold under government monopoly. In effect, the *gabelle* was therefore a form of direct taxation in disguise.[13] As the institutions charged with the sale of salt and collection of the tax, the *greniers* handled large sums of money. Their officers found plentiful opportunities to line their own pockets, and so lucrative were those posts (few other provincial offices were as profitable) that competition for them was fierce. The *grenier* at Chartres was staffed by a *président,* a *lieutenant,* a *procureur du roi,* a *grenetier,* and a variable number of *conseillers, contrôleurs,* and *mesureurs.* In the 1400s and 1500s many Aligres were officers of the *grenier.* Several were *grenetiers:* Jean Aligre's son Guillemin in 1474, another Jean in 1499, a Guillaume Aligre in 1529, and another Guillaume in 1537. Gérard Aligre was a *mesureur* in 1546, while in 1556 a Claude Aligre became *grenetier.* So the pattern continued into the second half of the century, the Aligres tightening their grip on the *grenier* which had almost become a family preserve.[14] By the late 1500s it was the most important single source of their income; more than anything else it provided them with the financial resources indispensable to their social advancement in the area.

Some Aligres may have been involved in the lace industry, although the evidence is highly suspect. When Etienne d'Aligre II became chancellor of France, somebody scrawled verse on a church wall in Chartres to the effect that d'Aligre had been a lace merchant earlier in his career. Again, in an undated letter François d'Aligre, *abbé* of Saint Jacques de Provins (1620-1712) warned his nephew

---

[12] See n.2.

[13] J. Pasquier, *L'Impôt des Gabelles en France aux XVII{^{e}} et XVIII{^{e}} Siècles* (Paris, 1905), 6-7.

[14] Lépinois, *Histoire de Chartres,* i, 67-71.

Etienne d'Aligre IV (1660-1725) that, 'toute votre richesse ne rendra pas notre famille plus ancienne, et j'aurois cru plus à propos de ne rien aller chercher au-dessus de notre premier chancelier [Etienne d'AligreII]'. The implication here, of course, is that the occupations and status of members of the family before Etienne II were unbecoming in a great noble dynasty. Finally, the duc de Saint Simon denigrated the d'Aligres for not even having been descended from solid merchant stock. He described Etienne d'Aligre II as, 'petit-fils d'un apothicaire et fils d'un homme qui, pour son petit état, s'étoit enrichi dans son négoce sans sortir de chez lui'.[15] Such scraps of evidence are too ambigious and speculative to be taken at face value. Indeed, we shall shortly encounter contrary claims by the d'Aligres to the effect that, far from stemming from humble origins, they were already noble in the fifteenth century! The extravagance of claims or accusations made in the seventeenth century about the social status of families two centuries earlier, will make familiar reading to students of this period. Anxious to demonstrate a noble lineage, or equally keen to disparage the pedigree of somebody else, seventeenth-century Frenchmen were prone to flights of the imagination, especially when hard evidence for or against was hard to find. As regards the d'Aligres, no facts have emerged to support the suggestion that they were involved in the lace industry, while Saint Simon's story is probably an invention; certainly the extant records of the family contain no trace of the apothecary's trade. The *abbé* d'Aligre's letter is worthy of respect, but he does not mention any occupation followed by his forebears. He simply warns that the family's status before Etienne II was unimpressive. The case for the lace industry or the apothecary's business is unproven. The most appropriate attitude is to take note of the 'accusations' without being unduly respectful towards them.

If financial prosperity helped the Aligres to penetrate the upper social strata of Chartres, so did their acceptance of positions of municipal leadership. Until 1572 the town's affairs were managed by twelve *échevins* elected from among the *bourgeois de Chartres* (citizens with voting rights and obligations to serve in the local militia) for periods of five years. In practice it was often difficult to persuade people to stand, the favourite excuses for refusing being either ill health or an inability to read. Potential candidates objected to the excessive demands on an individual's time, for one month in five had to be given in full-time attention to the post. Consequently the personal career or business of an *échevin* could suffer through lack of attention, especially as during the remaining four months there were still numerous

---

[15] A. De Boislisle (éd.), *Mémoires de Saint-Simon* (Paris, 1879-1930), xxii, 252-7.

meetings and public functions to attend. Financially, election could prove little short of disastrous. When the town's resources failed to meet its commitments it was usually the *échevins* who were expected to dip into their own pockets, particularly when the king sought a gift or a loan. On those occasions they were unlikely to see their money again. The frequency with which they bungled the town's affairs left them vulnerable at the very least to abuse from an unruly and volatile public, and to downright violence at the worst.[16] The amateurism with which they oversaw the town's interests was a source of tension between themselves and the *gens de robe* of Chartres. The *bourgeois* from whose ranks the *échevins* were chosen were predominantly merchants brought up in a practical school of commercial experience, but often lacking in advanced formal education. The plea that a particular *bourgeois* could not be considered for the *échevinage* on the grounds of low literacy, was by no means always a pretence. The *échevins* not infrequently encountered problems beyond their comprehension or capacity, in which case they invited lawyers from Orléans (significantly not from Chartres) to come and advise them. The legal community in Chartres generally exhibited a disdainful attitude towards the *échevins* regarding them as incompetent. The *échevins* replied in kind, denouncing outspoken *gens de robe* as self-opinionated lawyers all too ready to criticise. The fact was that the town's charter of 1296 excluded *gens de robe* from the *échevinage*. By the sixteenth century this was frustrating the ambition of the legal community and denying a badly needed legal expertise to the proceedings of the *échevins*. It made little sense when a fund of legal talent was ready to hand. Reform came in 1572. The number of *échevins* was reduced to eight, their term of office to two years, but most importantly *gens de robe* were made eligible as candidates.[17] In practice, elections thereafter were 'managed' to ensure that two lawyers and six merchants were returned. The merchants preserved their pre-eminence, but a respectable degree of legal competence was introduced among them.

In spite of the risks involved, service as *échevins* exerted an attraction that the Aligres could not resist: prestige. Chartres was a town which lacked a sizeable nobility for it possessed neither the institutions nor the attractions that could have drawn them. There was no *parlement,* no royal *château*, no great prince or aristocrat with a following of lesser nobles. The nobles of the region preferred to reside

---

[16]Chasles, 'Mouvement social', 624-5.

[17]Chasles, 'Mouvement social', 625; Lépinois, *Histoire de Chartres,* ii, 254-5; the *lettres* implementing the reform justified it on the grounds that the old system, 'forçait les électeurs à nommer aux fonctions d'échevin, des marchands illetrés ou des gens mécaniques'.

in their country *châteaux*, or if they did possess urban property it was normally in Paris. The d'Aligres de la Rivière themselves were eventually to conform to this pattern by building a *château* some twenty miles from Chartres, purchasing a residence in Paris, and gradually selling off the houses in Chartres. Chartres itself was solidly *bourgeois*, the only nobles of any distinction being the governor and the bishop. Otherwise the highest echelons of society were occupied by wealthy merchants and lawyers. It was a town where commoners could dominate the social scene and enjoy a prestige that larger towns would have denied them. Therein lay the attraction of the *échevinage*. It represented a peak of social respectability. It conferred lustre upon the *échevins* bringing them into contact with notabilities both local and national. It was, in short, an instrument of social ascension. The Aligres figured fairly prominently on its lists in the sixteenth century. Guillemin Aligre was elected in 1473, the year in which he became a *grenetier*. Others elected included Guillaume (1503), Etienne I (1528), Claude (1567), Jean (1580) and another Jean in 1598. In a community predominantly of common birth, the Aligres had reached the social summit by the end of the sixteenth century. Their property confirmed their status. They owned several *hôtels* in the rue Chantault in the parish of Saint André, and others in the rue des Lices in the parish of Saint Pierre, where the governor had his official residence.[18]

A further source to be exploited in an examination of the fortunes of this family is the marriages into which its members entered. In France marriage was held to be the union of two families rather than of two individuals, and therefore it was the interests of the families which took precedence when a match was contracted. Great emphasis was placed on the need to secure a partner of suitable social standing, for in addition to the normal material considerations, the honour and dignity of the families were at stake. The marriages of the Aligres can be taken up with Guillemin Aligre, who has already appeared as a *grenetier* and *échevin*, for it was with him that the three chief subsequent branches of the Aligres – those of la Motte-Saint-Lié, du Coudray, and la Rivière – originated.[19] It is the third of these that is of interest to this study.

Guillemin and his wife Marguerite Savard[20] had four sons and three daughters, although the order of their birth is uncertain. One son

---

[18]Lépinois, *Histoire de Chartres*, i, 456, 464-5, 475; *Procès-Verbaux de la Société Archéologique d'Eure-et-Loir*, xiv (1921), 107.

[19]*Encyclopédie Biographique du Dix-Neuvième Siècle: Extrait de la Troisième Catégorie: Illustrations Nobiliaires* (Paris, 1844), 3-4; see Appendix 1.

[20]Her status is not known, but the *Encyclopédie Biographique*, 4, remarks that she was, 'd'une ancienne famille de Chartres'.

Michel was trained in law and was styled an *avocat et conseiller*.[21] He brought honour to himself and to his family in 1477 when he commanded infantry helping to occupy Arras on behalf of Louis XI. The king rewarded him with a gift of 200 écus.[22] Michel's wife was Jeanne Chantault, who was probably a member of the distinguished legal family in Chartres after which the rue Chantault was named in the sixteenth century.[23] In 1494 another son Guillaume married Anne Boulineau, the daughter of a *receveur des tailles*; it was with him that the la Motte-Saint-Lié and du Coudray lines began.[24] All that is known of the next son Jean is that he married Marion le Coq whose father was an *avocat et conseiller* in Dreux. The final son was Etienne I, head of the la Rivière branch of the family. Before discussing him, however, a word is required on the daughters of Guillemin and Marguerite. Michelle, probably the eldest, married twice. Her first husband was Martin Pineau; her second was Michel Thomas, a *bourgeois de Chartres* and merchant. The next daughter Verdune married three times. Apart from their names nothing is known of the first two husbands, but the third, Jean Robert, whom she married in 1524, was a physician. The last daughter, Guillemine, also married in 1524, her husband being described simply as an *avocat*.

That leaves Etienne Aligre I (d.c.1545). Intending him for a career in law, his father sent him to study at the faculty in Orléans. It was a perspicacious choice, for in the late 1400s and early 1500s the university was at the height of its prestige. It possessed the most illustrious faculty in France for the teaching of Roman law,[25] but was also a vigorous centre of French humanism. For this latter reputation it was heavily indebted to certain exceptional individuals who championed the transformation of intellectual life in Orléans along humanist lines. François Deloynes, regent of the university in the late 1480s and one of the first professors to be fluent in classical Greek, patronised courses on Greek civilisation. One of his most notable successors Pyrrhus d'Angleberme, professor from 1506 until 1521,

---

[21]Throughout this study biographical details on the family are collated chiefly from B.N., Dossiers Bleus 11:275 and Pièces Originales 36, 37; from the standard genealogical compilations of Anselme, Courcelles and Moréri; from F. Duchesne, *Histoire des Chanceliers et des Gardes des Sceaux de France*... (Paris, 1680), the *Dictionnaire de Biographie Française* and the *Nouvelle Biographie Générale*.

[22]A[rchives] N[ationales], M[inutier] C[entral, Etude] LXXXVI [Liasse] 278: Preuve de chevalier de Malte de M. d'Aligre, 13 juin 1644 (quittance, 6 juillet 1479).

[23]Lépinois, *Histoire de Chartres*, i, 464-5; formerly the street was called rue Mur-en-Muret.

[24]His eldest son Jacques originated the la Motte line and a younger son Renault, the du Coudray line.

[25]*L'Université d'Orléans du XIIIe au XVIIIe Siècle* (Orléans, 1961), 10-16.

invited humanists from abroad to come and teach at the university. Probably the most celebrated of the many who accepted was Luther's redoubtable critic and opponent Aleander who spent seven months at the Hellenic Institute in Orléans.[26] There was created an ambiance of intellectual vitality which, associated with the law faculty's impressive reputation, attracted students from all over western Europe.[27] There was an invigorating cosmopolitan air at Orléans capable of stimulating the cultural sensibilities of students as much as their strictly academic interests. Many graduates returned home as changed men having come under the influence of current humanist trends in philosophy, theology or literature. Within easy reach of Orléans were splendid examples of the new Italian movement in architecture. The king patronised the new style. Between 1502 and 1510 his *château* at Amboise was extended, as was Blois from 1515. Closer to Orléans the great work at Chambord began about 1520. Between 1510 and 1520 other *châteaux* such as Chenonceaux, Bury and Azay-le-Rideau were either begun or enlarged. Orléans itself possessed a fine example of the Italian style in the alterations made to the town hall between 1503 and 1513.[28] Orléans, therefore, was no provincial backwater, no bulwark of tradition or conservatism. Along that entire stretch of the Loire change was in the air. It lay at the very heart of the French Renaissance. In such an environment only the dullest of minds could fail to be quickened, and there can be little surprise that the students of the university included people of the calibre of Jean Calvin and François Daniel.

The intellectual and cultural atmosphere of Orléans has been emphasised because it is very likely that those Aligres with law degrees took them there. There was Etienne I himself. In 1553 another Etienne Aligre from Chartres was a student there.[29] The reputation of the faculty and the proximity of Orléans to Chartres would also indicate it as the 'natural' university for sons of the family. In that case it means that we should think in terms of a family that was not only prosperous and active in public affairs in Chartres, but which had also come into contact with the latest intellectual movements and was familiar with the shift of current humanist ideas. In their case provincialism did not mean mental inertia or small-mindedness.

[26]*Ibid.*, 33-42.

[27] See papers on this theme by R. Feenstra, E. Génzmer, T.B. Smith, and S. Stelling-Michaud, in *Actes du Congrès sur l'Ancienne Université d'Orléans, 6 et 7 mai 1961* (Orléans, 1962).

[28] A. Blunt, *Art and Architecture in France: 1500-1700* (2nd. ed., London, 1970), 3-15.

[29] J. Doinel, 'Anne du Bourg à l'université d'Orléans', *Bulletin Historique et Littéraire* (Société de l'Histoire du Protestantisme Français), xxx (1881), 366.

On his return home Etienne I, following family tradition, assumed positions of importance in Chartres. He acquired the legal office of *greffier* which gave him the responsibility, among other things, for preserving the records of the court of the *bailliage*. Then in 1528 he was elected *échevin*. Strictly speaking this was probably in contravention of the rules excluding *gens de robe*. However, his father had been an *échevin*, Etienne was but a *greffier* and not a judge, and it was often hard to find suitable candidates for the *échevinage*.

His interests went beyond the law court and council chamber, for he was also a landowner. He had inherited from his father the two *seigneuries* of La Mothe and Chonvilliers. The dates when Guillemin had acquired these lands are unascertainable, but he had probably profited from the desolation of the area around Chartres left by the Hundred Years war[30] and purchased land cheaply from improverished nobles whose incomes from their ruined estates had been decimated. If this is what had happened then Guillemin had bought land at the best possible time; this assumes that he did so some time between 1470 and 1500, which would fit the known facts of his biography. After 1475 there was a movement of the population all over France, but especially between the Seine and the Loire, back to the countryside, thereby reversing the trend of the 1450s and 1460s. With peace established and the perils of rural life much reduced, more land was being cultivated and agricultural prices in general were rising.[31] It was in this period, from the 1470s to the early 1500s, that the urban *bourgeoisie* whose incomes had not been seriously depleted during the wars, began that 'invasion' of the countryside by which land changed hands on a large scale.[32] *Officiers* from the large towns who had surpluses of cash favoured investing in land, partly as a straightforward financial exercise, but just as importantly as an investment in prestige. Whatever cash returns came from land, it was the prestige that land conferred which made it highly attractive. Social status depended on prestige or honour; land therefore was a key to social advancement. The Aligres appear to have been beneficiaries of this phenomenon, moving into rural property and elevating their status correspondingly.

Etienne I married Jeanne Edeline from Nogent-le-Roy, a small town between Chartres and Dreux. They had nine children, most of

---

[30] R. Boutruche, 'The devastation of rural areas during the Hundred Years War and the agricultural recovery of France', P.S. Lewis (ed.), *The Recovery of France in the Fifteenth Century* (London, 1971), 25-6; J.H. Salmon, *Society in crisis: France in the Sixteenth Century* (London, 1975), 27.

[31] J. Jacquart, *La Crise Rurale en l'Ile-de-France: 1550-1670* (Paris, 1974), 42-5.

[32] *Ibid.*, 48.

whose careers and marriages resembled those of their uncles and aunts. One of the three daughters Marie, married Baltazar Hesselin who is described as an *avocat au parlement*. Anne's husband was a merchant from Dreux. Michelle married twice, her second husband Jean Pocquet, sieur de la Riendre, being secretary to the bishop of Chartres. Together they founded a famous school when in 1572 they granted to the town a large residence and land adjoining the episcopal palace for that purpose.[33]

The sons of Etienne I present less uniformity. Gérard was a *receveur du domaine de Chartres* (which involved administering the estates of the cathedral) and *mesureur du grenier à sel* (in 1546). Nicolas is simply termed a *contrôleur* at Gisors. Neither married. On a third son Florent no information has survived, but a fourth Jean was canon at Chartres cathedral. The one who contrived to live most adventurously and successfully was Claude. Unlike his brothers or uncles he opted for the military calling and fought at Pavia (1525) where he was captured with the king. He shared the imprisonment of François I, and according to one version of the story returned to France to assist in organising the king's ransom; another version maintains that he remained in detention with his master, only going back to France when François was released.[34] Whatever the truth, the monarch rewarded him handsomely by introducing him into the service of the royal family. He was nominated secretary to the queen mother, Louise de Savoie, duchesse d'Angoulême,[35] then in November 1528 *trésorier des menus plaisirs du roi*, which meant he was responsible for purchasing jewelry, furniture, paintings and other luxury items on behalf of the king.[36] Further advancement came his way. He acquired a noble title (baron d'Arcueil et de la Brosse) and land at Arcueil just south of Paris where he built his *château* of Arès. In 1533 he was promoted to *valet de chambre du roi*,[37] the final mark

---

[33] Lépinois, *Histoire de Chartres*, ii, 255-6; J-B. Souchet, *Histoire du Diocèse et de la Ville de Chartres* (Chartres, 1866-73), iv, 139-40; the first students arrived in 1572, but it was not until 1587 that the school received its charter as the 'Collège Royal de Chartres'; it was popularly known as the 'Collège Pocquet' until the present century.

[34] *Encyclopédie Biographique*, 8, claims that Claude was sent to France to raise the ransom; the testimony of Charles Desguez, sieur de la Potinière in the 'Preuve de chevalier de Malte, 1644', claims that Claude remained in captivity with the king; N.B. 'Lettres du roi reconnaissant qu'il a receu de Claude Aligre, commis à la gestion des finances envoyées de France en Espagne pour ses besoins, 3,773 livres 11 sous 9 deniers tournois pour travailler à sa délivrance et profiter des circonstances favorables à la conclusion de la paix avec l'Empereur, et 810 livres tournois pour en disposer à son plaisir'. (*Catalogue des Actes de François 1* [Paris, 1887-1908], v, 737, no.18507).

[35] *Catalogue des Actes de François 1*, i, 540, no.2874.

[36] *Ibid.*, i, 618, no.3240.

[37] *Ibid.*, ii, 495, no.6187.

of esteem coming in 1547 when he was chosen as one of the *cent gentilshommes du roi*,[38] a position which acknowledged him to be a noble of the highest merit. Although Claude's descendants never matched the achievements of the d'Aligres de la Rivière, they remained a noble family of great prestige, especially since their title originated in military service to the king and so fitted the purest ideal of how nobility ought to be earned.[39]

The remaining son of Etienne I and Jeanne Edeline was Raoul (c.1535-91), who represents the next link in the emergence of the d'Aligres de la Rivière. After a training in law he returned to Chartres where, like his father, he was a *greffier*; he was also *receveur du domaine de Chartres*, an office that he may have inherited from his unmarried brother Gérard. On the death of Etienne I he succeeded to the *seigneurie* of Chonvilliers (la Mothe went to Claude) and in addition possessed an *hôtel* in the rue Chantault in Chartres.[40] He purchased still more land, the most important in view of its subsequent role in the history of the family, being the *seigneurie* of La Rivière just outside the village of Pontgouin, seventeen miles to the west of Chartres. His marriage to Jeanne Lambert in 1559 included a feature of exceptional interest in that her dowry took the form of land: the *seigneurie* of Les Hayes in the village of Favières, some fifteen miles north-west of Chartres. The deceased father of Jeanne had been Pierre Lambert, sieur des Hayes, and it may be assumed that he had no male heir since normally land was not alienated in this way.[41] Raoul and his wife had only three children, one of whom died in infancy. Their daughter Marie married well. Her husband was Louis de Mineray, sieur de la Grande Nouë, *président* of the *présidial* in Chartres. Raoul's son Etienne II will be discussed at length in due course.

Raoul Aligre himself will reappear later in this study, but if stock is taken of his family during his lifetime the principal features of their condition and standing can be identified. They were firmly established in the higher reaches of society in Chartres, although in a larger town with a more elaborate social variegation their status would have been more modest. They owned land, *hôtels,* possessed legal and financial offices, and were prominent in municipal affairs. Suitable marriages were arranged with people of similar status, although the sons on the

---

[38]*Ibid.*, viii, 194, no.31059; B N , Dossiers Bleus 11:275, fos.23ᵛ-4.

[39]R. Mousnier, *Les Institutions de la France sous la Monarchie Absolue* (Paris, 1974), i, 103, 153-9.

[40]A[rchives] D[épartementales] d'Eure-et-Loir, MS G 1389, 1 nov. 1607.

[41]'Preuve de chevalier de Malte': Mariage, 18 avril 1559.

whole married more prestigiously than did the daughters. Nevertheless, several daughters married twice or even three times, which suggests that they were considered good matches by prospective husbands. Indeed, in their own restricted way the Aligres may have been the vehicle of the social advancement within Chartres of merchants and lawyers anxious to link themselves to this influential family. Whenever an Aligre daughter was available for marriage, there were suitors ready to propose.

One last issue calls for comment and it concerns the question of whether or not they were noble. Claude received a title, of course, but what about the others? The query arises because in 1644 Etienne d'Aligre III presented his son Jean for admittance to the ranks of Knights of Malta.[42] In the course of proving Jean's noble descent[43] he produced a document purporting to show that Guillemin Aligre, who has appeared in this chapter, was noble. Dated 6 July 1479 it was a receipt from Guillemin to the town of Chartres, acknowledging payment to his son Michel of the 200 écus which Louis XI had awarded him; the town had paid on behalf of the king.[44] It referred to Guillemin as *écuyer,* sieur de Chonvilliers. An *écuyer* was the lowest of noble rankings, but carried all the privileges of the second estate. The question simply is, was the title valid?

This is probably a case of usurped nobility such as historians frequently encounter in early modern France. The document in question was drawn up by a *tabellion: tabellions* performed functions similar to those of notaries, but were of inferior standing. In all probability this minor official would write as his important client dictated. If Guillemin Aligre, a citizen of influence and property, insisted that he was not only sieur de Chonvilliers (but *sieur de* was not a noble title) but an *écuyer* as well, who was a mere *tabellion* with an eye to the future of his business, to ask awkward questions? The receipt of 1479 cannot be taken at face value. Guillemin Aligre was probably resorting to the time-honoured practice of 'sliding' into nobility. He possessed two *seigneuries,* and was passing himself off as noble, doubtless hoping that with the passage of time he would be accepted as such locally, and would enjoy the status and privileges of *écuyer*. Again, he exercised functions that were incompatible with nobility. Since 1473 he had been an *échevin* and a *grenetier*. While it

---

[42] See n. 22.

[43] Noble descent over at least three generations on both sides of the family had to be demonstrated.

[44] See n. 22.

is just possible to square nobility and the *échevinage*,[45] the office of *grenetier* was emphatically derogatory to nobility. It is possible that he resigned the office before 1479, but it is more likely that he kept the office and his 'title' at the same time. If that is in fact what happened, it does not follow that Guillemin was uncommonly dishonest. The practice of 'sliding' into nobility, of acquiring a title through social consensus, was widespread in France, only coming under severe pressure from the late sixteenth century onwards. Indeed, it is open to question whether before the 1580s and 1590s somebody in Guillemin's position would have conceded that in any sense he was a usurper. He would probably have objected that possession of noble land, the adoption of a noble life style, and popular recognition in the neighbourhood as a noble, were sufficient criteria for a title. By the late sixteenth century, however, the state was institutionalising nobility by issuing *lettres de noblesse* and by selling offices which carried noble titles. In consequence, nobility by social consensus was increasingly being dubbed 'usurped' by the state, which was seeking to instil the idea of nobility based on legal documentation. This trend can be discerned in the *recherches de la noblesse* ordered by the Bourbon regime, and in some respects in protests from 'genuine' nobles against the prevalence of usurpation.[46] From a strictly legalistic position, therefore, Guillemin Aligre in all likelihood may be judged a usurper, but his situation was far from uncommon. Etienne I and Raoul Aligre also employed the title *écuyer*, but only in documents drawn up by *tabellions* in Chartres. By contrast, when Etienne II was living in Paris, legal documents in which he figured and which were composed by Parisian notaries, referred to him only as 'sieur de Chonvilliers', and never as an *écuyer*. He had doubtless learnt the appropriate lesson: it was one thing for the family to avail itself of a title back in Chartres, but another to risk exposure and shame as a usurper in the Paris of the new regime.

---

[45] A nobleman might be *bourgeois* if the word indicated domicile, not status (Mousnier, *Les Institutions*, i, 103).

[46] *Ibid.*, chap.4; D. Bitton, *The French Nobility in Crisis, 1560-1640* (Stanford U.P., 1969), chap.6.

2

ETIENNE D'ALIGRE II: HIS LIFE AND CAREER

Chartres and the Wars of Religion

Raoul Aligre's son Etienne II was probably born in 1560,[1] his infancy and youth coinciding with the outbreak and evolution of the wars of religion. The national religious crisis manifested itself in Chartres too. For all the vitality of catholicism there Chartres had been infiltrated by calvinist ideas, although to an extent that remains obscure. The disquieted *échevins,* bent upon keeping the peace, had their suspicions as to the chief culprits: certain impious *gens de robe*. In 1560 they complained to Charles de Bourbon, prince de la Roche-sur-Yon, governor of the Chartrain, that, 'Jusqu'à présent il n'y a eu aucun trouble sérieux au sujet de la religion. . . . Mais dernièrement à l'assemblée des états particuliers du bailliage, plusieurs députés ont fait des propositions grandement contraires à la foi catholique'.[2] Although little inclined to fanaticism themselves, they were apprehensive over the violence that could result from protestantism under the articulate and concerted leadership of intelligent lawyers. With the outbreak of national civil war they were forced to resort to harsh, but not ruthless, measures to save Chartres from bloodshed. A civil guard 150 strong was formed, and on 12 June 1562, 161 suspected huguenots (including several regular and secular priests, three *conseillers* from the *présidial*, as well as other lawyers), were expelled from the town.[3] With our knowledge of the fate that engulfed less fortunate towns because of religious feuding during the wars, it is difficult not to concede that the purge, rough as it was, was necessary. It served its purpose. Protestantism thereafter remained extraneous to Chartres, where questions of security subsequently concerned external, not internal threats. In December 1562 the huguenot leader Condé appeared with an army to demand the surrender of the town. The *échevins* refused. Unable to attack such well prepared defences Condé was forced to retreat.[4]

---

[1] Various years, 1559, 1560, even 1550, have been claimed for his birth; his parents' marriage contract was signed in April 1559 (chap. 1, n. 41), which would make 1560 most likely.

[2] Lépinois, *Histoire de Chartres,* ii, 203-4.

[3] *Ibid.,* ii, 209-11.

[4] Condé went on to his decisive defeat at Dreux on 19 December.

Etienne d'Aligre II

On the debit side, 1562 saw the appearance (although not for the first time), of that three-fold menace that was to prove so debilitating to Chartres over the next thirty years: the billeting of troops, the incidence of plague, and a combination of food shortages and inflation. Royal troops were quartered in Chartres in 1562 ostensibly for its protection. They caused such serious damage and disturbances as to provoke protests from the *échevins* to the king and solicitations for their removal. Plague arrived in August and reappeared frequently throughout the rest of the century. Royal expropriations left Chartres short of grain, a condition that again recurred throughout the wars. Furthermore, in January 1563 Charles IX and the queen mother, Cathérine de Médicis, spent the month there, upholding a royal tradition of using the town as a temporary residence. During the first phase of the wars of religion, therefore, Chartres rapidly assumed the posture and role which it maintained until all but the last years of the conflict. Self-interest dictated that it lock its gates, see to its defences, contribute as necessary to the royal cause, but otherwise avoid involvement.

It was put to the test in 1568 when a huguenot army which had penetrated the county of La Beauce besieged the town. Chartres came through with flying colours, the enemy retiring after two weeks having inflicted little damage. But the episode threatened the *échevins* with unwelcome consequences. The king decided that in view of the importance of Chartres he would install a permanent royal military commander with an appropriate force. The *échevins* opposed the plan. It endangered their authority and would impose a severe financial burden at a time when resources had been depleted by the costs of the siege. They selected Raoul Aligre, now a citizen of senior status and of high reputation, to present their objections to Madame Renée, duchesse de Chartres,[5] and to importune her to intercede with the king. Raoul's mission was a success. Charles IX rescinded the order, leaving the defence of Chartres in the hands of the *échevins*. Nevertheless, their financial problems continued, for over the next two years the king imposed extortionate demands for supplies for his armies. Moreover, to add to their worries huguenot assemblies sprang up in La Beauce and Le Perche, forcing the *échevins* to keep assiduous watch on visitors, for fear that protestantism would reappear in Chartres.

In the next decade, the 1570s, war impinged on life in Chartres less through military incidents of high drama (the chief arenas of

---

[5] She had been granted the *surintendance* of Chartres in 1566; since she was an influential huguenot, Cathérine de Médicis had no wish to offend her.

fighting moved away from the Ile-de-France during these years) than through the constant drainage of money and military necessities wrung from its over-tasked economy by a desperate monarch. This, furthermore, was at a time when the entire region between Paris and the Loire was afflicted by a series of harvest failures which drove people into towns in search of food.[6] The death of Charles IX and succession of Henri III made no difference, except perhaps in that Henri's numerous pilgrimages to Chartres reinforced the urgency with which he made his demands.

Here in outline is the cheerless urban environment, as distinct from the immediate family circle, in which Etienne II was raised. It provides a salutary corrective to any tendency to treat him simply as the product of a wealthy, successful family. A study of his domestic surroundings alone leaves out too many of the forces acting on him during the formative years of his childhood and youth. As we estimate the background from which he emerged, emphasis has to be placed on that complex knot of problems – religious, social, economic, political – which for several decades consigned Chartres, along with much of the country, to a valley of shadows.

The Early Years of Etienne II, to 1594

Although no detailed biography of these years is possible, the later course of his life permits certain assumptions. In particular it is evident that he was raised with a legal career in prospect. He had degrees in law, although whether from Paris or Orléans is not known. For reasons suggested earlier, the latter seems more likely. Hard facts about him appear in his twenty-fourth year when he took the first step that was to lead to the chancellorship forty years later. On 12 July 1584 he became a *conseiller* in the *grand conseil*.[7] It was an impressive office for a young man from the provinces, and questions are immediately raised. Who was acting as his protector and proposed him for the post? Was his uncle Claude still alive and using his influence at court? It will emerge shortly that Etienne II had connections with the comte de Soissons. Did a link already exist and was Soissons his champion? Or is the answer to be found in Chartres? Did his father meet the king on one of Henri III's visits and present a petition for his son? Whatever the explanation, the office was a

---

[6]Jacquart, *La Crise Rurale,* 174-9.

[7]B.N., Nouvelles Acquisitions 23419, fos 534-5; 'Preuve de chevalier de Malte': arrêt du grand conseil, 12 juillet 1584.

considerable coup. The *grand conseil*[8] was a sovereign court whose competence resembled that of the *parlements* with two major differences: firstly, unlike them it was not divided into *chambres* but sat as a single body; secondly, its authority extended over the whole kingdom, whereas that of a single *parlement* was geographically restricted. It often acted as a supreme court of appeal, a function which led to disputes with the *parlement* of Paris which held similar pretensions. It enjoyed a close relationship with the king, not least because until the 1570s it was peripatetic, accompanying the royal court on its travels. Other sovereign courts displayed a certain independence of will, but the *grand conseil* rarely did so. It was therefore regarded as a reliable royal instrument and its members as safe 'king's' men. When Etienne II joined, it included in addition to other staff, forty *conseillers* who each served one semester a year either from 1 April to 30 September or from 1 October to 31 March. They enjoyed a broad range of privileges, including exemption from *taille, aides,* and other standard financial obligations. When in Paris the *grand conseil* had normally met in the residence of the chancellor (who in theory, but rarely in practice, presided over its sessions), but by the 1570s was using the monastery of the Grands Augustins. In 1583 it moved yet again, this time to property belonging to and adjoining the church of Saint Germain l'Auxerrois.[9] A member of the *grand conseil* moved in court circles, could come to the attention of the king himself (and here it should be recalled that Etienne II may already have met Henri III in Chartres), and if he performed his duties diligently could anticipate promotion in royal service.

Etienne II was appointed at a time of acute political tension. In the same year as his admission the catholic league revived as the storm centre of civil war returned to Paris and its region. The city itself fell under the control of the league, the king being obliged to withdraw after the barricades of May 1588. The emergency engulfed the *grand conseil*, for it too split into league and royal factions. When Henri III ordered it to Tours in April 1589 its loyal members obeyed, but the rest constituted themselves a *grand conseil* under the league in Paris. The cleavage lasted for five years, the *grand conseil* not reuniting until Henri IV's entry into Paris in 1594.[10] Although Aligre's

---

[8] The passage that follows is based on M. Antoine, *et al., Guide des Recherches dans les Fonds Judiciaires de l'Ancien Régime* (Paris, 1958), 29-42, and E. Garçon, *Essai Historique sur le Grand Conseil* (Poitiers, 1876), 44-7.

[9] In 1686 the *grand conseil* moved again, to the hôtel d'Aligre in the rue Saint Honoré, which Etienne III was to acquire in 1656 (see p. 177); it remained there until 1754 when it transferred to the Louvre; the *grand conseil* was abolished in 1771.

[10] The last meeting of the league faction was on 18 March 1594.

movements during these years cannot be traced in detail, his chief decision is clear enough: he threw in his lot with the league.[11] In so doing he must have strained his relations with his father, for Raoul showed no cordiality towards the league and its aspirations, in fact losing his life in the struggle against it. But it also seems probable that Etienne II spent most of his time back in Chartres in the late 1580s. The lists of those *conseillers* who actively served in the rival assemblies of Tours and Paris make no mention of him;[12] if he was in neither city, where was he? Chartres seems the obvious answer. It is indicated by a further consideration.

In 1587 he acquired a second office, that of *président* of the *présidial* of his native Chartres. His main responsibility was thereby to maintain the chancellery of the court. Given the status of the *présidiaux* it was a highly prestigious post. But it was assumed at a time when the atmosphere in the town was turning more acrimonious than it had been since the early 1560s. In short, the league appeared in Chartres. At first the revival of the league in Paris had little consequence in Chartres where, because of his visits, Henri III was familiar and his cause well known. Nevertheless, his presence continued to be associated with extraordinary financial levies. For example, in 1585, a year of catastrophic harvests and bitter winter which drove starving peasants into Chartres, the king made two pilgrimages to the cathedral, using each occasion to demand more money and military supplies. Over the next two years he was often there, and it is a moot point whether the league faction that grew by 1588 was based more on sympathy with the league, or on exasperation with the king's impositions. If Etienne II was indeed in Chartres then he may well have been one of the leaders of the league faction. The event that sundered the town between its league and royal protagonists was the murder at the king's command of the duc de Guise and his brother the cardinal de Guise in September 1588, after which Chartres suffered the bitter internal divisions which the *échevins* had striven to forestall.[13]

The year 1589 marked the beginning of the brief heyday of the league there. Orléans had declared in its favour and called on Chartres to follow suit. During a general assembly of citizens called by the

---

[11] Although Louis XIV ordered the destruction of the records of the *grand conseil* during the years of the league, an outline of the affairs of the royal and league sections is in A.N., U622 and U633.

[12] A.N., U633, fos. 130-2, 154-5, 222-3, *passim*.

[13] A.N., KK638:'Ce qui se passa à Chartres après la mort de M. de Guise en l'an 1589', gives a detailed account.

governor of Chartres, de Sourdis, on 9 February to discuss the crisis, a group of leaguers opened the town gates to the duc de Mayenne, the new leader of the league, who was waiting outside with troops. He seized Chartres in the name of the league, imprisoning de Sourdis who refused to abjure his loyalty to the king. The coup had forced Chartres into the league camp, but it speedily became evident that the chief activity of the new masters was to continue requisitions of money and food, now to supply the enemies of the king. Political confusion and food shortages produced rioting throughout 1589, which the meagre resources of the *échevins* were unable to curb. The assassination of Henri III and much-disputed succession of Henri IV made little difference in the short run. In 1590, however, as Henri IV proved to be more than a transient pretender, the influence of royalist groups in Chartres revived. In an attempt to suppress the danger Réclainville, the league's appointee as governor, arrested six prominent *bourgeois* whom he suspected to be at the heart of the movement. One of the six was Raoul Aligre. Since nobody would testify against the suspects they were released.[14]

Raoul left the town to join the forces of Henri IV, now at the gates of Chartres. Henri, who had failed to take Paris at his first attempt,[15] laid siege to Chartres in February 1591 as part of his strategy of capturing key positions around the capital. Circumstances now were very different from those in 1562 and the siege of 1568. Over twenty years of tribute to the wars had taken a heavy toll. Chartres was no longer a well-stocked fortification. Moreover, if Henri IV truly was king, then only the most obdurate leaguer could reject the proposition that Chartres was in a state of rebellion. What revenge would Henri justly inflict if he won? His protestantism was a genuine stumbling block, but in negotiations with representatives of the *échevins* he promised that catholicism would suffer no molestation should the town surrender. It was this restraint on his part that turned the town against the league and in favour of the capitulation of 11 April. Uninhibited catholic worship was guaranteed by the king, with a corresponding pledge that huguenot worship was forbidden; all municipal officers were confirmed in their posts; troops of the league was allowed to leave.[16] On 19 April 1591 Henri IV officially entered Chartres.

---

[14] Souchet, *Histoire, , ,de Chartres*, 190.

[15] The great siege of 1590 pushed Paris to starvation, but Henri IV was forced back by a Spanish army in September 1590.

[16] Lépinois, *Histoire de Chartres*, ii, 334; Archives Communales de Chartres, S.a.3: 'Articles de capitulation accordés par Henri IV aux habitants de la ville de Chartres'.

The outlook for Etienne II was bleak. Personal tragedy had struck when, during the siege, his father Raoul was killed.[17] Etienne and Raoul had chosen opposite sides in the 1580s, and it may be presumed that their personal relations had suffered accordingly. Now, as a partisan of the league, Etienne II was doubtless fearing the worst. In the event he was fortunate. On 2 September 1591 Henri IV ordered an investigation into Aligre's recent conduct.[18] The results evidently were satisfactory, for on 10 September he was permitted to renounce the league and swear loyalty to the king.[19] The next day he was reinstated in his functions as a *conseiller* of the *grand conseil*.[20] As a further stroke of luck, the king chose Chartres as his temporary seat of government. For three years until Henri's entry into Paris in 1594, Chartres housed the *conseil du roi*, the *cour des aides*, and the royal version of the *grand conseil* (with Etienne II now a member). In the light of his future career it seems reasonable to suppose that Etienne used this opportunity to heal the breach with the king's entourage, to perform his duties with all diligence, to prove his loyalty, and to cast himself as a figure worthy of future honours. Just when his career in royal service looked finished, the Bourbon cause chose to centre on Chartres, the very base of Etienne's wealth and prestige, thereby enabling him to rescue himself from oblivion.

During this phase of his life, one other event of high importance should be observed. Amidst the confusion and excitement of the late 1580s he had married, in 1586 or 1587.[21] His wife was Marie-Elisabeth Chapellier (1573-1637), daughter of Jean-Jacques Chapellier, sieur de Buscatel et de Saint Cyr, a *conseiller d'état*. The Chapelliers were of solid Parisian *bourgeois* stock. Some members of the family, notably Jean-Jacques and his brothers, were legal and financial office bearers,[22] while others were *marchands bourgeois de Paris*.[23] One of Marie-Elisabeth's sisters Marie married Jacques Turpin, also a *conseiller d'état*; in 1629 their daughter Elisabeth was to marry Michel le Tellier, later marquis de Louvois. It was the protection given to le Tellier by Etienne II (then chancellor of France)

---

[17]'Preuve de chevalier de Malte': Testimony of Charles Desguez, sieur de la Potinière.

[18]A.N., U633, f.233.

[19]A.N., U622, p. 141; U633, fos. 234-5.

[20]A.N., U622, p. 140; B.N., Dossiers Bleus 11: 275, no. 5.

[21]The marriage contracted was dated 20 Nov. 1586 ('Preuve de chevalier de Malte': Mariage, 20 nov. 1586).

[22]B.N., Dossiers Bleus 168, f.2.

[23]A.N., M.C., LXXXV1-125: Quittance, 21 nov. 1586, refers to 'Jacques Chapellier. . . . marchand bourgeois de Paris'.

which was to launch le Tellier on his career when in 1631 he became *procureur du roi au Châtelet*.[24] Thereafter the relations between the two families remained close and will reappear in this study.

Property and Career to 1613

Having survived the crisis of 1589 to 1591 in Chartres, and having allied himself by marriage to the Chapelliers, Etienne devoted his energies to his career and to the management of his property. A comprehensive analysis of his property must be delayed until later; in the short term, however, he had inherited from his father considerable holdings, the chief portions being the *seigneuries* of La Rivière, Les Hayes, and Chonvilliers. He chose La Rivière as his principal provincial residence, undertaking the construction of a *château* in 1615. As so often happened, this successful son of Chartres chose not to reside in his native city, but to opt for *la vie noble*. Between 1606 and 1609 he began to purchase land which would fill out his estates: about 1 acre at Chartres for 150 livres;[25] at Pontgouin 1 arpent (1.04 acres) of pasture, plus another perche (about 50 square yards) together costing 27 livres;[26] at Chonvilliers in two separate transactions, 22 sétiers (18.25 acres) of *terre labourable* in several pieces for 648 livres,[27] and 1 sétier for 24 livres.[28] His other property consisted of a *hôtel* in the rue Chantault in Chartres[29] and 20 arpents of land at La Forêt, close to La Rivière.[30]

Meanwhile his career was making progress thanks partly to judicious moves on his own part, but also to his association with a powerful aristocrat and prince of the blood, Charles de Bourbon, comte de Soissons. The role of Soissons in this phase of Aligre's life is hard to evaluate chiefly because the date of their first collaboration cannot be ascertained. In 1607, however, Soissons appointed Aligre

---

[24] J. Roujon, *Louvois et son Maître* (Paris, 1934), 24; L. André, *Michel le Tellier*, 34-5.

[25] A.N., M.C., XXIV-226: Vente, 27 avril 1606.

[26] A.N., M.C., XXIV-232: Vente, 2 mai 1608.

[27] A.N., M.C., XXIV-232: Vente, 2 juin 1608.

[28] A.N., M.C., XXIV-236: Vente, 31 juillet 1609; if these figures are scaled up, land at Chartres cost 148 livres per arpent, pasture at Pontgouin 26 livres, and *terre labourable* at Chonvilliers from 29 livres to 35 livres; the high price of land at Chartres stands out here.

[29] A.D., Eure-et-loir, MS G 1389, 1 nov. 1607.

[30] A.N., M.C., XXIV-222: Procuration, 22 avril 1605.

his *intendant*.[31] It was a highly responsible position, putting him in charge of the comte's finances and of the general administration of his household. A prince of the blood was an invaluable protector to a royal officer; further evidence of his confidence in Aligre came on the comte's death in 1612 when he left Etienne as *tuteur honéraire* to his son and heir Louis (born in 1604). The link with the Soissons continued, for when Aligre's son Etienne III married in 1617 the two principal witnesses to the marriage contract were Louis, the new comte de Soissons, and his mother.[32]

The elder Soissons may have had a hand in advancing Aligre's career at the turn of the century. About 1605 Etienne II shifted his permanent residence from Chartres to Paris, joining those droves of provincials who flocked into the capital after its pacification by Henri IV. Unlike many who came he was no new-fledged opportunist seeking a fortune; he was in his forty-fifth year and a respected member of the *grand conseil*. At first he rented a house in the rue d'Avron[33] in the parish of Saint Germain l'Auxerrois. He remained there until 1614 when he moved into the rue Jean Tison (which ran off the rue d'Avron), where at 900 livres a year he rented a two-storey residence: '... deux caves étant soulz la grand salle. Ladite grande salle et la sallette joignant, avec les chambres, garderobbes, gallères et greniers audessus et une chambre... au deuxiesme étage du corps'.[34] In the following year he returned to the rue d'Avron where he purchased the house in which his family was to live until the 1650s.[35] The quarter of Paris where he resided was highly desirable. Henri IV and Louis XIII both used the Louvre, within two minutes walk of the rue d'Avron, as the principal royal palace, thereby stimulating a voracious demand for property in the neighbourhood. The area around the Louvre developed rapidly as aristocratic *hôtels* were built, and lesser courtiers scoured what had become an upper-crust part of the city, for rooms or lodgings.[36] With Paris at last undergoing systematic planning to turn it into a worthy capital, Etienne Aligre resided in what was a modish part of the city.

Another mark of his advancement which again he may have owed to the intercession of Soissons, was his nomination by the king as

[31] B.N., Dossiers Bleus 11: 275, f.43.
[32] A.N., M.C., XXXV1-103: Mariage, 5 fév. 1617.
[33] A.N., M.C., XXIV-223: Constitution, 8 juillet 1605.
[34] A.N., M.C., XXIV-249: Bail, 5 fév. 1614.
[35] A.N., M.C., XXIV-348: Partage, 9 mars 1638.
[36] R. Mousnier, *Paris, Capitale au Temps de Richelieu et de Mazarin* (Paris, 1978), 125-6.

president of the estates of Bretagne. Several witnesses testify to his selection, but do not indicate the date except to say that it occurred under Henri IV.[37] They also go on to say that ill-health prevented him from going on his mission. Even so, the episode indicated that his former misdemeanours had been forgiven, that he was considered suitable material for other honours in due course.

They came in January 1613 with his promotion to the rank of *conseiller d'état*.[38] He thus entered one of the elite corps in central administration, for if there was any branch where advancement depended on talent as well as on influence, this was it. The office was not venal and therefore could not turn into a hereditary possession. If certain families reappeared among the *conseillers d'état* from generation to generation, it was because of their capacities for the office. Expert in law, of proven administrative ability, often having first served in the *grand conseil* or in one of the *parlements,* they sustained the bulk of administration in the *conseil du roi*. Frequently they were employed in supplementary roles such as special commissioners or *intendants* in the provinces.[39] Amidst the complexities of sixteenth and seventeenth century French government they represented an impressive source of expertise able to keep the cumbersome wheels in motion. Etienne Aligre was an eminently suitable choice. In 1613 he was fifty-three years old; he was at the height of his professional powers; he had detailed knowledge of the *grand conseil* and its procedures; he had many contacts in the government and the *parlement* in Paris. In short he possessed the qualities required in a successful *conseiller d'état*. For the time being he also retained his office in the *grand conseil*, but only until 1616 when he resigned it in favour of his son Etienne III.[40]

Steps to the chancellorship

During these years the omens for France were again disquieting in the extreme. The assassination of Henri IV left the country on the edge of a morass of civil conflict in which retrogressive forces threatened to

---

[37] All the standard biographical souces refer to this episode; the most reliable source is Bibliothèque de l'Institut, MS Godofroy 519, f.233; this is part of a *mémoire* drawn up by Etienne d'Aligre IV (1660-1725) outlining the history of his family and submitted to Pierre de Guibours, le père Anselme de Sainte Marie for his *Histoire Généalogique de la Maison de France*.

[38] 'Preuve de chevalier de Malte': Brevet de conseiller d'état, 5 jan. 1613.

[39] R. Bonney, *Political Change in France under Richelieu and Mazarin, 1624-1661* (Oxford, 1978), 105-8.

[40] B.N., Dossiers Bleus 11: 275, f.52.

undo much of what he had accomplished. The aristocratic cliques centred on mighty figures like Condé, Vendôme, Conti, Bouillon and others who tried to exploit the defects of a regime headed by a vacillating regent, surely could offer nothing positive in terms of the life of the nation with its vivid memories of the wars of religion. The estates general called in 1614 largely at their insistence proved to be an instrument of social division rather than of harmony. Refusing to serve as the tool of infractious princes, it nevertheless lacked the will or the capacity to serve a progressive purpose in legislation or government.[41] The first phase of the rebellion of the princes had ended with the treaty of Saint Ménéhould in May 1614, but the refusal of the estates general to comply with their aspirations drove them into a second phase led by Condé, which lasted from August 1615 to May 1616, when peace was concluded between the princes and the regent at Loudun.

While Etienne II shared the fears and apprehensions of his countrymen in a general sense, he had personal interests at stake in the events of 1614 and 1615. In September 1615 Condé was moving through the region between Chartres and La Rivière with, it was reported, 10,000 infantry and 1,800 cavalry.[42] Aligre was afraid for both his family and his property. He wrote to his friend Chouane, president of the *présidial* of Chartres, asking him to shelter his (Aligre's) mother while troops were in the offing; he was equally fearful for La Rivière, hoping that Condé would pass through quickly before the estate was damaged.[43] On a more strictly political level he was pulled into the margins of the conflict between the princes and the regent through his association with the Soissons. The mother of Louis, comte de Soissons, Anne de Montafié, a seasoned schemer, had broken with the regent Marie de Médicis. Marie was seeking reconciliation through her intermediary Villeroy; he in turn approached the comtesse through Aligre, the trusted servant of her deceased husband Charles. Etienne II held emphatic views on the turmoil of 1614 and 1615. He considered the party of the princes to be fundamentally weak, for the huguenots apart, nobody was willing to support them. There was a widespread and irresistible desire for peace in the country.[44] It made sense to Aligre that the breach between

---

[41] See J.M. Hayden, *France and the Estates General of 1614* (Cambridge, 1974).

[42] Etienne d'Aligre II to Villeroy, 5 sept. 1615 (B.N., MS Français 15582, f.49).

[43] Etienne d'Aligre II to Chouane, 15 sept. 1615 (Bibl. de l'Institut, MS Godefroy 268, f.34).

[44] See no.42; after the assassination of Henri IV and their assembly at Saumur in 1611 the huguenots were prepared to ally with Condé and others: see A.D. Lublinskaya, *French Absolutism: the Crucial Phase, 1620-1629* (Cambridge, 1968), 165, and D.

the comtesse and the regent should be healed quickly. To this end he was able to report to Villeroy in December 1615 that Marie's blandishments had succeeded, for the comtesse now favoured general peace and was amenable to a *rapprochement*.[45] It cannot have escaped the notice of Marie de Médicis that Aligre had eased the path to reconciliation. This ex-leaguer was by now sceptical of the ambitions of aristocratic coteries.

Meanwhile the political instability of the 1610s and 1620s continued to be exacerbated by the emergence at court of cliques gathered around parvenus like the Concinis and the Luynes. As they locked in combat, favourites, ministers, secretaries of state, advisers, came and went in an extraordinary procession. For over ten years government was plagued by a chronic lack of continuity of personnel in its topmost ranks. In 1616 the Concinis purged the government. They in turn were ousted after the murder of Concini in 1617. The Luynes faction ruled the roost until the death of the duc de Luynes in 1621. Then the Brûlarts took over until their overthrow in 1624.[46] Under such circumstances it was little short of impossible for policy to be elaborated and executed with any satisfactory degree of consistency. On both domestic and foreign fronts French policy lacked consistent guiding principles. At the best of times this was a risky state of affairs, but its perils were multiplied in those momentous years from 1618 to 1622 when events inside and outside France confronted the government with a series of crises which only a united, resolute regime could have handled confidently. There was the Bohemian rising of 1618 and its collapse in 1620; the occupation of part of the Palatinate by the Spanish; the Spanish seizure of the Valtelline in 1620; the resumption of the Dutch-Spanish conflict in 1621; the rising of the huguenots in 1621. With turmoil in Europe encouraged and exploited by the Habsburgs, whose offensives looked unstoppable in the 1620s, France could not afford a fissiparous government and rebellious country.

Throughout those turbulent years Aligre resisted absorption into any of the warring cabals, even though his long-standing association with the house of Soissons was well known. Instead he was earning a reputation as a *conseiller d'état* of the highest calibre. By the early 1620s he was appearing in the king's entourage and advising on an

Parker, 'The social foundation of French absolutism, 1610-1630', *Past & Present,* no. 53 (1971), 68

[45] Etienne d'Aligre II to Villeroy, 28 déc. 1615 (B.N., MS Français 15582, f.82).

[46] Outlines of these manoeuvres are in Lublinskaya, *French Absolutism,* 243-60, and V-L. Tapié, *France in the Age of Louis XIII and Richelieu* (London, 1964), chaps. 2 & 3.

impressive range of topics.[47] He was also being mentioned as a possible candidate for the chancellorship. This office had shared the vicissitudes of the government as a whole, for between November 1616 and January 1624 when Aligre eventually was commissioned there were six *gardes des sceaux* or chancellors.[48] The thread of the story can be taken up on 22 September 1622 when the *garde des sceaux,* Méry de Vic, sieur d'Ermenonville, died. Louis XIII considered appointing Aligre who, now that he was in his early sixties, possessed the appropriate seniority of years and experience as well as the necessary talents. Most significantly of all he looked politically independent, a qualification which made him highly attractive to a monarch despairing of factionalism and searching for servants dependent entirely on himself. But Aligre was not chosen. According to Bassompierre[49] who was involved in the manoeuvres, Aligre's chances were dashed when Schomberg and Condé, to whose group de Vic had belonged, decided to champion him against the Brûlarts. His independence was immediately suspect. Bassompierre, who was backing the Brûlarts, claims that it was he who convinced the king that should Aligre be selected, Aligre along with Schomberg and Condé would be, 'trois testes en un chaperon qui manieront l'estat à leur fantaisye'.[50] Louis turned instead to Louis Lefèvre, sieur de Caumartin who was duly charged with the guardianship of the seals. He held the seals for only four months, but on his death in January 1623 it was again a Brûlart who replaced him: Nicolas de Brûlart, sieur de Sillery, chancellor of France since 1607, was now restored to favour. Almost

---

[47] H. de Surirey de Saint Rémy (ed.), *Registres des Déliberations du Bureau de la Ville de Paris,* xviii (1953), 198-9, 426.

[48] The full list of chancellors and *gardes des sceaux* in the reign of Louis XIII is: Nicolas Brûlart, sieur de Sillery (chancellor 1607 to his death on 2 Oct. 1624); Guillaume du Vair, bishop of Lisieux, *premier président du parlement de Provence (garde des sceaux,* May 1616 to his resignation on 25 Nov. 1616); Claude Mangot, *conseiller d'état (garde des sceaux,* 25 Nov. 1616 to 24 April 1617 on the death of Concini); Guillaume du Vair (reappointed 25 April 1617 to his death on 3 Aug. 1621); Charles Albert, duc de Luynes, *pair et connétable de France (garde des sceaux,* 2 Aug. 1621 to his death on 24 Dec. 1621); Méry de Vic, sieur d'Ermenonville, *conseiller d'état (garde des sceaux,* 24 Dec. 1621 to his death on 22 Sept. 1622); Louis Lefèvre, sieur de Caumartin, *président du parlement de Paris (garde des sceaux,* 23 Sept. 1622 to his death on 21 Jan. 1623); chancellor Sillery (resumed seals 23 Jan. 1623 to his dismissal 23 Jan. 1624); Etienne d'Aligre II, sieur de la Rivière, *garde des sceaux,* 24 Jan. 1624 to 2 Oct. 1624, then chancellor to his death on 11 December 1635; exiled from court 1 June 1626); Michel de Marillac, *surintendant des finances (garde des sceaux,* 1 June 1626 to his disgrace 14 Nov. 1630); Charles de l'Aubespine, *conseiller d'état (garde des sceaux,* 14 Nov. 1630 to his arrest 28 Feb. 1633); Pierre Séguier, *président du parlement de Paris (garde des sceaux,* 28 Feb. 1633; chancellor on death of Etienne d'Aligre II to his own death in 1672).

[49] A. de la C. de Chantérac (ed.), *'Journal de ma Vie': Mémoires du Maréchal de Bassompierre* (Paris, 1870-7), iii, 131-40.

[50] *Ibid.,* iii, 135.

a year to the day later he, along with all the Brûlarts, was dismissed. On 24 January 1624 Etienne Aligre at last was chosen as *garde des sceaux*,[51] and when Sillery died in October 1624 d'Aligre succeeded to the chancellorship, taking the oath on the third of the month.[52] He received a title ('La Rivière') with the rank of *chevalier*,[53] and the right to prefix his name by 'de'. His promotion in 1624 took place in circumstances different from those of 1622. Schomberg had been dismissed in 1623 and Condé was out of the country. Nobody wrecked his chances by 'supporting' him.

The Chancellorship

What of the charge that he now exercised?[54] In the words of Guillaume Budé it was, 'le solstice des honneurs, au-dessus duquel il n'y a plus d'avancement dans la robe'.[55] The jurist Peleus deemed it, 'le plus haut sommet des honeurs outre lequel un homme de robbe longue ne peut espérer aucune chose. . . .'[56] The office was of dual character, the chancellor being, 'un magistrat qui réunit à la dignité et fonctions du premier Grand Officier de la Couronne, les fonctions et la dignité de Chef de la Justice'.[57] His obligations as *grand officier* were less striking than as head of justice, but they were by no means negligible. Some were of ceremonial character, for instance at a coronation or a royal wedding. He might be charged with command of

---

[51]'Provisions en faveur du sieur Haligre de l'office de Garde des Sceaux. . . données à Paris, janvier 1624' (B.N., MS Français 18274, fos.343-5) the *lettres* specified that when the chancellorship fell vacant Etienne II should have it; the Venetian ambassador, Giovanni Pesaro, described Etienne II as, 'uomo di bassi natali, ma di buon condizioni, buon francese, di soavissime maniere. E servitore della casa di Soissons, nella quale ha fabbricato la sua fortuna: inimico all concelliere, obbligato al principe di Conde che gli procuro una carica nell'armata' (*Relazioni degli Stati Europei Lette al Senato degli Ambasciatori Veneti*, serie ii – Francia – ii [1859], 176).

[52]'Lettres par lesquelles le roi donne à M. Haligre l'office de chancelier de France, octobre 1624' (B.N., MS Français 18274, fos. 349 ᵛ-53).

[53]This was the rank traditionally assumed by chancellors and other holders of great office (Mousnier, *Les Institutions*, i, 103); in order of precedence, noble ranks were: prince, duc, marquis, comte, baron, chevalier, écuyer (H.J. de Morénas, *Grand Armorial de France* [Paris, 1934], i, 12-13).

[54]Outlines of the chancellorship are in Doucet, *Les Institutions*, i, 103-8; H. Michaud, *La Grande Chancellerie et les Ecritures Royales au Seizième Siècle* (Paris, 1967), 23-61; R. Mousnier, *Lettres et Mémoires Adressés au Chancelier Séguier (1633-1649)* (Paris, 1964), i, 21-6.

[55]Quoted in M. J B. Poigue, *Histoire des Chanceliers de France et des Gardes-des-Sceaux de France depuis Clovis I jusqu'à Louis XVI* (Clermont-Ferrand, 1847), 27.

[56]J. Peléus, *Le Chancelier de France* (Paris, 1611), 30.

[57]M. Guyot, *Traité des Droits, Fonctions, Franchises, Exemptions, Prérogatives, et Privilèges Annexés en France à chaque Dignité. . .* (Paris, 1786-8), iv, 111-12.

a military campaign as happened when chancellor Séguier was sent to Normandie in 1639, or he might be used in a diplomatic capacity. He was senior member of the inner council (*conseil étroit* or *secret*), that small body of advisers that helped the king to formulate policy; in the king's absence he chaired its meetings.

Yet it was justice that occupied most of his energies. As head of the judicial machinery of the kingdom, in which regard he had no peer but the king, the chancellor exhibited certain attributes of monarchy: he held office for life as did the king, and his writ ran throughout the realm as did that of the king. His outstanding function was to draft and send to the sovereign courts the royal *ordonnances, édits, déclarations* and *lettres patentes*. To this end he was head of the *grande chancellerie*, a large institution of between 200 and 300 staff concerned exclusively with this branch of judicial administration.[58] In addition he was head of the sovereign courts.[59] He had right of presence at their assemblies and of nomination to many of their offices. Venality of office had diminished the effectiveness of this latter function, but nevertheless a chancellor could still modify the composition of a court. The weight of his presence was felt especially in the chancelleries of the sovereign courts, for it was to him that their officers were responsible. All of these functions, combined in the chancellor, were indispensable to the unified state. Since France could be bound together effectively only if royal law was standard everywhere, in all questions of the interpretation of legal texts his was the ultimate authority. The unification of the state required royal legal documents that were consistent, uniform and based on precedent. For the king's will to be enforced equally throughout the realm, documents despatched to every part of it must be exactly the same down to every last comma and point. The guarantee of their purity and uniformity was the responsibility of the chancellor.

Under the heading, 'head of justice', came other functions deriving from his status as *garde des sceaux*. They involved not simply keeping the seals but applying them to royal acts, which only came into force after the ceremony had been performed; an unsealed royal act had no standing. In this connection the chancellor was empowered to withhold the seal from an act which he considered unconstitutional or otherwise unsatisfactory; in that case the act had to be reconsidered or

---

[58] See Michaud, *La Grande Chancellerie;* its structure is outlined in Guyot, *Traité des Droits,* iv, 107-8.

[59] The *parlements,* the *cours des aides,* the *chambres des comptes,* the *grand conseil,* the *cour du trésor,* the *cour des monnaies.*

even abandoned.[60] D'Aligre himself was keeper of three seals: the *grands sceaux* of 1610, 1616 and 1617.[61] The necessary seal was affixed to royal acts in a ceremony usually held in the private residence of the chancellor twice or three times a week. It could last from two to five hours, depending on the number of acts to be dealt with.[62]

Was there any distinction between the office of chancellor and that of *garde des sceaux?* It appears probable that the latter charge had become independent in the sixteenth century.[63] By the seventeenth, it could be filled by somebody other than the chancellor under one of two conditions: should the chancellor be in disgrace and deprived of his responsibilities (although not of the office itself, which was held in perpetuity), or should no chancellor be appointed. An example of the first is Etienne II himself. It was the dismissal of chancellor Sillery in January 1624 which led to Etienne's appointment as *garde des sceaux*; when he too was discarded in 1626 his functions were assumed by a new *garde des sceaux*, Marillac. An example of the second condition is found in d'Aligre's son, Etienne III. On the death of chancellor Séguier in 1672 Louis XIV held the office in abeyance. Meanwhile Etienne III was chosen as *garde des sceaux*, and it was not until 1674 that Louis rewarded him with the chancellorship. The keeper of the seals fulfilled all the strictly judicial functions of the chancellor, and enjoyed their accompanying privileges. On the other hand, there is strong evidence that he was not considered a *grand officier de la couronne*.[64] His status correspondingly was lower than that of the chancellor. But of all the distinctions between the two the clearest is that the *garde des sceaux* served at the royal pleasure. His office was revocable at any time. There was no question of its being immune from the king's will.

One last set of chancellor's obligations that should be noted is his headship of the universities and academies. In practice this made him

---

[60]Etienne II exercised the right in 1625 when he refused to seal *lettres* imposing another tax on wine imported into Paris; he did so on the grounds that, although the tax was intended for poor relief, it would be ineffective while placing another burden on excessively-taxed wine (Saint-Rémy [ed], *Registres... de la Ville de Paris*, xviii, 59-60).

[61]L. Rouvier, *Les Sceaux de la Grande Chancellerie de France de 458 à nos Jours* (Marseille, 1935), 63-5; there was also a *sceau secret* of 1615 which the king retained personally.

[62]The ceremony of applying the seals is discussed in E. Schwob, *Un Formulaire de Chancellerie au XVIIIe Siècle* (Paris, 1936), 46-50, and G. Tessier, 'L'Audience du sceau', *Bibliothèque de l'Ecole des Chartes*, cix (1951), 51-95.

[63]Peigue, *Histoire des Chanceliers*, 28, puts the break at 1551; Michaud, *La Grande Chancellerie*, 59, puts it earlier without suggesting a date.

[64]Peigue states categorically that he was not; Michaud is uncertain.

responsible for upholding intellectual and religious orthodoxy within them. This was done less through direct involvement in the day-to-day affairs of these institutions, than through surveillance of printers, bookshops and libraries. It was with the printed word rather than with the lecture theatre that the chancellor was occupied.

Even this brief sketch of the chancellor's activities can serve to confirm his eminence and distinctiveness. It was therefore fitting that he enjoyed privileges commensurate with his status.[65] Not least were the visible symbols of office. In a France, indeed a Europe, where details of ritual could carry heavy implications, outward signs of rank, or the privileges attaching to office, helped to signify and preserve the differentiations essential to a hierarchical society. In public ceremonies the chancellor took precedence over all royal officers, coming immediately after the princes of the blood. He had his own regular form of dress – a crimson robe decorated in gold and pearls – with variations for different occasions. He had the unique right to adorn his private residence with tapestries presented by the king, and bearing the *fleur de lys* as well as his own coat of arms. He was provided with a coach and six horses, as suited one of his standing. Then there were gifts: from the king, a silver-decorated velvet hat at the beginning of each year; 12 aunes (about 15 yards) of velvet from each *trésorier de France* at his appointment, and 4 aunes from each *secrétaire des finances*. He enjoyed ecclesiastical privileges. There was the *droit d'indult* by which he could nominate once to a benefice during his term of office. Thus Etienne II nominated a distant cousin, frère Jean Edeline to a benefice in 1630.[66] Again, any of his children who were in holy orders were exempt from the *décime*.[67] Etienne II's son Nicolas profited from this as *abbé* of Saint Evroul; in the next generation so did two of the sons of Etienne III. The chancellor disposed of a host of other privileges of a financial nature. Given their number and complexity, however, it is proposed to delay discussion of them until Etienne II's own finances are examined.

Etienne d'Aligre in Office

When d'Aligre received the seals governmental change was still in the air. In January 1623 there had been appointed in place of the comte

---

[65] B.N., MS Français 16218, fos.321-4: 'Estat des Droits qui appartiennent à Monseigneur le Chancelier'.

[66] Guyot, *Traité des Droits*, 164.

[67] Financial contribution from church to crown.

de Schomberg as *surintendant des finances,* Charles, marquis de la Vieuville. Warmly trusted by Louis XIII, he was also linked by marriage to the great financier Beaumarchais. The dismissal of the Brûlarts was in no small measure his doing.[68] The coup left him effectively chief minister, but not for long. On 29 April 1624 Louis XIII, with many misgivings, admitted Richelieu into the inner council where there was a great need for somebody with a talent for international affairs. Richelieu in turn undermined la Vieuville's position, encouraging a pamphleteering campaign which impugned his handling of state finances, and in particular deprecating the extortionate rates of interest (up to 16.6%) which financiers were permitted to charge on loans to the government. At court the queen mother and her clique urged the king to rid himself of la Vieuville, whose relationship with Louis was further imperilled by his failures on the international scene. His mishandling of the Valtelline question and his inability to conclude negotiations with the English over the most imaginative of his projects (although it had been talked about for several years), a marriage between the king's sister Henriette and the prince of Wales, left him dangerously exposed to his powerful enemies. On 12 August he was arrested and incarcerated in the *château* of Amboise.[69]

D'Aligre was involved in the aftermath of la Vieuville's disgrace. To complete his triumph, Richelieu in September proposed the creation of a *chambre de justice* along the lines of those of 1584, 1597, 1604 and 1607, which would investigate the malpractices of financiers and royal *officiers* who had dealt with them on behalf of the crown.[70] It was d'Aligre's responsibility as *garde des sceaux* to oversee the drafting and registration of the edict which would establish the *chambre*. Work proceeded speedily, the edict being issued on 21 October 1624.[71] It authorised a twenty-strong commission to probe as far back as 30 September 1607 when the last *chambre* disbanded; in fact the intention was to concentrate on recent years and so underline la Vieuville's ignominy. The *chambre* was effective: it

---

[68]Details are in Lublinskaya, *French Absolutism,* 244-58.

[69]He escaped in 1625; he published an apologia addressed to d'Aligre as chancellor: *Lettre de Monsieur le Marquis de Vieuville à Monseigneur le Chancelier* (1625) (B.N., MS Clairambault 1133, fos.472-82).

[70]P. Grillon (ed.), *Les Papiers de Richelieu* (Paris, 1975-), i, 116-22; see F. Bayard, 'Les chambres de justice de la première moitié du XVII⁰ siècle', *Cahiers d'Histoire,* xix, no. 2 (1974), 120-40.

[71]B.N., Collection Dupuy 848, fos.135-42: 'Edict du Roy pour l'establissement d'une Chambre de Justice... 21 oct. 1624'; the hasty passage of the edict through the *parlement* of Paris was aided by the co-operation shown to d'Aligre by Mathieu Molé, *procureur general* in the *parlement* (see A. Champollion-Figeac [éd.], *Mémoires de Mathieu Molé* i, [Paris, 1855], 334-9).

imposed fines totalling 10,800,000 livres,[72] and further penalties on thirteen culprits, five of whom were condemned to death. Richelieu had made his point: la Vieuville had tolerated such shady financial practices as warranted official investigation.[73]

The other outstanding issue of 1624 was the English marriage. Once again d'Aligre was involved. In August 1624 a new team of French negotiators was selected to meet the English representatives, the earl of Carlisle and Henry Rich, later earl of Holland. The team was composed mainly of new men in the *conseil étroit*, or old ones restored. There was Richelieu himself; d'Aligre as the new *garde des sceaux*; Schomberg, recently reintroduced into the inner council at Richelieu's insistence, and an authority on England having served there as ambassador in 1615 and 1616; cardinal de la Rochefoucauld, the senior member of the *conseil étroit*;[74] and Loménie de Brienne, sieur de la Ville-aux-Clercs, only twenty-nine years old, but already admired by Richelieu. This time discussions ended satisfactorily, although Carlisle and Rich drove a hard financial bargain. Henriette's dowry of 800,000 écus (2,400,000 livres) was higher than those of her two elder sisters.[75] In return there were English concessions on the question of religion. Henriette and her entourage would worship as catholics in England, where the recusancy laws would be lifted and all catholics released from prison. These provisions were invaluable to Richelieu. He was genuinely concerned to preserve Henriette's catholicism, but also needed defence against inevitable criticism at home of a 'protestant' marriage, especially since in July 1624 an alliance had been signed with the protestant Dutch Republic. Most of the details of the terms were the work of Richelieu, Schomberg and Brienne. D'Aligre's functions were to advise on legal matters and to assume responsibility for drafting the marriage contract of 3 May 1625 which followed on the settlement. He saw it through the necessary procedures, including registration with the *grand sceau*.[76]

Meanwhile chancellor Sillery died on 1 October 1624, d'Aligre assuming the chancellorship on 3 October. Congratulations came in

---

[72]J. Dent, *Crisis in Finance: Crown, Financiers and Society in Seventeenth-Century France* (Newton Abbot, 1973), 104.

[73]The *chambre* disbanded in May 1625.

[74]Normally the chancellor was the senior member, but Sillery was in disgrace; the honour thus devolved upon the cardinal.

[75]Elisabeth de France married Philip III of Spain with a dowry of 500,000 écus; Christine married Victor-Amadeus of Savoy with one of 400,000 écus (M. Valtat, *Les Contrats de Mariage dans la Famille Royale en France au XVIIe Siècle* [Paris, 1953], 117).

[76]*Ibid.*, 24-5, 28-9.

from many sides, including the *parlement* of Aix[77] and his home town of Chartres.[78] The usual crop of adulatory pamphlets appeared such as *Discours à Monsieur d'Haligre, Chancelier de France* and *Discours sur la Promotion de Monseigneur le Chancelier...*[79] These and others like them pursued fairly uniform themes: the state suffers chronic maladies; justice is flouted everywhere; financial chicanery is rife; where can the king find advisers who will guide him wisely and in constancy? In d'Aligre Louis has discovered a servant whose sagacity, learning, knowledge of law, and probity, are worthy of the chancellorship. One pamphlet adopted an independent line in that it proffered advice to d'Aligre; it carries a further interest in that it was written by Jacques l'Huillier, a member of a distinguished legal family with which the d'Aligres were by now allied through marriage.[80] The objective of the chancellor, so it argued, was to uphold justice and to serve the financial requirements of the king. To these ends it counselled four guiding principles: vigilance against corruption, harmonious relations with those nearest to the king, cooperation with the *maîtres de requêtes*, and resolute defence of the royal interest in the *parlement* of Paris.[81] Such pamphlets were routine when a figure as important as a chancellor was appointed. If none of them penetrated very deeply into the problems of the day, they nevertheless bore testimony to the ever-present public concern at those two essentials of government, justice and finance.

Among the institutions complimenting d'Aligre on his promotion was the *parlement* of Paris, which on 7 October sent a delegation bearing its felicitations.[82] It registered his *lettres de provision* on 5 December,[83] after which, on 18 December, he made his first official visit to the assembly in his new capacity.[84] The ceremony, preceded by a lengthy procession through the streets of Paris, was held in the Sainte Chapelle. At an appropriate point in the proceedings d'Aligre gave a speech which took as its theme the relationship between king

---

[77]Bibliothèque de Carpentras, MS 1780, f.366.

[78]Lépinois, *Histoire de Chartres*, ii, 398.

[79]Copies in B.N., Ln^{27}242,246.

[80]See below p. 77.

[81]*Advis a M. Haligre, garde des sceaux de France, a sa promotion 1624 [à chancelier]* (B.N., MS Dupuy 851, fos.145-8).

[82]B.N., MS Français 7545, fos.224-4^v,

[83]B.N., MS Français 7545, fos.226-7.

[84]An account of the ceremony and speeches is in B.N., MS Français 7545, fos. 226-43; Collection Dupuy 647, fos.91-100; A.N., K649, no.5(2), and Duchesne, *Histoire des Chanceliers*, 767-9.

and parlement. He began by acknowledging the prestige of the parlement, which he compared to a temple, 'où la vraye justice réside'. It was, 'embaulmée de la bonne odeur qui procède des rares vertus de tant de grands personnages qui y sont establis....' But its status should not be exaggerated. It was a temple to the image of God and nothing more. It was not in itself the image of God. Only kings, 'sont les vrayes Images de Dieu et se peuvent dire les vrays Dieux en terre, car ils ont des marques visibles de la Divinité'.[85] The right to judge men, therefore, belonged exclusively to the king. In the exercise of their functions judges and magistrates were like sons acting on behalf of their father. Indeed, a family-like relationship existed between king and magistrates (and especially between king and *parlement* of Paris, which was held in unique esteem) wherein the king was anxious to uphold their legitimate rights. In this role of protector he was acutely conscious of their sense of grievance on certain matters. But he considered that abuses had crept into the *parlement*. He disliked the tendency for individual families to monopolise particular offices, for judges to approach cases in a partisan spirit, for the number of *officiers* to go on multiplying throughout the realm. Of the grievances of the *parlement*, three were most urgent. Firstly, there were complaints about the large number of edicts that the *parlement* received for registration, many of which it could not consider fully. The reason for the plenitude of edicts was that, 'le Roy avoit esté constraint de venir à ces moyens extraordinaires pour pouvoir fournir aux grandes despenses qu'il luy a fallu faire pour remédier aux désordres de son Estat'. Secondly, a large back-log of cases requiring judgement by the *parlement* had accumulated. How could it rid itself of this encumbrance? The problem in fact was of the *parlement's* own making because of disorder in its proceedings over many years, and 'n'y pouvait remédier que par le temps'. Thirdly, the number of *officiers* in law courts was excessive. This echoed the crown's opinion, and was a problem to which d'Aligre would devote much attention.

How should the speech be interpreted? On one level it was a formal address suited to the occasion. It was prudent, conservative, cautious. Set in a broader context, however, it assumed wider implications.[86] During these years, as throughout his reign, Louis XIII sought to restrict the *parlements* to their judicial functions, to

---

[85] The reference is to the coronation, when the king was anointed with holy oil and was deemed to possess powers of healing.

[86] R. Mousnier, 'Le conseil du roi de la mort de Henri IV au gouvernement personnel de Louis XIV', *La Plume, la Faucille et le Marteau* (Paris, 1970), 142-6; J.H. Shennan, *The Parlement of Paris* (London, 1968), 246-9.

oblige them to relinquish their ambition to deal with political affairs of state. This was to be a strategy championed by Richelieu and may well have underlain d'Aligre's speech. Although there is no documentary proof, it seems likely that in view of the importance of the occasion on which it was given, he had discussed the speech with the *conseil étroit*. He treated the *parlement* exclusively as a judicial assembly; the problems he raised and discussed were of a judicial nature; there was no concession to the principle that there was a political dimension to the *parlement's* functions. This was to be a source of constant tension between crown and *parlement* down to the Fronde rebellions, neither side being willing to compromise on a matter of fundamental principle. On 18 December 1624 d'Aligre adhered faithfully to the crown view: the *parlement* was a judicial instrument of state and nothing more.

The year 1624 was dominated for d'Aligre in his capacity as *garde des sceaux* and chancellor, by the English marriage and the *chambre de justice* of that year. In 1625 the quinquennial general assembly of the clergy met, drawing him into its deliberations over two matters. Firstly, the assembly made its usual allegations that the crown had been trespassing on the financial and judicial rights of the church. A deputation headed by cardinal de Sourdis presented a proposal to the chancellor that they should meet representatives of the king's council to discuss their grievances face to face. D'Aligre resisted, foreseeing a dangerous precedent; but to his friend and colleague Molé, *procureur général* in the *parlement* of Paris, he confessed that he had been hard pressed and earnestly requested Molé's support in defending the royal interest.[87] Secondly, he was pulled into a dispute that arose from the publication of two anonymous pamphlets deploring the 'protestant' foreign policy of the government: *L'Avertissement au Roi Très Chrestien* and *Mysteria Politica*. The assembly condemned the pamphlets, but the papal nuncio, Spada, objected that it had done so in terms implying that the pope had no authority over kings. Meanwhile the *parlement* of Paris, using similar language, had also denounced the pamphlets and issued a decree against them. Spada appealed to d'Aligre to use his influence to have the decree revoked. Likewise bishops from the assembly met him at the end of February 1626 with the same request (the assembly had revised its position in the light of Spada's protest). By now, however, there had been introduced into the affair the question of the autonomy of the *parlement*. Matters dragged on irresolutely, d'Aligre receiving one

---

[87] Champollion-Figeac (ed.), *Mémoires de Molé*, i, 342-3; P. Blet S.J., *Le Clergé de France et la Monarchie: Etude sur les Assemblées Générales du Clergé de 1615 à 1666* (Rome, 1959), i, 278-82.

deputation after another. They were still unresolved when he lost the seals later in the year.[88]

D'Aligre was highly accomplished in the routine work of the chancellor; his days were filled with the drafting of edicts, the expedition of letters, and so on, in addition to weightier matters concerning the English marriage and the assembly of the clergy, the meetings of the *conseil étroit* and the host of other obligations which came the way of a chancellor. However, when it came to political infighting, he was bereft of talent, too easily surrendering to the momentary impulse that would rescue him from an embarrassing position yet damage his longterm prospects. It was this tendency that led to his undoing in 1626. Richelieu, with characteristic clarity of thought and purpose, was endeavouring to impose a coherent pattern on both domestic and foreign policy. But his attack on social and political problems kindled an aristocratic cabal with strong *dévot* overtones, pledged to his overthrow or even assassination. The figure around whom this opposition grouped was the king's eighteen-year-old brother Gaston duc d'Anjou (duc d'Orléans from August 1626). Various powerful intriguers saw in him the instrument of their purpose: the queen mother, Condé and Soissons to name but three. In the short term it was Anjou's governor, the maréchal d'Ornano, who made the running. His demand in 1626 that if his master were to be admitted to the *conseil étroit* then he should too, was an ominous and naked sign of political ambition. To forestall this nascent menace and to discourage others, Richelieu persuaded the king to authorise the arrest of d'Ornano. On 4 May d'Ornano and Claude de Chaudebonne, a favourite of Anjou, were imprisoned in Vincennes; the following day two friends of d'Ornano, Modène and Déageant, and d'Ornano's brothers, de Mazargues and the *abbé* de Montmajour, were seized; d'Ornano's wife was ordered to leave Paris.[89] Anjou reacted violently and hot-headedly, uttering lurid threats against the king's ministers. In this mood he encountered d'Aligre, abusing him for having complied in the arrest. D'Aligre committed a fatal error: overawed by the anger of the prince, he denied any part in the affair. That denial ended his career.

In the words of Richelieu, d'Aligre 'n'avoit pas osé soutenir à Monsieur [Anjou] la justice du conseil de sa Majesté sur l'arrêt du maréchal d'Ornano'.[90] That the chancellor of France should shrink

[88] Blet, *Le Clergé de France,* 335-61.

[89] Grillon (ed.), *Les Papiers de Richelieu,* i, 317-18; Tapié, *France in the Age of Louis,* 155-6.

[90] J-F. Michaud et J-J. F. Poujoulat (eds.), *Mémoires du Cardinal de Richelieu* (Paris, 1837), iii, 84.

from associating himself with a royal command was unforgiveable. D'Aligre's retreat before the ill-temper of Anjou marked him, in Richelieu's eyes, as a weakling unfitted to his charge. Of what use to the king and to Richelieu, who rightly anticipated a fierce struggle with court cabals,[91] was a chancellor who could be brow-beaten by an eighteen-year-old youth? Rumours spread that d'Aligre was to lose the seals. On 12 May the king dropped a heavy hint to Michel de Marillac, a creature of Richelieu and one of the two *surintendants des finances* appointed to replace la Vieuville, that greater honours soon would be coming his way.[92] On 14 May d'Aligre asked the king if the gossip had anything to it. While refusing to give a straight answer, Louis indicated that he was dissatisfied with him, especially because of the conversation with Anjou. D'Aligre attempted to bluff his way out by pretending that Anjou and he had not in fact spoken about d'Ornano. He received a blunt reply: 'Vous en avez menti, car mon frère me l'a dit et il est bien plus croyable que vous.'[93] The anticipated blow came on 1 June. D'Aligre was instructed to surrender the seals to Marillac, now *garde des sceaux,* and to retire to his estates at La Rivière. He was still chancellor and continued to enjoy all the rights and emoluments of the chancellorship, but his active career was over. Richelieu seized the opportunity to fortify his own position further: another of his men, d'Effiat, replaced Marillac as *surintendant des finances.*[94]

The turbulent political currents that had raised d'Aligre to the surface in 1624 thus submerged him again in 1626. But although it is undeniable that his conduct during the d'Ornano affair was dishonourable and feeble in the extreme, it is more than possible that Richelieu in any case had his eye on a charge as important as the guardianship of the seals; that he was looking for a pretext to nudge the chancellor into retirement. The charitable interpretation of d'Aligre's pusillanimity during his interview with Anjou is that he was simply in a funk when confronted by the duke. Yet the more unfavourable possibility cannot have escaped Richelieu, that a calculating d'Aligre who in the past had close links with the house of Soissons, and as recently as 1622 had been backed by Condé for the guardianship of the seals, had attempted to play for safety, to cover himself should the cardinal's enemies indeed secure his removal. Either way d'Aligre

---

[91] On 20 May 1626 Richelieu was provided with a bodyguard (Grillon [ed.], *Papiers de Richelieu,* i, 339).

[92] *Ibid.,* i, 320.

[93] E. Griselle (ed.), *Lettres de la Main de Louis XIII* (Paris, 1914), ii, 520.

[94] Lublinskaya, *French Absolutism,* 287.

was finished. Later, in retirement at La Rivière, in one of his many conversations with Jean-Baptiste Souchet, historian of Chartres and frequent visitor to the *château,* d'Aligre confessed that after the initial bitterness had subsided he was not displeased to be away from the court with its incessant intrigues and factions.[95] In his mid-sixties he had proved ill-suited to that labyrinth. His dismissal appears to have provoked little surprise. The general opinion was probably that of Pierre Dupuy: 'Nous nous pleignons du chancelier qu'il estoit mol; l'on l'a osté et l'on nous en donne un autre que a de la vigueur'[96]

A Comment

Within d'Aligre's career up to 1626 two periods made an exceptional contribution to his ascension to the chancellorship: 1591-4 when Henri IV's base was at Chartres, and 1616-24 when there existed frequent vacancies in the upper reaches of government. He was a beneficiary of that social and political turmoil which scourged France during his lifetime. Without consciously aiming at the chancellorship, he was in the right place at the right time, and had a valuable association with the Soissons. The civil wars of the late 1500s and early 1600s displayed few creative features, yet among them may be numbered the opportunities for preferment that they gave to people like d'Aligre. In more settled times, he and others who emerged from obscurity, might well have settled for provincial or minor Parisian careers. The Colberts, Pussorts, Foucquets, Phélypeaux are others who, like the d'Aligres, prospered in business, acquired legal and financial offices in the provinces, bought land, claimed a title, attached themselves to great aristocratic families, came to Paris in search of positions in central government or administration, married shrewdly, and then proceeded to flourish in the service of the king. A *château* would be built in the country where the head of the family could live *noblement* when he desired. By disturbing social stability, by forcing the crown to cast far and wide in the search for reliable servants, civil strife encouraged a social mobility of great potential value to the kingdom, if only in the sense that it could let new and talented blood into central government. Yet one should be wary of making the facile assumption that new blood meant more perceptive or effective government. D'Aligre's career, in fact, illustrates one of the most knotty problems facing Louis XIII.

[95] Souchet, *Histoire. . .de Chartres,* iv, 347-8.

[96] Pierre Dupuy to Peiresc, Paris, 8 jan. 1627 (P. de Tamizey de Larroque [éd.], *Lettres de Peiresc aux Fréres Dupuy* [Paris, 1888], i, 807; the reference to 'un autre' is, of course, to Marillac.

However valid the theory that later in the century Louis XIV brought people of bourgeois origins into government as part of his absolutist programme, no such comment would be convincing for the 1610s and 1620s. In so far as d'Aligre and others advanced in royal service, it was a symptom of the crown's infirmities, not of a conscious governmental revolution. Rather than pointing to the future *embourgeoisement* of French government, d'Aligre exemplifies Louis XIII's current difficulties in creating a settled team of advisers. Under Louis XIII and during much of the reign of Louis XIV, the answer to the puzzle of how stability could be introduced into central government, was to be found in the emergence of family 'clans' with their 'creatures' and *fidèles.* families like the Colberts or Phélypeaux were to create networks of influence in central government through the careful promotion of members of the family and their 'creatures'. The head of the family, once in a position of political influence would practise nepotism even of the most blatant type in order to amass power for the 'clan'. In this way, as the king controlled the head of the 'clan', so he controlled an extensive band of servants associated with it. Richelieu, Mazarin, the great ministers of Louis XIV all adhered to this pattern. It remains to be seen whether the d'Aligres did too.

3

THE PROPERTY AND FAMILY OF ETIENNE D'ALIGRE II

From d'Aligre the careerist we turn to d'Aligre the man of property and head of a branch of his family. This is not to suggest that the themes of career, property and family were separate and distinct in his life. One purpose of this chapter is to illustrate the opposite: that his public career had implications for his property and family. If his appearance at the centre of the national stage was to prove more than a brilliant but transitory episode in the history of the d'Aligres de la Rivière, it was imperative that he use his eminence to augment their wealth and social standing. As a preliminary step, it is proposed to consider some of the roles that property, the first subject under discussion, played in family life in seventeenth-century France.

Property and the Family

Of all forms of property land was most prized, for it was a source of prestige as well as of wealth. Yet no simple equation existed between the amount of land possessed and the degree of prestige subsequently enjoyed. More lustre attached to land near Paris or one of the other great cities, or to the rich soil of a province like Normandie, than to the barren mountains of Auvergne. A *fief de dignité,* that is land with a noble title and a variety of seigneurial rights and obligations, was preferable to land *en roture,* that is non-noble land. On a fief a *château* could be built or an existing one occupied or improved. The head of the family could live there *noblement,* which is to say that he could hunt (an exceedingly 'noble' pastime), enjoy his seigneurial dues and administer seigneurial justice; this last activity also helped to ensure the general subordination of tenants to his will. The income from dues and justice may not have amounted to much, but the prestige associated with them was considerable[1] A fief guaranteed its possessor a certain role in local society. He had his special seat in the parish church. He was invited to baptisms, marriages, funerals. He would certainly be popular if he defended his tenants against outside

---

[1]G. d'Avenel, *La Noblesse Française sous Richelieu* (Paris, 1901), 145-7; P. Lemercier, *Les Justices Seigneuriales de la Région Parisienne de 1580 à 1789* (Paris, 1933), 65-128.

interference[2]. The *château* could be the centre of local cultural life. In short, if he wished, the *seigneur* could cut a figure of some dash in his locality.

As a source of wealth, land had a cash value. This would not normally be realised, except as regards land peripheral to the central requirements of a family. Small parcels might be bought or sold as circumstances dictated, but the principal holdings, especially any fiefs, would be bequeathed from one generation to another. Only the most desperate conditions would lead to their alienation. It further produced an annual return in cash and in produce. That proportion of land which a *seigneur* required for his personal maintenance supplied his household with necessities such as food, timber, medicinal herbs. There was often a mill which his tenants used, paying in either cash or kind. Any surpluses from his personal domain could be sold off; timber was a highly profitable commodity in this respect.[3] Other land could be leased on a cash or kind basis. Again, it was excellent security on which to raise a loan. It was much easier for a landowner to borrow a large sum than a non-landowner. In other words, land was a source of wealth in that it raised the owner's credit-rating.

Another form of property to be considered is buildings and their contents. Buildings did not confer prestige as did land (no *château*, for instance, ever carried a noble title), but they did reflect it. This is especially true of Paris under Henri IV and Louis XIII, where the *hôtels* of the fashionable Marais, in addition to representing considerable investments of capital, reflected the honour of their proprietors who frequented the royal court. Among the contents of such buildings some were of primarily practical value: kitchen implements, everyday furniture, draperies, bedding, horses, carriages, and so on. Others served different purposes. There were luxury items such as tapestries, paintings, carpets, mirrors, jewels. Symbols of prestige, they also formed part of the material resources of a family, to be transmitted over the generations as part of the family heritage. They were also a safe form of investment or hedges against inflation, particularly when governments readily resorted to currency manipulations. Furthermore, luxury items were easily convertible into cash should that be necessary. Their sale or mortgage was less damaging to family

---

[2] This could even extend to supporting rebellion against tax agents of the crown; there is much literature on the subject, e.g. R. Mousnier, *Peasant Uprisings in Seventeenth Century France, Russia and China* (London, 1960), 49-52.

[3] Forest also facilitated the noble occupation of hunting, and was prized as such: see J. Meuvret, 'Domaines ou ensembles territoriaux? Quelques exemples de l'implication du régime de la propriété et de la structure sociale dans la France des XVIIe et XVIIIe siècle', *Etudes d'Histoire Economique* (Paris, 1971), 186-7.

prestige than was the alienation of land, and may even have sold more easily. After all, more people would be ready to buy a diamond necklace than a piece of land that might be in a rural back-water. The contents of a residence would also include items connected with leisure and cultural pursuits: a library, musical instruments, weapons, perhaps even a collection of scientific and antiquarian curiosities. This category, unlike the others, was potentially a source of prestige rather than just a reflection of it. In the early 1600s the cultural life of Paris and other cities was aided by the emergence of literary and scientific *salons,* many of which were organised by ladies of high society. There, leading figures of the Paris intelligentsia met nobles, churchmen, courtiers, members of the government, to discuss matters of scientific, philosophic, and literary interest. The host or hostess of a thriving *salon* thereby acquired much social and cultural prestige.

A discussion of property should include public offices, which by the 1600s had become virtually the hereditary possessions of their 'owners'.[4] Many offices had a cash value which could be realised through a sale; but as with land, families preferred to retain them. There was also an annual income stemming from the functions associated with an office. But offices conferred prestige too. Some, such as an eminent position in a *parlement,* even bore a noble title. Over several generations families would steadily accumulate more and costlier offices (perhaps selling some lesser ones in the process) so as to appreciate both their wealth and status.

Under the heading of property the final item to be considered is *rentes.* Some took the form of state bonds. The government would borrow from the public, paying an annual interest or *rente,* usually of about 8 per cent.[5] Others were *rentes constituées,* which in fact were loans between individuals intended to circumvent the laws on usury. The procedure was that the lender 'gave' money to the borrower; it was genuinely alienated for he could not insist on its repayment, nor could he 'give' it for a fixed period. In return the borrower constituted a *rente* to the lender, usually the equivalent of 5 per cent of the sum borrowed. In practice this *rente,* paid annually, was the interest on the loan; but only if the borrower failed to pay it over five consecutive years could the lender take steps to reclaim his original money.[6] The attraction of *rentes constituées* as against state *rentes* in the eyes of investors will be discussed in connection with Etienne II's finances,

---

[4]See R. Mousnier, *La Vénalité des Offices sous Henri IV et Louis XIII* (2e. ed., Paris, 1971).

[5]See B. Schnapper, *Les Rentes au XVIe Siècle* (Paris, 1957), 169.

[6]F.B. de Visme, *La Science Parfaite des Notaires* (Paris, 1771), i, 511-13.

but in the present context it can be noted that a *rentier* not only would expect an annual return of 5 to 8 per cent on his investments; he further derived prestige in that he did not need to live by manual labour.

Land, buildings and their contents, offices and *rentes* are the categories according to which Etienne II's property will be analysed. It should be emphasised that at every stage it was not simply wealth that was at stake; prestige was too.

Land[7]

Etienne d'Aligre's principal estate and residence after 1626 was, of course, La Rivière. In addition to the *château* and its grounds there were 316.5 arpents (about 330 acres) of land: 55 per cent was *terre labourable,* 33.5 per cent woodland, 11.5 per cent meadow and pasture; there was also a water mill. Almost two-thirds were held in fief to the bishop of Chartres,[8] namely all the woodland (106 arpents), the mill, 78 arpents of *terre labourable* and 16.5 arpents of meadow and pasture. This portion was d'Aligre's *domaine proche,* or that which supplied his household. The remaining 116 arpents were *en roture* (96 arpents of *terre labourable* and 20 of meadow and pasture); they were leased at 1,800 livres per annum,[9] or 12 per cent of their value which was 14,800 livres. If it is assumed that the land held in fief, whose value was 23,480 livres, also gave a return of some 12 per cent (about 2,820 livres), then the entire estate of La Rivière probably gave an annual return of some 4,620 livres. This excludes the water mill and the produce of the *château* gardens. The value of the estate less the *château* and its grounds was 38,280 livres, or 122 livres per arpent.

A few miles from La Rivière in the parishes of Pontgouin and Le Favril, and in the *seigneurie* of La Forêt, d'Aligre owned more land *en roture,* which he also leased for cash in four lots. Details of these are given in Table 1.

---

[7]Unless otherwise stated the information in this section is from A.N., M.C., XXIV-348; Partage, 9 mars 1638 (this document lists and evaluates most of Etienne II's property at his death and prior to its division), and B.N., Pièces Originales 36 & 37 (which contain details on some of his *rentes*).

[8]There is no indication of any dues that Etienne II owed.

[9]There is no indication of the length of the lease.

Table 1

Title		Area in arpents	Value in livres	Lease per annum	Value per arpent
Ferme de Bellevoir	77 8	*terre lab.* meadow & pas.	7,040	352 (5%)	83
Pré de Gérainville	21.5	*terre lab.*	2,080	140 (5%)	97
Métairie de la Rousselière	44 6 1	*terre lab.* meadow & pas. woodland	6,000	300 (5%)	118
—	7.5 2.5 0.5	*terre lab.* meadow & pas. woodland	1,040	52 (5%)	100

Together these plots totalled 168 arpents: 150 of *terre labourable*, 16.5 of meadow and pasture, with only 1.5 of woodland. Set in open country the value of these pieces of land varied considerably from 83 to 118 livres per arpent. Given their proximity to La Rivière they rounded it off, providing d'Aligre with a continuous belt of land from the banks of the Eure to the village of Le Favril.

Just north-east of La Rivière was his *seigneurie* of Les Hayes. Part was held in fief to the duc de Mantoüe in his capacity as baron de Châteauneuf-en-Thymerais. Into this category came 164 arpents of *terre labourable*, 16 of woodland, 4.5 of meadow and pasture, and a house with 2 arpents of land. 104 arpents of the *terre labourable* and the 16 arpents of woodland were *censive*, which is to say that although d'Aligre possessed seigneurial rights, the tenants paid a fixed annual sum or *cens* which gave them practical if not legal proprietorship.[10] The rate of *cens* was 22 sols per 7.5 arpents, or 17 livres 12 sols in all. A further 2 or 3 arpents were held in fief to another, un-named *seigneur*, while *en roture* there were 49 arpents of *terre labourable* and 4.5 of meadow and pasture. Les Hayes thus comprised 216 arpents of *terre labourable*, 16 of woodland, and 9 of meadow and pasture; the remainder adjoined the house. Valued at 12,630 livres, the whole *seigneurie* was let at 564 livres (4.4 per cent). The land per arpent was worth less than at La Rivière: only 52 livres. This may help to explain the low rate of 4.4 per cent that d'Aligre charged for the lease; other factors could include the comparatively low area of woodland, and the 'loss' of the land *en censive*, whose tenants paid a fixed sum.

The third *seigneurie* of Chonvilliers lay south-east of Chartres. There was a house with 4 arpents of fruit bushes and trees, 394

[10] Doucet, *Les Institutions*, ii, 474-5.

arpents of *terre labourable,* 3 arpents of vine, and a water mill. About one third was held in fief to the sieur de Truitin and carried a seigneurial obligation of 9 muids (about 530 gallons) of wine. The rest was held *en franc; franc fief*[11] was paid at 2 muids (102 bushels) of wheat and 23 livres in *rentes* to the blind of Chartres. Valued at 15,000 livres Chonvilliers was leased at 700 livres (4.6 per cent). Once again, the charges in grain and *rentes* and the absence of woodland, may explain its poor value.

Of the three *seigneuries* La Rivière was by far the most valuable and profitable. This doubtless explains why d'Aligre built his *château* there rather than at Les Hayes or Chonvilliers. On the banks of the Eure, containing a generous portion of woodland which fitted *la vie noble*[12], it met his requirements more aptly than did the other two *seigneuries.* As sieur de la Rivière, d'Aligre owed *foi et hommage* to the bishop of Chartres[13]. He may have chafed at this, for as chancellor of France he stood higher in the social hierarchy than did the bishop. But even this was preferable to Chonvilliers which obliged him to a mere 'sieur'; at least through Les Hayes he owed homage to a duke, albeit through the inferior title of baron.

By 1635 d'Aligre possessed extensive tracts and small pieces of land elsewhere: this is described in Table 2.

Although the document on which the information in Table 2 is based converts all the leases into cash as depicted in the table, in fact d'Aligre let Gellainville, Chaunay, Chartainvilliers and Brainville in kind. In its conversions the document employs the rate of 5 livres per sétier of grain.[15] Gellainville was let at 2.5 muids (30 sétiers or 129 bushels) of wheat and 2.5 muids of *méteil* (a mixture of wheat and rye); the cash equivalent is 300 livres. Chaunay was let at 5 sétiers (4.3 bushels) of grain: 25 livres; Chartainvilliers at 4 muids (48 sétiers or 206 bushels): 240 livres; and Brainville at 13 sétiers (56 bushels): 65 livres. In other words d'Aligre adopted a policy of mixed leasing, some land in cash, some in kind. That let in kind guaranteed him 126

---

[11]*Franc fief* was a sum payable by non-noble holders of fiefs; Etienne II would have ceased paying it when he became noble in 1624.

[12]See n. 3.

[13]A.D., Eure-et-Loir, MS G 116, fos. 16-17^v.

[14]This is a notional figure, the prices of grain per sétier in Charters in the 1630s being:

1630	12	1	8 s.	0 d.	1635	6	14	0
1631	9		6	0	1636	7	5	0
1632	8		7	0	1637	6	15	0
1633	6		15	0	1638	6	0	0
1634	6		9	0	1639	5	19	0

(Doyen, *Histoire. . . de Chartres,* ii, 377).

Table 2

Title	Arpents	Type	Value	Annual Return
S. Baite	65	terre lab.	11,500	500 (4.3%)
Neuilly[15]	3.5	meadow	1,035	45 (4.3%)
Uscouan	4	terre lab.	690	30 (4.3%)
Ensonville	100	terre lab.	4,100	186 (4.5%)
Gellainville	85	terre lab.	5,400	300 (5.5%)
Chaunay	5	terre lab.	400	25 (6.2%)
Chartainvilliers	67	terre lab.	4,800	240 (5.0%)
Challet	10	terre & vine	265	18-5-0
Sérèsville	0.75	vine	45*	2-5-0*
Brainville	65*	terre lab.	1,300*	65*
S. Barthélemy	1	vine	60*	3*
S. Prest	165*	meadow	16,600*	830
	571.25		46,195	2,244-10-0
La Rivière	316.5		38,280	4,620*(12%)
Pontgouin & Le Favril	168		16,160	844 (5.2%)
Les Hayes	243		12,630	564 (4.4%)
Chonvilliers	401		15,000	700 (4.6%)
	1,699.75		128,265	8,972-10-0
Chartres		Some gardens on the outskirts of the city: size and value not known.		

*estimated

sétiers (almost 542 bushels) of grain each year irrespective of harvest fluctuations. Since he resided at La Rivière from 1626 to 1636 and at times would have had a large household to maintain, a direct supply of grain in this way was self-evidently of great practical value. Brainville has the added interest that d'Aligre had acquired it from the family of Benoist Nolent. Nolent had once been d'Aligre's *fermier* of Chonvilliers but had fallen behind in his payments by 2,627 livres 12 sols. On Nolent's death his property at Brainville had passed to d'Aligre in payment of the debt.

The rate of return which the land leased in kind brought to d'Aligre was higher than leased in cash: between 5 per cent and 6 per cent as against 4 per cent to 5 per cent. Is it possible to estimate how heavy a burden this was on the lessees? In an exact sense it is not, but an approximation is feasible. The fluctuations and uncertainties of harvests were such as to make the annual payment of grain to d'Aligre a varying proportion of the actual produce of the land. Certain considerations should be borne in mind. Gellainville, Chaunay, Chartainvilliers and Brainville were measured not in area but in productive capacity. In that part of France, however, the custom was

---

[15] It is uncertain whether this is Neuilly west of Paris, or Neuilly-sur-Eure, about fifteen miles north-west of La Riviere.

to have only two-thirds of land under cultivation, the other third remaining fallow for a year; there were two harvests a year, one from a spring sowing and the other from an autumn sowing.[16] To take Gellainville as an example, its 'area' or productive capacity was 8 muids 10 sétiers (106 sétiers); two-thirds under cultivation gives about 70 sétiers, which after two harvests is 140 sétiers (about 600 bushels). D'Aligre took 5 muids (60 Sétiers), or about 43 per cent of the theoretical annual grain produce of Gellainville. Gellainville was thus let on a share-cropping basis (or *métayage*), the tenant paying his rent not in cash, but by a portion of his annual crop. By the same estimates d'Aligre took about 40 per cent of the produce of Chartainvilliers, and 60 per cent of the small piece of land at Chaunay. There is insufficient information to suggest a figure for Brainville.

A glance at the map indicates the location of his land. It was all within the Chartres region, overwhelmingly within the grain-producing area that surrounded the city. Given the outstanding role played by grain in the seventeenth century diet and given the big market in Paris, d'Aligre's land was of the most profitable type possible. To summarise, he owned about 1,700 arpents valued at some 128,265 livres, which in cash terms gave an annual return of about 9,000 livres.

Château and houses

In addition to the houses at Les Hayes and Chonvilliers, d'Aligre owned the *château* at La Rivière, the house in the rue d'Avron in Paris, and another in Chartres in the parish of Sainte Foy. The residence in the rue d'Avron consisted of, 'un corps de logis, court privé, jardin, aisances et apartenances';[17] its value was 57,000 livres.[18] Although a detailed account of its contents is impossible, some information has survived relating to the year 1635.[19] The silver vessels in the house were valued at 12,616 livres, the furniture at 10,746 livres, the *linge* at 2,577 livres: 25,939 livres in all. There were also 17,957 livres in cash belonging to Etienne II. Excluding cash, the house and contents (incomplete as the list is) stood at a minimum value of 82,939 livres.

---

[16]M. Bloch, *French Rural History* (London, 1966), 26 35; E. le Roy Ladurie et M. Morineau, *Histoire Economique et Sociale de la France* (Paris, 1970-7), i, 537-42.

[17]A.N., M.C., XXIV-348: Echange, 23 jan. 1638.

[18]A.N., M.C., LXXXVI-319: Inventaire après-décès de Jeanne l'Huillier, 22 oct. 1641: ('Titres et papiers concernant les propres du sr. d'Aligre', no. 72).

[19]*Ibid.*, nos. 5-9.

54

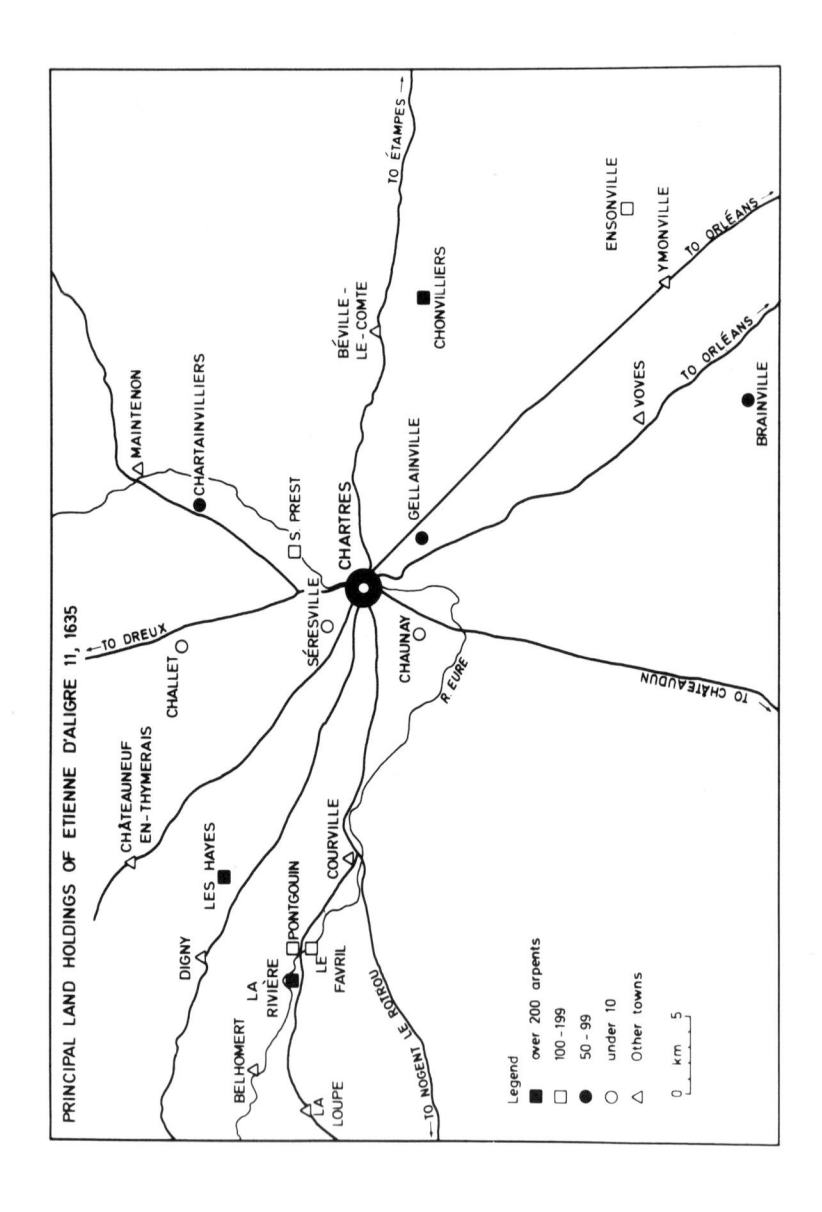

The house in Chartres similarly presents problems, but again it may be possible to suggest a reasonably accurate figure. Etienne III, who inherited it, sold it in 1653 for 5,400 livres.[20] The difficulty is the gap between 1635 when Etienne II died and 1653, for there is no convenient measure by which to assess the property market in Chartres as there is for Paris.[21] In order to err on the side of underestimating the wealth of Etienne II, the somewhat arbitrary sum of 4,000 livres will be taken for 1635. The value of the contents cannot be estimated.[22]

That leaves the *château*. Here a hiatus exists for neither the building nor its contents can be valued. There is simply insufficient information on which to attempt an evaluation. It must remain a regrettable but unavoidable lacuna in our estimation of his wealth at his death.

Offices[23]

During his lifetime d'Aligre held five offices: *conseiller* in the *grand conseil*, *président* of the *présidial* in Chartres, *consiller d'état, garde des sceaux*, and chancellor. The first two were venal, but the remaining three were not. On his promotion to the chancellorship the income from the councillorship of state and the guardianship of the seals ceased; down to 1635 he henceforth enjoyed the vast financial rewards of the chancellor. There were his *appointements*, or annual payment by the crown of 30,000 livres. Next, the chancellor had right of appointment to a long list of offices in the *grande chancellerie*, the *parlements*, the various *cours des aides*, one hundred *présidiaux*, and the chancelleries of about thirty towns or provinces. Not only did he receive a percentage of the sale of these offices, but the *droit annuel* or *paulette* which their holders paid, went to him; this sum alone came to about 43,000 livres a year. The chancellor had the *droit de visa*, which was a charge on every document despatched by the *grande chancellerie;* this normally totalled about 2,000 livres per annum. The regular, annual income of the chancellor was thus of the order of

---

[20]A.N., M.C., LXXXVI-292: Vente, 25 avril 1653.

[21]Vol. 1 of G. d'Avenel, *Histoire Economique de la Propriété... 1200-1800* (Paris, 1894-1912) contains much information on the Parisian property market.

[22]The source cited in n. 18 says (no. 74) that the contents of the house in Chartres were also sold in 1653, but it does not say for how much.

[23]The information in this section is based on A[rchives du Ministère des] A[ffaires] E[trangères]: M[émoires et] D[ocuments]: France 134: 'Evaluation des offices qui sont à la nomination de Monseigneur le Chancellier' (1698).

75,000 livres. To this sum should be added less regular but highly lucrative payments. Mention has been made that the chancellor received a portion of the sale of the offices at his disposal; there is no way of knowing how much d'Aligre derived from this source. In addition there were ten offices in the *grande chancellerie* where the *droit de survivance,* totalling 52,000 livres, was payable to him; he possessed the same right with another 170 offices in different branches of central administration, whose joint *droit de survivance* came to 76,500 livres. Again, in d'Aligre's case it is impossible to know how many *officiers* paid him the *droit de survivance,* or on how many occasions. If we make the assumption that during the eleven years of his chancellorship it was paid once by each office holder, that would have brought him 128,000 livres. From 1624 to 1635 d'Aligre therefore drew a minimum of 75,000 livres per annum from the chancellorship, plus whatever came from the sale of offices and the *droit de survivance;* this could have been on average between 10,000 and 15,000 livres a year. Since, however, those latter figures are speculative, only his income of 75,000 livres will be used in further calculations. Once again, this is an underestimation.

Rentes[24]

The *rentes* which d'Aligre drew, both on the state and through *rentes constituées,* can best be described in tabular form.

Table 3

Source	Principal	Percentage of total	Rente	Percentage of total
Hôtel de ville	10,000	3.4	693- 3-11	3.6
Clergy	1,210	0.4	121	0.6
Recettes générales	2,938- 2-0	1.0	489-13-8	2.5
Aides	11,355-17-9	3.8	983-19-9	5.2
Gabelles	28,656-16-0	10.0	2,129- 5-0	11.2
Private loans (rentes constituées)	238,558	81.4	14,703- 6-4	76.9
	292,718-15-9		19,120- 8-8	

The outstanding feature of d'Aligre's investment in *rentes* is his strong preference for *rentes constituées* or private loans, as against the various state bonds which together comprised only 18.6 per cent of his investment and 23.1 per cent of his *rentes.* Several reasons can be

[24]See n. 7.

suggested for this policy. Although the state generally paid 8 per cent interest, it was a risky debtor often falling into arrears with its payments or even paying less than the official rate. An individual who reneged was easier to deal with. *Rentes constituées* were more versatile than those on the state. They could form part of a dowry or the purchase price of, say, property. In rural districts where financial services were non-existent they were a means whereby a noble or landowner could 'maintain' his tenants or followers by loaning cash when they needed it. They could be used to create good will among aristocrats and other people of influence in need of a loan. They could be employed to create a network of influence among officials and other servants of the crown. By comparison, state bonds were a clumsy form of investment.

D'Aligre's *rentes constituées* varied considerably in size. In 1635 there were being paid to him one on a principal of 150 livres, one on 192 livres, one on 300 livres, one on 336 livres, one on 400 livres, one on 430 livres, one on 450 livres, one on 6,000 livres, two on 8,000 livres, three on 9,600 livres, one on 10,000 livres, one on 12,000 livres, one on 13,500 livres, four on 16,000 livres, one on 18,000 livres, one on 20,000 livres, and two on 24,000 livres; loans of 238,558 livres in all. The average rate of repayment was fairly high at 6.25 per cent. As regards the dates when these loans were made, three are unknown, but one was in 1605, another in 1613, a third in 1622, with the rest in the period between 1624 and 1635. The bulk of the *rentes constituées* therefore were negotiated during the years of the chancellorship when he had enormous funds at his disposal; the capital which those eighteen *rentes* represent is 227,850 livres. Nor does that sum indicate all the *rentes constituées* of those years, for some loans that he made were redeemed before his death. On 30 May 1625 Jean Habert, sieur de Montauret, a *trésorier général de l'ordinaire des guerres,* Simon Collin, a *trésorier général de l'extraordinaire des guerres,* and Anne Jacqueline, a *trésorier général des bâtiments du roi,* borrowed 24,000 livres on a *rente* of 1,500 livres; they redeemed it in 1628.[25] In 1627 the same three people borrowed another 34,000 livres which they also redeemed in 1628.[26] These two loans raise the amount invested by d'Aligre in *rentes constituées* while he was chancellor to 285,850 livres.

Who approached him for loans? The small sums that he distributed were usually to people from Chartres and its region who turned to him for help. In 1622 he loaned 300 livres to a widow in Chartres. In 1632

[25] A.N., M.C., XXIV-322; Quittance, 6 avril 1628.
[26] A.N., M.C., Ll-89: Rachat, 20 juillet 1628 (2 contracts).

the village of Pontgouin borrowed 450 livres, perhaps to finance some community enterprise. In the same year a small landowner from Pontgouin received 400 livres. Local nobles such as the sieur de Mainvilliers[27] and the sieur le Prestre[28] came to him. In such instances he was serving the neighbourhood as a source of finance. Parisian *officiers* were among his debtors. Habert, Collin and Jacqueline have been observed, but there were *conseillers d'état* such as François de Villemontée, sieur de Montaiguillon[29] and Guillaume Perrochet;[30] or others from financial administration like Antoine Hérouard, sieur de la Boisseur, *trésorier de France;*[31] there was also Pierre de Lalane, sieur de la Roue, a *greffier et garde des procès du conseil prive.*[32] Aristocrats constituted *rentes* to d'Aligre. The comte de Lude borrowed 24,000 livres,[33] François de Béthune, comte d'Orval 19,200 livres,[34] Henri de Schomberg, duc d'Alluye 24,000 livres,[35] and not long after d'Aligre's death the duc de Condé approached the family and borrowed 9,000 livres from Etienne II's funds and another 13,500 from Etienne III.[36] The pattern of d'Aligre's *rentes constituées* is reasonably clear: with the exception of clients from the area around La Rivière, his money was loaned to Parisian *officiers* or to aristocratic families who could provide excellent security and were useful contacts for the family.

A Summary of the Fortune

Bearing in mind that d'Aligre's fortune has been underestimated in those areas where doubt exists, the broad outlines of his wealth are available. If the *château* at Rivière had been included, the value of the fortune would have been well in excess of 500,000 livres, and if all the emoluments attaching to the chancellorship had been added, then d'Aligre's annual income would have been nearer 150,000 livres than

---

[27] A.N., M.C., XXIV-323: Constitution, 18 août 1628.
[28] A.N., M.C., XXIV-348: Partage, 9 mars (constitution, 25 avril 1633).
[29] A.N., M.C., XXIV-323; Constitution, 14 août 1628.
[30] A.N., M.C., LI-106: Constitution, 6 avril 1635.
[31] A.N., M.C., LI-98: Constitution, 26 Avril 1632.
[32] A.N., M.C., LI-94: Constitution, 19 avril 1630.
[33] A.N., M.C., XXIV-322: Constitution, 6 avril 1628.
[34] A.N., M.C., XXIV-327; Constitution, 13 sept. 1629.
[35] A.N., M.C., XXIV-348: Partage, 9 mars 1638 (constitution, 31 juillet 1633).
[36] A.N., M.C., XXIV-346: Constitution, 5 fév. 1637 (2 contracts).

Table 4

	Value	Percentage	Annual Return	Percentage
Land	128,265	25.3	9,000	8.7
Other Property	86,939	17.1		
Chancellorship			75,000	72.1
Rentes	292,718	57.6	19,120	18.6
	507,922		103,120	

100,000. Some notion of the size of the fortune can be indicated by the consideration that an income of over 100,000 livres was sufficient to feed a sizeable village and two or three regiments over twelve months, while a sum of about 550,00 livres was roughly the annual *taille* paid by the province of Dauphiné in the 1630s, and greater than that paid by Bretagne, Provence and Bourgogne.[37] It is a fortune profoundly influenced by the chancellorship. The income from that charge enabled him to act as a banker on a large scale, and it is noticeable that after 1626 he put his money into *rentes constituées* rather than into the purchase of yet more land. This was a wise decision. Land was, of course, a source of wealth and prestige, but it tied up capital in a way that *rentes* did not. D'Aligre disposed of plenty of land, while the prestige of his family was beyond question once he was chancellor. Given that he and his son Etienne III needed a plentiful supply of cash to promote the careers and marriage of members of the family, and given that the colossal income from the chancellorship would cease at Etienne II's death, it was imperative that a large block of capital in the form of *rentes* be set aside as a fund to finance the d'Aligres de la Rivière over the next generation.

This survey of Etienne II's fortune perforce has concentrated on the last years of his life, which is the only period for which adequate documentation is available. If it is vulnerable to the comment that the final years were hardly typical of his life as a whole, nevertheless the most important question for the prestige and material standing of his family was, what property and wealth did he bequeath to the next generation? The preceding pages have provided a clear answer.

How were his assets divided after his death? According to the *coutume* of Le Perche the tradition was for the eldest son to inherit the

---

[37]B.N., MS Français 7736, fos. 4-5; the calculation on how many people could be fed is based on a similar point made by R. Pillorget, 'Henri Pussort, oncle de Colbert, sa carrière, ses demeures parisiennes, son portefeuille', *Bulletin de la Société de l'Histoire de Paris et de l'Ile-de-France* (1967-8), 133-4.

principal *château* and estate, along with their associated rights; the rest of the property was apportioned on the basis of 50 per cent to the eldest son and 50 per cent divided equally among the remaining inheritors; children in holy orders were excluded.[38] But only part of Etienne II's property lay in Le Perche. Some was inside the Chartrain and some in the area of the *coutume* of Paris, two regions where there was much variety in inheritance practices.[39] In his final will written in 1631, Etienne II provided that although in the first instance all his possessions would transfer to his wife, on her decease the inheritance would be divided equally three ways: between his sons Etienne III and Louis, and his son-in-law François de Courseulles, sieur du Rouvray.[40] In fact, when the inheritance was apportioned between them in 1638, only part of the property and *rentes* were shared. It was agreed that Etienne III should acquire land to the value of 49,175 livres 8 sous 4 deniers, Louis to the value of 35,713 livres 15 sous, and du Rouvray to 32,635 livres 16 sous 8 deniers: that is in the proportions of 42 per cent to Etienne III, 30 per cent to Louis and 28 per cent to du Rouvray. Accordingly Etienne III received La Rivière, the land at Pontgouin and Le Favril, and Gellainville. Louis succeeded to Chonvilliers, Saint Baite, Neuilly and Uscouan. Du Rouvray acquired Les Hayes, Ensonville, Sérèsville, Chaunay, Chartainvilliers and Challet. When the values of these lands were totalled they did not correspond to the sums that had been agreed; in particular Etienne III's new land exceeded in value his 49,175 livres. He therefore transferred to Louis and du Rouvray cash to make up the difference. The property that was not specifically distributed by the *partage* of 1638 (Brainville, Saint Barthèlemy, Saint Prest, the houses in Paris and Chartres, and one or two other small pieces of land) was held jointly until decisions could be taken later. The *rentes* were divided equally, each receiving *rentes* of 637 livres 9 sous 7 deniers on a principal of 97,572 livres 18 sous 7 deniers. Etienne III thus inherited to the value of some 146,750 livres, Louis to some 133,285 livres, and du Rouvray to some 130,207 livres, apart from the property still held in common. These figures give the proportions of 35.7 per cent to Etienne III as the eldest son, 32.5 per cent to Louis, and 31.8 per cent to du Rouvray.

[38] *Coustume des Pays, Comté et Bailliage du Grand Perche...* clauses cxxxvii-cxlv, clxv (printed in G. Bry, *Histoire du Pays et Comté du Perche* [1620], 2éme. éd., revue et augmentée par P. Siguret [Paris, 1970]).

[39] E. le Roy Ladurie, 'Family structures and inheritance customs in sixteenth-century France', J. Goody, J. Thirsk, E.P. Thompson (eds.,), *Family and Inheritance: Rural Society in Western Europe, 1200-1800* (Cambridge, 1976), 40-1.

[40] A.N., M.C., XXIV-347: Testament d'Estienne Haligre, 24 oct. 1637.

D'Aligre's Children: the Daughters[41]

In view of the dramatic changes in Etienne II's social and material standing during his lifetime, the consequences for his family call for examination. Of his seven children, four were daughters. Three entered holy orders. Marguerite, probably the eldest, joined the convent of Belhomert to the north-west of La Rivière. She was ultimately prioress, and was still living as late as 1664.[42] Her sisters who took religious vows are enveloped in anonymity, not even their names being known; one was a nun at Belhomert, the other at Gef.[43] They introduce what was to be a prominent theme in d'Aligre family history throughout the rest of the century: the taking of religious vows. To what extent the daughters of Etienne II entered the convent willingly is open to speculation, but it will transpire that of those d'Aligres opting for the religious life several showed signs of genuine vocation. Financially it was in Etienne II's interest that he had to provide a marriage dowry for only one daughter Elisabeth, who married du Rouvray, a *lieutenant de la vénerie et gentilhomme de la chambre du roi*. As a courtier he was a most suitable match. He originated from near La Rivière, his *seigneurie* of Le Rouvray being contiguous to Etienne II's *seigneurie* of Les Hayes. Elisabeth predeceased her father, but left a son François, on whose behalf du Rouvray shared in the *partage* of 1638. That such a large portion of Etienne II's property was alienated by Etienne III and Louis indicates that they esteemed the link with du Rouvray, and considered their nephew one of the family in the settlement.

D'Aligre's Sons: Louis (d. 1643)

Only one of Etienne II's sons married: Etienne III, the eldest, who will be studied in due course. The date of birth of the next son Louis, is unkown. It was some time between 1592 and 1609 when Etienne III and Nicolas were born. He did not pursue a career. There is nevertheless evidence that at one stage he may have been a *trésorier général des finances* attached to the *bureau* at Bourges.[44] In principle the *trésoriers* administered the financial policy of the government in their particular *généralité*. In practice some held the office for reasons of prestige or in order to enjoy the income, but were absentee, taking

---

[41]See Appendix 2.
[42]A.N., M.C., LXXXVI-397: Donation, 6 sept. 1664.
[43]B.N., Dossiers Bleus 11: 275, fos. 24, 27.
[44]B.N., Dossiers Bleus 11: 275, f.8ᵛ.

no active part in the activities of their *bureau*.[45] Louis seems to have fallen into this category; there is no indication that he ever visited Bourges or participated in the affairs of the *bureau*. If he did hold the office he must have disposed of it before the early 1630s,[46] for none of the records that cover the last ten years of his life (the period for which they are the most numerous) speak of it.

It is probable that in 1625 Louis was being edged by his father towards public office. In the autumn of that year there was much discussion in court circles as to how to handle the huguenot rebellion.[47] Richelieu's school of thought contended that the menace of Spain was paramount, that peace must be signed with the huguenots and the bulk of the king's forces devoted to the anti-Habsburg struggle. Conversely, influential *dévot* opinion held that the existence of heresy placed a curse on catholic France, that ruthless measures against the huguenots were necessary, along with *rapprochement* with Spain. Louis d'Aligre contributed to the debate. Possibly with his father's help he composed a document entitled, 'Discours sur les affaires présenté par M. Aligre, fils de M. le Chancelier';[48] a later hand has appended the date, 'February 1626', but this must be an error, for peace with the huguenots was signed on 5 February 1626 and the matter put beyond question. As M. Grillon has said in a similar case,[49] it is likely that Louis wrote the 'Discours' for the meeting of the king, queen mother, ministers, leaders of church, army and *parlement* at Fontainebleau in September 1625 to discuss peace terms.

He presents an astutely argued case for peace with the huguenots and continued resistance to Spain. He grants that it would be easier to fight the huguenots and appease the Spanish; but the easiest tasks are not necessarily the most useful or glorious. Warning that, 'La réputation sert de beaucoup à tous princes, spécialement aux grands et puissants roys qui désirent se conserver en crédit', he asserts that surely it is more illustrious to combat the king of Spain than miserable

---

[45] Dent, *Crisis in Finance*, 141-2.

[46] In a letter of 1627 Etienne II referenced to 'la démission de son second fils', but did not say from what Louis was resigning (Le Chancelier d'Aligre au Cardinal de Richelieu, S.L., fév. 1627 [Grillon (ed.), *Les Papiers de Richelieu*, ii, 100]).

[47] *Ibid.*, i, for the period from August 1625 to February 1626 contains material on this question.

[48] A.A.E., M.D., France 246, fos. 53-59; that Louis, and not one of his brothers, was the son mentioned in the title is indicated by Etienne III's absence in Venice at this time and the fact that Nicholas was only sixteen.

[49] Grillon (ed.), *Les Papiers de Richelieu*, i, 218.

wretches, 'dont le désespoir et la nécessité sont les forces principalles'. If Spain were appeased, France's friends would be abandoned:

> Et pour récompense il nous souffrira de nous consommer tout à notre aise en guerres civiles sans nous menacer ni d'Espinola ni de Tilly. Et ainsi penserons avoir fait des merveilles lorsque nous aurions mis le feu dans quelques bicoques, bien qu'elles soient à nous. C'est cette facilitè qui porte la plupart de nos cavaliers à demander la guerre contre les Huguenots, étant accoutumés à marcher en campagne en toute liberté, et toujours attaquer sans avoir jamais besoin de se défendre.

Those who demand war with the huguenots and peace with Spain practise the deceit of the quack doctor who treats symptoms not causes. The cause of France's problems must be attacked, and that cause is Spain: 'L'on voit visiblement que l'Espagne travaille à la domination universelle; son seul obstacle est la France. Elle n'ose l'attaquer ouvertement. Elle essaye donc d'y semer la division pour nous afaiblir.' But the cause of France's ills is known; it will not be ignored. Admittedly France would be stronger without the huguenots, 'mais nous les avons, et depuis cent ans nos pères ont travaillé pour les ruiner. C'est un malheur auquel sagement il se faut accommoder.' Modern-day huguenots do not have the bellicose courage of their predecessors; they must be treated carefully so as not to rekindle the old fires. So far they have fought only spasmodically and continue to recognise the sovereignty of the king. Threats of annihilation will simply drive them into the arms of foreigners and force them to resist more fiercely. So why do some advisers still urge the king to launch all-out war on the huguenots? Some through silly religious zeal, but others, especially *les grands,* for pernicious reasons. Some think that victory over the rebels will bring them rich rewards from a grateful monarch; others contemplate blackmailing the king into concessions by threatening to aid the huguenots; all envisage the king having to turn to them for help, for which they will demand a price. Thus, for all their talk, 'ils ne veulent point la ruine entière des Huguenots'. Under these circumstances, 'La paix est le souverain remède'. Even if the huguenots do not desire it, it must be forced on them like medicine on an unwilling patient. They will come to see that the king accepts them as his subjects and has no intention of ruining them. They will become loyal subjects who will allow the king to concentrate on the real enemy, Spain.

In the document Louis appears squarely on the side of Richelieu. There is no reason to suppose that the 'Discours' does not fairly represent his views; but is was a shrewd move to back the cardinal at this difficult historical juncture. Etienne II knew Richelieu's mind on the subject and doubtless gave appropriate advice to his son during the drafting of the 'Discours'. Even so it was a clear declaration of loyalty on a most controversial topic. It was bound to ingratiate Louis with the cardinal and to mark him for possible advancement. Moreover, with his father as chancellor, promotion surely would not have been long delayed. But within months of the 'Discours' appearing Etienne II was exiled from court and Louis's chances correspondingly dashed. He never received public office, devoting the rest of his life to *la vie noble;* his father's disgrace meant the end of his own aspirations.

Given his *vie noble,* he was employing the title, 'sieur de Chonvilliers', by the early 1630s. That indicates that his father effectively, if not yet officially, might already have turned it over to him.[50] He was also spending much of his time in the scientific and literary *salons* of Paris.[51] By the *partage* of 1638 he acquired the territories of Chonvilliers, Uscouan, Neuilly and Saint Baite, along with a generous sum of money in the form of *rentes.* Thereafter he handled his interests in finance and property with admirable sagacity and much effect.

Now possessing large capital resources he proceeded to purchase land. He adopted the strategy that his father had pursued near La Rivière: he purchased a *seigneurie,* but then bought more land on its border so as to enlarge the domain. In 1640 Louis acquired the *seigneurie* of Boislandry which he held in fief to the duc de Sully.[52] It lay in heavily-wooded country just off the road between Courville and Nogent-le-Rotrou; it extended to the villages of Champrond-en-Gatiné, Montlandon and Frétigny. It included a *château* and grounds covering 3 arpents, 12.25 arpents of *terre labourable,* 22.25 arpents of meadow and pasture, 47.25 arpents of woodland, a further 42 arpents whose nature is undefined (although much would have been woodland given the heavy forestation round Boislandry), two lakes of 35 and 4 arpents respectively, and a windmill. At 165.75 arpents it was about half the size of La Rivière and two-fifths of Chonvilliers. As *seigneur* Louis retained various rights: high, middle and low justice, the receipt of fines or seizures that his court imposed, hunting and fishing rights (*droit de garenne á poile, à connils et à eau*), the right to insist that his tenants grind their corn at his mill, and so forth. He further drew *cens* and other obligations in cash and in kind which totalled about 60 livres in cash, between 30 and 40 chickens, about

---

[50] A.N., M.C., Ll-101: Obligation, 25 mai 1633, refers to him as 'sieur de Choinvilliers'.

[51] See below, pp. 72-6.

[52] A.N., M.C., XXIV-417: Advert, 30 nov. 1640.

100 lbs. of butter, and about 30 cheeses a year. Louis leased Boislandry for cash. In 1643 he negotiated a contract to let it for twelve years at 3,300 livres per annum.[53] If 3,300 livres is assumed to be 4.5 per cent of the value of Boislandry (this was the rate at which his father leased out seigneurial land), then the *seigneurie* was worth some 73,300 livres. Presumably he paid roughly this sum when he bought it. If this assumption is correct, then Boislandry at almost 166 arpents and let at 3,300 livres, was considerably more valuable than Chonvilliers at about 400 arpents and let at 700 livres, or Les Hayes at about 240 arpents and let at 564 livres. If not the largest *seigneurie* of the d'Aligres de la Rivière, it was by far the most profitable. To this core he added more land. From Sully he bought 43 arpents contiguous to Boislandry, while from Madeleine de Fervel, widow of Gillies de Villeroy, *président* in the *parlement* of Paris, he acquired the fief of Frisegère near Frétigny. It included a house, stables, other buildings, and eighteen pieces of land.[54]

Although Louis followed his father's example closely when he purchased land, his financial investments displayed some contrasts. Etienne II had loaned large sums through *rentes constituées*, and to a much lesser degree had purchased state bonds. Louis bought no state bonds, and only rarely entered into *rentes constituées*. Only two instances have survived. In 1641 Philippe Hotman, sieur de Mortefontaine, a *loueur des rivières de Loire et Cher*, borrowed 10,200 livres on a *rente* of 566 livres 13 sous 4 deniers (5.5 per cent); he redeemed it less than two years later.[55] In 1643 Louis loaned 12,000 livres on a *rente* of 600 livres (5 per cent) to Charles de Maignart, sieur de Baronière, who sought it as part of 180,000 livres which he needed to purchase the office of *maître des requêtes*.[56] This *rente* was redeemed in 1646.[57] Louis sometimes loaned money on a variation of the *rentes constituées*: the *transport de rentes*. A typical example would be as follows: A lent money to B who then paid a *rente* to A (i.e. they contracted a conventional *rente constituée*); A later required cash, but of course could not demand back the capital he had loaned to B, since in a *rentes constituée* his capital was alienated; A thus had to borrow money and turned to C,

---

[53] A.N., M.C., LXXXVI-276: Bail, 27 mai 1643.

[54] A.N., M.C., XXIV-417: Advert, 17 nov. 1640 (2 contracts), they do not indicate the area of the land.

[55] A.N., M.C., XXIV-418: Constitution, 17 mai 1641.

[56] A.N., M.C., LXXXVI-275: Constitution, 10 fév. 1643; by a second contract of the same date Maignart borrowed 8,000 livres from Etienne III for the same purpose.

[57] A.N., M.C., LXXXVI-375: Quittance, 18 août 1646 (both *rentes* were redeemed).

from whom he received a sum equivalent to that which he had originally loaned to B; instead of contracting a *rente constituée* with C, A simply transferred to him all his rights in connection with his (A's) loan to B; B henceforth paid his *rente* to C, and when he eventually redeemed it, did so by paying the capital to C. This procedure, an exceedingly common one,[58] appears on three occasions in Louis d'Aligre's records, with himself playing the role of C. In 1643 he was drawing *rente* of this type at 625 livres, 1,000 livres and 500 livres.[59] At 5 per cent they represented a joint capital of 42,500 livres.

A form of lending which he favoured was the simple fixed-term loan which carried no interest, at least on paper. For instance, in 1632 he loaned 12,000 livres to three nobles from Le Perche; they repaid him in 1640.[60] Again, in 1634 Louis Gareau, a *receveur général des finances* residing in Paris, borrowed 4,000 livres which he promised to repay within six months.[61] At his death in 1643 Louis d'Aligre was owed 47,930 livres under six such contracts of 1630, 1633, 1635 (2), 1638, and 1643.[62] What was the attraction to him of this form of 'investment'? As against the *rente constituée* when the lender alienated his capital, a simple loan (*acte d'obligation* or *de promesse*) was normally for a fixed period; the lender knew when his money would be repaid. Yet a loan of this type carried no interest, so why should somebody like Louis advance money at all? It could be that he or any lender was simply helping a friend or associate for a short period. But of greater weight is the consideration that such loans were often accompanied by verbal agreements, whose content never appears in contracts. It could happen that the lender insisted on more than the legal 5 per cent interest of a *rente constituée*, he and the borrower drawing up a simple *acte de promesse* but the borrower privately agreeing to pay an interest of 8 or 9 per cent. Again, a borrower might compensate the lender through the performance of services of one kind or another. In a *rente constituée*, interest was written into the contracts; accompanying an *acte de promesse* there were often verbal agreements serving a similar purpose.[63] Further-

---

[58]There are many such examples in the *liasses* of the Minutier Central; they bear further testimony to be flexibility of *rentes constituées*.

[59]A.N., M.C., LXXXVI-320: Inventaire après-décès de Louis d'Aligre, sieur de Chonvilliers, 21 nov. 1643 (actes de transport, 30 août 1637, 1 août 1639, a third undated).

[60]A.N., M.C., XXIV-416: Quittance, 24 fév. 1640.

[61]A.N., M.C., LI-105; Obligation, 29 déc. 1634.

[62]A.N., M.C., LXXXVI-320: Inventaire. . . de Louis d'Aligre, 21 nov. 1643 ('Papiers privés. . .', nos. 10-15).

[63]This comment was suggested to the writer by Prof. R. Pillorget.

more, if the debtor-party to such a contract failed to meet the date of repayment, the creditor was in a powerful position in law to impose a penalty; it could involve the seizure of property or, if the loan was allowed to remain outstanding, compensation in some other form. In 1633, for instance, Louis d'Aligre loaned 14,000 livres for one year to Guillaume Menart (status unknown) and Guillaume Philippe, a *bourgeois de Paris*.[64] In 1643 the debt was still unpaid.[65] It is inconceivable that Louis left 14,000 livres, which should have been repaid in 1634, outstanding for nine years without insisting on compensation; but what form it took is unknown.

From the foregoing pages it is possible to reconstruct, in Table 5, at least some of the chief elements in Louis's fortune in 1643.

Table 5

Property & Cash	*Value*	*Annual Return*
Chonvilliers, Neuilly, Uscouan, S. Baite	28,225	1,275
Boislandry	73,300*	3,300
Other land near Boislandry	?	?
Offices in the *grenier à sel* in Chartres	44,000**	2,200
Rentes	64,700*	3,291
Promesses	47,930	?
	258,155	10,066

* estimated
** it is not known when he acquired them

It must be emphasised that these figures are far from complete; those concerning Louis's income are particularly deficient. More information comes from another source which, while it still leaves the picture incomplete, helps to rectify some of the shortcomings. Louis spent much of his time at the rue d'Avron where he rented rooms from his brother Etienne III, now the proprietor of the family residence.[66]

[64] A.N., M.C., Ll-101: Obligation, 25 mai 1633.

[65] A.N., M.C., LXXXVI-277. Obligation, 18 août 1643.

[66] Etienne III bought up Louis's and Courseulles's shares of the house (A.N., M.C., XXIV-348: Echange, 23 jan. 1638 and 4 mars 1638): Louis later rented rooms there at 1,400 livres per annum (A.N., M.C., LXXXVI-320: Inventaire... de Louis d'Aligre, 21 nov. 1643 [accord, 22 mai 1643]).

When Louis died in November 1643, Etienne III authorised an inventory of his belongings there.[67] It bears the limitation that it deals only with Louis's appurtenances at the rue d'Avron; he may well have had possessions at Chonvilliers and Boislandry. But since he lived principally in Paris, it is possible to perceive at least something of his life-style. He did not live in the grand manner, the value of his clothing, furniture, paintings, mirrors, carpets, linen, and cutlery being only 1,681 livres. He owned a coach and two horses worth 900 livres. Of much greater value was the cash he left in the form of gold or silver coins and medallions: they totalled 28,203 livres. Most coins were French, but some were Italian (worth 62 livres 8 sous) and some Spanish (worth 2,700 livres); there were two medallions worth 5,000 livres each. He possessed a library of 1,098 volumes; it is frustrating from a historical point of view that the inventory simply enumerates them without giving the titles for, as it will emerge, Louis had wide intellectual tastes. The library was evaluated at 1,270 livres, but that is no guide to the role that it played in his life. When the information in the inventory is added to what is already known, then in 1643 Louis left property and cash to the value of 290,209 livres, or 300,000 livres in round figures. It is not suggested that this is an accurate figure, but it probably approaches the minimum of his wealth.

Any reflection on Louis's life must emphasise that it was after 1635, when he inherited part of his father's estate, that he was able to exercise his financial talents to the full. The acquisition of Boislandry was his principal contribution to the long-term prospects of his family, for it meant that future generations would have yet another *seigneurie* to distribute among their sons. In any case, since Les Hayes passed out of d'Aligre possession in 1638, it was advisable to introduce a replacement into the family. Louis did not marry; on his death, therefore, his property reverted to his brother Etienne III.[68] He profited from his father's success in that he was able to enjoy a noble life unhindered by financial worries, but he was in no sense a drain on family resources. When he died, he returned to the common funds of the d'Aligres far more then he ever withdrew.

Nicolas (1609-36)

Etienne II's son Nicolas lived an independent life as did Louis. He never held office or pursued a career. He was a beneficiary of his

---

[67] See n. 59.

[68] Although 'propres' of 60,000 livres went to nephews (A.N., M.C., LXXXVI-277: Accord, 1 déc. 1643).

father's promotion in 1624 in that, in the same year, Etienne II purchased for him two monasteries of which he became *abbé commendataire* i.e. he drew their revenues but was not obliged to take holy orders. One was the Benedictine house at Saint Evroul in the diocese of Lisieux, the other was the Augustinian house of Saint Jacques at Provins. Saint Jacques was to assume considerable importance for the d'Aligres, three of whom succeeded Nicolas as *abbés*.[69] Etienne II bought it from the Séguier family, its previous *abbé commendataire* having been Nicolas Séguier (d. 24 September 1624), son of the great chancellor.[70] It was an easy-going foundation whose nine monks exhibited serious shortcomings. From the townspeople of Provins came charges of misbehaviour and absenteeism among the monks, who appear to have made up in a vigorous social life what they lacked in piety. Etienne II himself lamented that, 'ces religieux étaient plus habitués à l'arquebuse qu'à leurs bréviaires'.[71] The first attempt to reform the monastery had met with humiliating failure. In 1623 cardinal de la Rochefoucauld sent père Robert Baudouin to conduct an inquiry. He was sent packing by the monks who calculated that the Séguiers would brook no interference. For a time when Nicolas d'Aligre was *abbé*, la Rochefoucauld left Saint Jacques to its own devices, but it was inevitable that another bid for reform would be made. Nicolas, although ony in his teens, favoured change, while his father, who was distressed at the state of the monastery, advocated a strong dose of discipline. In 1632 there were introduced into Saint Jacques eight members of the Congrégation de Sainte Marie (founded 1622-4), who began a process of reform and improvement that was to continue under Nicolas's successors, culminating in the impressive life of the saintly and austere François d'Aligre.

Meanwhile Nicolas resided in the rue d'Avron. As was the case with Louis, he too moved in the society of the *salons*. According to one unsubstantiated source, he spent a period in the army.[72] He died when only twenty-seven, possibly in Spanish custody. In September 1634 the Spanish governor of Perpignan was arrested on French

[69] A. Barrault, 'Les d'Aligre, Abbés de Saint Jacques de Provins au XVIIe siècle: la réforme des chanoines réguliers (1623-1643)', *Bulletin de la Société d'Histoire et d'Archeologie de l'Arrondissement de Provins* (1958), 11-28.

[70] *Ibid.*, 14.

[71] Etienne d'Aligre II to Molé, [La Rivière], 4 jan. 162[8] (Champollion de Figeac [ed.], *Mémoires de Mole*, I, 285); in the *Mémoires de Molé* the letter is dated incorrectly as 1623; on the correction see Barrault, 'Les d'Aligre', 16.

[72] *Encyclopédie Biographique*, 11, says he was *maître de camp de cavalerie*, while the *Dictionnaire de Biographie Française* claims simply that, 'il servit la carrière des armes'; the writer has not been able to verify this.

territory, allegedly for spying on French defences. With relations between the two governments rapidly deteriorating (war was to break out in May 1635), negotiations failed to secure the governor's release. Nicolas d'Aligre had been travelling in Spain, and on his return in February 1635 was detained by the Spanish at Perpignan as an act of reprisal. As son of the chancellor of France he was a suitable hostage. The news figured in the *Gazette* (3 March) and provoked protests from many sides.[73] Still in custody when his father died, he may have been in Spanish hands when he too met his death on 26 October 1636.[74] Coming so soon after the decease of Etienne II and within a few years of that of his sister Elisabeth, it meant that three d'Aligres had expired within a relatively short time. The abbey of Saint Evroul passed into the hands of Antonio Barberini; Saint Jacques de Provins remained with the d'Aligres.[75]

The d'Aligres and their Times

Modern historians are acutely conscious of the strategic importance of the 1620s and 1630s in the history of seventeenth-century France.[76] Truly notable struggles were being waged concerning the nature of the state, its relation to the king's subjects, and France's position in Europe. Louis XIII's regime fought hard to transcend the turmoil, the uncertainties, the internal divisions inherited from the sixteenth century but only partially resolved by Henri IV. Within this historical context Etienne II, like many of his contemporaries, saw his life transformed. In his youth he had tended towards the catholic league, but he came to appreciate that Bourbon kingship, with all its faults, was the only effective antidote to the country's ills. If he was ever again politically suspect after his defection from the league, it was throught his obligations to the house of Soissons. Yet even in 1615 when aristocratic factions threatened the monarchy, Etienne II used such influence as he possessed to reconcile crown and aristocrats who, he perceived, could offer little to the country by way of creative political or administrative ideas. Thereafter he was promoted in royal service, his talents and the circumstances of the day carrying him to

---

[73] For instance Peiresc wrote: 'Je plains bien cependant le pauvre abbé de St. Euveroul, et Messieurs ses parents, car cette affaire est pour tirer long traict...' (Peiresc to M. de S. Saulveur de Puy, Aix, 26 fév. 1635 [Tamizey de Larroque (ed.), *Lettres de Peiresc,* ii, 277]).

[74] On the dating of his death see Barrault, 'Les d'Aligre', 21-2.

[75] G. d'Avenel (éd.), *Lettres, Instructions Diplomatiques et Papiers d'Etat du Cardinal de Richelieu* (Paris, 1853-77), v, 296, n.3.

[76] E.g. Lublinskaya, *French Absolutism.*

the supreme office of chancellor. He lacked the qualities necessary for lengthy survival at that level, which may explain in part one of his 'failures': his ineffectiveness is establishing a d'Aligre 'clan' in central government. But that presupposes that he ever seriously entertained such a project. On the contrary, his brief experience of the active chancellorship may have left him largely indifferent to such an enterprise. The survey of the lives of Louis and Nicholas has shown no great exertion towards inserting them into public office with their brother Etienne III. In 1626 Etienne II retired to La Rivière where he spent the rest of his life in quiet retreat. But he was not a forgotten man. He launched le Tellier on his career,[77] people of eminence approached him for money, while as late as 1633 the hospital of La Charité in Lyon wrote to him as chancellor, appealing for help with its financial problems.[78] He remained in touch with events at court, and whatever his sentiments towards Richelieu, he remained committed to the general conviction that monarchy was the only institution capable of welding state and society into a durable whole.

Such few indications as we possess concerning his thoughts on religion suggest that in his post-league years he sympathised with the reforming movement in French catholicism. He was genuinely exasperated at the unedifying spiritual condition of Saint Jacques de Provins, and took a lead in planning its reform. He was regularly in touch with his daughters in the convent at Belhomert, where he and his wife were to be buried. In his will he made suitable provision for the repose of his soul, including an annual mass on the anniversary of his death.[79] If there are no signs that he held novel religious ideas, he did show real concern for the condition of the church. In this he was backed by his wife. Marie-Elisabeth Chapellier appears but rarely in the family's documents. She was considerably younger than her husband, by fourteen years, and was to outlive him by two. After 1626 she spent lengthy periods in Paris, usually to supervise Etienne's financial transactions. In an age when premature death could take a husband or wife, with serious consequences for family life, the d'Aligres were fortunate that Etienne II and Marie-Elisabeth remained together for almost fifty years. There was a continuity and stability to d'Aligre family life that was by no means the rule in the seventeenth century. Her will indicates religious piety and a social conscience.[80]

[77] See pp. 26-7.

[78] Directeurs de l'Aumône Général de Lyon à Etienne d'Aligre 11 mars 1633 (Bibl. de l'Institut, MS Godefroy 271, fos. 6-7).

[79] A.N., M.C., XXIV-347: Testament d'Estienne d'Haligre, 24 oct. 1637.

[80] A.N., M.C., XXIV-347: Testament de Marie-Elisabeth Chapellier, 24 oct. 1637.

After commending her soul to God (there is no mention of the Virgin or a saint), she left 100 livres to the convent at Belhomert for masses on behalf of her husband and herself. A further 50 livres were bequeathed to the Capuchins at Chartres for 100 masses, with the same arrangment for the Augustinians, the Jacobins and Recollets; 25 livres were left to the Cordeliers and the Minimes for fifty masses. Charitable legacies included 2 sétiers of wheat and rye for the poor, 2 sétiers for the poor of Pontgouin, 8 sétiers to be distributed on the anniversary of her death, 100 livres for work among prisoners in Chartres and Paris, and another 100 to be distributed among the poor of both cities. There was provision for her servants: 400 livres for her chamber maid, 90 livres for her lackey and one year's wages for her other servants.

It is in their intellectual tastes that some of the most fascinating aspects of the d'Aligres are to be found: they moved in Parisian philosophic and scientific circles associated with *libertinage philosophique*,[81] and were up to date with the movement of ideas on a European scale. In this regard they had close contact for many years with Nicolas-Claude Fabri de Peiresc (1580-1637), *parlementaire* at Aix, *savant*, and correspondent with many of Europe's leading scholars. The first association between Peiresc and the d'Aligres is not documented, but as early as the 1610s one of Etienne II's predecessors as *garde des sceaux*, Guillaume du Vair, had spoken of him to Peiresc in glowing terms.[82] On Etienne's promotion to the seals and subsequently to the chancellorship Peiresc sent his congratulations,[83] thereafter maintaining a steady if not profuse correspondence. Some dealt with Peiresc's duties as a *parlementaire*, but others reflected his ceaseless enthusiasm for the world of scholarship. When the distinguished Dutch statesman and jurist Hugo Grotius was a refugee in Paris, Peiresc expressed his gratification that Etienne II was among those who afforded him protection.[84] In 1636 the French classical scholar and linguist Claude de Saumaise was visiting his native country, his permanent base being the University of Leyden. Peiresc, anxious to attract such fine talent back to France implored one of the d'Aligres,

---

[81]See A. Adam, *Les Libertins au XVIIe Siècle* (Paris, 1964) and R. Pintard, *Le Libertinage Erudit dans la Première Moitié du XVIIe Siècle* (2 vols., Paris, 1943).

[82]Peiresc to Etienne d'Aligre 11, Boisgency, 18 déc. 1629 (Bibl. de Carpentras, MS 1871, fos. 293-3^v).

[83]The same, Aix, 24 jan. 1624 (*Ibid.,* fos. 302-3), 17 oct. 1624 (MS 1780, fos. 368-8^v).

[84]The same, Aix, 4 fév. 1624 (Tamizey de Larroque [ed.], *Lettres de Peiresc,* i, 26).

Etienne III, to exert his influence with Richelieu to secure the offer of a pension to Saumaise.[85]

Within Paris one of the most celebrated scientific *salons* or *cabinets* was that of the brothers Pierre and Jacques Dupuy.[86] Its meetings were attended by some of the finest minds of the age: Grotius, Gassendi, Chapelain, Bigot, Godefroy to name but a few. But there were also in attendance nobles, *officiers, parlementaires,* interested amateurs who were attracted by the creation and dissemination of knowledge. Among them were the sons of Etienne II, some of whose closest friends were members of the Dupuy *cabinet.* Indeed, one of Etienne III's most intimate friends was Jacques Dupuy himself. It was to him that Etienne III turned for solace when his father died on 11 December 1635:

> Cet accident... me touché néantmoins si sensiblement que je ne m'en puis remettre; et ne me sens point assez fort pour résister à cette rude attaque, ne me restant qu'à grande peine assez de vigueur pour vous escrire ce mot et me consoler avec vous comme avec l'un de mes meilleurs et plus chers amis, dans le sein duquel je verse librement mes pleurs et dépose mes desplaisirs... Je ne me souhaitterois présentement, aultant que jamais, dans votre cabinet pour y recevoir quelque soulagement et consolation.[87]

The Dupuy *cabinet* earned a reputation for anti-Aristotelianism, anti-Cartesianism, indeed anti-dogmatism in any form be it scientific, philosophic or religions. Its *libertinage* had nothing to do with the atheism or amorality popularly attributed to that movement. Instead it championed certain attitudes of mind, a scepticism towards rigid intellectual systems and cosmic propositions, a liking for free thought untrammelled by cloying orthodoxy, a disposition to hear new ideas without necessarily testing them according to received tradition. The Dupuy *cabinet* created a distinctive intellectual ethos which labelled its adherents 'Dupuy men'. Of the *savants* whom Etienne III, Louis and Nicholas encountered at the *cabinet,* the one to whom they were especially drawn was Pierre Gassendi (1592-1655). In his own lifetime, Gassendi's influence in France as a philosopher and mathematician surpassed that of Descartes, whose method he severely censured. The d'Aligres knew Gassendi partly through the *cabinet,* but also through their cousin François l'Huillier, another *habitué* of

---

[85]Peiresc to Etienne d'Aligre III, Aix, 22 juillet 1636 (Bibl. d'Aix, MS 1019, fos. 122-3).

[86]H. Brown, *Scientific Organisations in Seventeenth Century France* (Baltimore, 1934), 6-17.

[87]Etienne d'Aligre III to Dupuy, La Riviére, 12 déc. 1635 (B.N., Collection Dupuy 675, f. 215).

the *cabinet,* who accompanied Gassendi on some of his travels.[88] Gassendi was a frequent guest at the rue d'Avron;[89] indeed, he and Peiresc (both Provençaux) regarded it as a standard meeting place in Paris for scholars from that province.[90]

Another member to the Dupuy group with whom the d'Aligres were linked was François-Auguste de Thou (1607-42), first cousin to the Dupuy brothers and son of Jacques-Auguste de Thou the great historian and jurist. As the son of a distinguished father he was a *conseiller* in the *parlement* of Paris at the age of twenty-one, and subsequently a *maître des requêtes.* But for all his undoubted intelligence his was an unstable personality; he was to die the death of a traitor through his involvement in the Cinq-Mars conspiracy. In happier days he travelled extensively, often in the company of one of the d'Aligres. In the summer of 1629 Etienne III was in Provence with the royal court.[91] With two companions, le Grand a *maître des requêtes* and le Pelletier son of the *premier président* of the *parlement* of Paris, he visited and stayed with Peiresc in Aix. The group then accompanied Peiresc to Marseille where they all met de Thou who had just returned from a tour of Spain, Italy and the Levant.[92] Together they explored Provence before leaving Peiresc at Aix and heading back to Paris.[93]

Louis d'Aligre, another habitué of the meetings of the Dupuy *cabinet,* followed literary trends closely. He was a particular friend of Jean Chapelain and Jean-Louis Guez de Balzac, at least until Balzac exiled himself from Paris in 1631 after the attacks of his critics. Chapelain wrote to Balzac in 1627: 'Mr. d'Haligre me fit, hier, une visite, et toute nostre conversation fut de vous aux termes que vous le

---

[88] Gassendi to Peiresc, Paris, 28 août 1629 (Tamizey de Larroque [ed.], *Lettres de Peiresc,* iv, 203-4); on l'Huillier see Pintard, *Le Libertinage,* i, 191-5, and P. Gassendi, *Lettres Familières à François Luillier, pendant l'Hiver 1632-1633,* ed. B. Rochet (Paris, 1944).

[89] Peiresc to Etienne d'Aligre III, Boisgency, 18 déc. 1629 (Bibl. de Carpentras, MS 1871, fos. 293^v-4).

[90] Peiresc to Gassendi, Boisgency, 18 jan. 1630 (Tamizey de Larroque [ed.], *Lettres de Peiresc,* iv, 238-9).

[91] Gassendi, *Lettres Familières,* 59, n. 96; P. Gassendi, *The Mirrour of True Nobility & Gentility, being the Life of the Renowned Nicolaus Claudius Fabricius, Lord of Peiresk, Senator in the Parliament at Aix,* Englished by W. Rand (London, 1657), book 4, p. 37.

[92] Peiresc to Dupuy, Aix, 16 juin 1629 (Tamizey de Larroque [ed.], *Lettres de Peiresc,* ii, 115; also 118, 120, 121).

[93] Peiresc gave Etienne III an important packet of notes to deliver to Gassendi; they included Gassendi's notes for his work on Epicurus (Gassendi, *Lettres Familières,* 59, n. 96).

pouvés souhaitter. C'est une cervelle d'homme aussy bien faitte qu'il y en ait entre Paris et Angoulesme, et vous pouvés sur ma parole vous resjouir de l'avoir pour ami.'[94] Again the following year: 'Ces jours passés, Mr. d'Aligre et Mr. l'Huillier me firent une visite exprès pour parler de vous et lire quelques unes des lettres que vous m'avez écrites. Vous devez estre fort satisfait d'eux, car ils le sont extrêmement de vous.'[95]

Such glimpses into the social and intellectual interests and activities of Etienne III, Louis and Nicolas help to rectify any impression that they devoted their lives only to the accretion of property and money. Philistinism was no part of their existence; they moved in *savant* circles, while their home in the rue d'Avron was a gathering place of scholars. In however humble a way they played a part in sustaining those sceptical and enqiring tendencies in Parisian cultural life which helped to place that city in the forefront of much of Europe's most adventurous thought. The d'Aligres themselves were not especially gifted in matters of science or philosophy, but they and others like them helped to preserve an environment where there could be created and disseminated ideas which in the long run helped to transform western thought. In an age when political and religious establishments could not be relied upon to tolerate unorthodox propositions, wealthy and influential citizens like the d'Aligres who conferred protection and respectability on *salons* and *cabinets,* made necessary if unspectacular contributions to the cause of free intellectual investigation. Etienne III and his brothers manifested unmistakeable sympathy for 'advanced' thought. Whereas their father temperamentally remained a provincial more at ease in Chartres or at La Rivière than at court, the sons were truly 'Parisian': intelligent, educated, travelled, men of intellectual fashion.

In the course of tracing the d'Aligres de la Rivière thus far we have touched on problems of general historical significance: the political and social turmoil of the late 1500s and early 1600s, questions of land tenure and the management of private finances, patterns of marriage and inheritance. Within them we have observed the family emerge from a provincial background in Chartres, albeit one of respectable prosperity and status, to the *noblesse de robe.* If any factor deserves special emphasis in the story it is service to the crown. The crown rewarded its servants generously, transforming lives through the distribution of titles, money and power. The d'Aligres were

[94]Chapelain to Balzac, Paris, 7 août 1637 (P. Tamizey de Larroque [ed.], *Lettres de Jean Chapelain* [Paris, 1880-3], i, 161).

[95]The same, Paris, 6 juin 1638 (*Ibid.,* i, 245).

beneficiaries of this phenomenon, for while they may have deplored Etienne II's rough treatment in 1626, they had to acknowledge that as a family they did exceedingly well out of Louis XIII. To him they owed everything that distinguished them: title, wealth, prospects for the future. Yet that future was not without its shadows. Premature death had removed Elisabeth, Nicolas and Louis by 1642, as well as their parents. Nicolas and Louis left no children; only Etienne III remained to continue the family name, with all the responsibilities thereto attached. Who could tell whether he would flourish or be smitten by some disaster threatening the extinction of the line? The marriage of only one son to protect a family into the next generation, was too slender a thread for comfort in an age acutely conscious that: 'La mort de ses rigueurs ne dispense personne.' Happily such apprehensions proved groundless. Etienne III was to prove prolific in children as well as in work. The rest of the 1600s were to demonstrate that, in the d'Aligres de la Riviére, there had entered the *noblesse de robe* a family of great talent, worthy of nobility and capable of more distinguished service to state and church.

4

ETIENNE D'ALIGRE III AND THE VALTELLINE CRISIS

Etienne III is a central figure of this study. His career far excelled that of his father in variety and durability. Yet it is significant that while the early years seemed to presage political distinction, the promise was not fulfilled. At an advanced age it was with the chancellorship that he was rewarded, not a secretaryship of state; and this more as a sign of gratification for years of assiduous service than as the climax to glory. The withdrawal of his father from court in 1626 and the absence of his brothers from government left him isolated when leadership of a 'clan' was the *sine qua non* of political success.

His youth nevertheless suggested great things. Born in Chartres in 1592, he was groomed by his father for public office. In 1616 he succeeded to Etienne II's councillorship in the *grand conseil*.[1] The following year he married into one of the best known families of the *noblesse de robe,* the l'Huilliers.[2] His wife Jeanne (1603-41) was youngest child of François l'Huillier, sieur d'Interville, a *conseiller d'état,* and his wife Anne Brachet (the Brachets were another prominent *robe* dynasty). The l'Huilliers and Brachets possessed *seigneuries* in the Chartres region, so that geographically as well as professionally they and the Aligres had much in common. To the Aligres it was an estimable marriage: Jeanne belonged to a titled family, influential in court and *parlement.* To the l'Huilliers it was a suitable match for a youngest daughter (it should be recalled that in 1617 the Aligres were still of only middling social status).[3] Jeanne was endowed with a respectable if not extravagant dowry of 60,000 livres: 12,000 in cash, the rest in *rentes.* She and Etienne resided in the rue d'Avron, where the first child Louis was born in 1619. Fourteen others were to follow.

For several years Etienne III pursued his career in the *grand conseil*. The breakthrough came in the same year that his father received the seals and the chancellorship. In 1624 he was designated to a post which he could hardly have anticipated and for which his training thus far gave singularly little preparation: French ambassador

---

[1] B.N., Dossiers Bleus 11: 275, f.52.
[2] A.N., M.C., XXXVI-103: Mariage, 5 fév. 1617.
[3] On the early history of the l'Huilliers see, A. de Salinis, *Madame de Villeneuve, née Marie l'Huillier d'Interville, Fondatrice et Institutrice de la Société de la Croix (1597-1650)* (2e. éd., Paris, 1918), 3-13.

to Venice. Given his youth and inexperience he may appear an improbable choice.[4] The delicate state of Franco-Venetian relations in 1624 stipulated an ambassador capable of blending tact and trenchancy, of grasping the intricacy of north Italian politics, and of upholding French prestige under what were to be gruelling circumstances. Could an untried young man of thirty-two realistically be expected to make the grade? It must be assumed that Louis XIII and Richelieu considered that he could. Moreover, it should be recalled that although by the standards of the times France maintained a large diplomatic corps, there existed as yet no profession of diplomacy. No particular category of person was employed on ambassadorial missions (apart from the general principle that he would be noble), nor was a specific training mandatory. No 'diplomatic tradition' supplied the king with his envoys.[5] The absence of diplomatic experience on Etienne III's part was therefore unremarkable. Strongly in his favour was the consideration that he possessed the means to maintain himself and his staff in the required style. Although he was to receive 18,000 livres per annum (which was also the sum paid to the ambassadors in Madrid and London, but only half that paid to the ambassador in the Levant, and less than half the 42,000 livres paid to the ambassador in Rome),[6] there was no guarantee that it would be forthcoming. Furthermore, since governments did not maintain regular embassy buildings abroad, an ambassador was obliged to arrange his own accommodation which had to be of appropriate size and dignity. This too was a drain on his personal resources, at least in the short run. Prestige-conscious but impecunious governments often selected ambassadors as much for their wealth as for any supposed abilities. Etienne III passed this test. His father could support him if necessary from the enormous returns on the chancellorship; but Etienne III also fortified himself financially by selling his office in the *grand conseil* for 64,000 livres.[7] But the deciding factor leading to his appointment was probably that he was his father's son. Etienne II was one of the new faces in central government; by extension Etienne III was awarded this important post. He received his instructions at the end of September.[8] Shortly afterwards he departed with his wife and family (there were now four children; two more were to be born in Venice)

[4] Although in 1624 he was made *conseiller d'état* ('Preuve de Chevalier de Malte' [*brevet*, 25 nov. 1624]).

[5] C.G. Picavet, *La Diplomatie Française au Temps de Louis XIV (1661-1715)* (Paris, 1930), 73-80.

[6] A.A.E., M.D.: France 246, f. 157.

[7] A.N., M.C., LXXXVI-319; Inventaire. . . de Jeanne l'Huillier, 22 oct. 1641 (Titres et papiers concernant les propres du sr. d'Aligre', no. 1).

[8] A.A.E., C [orrespondence] P[olitique]: Vénise 43, fos. 121-2^v).

arriving in Venice on 5 December after an arduous journey. His official reception occurred on 12 December.[9]

Franco-Venetian Relations

Relations between the two states in 1624 were dictated by the Valtelline crisis.[10] Since the rising of the catholic Valtellins in 1620 against their protestant Grison overlords, followed by the erection of a provisional government under Spanish protection and the installation of Spanish strongholds in the valley, events there had assumed international implications. They coincided with the early stages of the Thirty Years war in Germany, the reopening of the Spanish-Dutch war in 1621, the rising of the huguenots in France: three substantial threads which, with the Valtelline, formed a bewilderingly tangled knot. The Venetian attitude to the Valtelline was governed by one obsession: security. If the Spanish succeeded in wresting the valley from the Swiss, or even if they simply secured right of passage for their troops from the Spanish Habsburg Milanese to the Austrian Habsburg Tyrol, Venice would be severed from non-Habsburg Europe, at least by land.[11] Venetian trepidation concerning Spanish hegemony in northern Italy was shared by neighbours: the pope, the dukes of Savoy and Mantua, the Swiss cantons; at a greater distance by the Dutch Republic and German protestant states. The only country with the resources to restore the Valtelline to the Grisons was France, and it was to the French that the Venetians and the others turned. Yet even here intricacies were involved. France would not risk open war with Spain; the Venetians therefore must not subscribe to measures that might provoke a Spanish assault on themselves; nor must they permit the French to extract too high a price for aid; and how could they be sure that French action would accord with Venetian interests? The facts of life were driving the Venetians into the arms of the French, but at times those arms could look uncomfortably like tentacles.

The French too were apprehensive at the dramatic amelioration of the Habsburg position in Italy.[12] Their first attempt to dislodge the

---

[9]D'Aligre to Herbault, Vénise, 12 déc. 1624 (*Ibid.,* fos. 121-2ᵛ).

[10]Surveys are in Lublinskaya, *French Absolutism, passim,* and Tapié, *France in the Age of Louis XIII,* ch 4

[11]On the Venetian position see, B. Nani, *Histoire de Vénise* (Paris, 1679-80), ii, 57-78.

[12]On the French position see, R. Pithon, 'Les débuts difficiles du ministère de Richelieu et de la crise de Valtelline (1621-1627)', *Revue d'Histoire Diplomatique,*

Spanish from the Valtelline appeared to work: in April 1621 by the Franco-Spanish treaty of Madrid the full restoration of the *status quo ante bellum* in the valley was agreed. This surprising tractability on the part of the Spanish is to be explained by two factors: Philip III had died on 31 March, leaving a degree of confusion as his sixteen years old son succeeded; more importantly, in 1621 the Spanish-Dutch truce of 1609 was due to expire and it was widely assumed that hostilities would reopen. Virtually on his death-bed, Philip III had urged that French enmity over the greater Dutch struggle be not provoked by intransigence over the Valtelline. But the Spanish governor of Milan in command of the occupation of the Valtelline, de Feria, made the treaty inoperable. Recognising the weakness of the French he obstructed, with the connivance of his masters in Madrid, the international commission appointed to implement the treaty. French impotence was cruelly exposed later in 1621 when the Grisons attempted to reconquer the valley. Their forces were crushed; the Venetians called on the French to intervene, but they could not. Amid recriminations against France and Venice the beaten Grisons signed away their claims to the Valtelline by the treaty of Milan in January 1622. The year 1622 was the nadir of French fortunes in the region. The Spanish, now embroiled in war elsewhere in Europe, transferred their bases in the Valtelline to the pope, while reserving right of passage for their troops. By this master-stroke they continued to enjoy the advantages, but not the cost and responsibility of command of the valley. They also placed catholic France in the embarrassing position that military intervention now would be against the forces of the head of the church.

The first signs of French recuperation came in 1623. In February there was formed a league of France, Venice and Savoy, whose purpose was to implement the treaty of Madrid and to encourage military diversions in Germany. A full alliance was declined since neither France nor Venice was ready for an open breach with Spain. But it was in 1624, with the arrival of the new men in the inner council of Louis XIII — Richelieu, d'Aligre and the others — that serious measures were at last adopted to recoup lost ground. The marquis de Coeuvres in 1624 and Bassompierre in 1625-6 were despatched to Switzerland where, by a judicious combination of diplomacy and offers of subsidies, they convinced the cantons and the Grisons that the restoration of Grison authority in the Valtelline along with the

---

lxxiv (1960), 298-322, and R. Pithon, 'La Suisse, théâtre de la guerre froide entre la France et l'Espagne pendant la crise de Valtelline (1621-1626)', *Schweizerische Zeitschrift für Geschichte,* xiii, no. 1 (1963), 33-53.

abrogation of the Spanish right of passage were realistic possibilities. Troops of the league were sent to the valley, where a sporadic campaign was fought over the next three years. Etienne III therefore was an instrument of the new initiative. His was no routine appointment. To him fell the far from enviable task of convincing the Venetians that a new beginning had been made, that in France there was now a government of resolution in which they could place their confidence. According to his written instructions his priorities were, to press the Venetians to maintain supplies of troops, weapons and money to the armies of the league; to sustain any diversions in Germany that might transpire; to cultivate harmony between two of the senior north Italian princes, the dukes of Mantua and Savoy. In other words, he was to be preoccupied less with the implementation of French policy in a direct sense, than with the creation of a climate within which that policy could be executed by others.

Etienne III in Venice

His three years in Venice were to be among the most demanding of his career. Charged with a delicate task, few advantages were to hand as he laboured to sustain trust in France among a people he found antipathetic. He never came to terms with what he took to be their obsessive secrecy and circuitousness. Within two weeks of his arrival he was complaining of the impossibility of receiving a straight answer to any question.[13] To his colleague Béthune, ambassador in Rome, he expressed exasperation at the meagre information given to foreign ambassadors by the Venetians; how then could ambassadors do more than guess Venetian intentions?[14] To his friend Peiresc he wrote:

> Nous sommes en un lieu qui présentement produit peu de nouvelles, parmi des gens qui ne communiquent jamais avec les estrangers et dont les esprits sont si rudes et grossiers qu'à peine peut on croire que ce soient Italiens. Le désordre et la corruption se meslent parmi eux comme dans les autres estats. Les brigues et les partialités y règnent puissament. . . .[15]

Coming as he did from a wholly different political tradition (albeit one that itself was not without its 'brigues et partialités'!), he was constantly perplexed by the changing attitude of the *collegio* on the

---

[13] D'Aligre to Herbault, Vénise, 20 déc. 1624 (A.A.E., C.P.: Vénise 43, fos. 129-30).

[14] D'Aligre to Béthune, Vénise, 26 juin 1627 (B.N., Collection Cinq Cents de Colbert 371, pièce 1).

[15] D'Aligre to Peiresc, Vénise, 8 déc. 1626 (B.N., MS Français 9542, f.169).

great matters of the day. One of the few constants on which he could rely in his dealings with the Venetians was their fear of the Spanish.[16] Even this was not a simple, uncomplicated dread. Some of the more belligerent members of the *collegio* argued that the Valtelline was but a symptom of Spanish power whose real centre was Milan, and that logically it was Milan that should be attacked by the league.[17] D'Aligre nevertheless knew that there were others who might be tempted by Spanish offers when an ambassador arrived from Spain in June 1626.[18] His fears in this regard were heightened at the end of the month when word arrived of the surrender of the Dutch to the Spanish at Breda. Spaniards in Venice quickly boasted of their invincibility. No government, they warned, should be so foolish as to join anti-Spanish coalitions.[19] Throughout his period in Venice d'Aligre was forced to devote an inordinate amount of time to countering Spanish-inspired rumours concerning intended French treachery. Frequently he urged that ministers back at home ought to emphasise to the Venetian ambassador France's abiding commitment to the Republic and to their joint venture in the Valtelline.[20] He was afraid that if Venetian awe of the Spanish were allowed to reach extremes, it could lead to the emergence of a 'peace party' contrary to French interests. It required no little skill on his part to conjure up the Spanish bogey sufficiently to stiffen Venetian resolve, without allowing that resolve to turn into defeatism.

Shortly after his arrival in Venice, his cause was assisted by news that the marriage of Henriette and the prince of Wales had been negotiated.[21] This was the kind of restorative that French prestige needed. Even so, rumours spread that the marriage might come to nought,[22] and it was not until couriers arrived in June confirming that the ceremony had actually occurred that its benefits to French prestige were assured.[23] They were short-lived, for Louis XIII's reputation was grievously harmed by the recurrence in 1625 of huguenot rebellion. When they heard of it, the Venetians were quick to ask searching questions of Etienne: would Louis XIII not be obliged to withdraw some of his forces from the Valtelline; would he

[16]D'Aligre to Herbault, Vénise, 20 déc. 1624 (A.A.E., C.P.: Vénise 43, fos. 129-30).
[17]The same, 22 déc. 1624 (*Ibid.*, f. 135).
[18]The same, 10 juin 1625 (*Ibid.*, f. 211).
[19]The same, 24 juin 1625 (*Ibid.*, fos. 216-18).
[20]The same, 24 mai 1625 and 6 sept. 1625 (*Ibid.*, fos. 182-3^v, 263-5^v).
[21]The same, 20 déc. 1624 (*Ibid.*, fos. 128-8^v).
[22]The same, 22 avril 1625 (*Ibid.*, fos. 195-7).
[23]The same, 10 juin 1625 (*Ibid.*, fos. 209-9^v).

not, at the very least, reduce his financial contributions to the cause; would not Venice thus be faced with excessive military and fiscal burdens; and how sound an associate was a monarch who could not keep his own house in order?[24] Naturally the Spanish exploited Etienne's embarrassment by disseminating two stories whose contradictions troubled them not at all: that Louis XIII was in desperate straits because of the rebellion, but that he also entertained the ambition of 'la monarchie d'Europe'.[25] D'Aligre moved quickly to put the French case. In January 1625 he requested permission to present to the *collegio* a comprehensive statement on the situation in France.[26] Malcontents, he submitted, had rebelled with the aid of mercenaries; but they were a minority repudiated by most huguenots, who had sworn loyalty to the king. Governors of the western provinces were amassing forces which would nip the trouble in the bud. So plentiful were their resources that the king had no need even to consider withdrawing troops from the Valtelline, while as evidence of his good faith he had authorised Etienne III to receive another 300,000 livres to pay the troops there. France was an exceedingly rich country; Louis XIII could both crush rebellion and sustain an undiminished policy in the Valtelline.

The realities did not match such confident predictions. As the rebellion persisted, d'Aligre was obliged to repeat frequently the assurance that French commitment to the Valtelline would not suffer.[27] He was most hard-pressed in August. He execrated Spanish catholics who gloated over the advances of heresy in a fellow-catholic state.[28] He again addressed the *collegio,* driving home the community of interest of France and Venice in the Valtelline; but he knew that many members of the *collegio* still considered that sooner or later the king would have no option but to recall troops.[29] In September he as much as the Venetians was relieved to hear that Louis had offered terms to the rebels.[30] Even more was he delighted with the peace that was signed at La Rochelle in February 1626.[31]

Even so, much damage had been done to the French position. The huguenot rising had been costly in the damage done to French

[24]The same, 24 mai 1625 and 4 août 1625 (*Ibid.,* fos. 182-3ᵛ, 239-41).
[25]The same, 10 juin 1625 (*Ibid.,* fos. 209-10).
[26]The same, 28 jan. 1625 (*Ibid.,* fos. 149-50).
[27]The same, 24 mai 1625 (*Ibid.,* fos. 182-3ᵛ).
[28]The same, 4 août 1625 (*Ibid.,* f. 241).
[29]The same, 26 août 1625 (*Ibid.,* fos. 252-4ᵛ).
[30]The same, 23 sept. 1625 (*Ibid.,* f. 273).
[31]The same, 26 fév. 1626 (A.A.E., C.P.: Vénise 44, fos. 20-1).

prestige; it also hindered d'Aligre in the execution of other of his duties. Nowhere was this clearer than in the case of German diversions. By its membership of the league with France and Savoy, Venice had agreed to assist military measures in Germany designed to force the Spanish to ease the pressure in Italy. In 1624 Richelieu signed an accord with the protestant mercenary Mansfeld by which Mansfeld would receive subsidies to finance a campaign predominantly against the Spanish in the Palatinate. D'Aligre was instructed to press the Venetians to contribute as members of the league.[32] Early in May 1625 he met representatives of the *collegio,* explaining the advantages that Venice itself would derive from Mansfeld's campaign. They refused aid, partly through fear of Spanish reprisals, but chiefly for financial reasons. Already, they insisted, Venetian resources were stretched beyond reasonable limits; a further burden on the populace would be intolerable. D'Aligre for once sympathised. Reporting to Herbault, he outlined the existing financial position of the Republic which, he implied, could not absorb many more strains.[33] As duty obliged, he repeated the appeal to the Venetians on more than one occasion; in October 1625 Mansfeld even sent his own representative to plead for aid.[34] The Venetians continued to refuse. Apart from understanding their objections, d'Aligre in any case was reluctant to push them too far: he would not unduly risk their hostility while the huguenots were in revolt and Venetian confidence in the ability of France to meet all its foreign commitments consequently was shaken.

Another irritant as he tried to encourage Franco-Venetian co-operation, was the attitude of the papacy. In June 1625 the nuncio in Venice proposed that the Republic quit the league in favour of one with the Papal States and Florence. This alternative association, it was asserted, would resolve Italian problems efficiently.[35] At the same time the nuncio in France was arguing that the performance of the league had not come up to expectations. Was it really in France's interest to be tied to a state like Venice? These papal manoeuvres accomplished nothing for the moment, except that they obliged d'Aligre all the more solicitously to assure his hosts that Louis XIII was immune to papal machinations.[36]

---

[32] The same, 6 mai 1625 (A.A.E., C.P.: Vénise 43, fos. 183-8).

[33] The same, 6 mai 1625 (*Ibid.*).

[34] D'Aligre to the King, Vénise, 23 oct. 1625 (*Ibid.,* fos. 287-9).

[35] D'Aligre to Herbault, Vénise, 16 jan. 1625 and 6 mai 1625 (*Ibid.,* fos. 147-7^v, 187-7^v).

[36] The same, 24 mai 1625 (*Ibid.,* fos. 182-3^v).

His remaining major responsibility was relations between Savoy and Mantua. He had visited both *en route* to Venice, lecturing their rulers on the importance of mutual trust.[37] Thereafter geography largely removed Savoy from his orbit, but he maintained close contact with Mantua on the Venetian border. The duke insisted on neutrality. With the Spanish base at Milan but three hours march away what option did he have; moreover, he asked, what could he do but tolerate the Spanish troops that passed through his territory? He was in no position to prohibit them. Their presence should not be interpreted as a sign of Mantuan hostility to France and its associates.[38] D'Aligre made sympathetic responses, but when in October 1625 the duke appeared in Venice to discuss the possibility of a military league (also holding discussions with d'Aligre), Etienne as well as the Venetians was suspicious.[39] Why had the duke suddenly changed his tune? The Spanish 'threat' to Mantua had not dissolved; therefore either the duke's earlier insistence that he had no option to neutrality was a deception, or the present offer was a trap. Was the duke perhaps a tool of the Spanish as the Venetians suspected?[40] As gifted as the duke in the skills of evasion, they sent him away with ambiguous replies.

During his first year d'Aligre encountered all the outstanding problems that attached to his office. It was a testing period with which he coped satisfactorily for one new to international diplomacy. The second year was even more demanding. Early in 1626 the Venetians taxed him with unpleasant rumours that betrayal was in the air, that the French were countenancing a bargain with Spain, even one reached without consulting Venice and Savoy.[41] Etienne discounted such shameful slander, promising that Louis XIII would never act independently of his friends. Later the Venetians insisted that indeed they possessed information that Louis XIII was negotiating with Philip IV behind their backs. Etienne, slighted that the word of his king should be doubted, wrote to Herbault on 1 March: at all costs such malicious untruths — doubtless originating with the Spanish — must be countered if serious Franco-Venetian discord was to be avoided.[42] But at the end of March arrived the news that the French ambassador in Spain, du Fargis, had indeed agreed terms with

---

[37] The same, 9 nov. 1624 and déc. 1624 (*Ibid.*, fos. 113-13ᵛ, 117-19).

[38] The same, 13 jan. 1625, 16 jan. 1625, 27 fév. 1625, 12 mars 1625 (*Ibid.*, fos. 141-2, 144-4ᵛ, 163-3ᵛ, 165-7ᵛ).

[39] The same, 17 oct. 1625 (*Ibid.*, fos. 219-9ᵛ, 282-3).

[40] The same, 23 oct. 1625 (*Ibid.*, fos. 290-3).

[41] The same 14 jan. 1626 (A.A.E., C.P.: Vénise 44, fos. 8-9ᵛ).

[42] The same, 1 mars 1626 (*Ibid.*, fos. 24-6).

Olivares at Monzón. D'Aligre was as shocked as anybody. On 1 April he was haled before the *collegio* where he was subjected to denunciations of French treachery.[43] The *collegio* was, 'remply de plaintes contre la france qui faict la paix sans eux au mesme temps qu'elle les solicite à la guerre'.[44] His reply, with which he had been furnished from Paris, was ready: he was displeased to be in this position, for he had dealt with the *collegio* in all sincerity; he regretted du Fargis's behaviour as much as they; by negotiating secretly with Olivares, du Fargis had acted on his own initiative and without the knowledge of Louis XIII; the king disapproved of such conduct, but nevertheless considered that since a form of agreement had been reached, the opportunity should not be lost to exploit it; further discussions with the Spanish would be held, but the king gave his assurance that no treaty would be ratified until his Italian friends had expressed an opinion; meanwhile French forces in the Valtelline would be strengthened as a guarantee that the valley would not simply be abandoned. Later that day a member of the *collegio* asked d'Aligre whether he possessed the terms of the treaty. He did, but denied it, 'scachant bien qu'elles [the terms] leur sont touttes désagréables puis qu'elles n'assurent en aucune façon la vallée aux Grisons, mais en démolissant les forts la laissent ouverte à l'Espagnol qui ne garde sa parole qu'en tant que son interest le permet. . . . '[45]

In the absence of publicised terms, there emerged during the next few weeks the inevitable rumours as to the details of Monzón. D'Aligre was forced to resume his familiar but now discredited role as champion of the credibility of the king. But by the end of April, as Venetian bitterness gave way to a more rational assessment of the Republic's position, d'Aligre could discern the beginnings of a considered stance by the *collegio*. As ever, security was its chief preoccupation. There were three principal considerations: firstly there existed the danger that the Valtellins, now incurably Hispanophile, would in future serve as agents of Spanish influence in the Valtelline; secondly if, as appeared likely, the Valtellins secured the right to elect their own magistrates, who also would be pro-Spanish, that must be balanced by the Grisons nominating governors in the valley; thirdly forts there must not be dismantled but handed over to Grison garrisons, otherwise nothing could prevent the Spanish later reoccupying the valley at will.[46] D'Aligre estimated that there existed a war-

[43]The same, 1 avril 1626 (*Ibid.*, 40-1ᵛ).
[44]The same, 1 avril 1626 (*Ibid.*, f. 42).
[45]*Ibid.*, f. 44.
[46]The same, 22 avril 1626 (*Ibid.*, fos. 50-2ᵛ).

weariness in the Republic which, provided proposals were forthcoming from the French on these three essential matters, could compel the *collegio,* albeit reluctantly, to consent to Monzón. Above all, 'La restitution des forts les presse le plus, d'autant que par ce moyen tout le fruict de leur despense est perdu'.[47] The Venetians continued to pester him for details of the agreement at Monzón. Still he insisted that he knew nothing. The more they pressed him, the more his contempt for them grew. He advised Herbault: 'songer à nos Interests comme ils pensent aux leurs. Le temps les adoucira peu à peu et les résoudra á recevoir les articles selon la Volonté du Roy sans qu'il soit besoign d'autres persuasions que de la nécessité. Car les paroles ne servent pas beaucoup auprès d'eux'.[48]

At the end of May he received an important despatch. The king had at last decided to ratify the agreement. D'Aligre was not to reveal this to the Venetians, but was to inform them that an extraordinary ambassador, Châteauneuf, would be arriving to explain the circumstances surrounding Monzón, its contents, and Louis's steps to protect Venetian security.[49] This exercise in appeasement duly proceeded. Châteauneuf arrived several weeks later, being received officially on 28 July. He remained in Venice for a month, during which either he alone or he and Etienne had a series of meetings with nominees of the *collegio.* As d'Aligre already had predicted, Venetian concern concentrated on the forts in the Valtelline, the Venetians even contemplating occupying them themselves.[50] Although his reception at first was hostile,[51] Châteauneuf's skills as a negotiator persuaded the Venetians to subscribe to the settlement in principle, pending an equal agreement by the cantons and the Grisons. He and the Venetians arrived at four principles to be put to the Swiss: the Valtelline should be closed to troops of the emperor (though not to those of Spain); the Grisons should concede the right of the Valtellins to elect magistrates; but the Grisons should maintain a militia in the valley with French and Venetian assistance; there would be a general offer of Franco-Venetian aid to the Grisons as a guarantee of their authority in the Valtelline.[52] In late August Châteauneuf left for

---

[47]The same, 7 avril 1626 (*Ibid.,* fos. 48-8ᵛ).

[48]The same, 6 mai 1626 (*Ibid.,* f. 50).

[49]D'Aligre to the King, Vénise, 4 juin 1626 (*Ibid.,* fos. 74-5).

[50]D'Aligre & Châteauneuf to the King, Vénise, 13 août 1626 (A.A.E., M.D., France 246, fos. 105ᵛ-6).

[51]D'Aligre to Herbault, Vénise, 13 août 1626 (A.A.E., C.P.: Vénise 44, fos. 207-8).

[52]The same, 27 août 1626 (*Ibid.,* fos. 281-1ᵛ).

Switzerland to canvass support for Monzón,[53] leaving behind him a *collegio* still suffering from a wounded pride whose mollification fell to d'Aligre. Throughout the autumn and winter of 1626-7 he reassured the Venetians of French good will, all the while keeping Châteauneuf informed as to the changing moods of the *collegio*.[54]

Meanwhile there arrived disastrous news: his father had been dismissed from court. D'Aligre immediately supposed his own position to be in jeopardy. Recent history gave weight to his apprehensions, for when the Brûlarts were dismissed so were their associates. Simply by being the son of his disgraced father he was in danger. He immediately sent a suitably-phrased letter to Richelieu which, he hoped, would save himself from recall:

> L'esloignement de la cour m'oste les moyens d'excuser monsieur le chancelier mon père auprès de vous n'ayant cognoissance du particulier de sa disgrace, ny des raisons qui ont rendu son service désagréable à Sa Majesté; aussy n'entreprene je pas de les examiner, puis qu'il est expédient aux affaires publiques. Mais je me jette entre vos bras et recherche vostre protection, en laquelle seule j'ay toujours espéré, sachant que je vous doibs l'honneur d'estre employé en cette Ambassade, où si je n'ay servy avec la prudence et conduite nécessaire, j'y ai au moins aporté l'affection, la fidélité et la diligence qui dépendaient de moy, dont je ne recherche autre tesmoing que vous Monseigneur, et auquel j'en ay toujours rendu compte, sinon par lettres séparées pour n'estre importun, au moins par mes despêches qui ont toujours passé soubs vos yeux. Dieu ne m'a pas donné les aultres parties dont je vous supplie très humblement de couvrir les défauts comme de vostre créature. Je ne scay quelle sera l'intention du Roy pour mon regard... mais s'il luy plaist de me continuer... je n'ay autre apuy que le vostre Monseigneur pour conserver sa bonne volonté ny aultre garend de ma fidélité; je vous supplie très humblement de ne me point abandonner.[55]

He received word of the confirmation of his post, but the fact that the decision was taken before his letter reached Richelieu[56] indicates that the question whether he should be recalled had been posed in Paris. He thus survived a moment of acute danger, but also drew the appropriate conclusion: if his long-term prospects were to be safeguarded he required a new patron at court now that his father had been

---

[53]D'Aligre to Châteauneuf, Vénise, 27 août 1626 (*Ibid.,* f. 272).

[54]Correspondence is in A.A.E., M.D.: France 246, fos. 82-7ᵛ, 90, 93, 95, 101ᵛ-2ᵛ, 105ᵛ-6, 191.

[55]D'Aligre to Richelieu, Vénise, 30 juin 1626 (A.A.E., C.P.: Vénise 44, f. 94).

[56]The same, 14 juillet 1626 (*Ibid.,* f. 125).

removed. He turned to Richelieu. Thereafter he wrote periodically to the cardinal, and if the spectacle of d'Aligre attaching himself to the man who had destroyed his, Etienne's, father appears finely calculated and unedifying, we should not be too ungenerous in our judgement. The mode of an age which threatened to visit the sin of the father on the son left little room for sentiment. Etienne III could secure his future only by adhering to a suitable 'clan'; that of Richelieu appeared to him the most effective; family pride could not therefore stand in the way.

Having survived this potential crisis and with the centre of negotiations on the Valtelline having shifted to Switzerland, d'Aligre were relieved of the weightiest of his responsibilities. His correspondence subsequently sought chiefly to adumbrate the changing moods of the *collegio* as they affected France. By the end of 1626 the defeat of the Danes by the forces of the emperor, the death of the only outstanding protestant general Mansfeld, and that of the duke of Mantua whose successor was suspected of being pro-Spanish (although he too was to expire within a few months, leaving a succession crisis involving a French claimant), again raised queries among the Venetians as to whether the movement of history was not irretrievably in favour of the Habsburgs.[57] In December 1626 d'Aligre warned that they, 'fassent maintenant l'amour à l'Ambassadeur d'Hespagne et qu'ils se préparent à quelque accommodement'.[58] The Venetian predicament remained as perplexing as ever: should they play for high stakes by adhering to the anti-Habsburg cause which nevertheless placed them in danger of the vengeful wrath of the Spanish, or should they settle for a modicum of independence by simply living with Spanish hegemony in northern Italy? The latter viewpoint was inevitably encouraged by the European balance at the end of 1626.

D'Aligre's third and final year as ambassador was rendered somewhat nugatory by the occurrence of one of those disputes over diplomatic rights that could disrupt normal relations for long periods. In Venice there had arisen a particular nuisance through rowdy young nobles hiring gangs of hoodlums or 'braves', who fought battles between themselves, but also terrorised and violated ordinary citizens. Since more than one of his staff had been molested, d'Aligre authorised them to carry weapons when moving around the city. In January 1627 his *valet de chambre* was arrested for carrying a sword and pistol in violation of the latest edict against weapons in public.

[57]D'Aligre to Herbault, Vénise, 9 déc. 1626 (*Ibid.,* fos. 426-7^v); d'Aligre to Châteauneuf, Vénise, 15 jan. 1627 (A.A.E., C.P.: Vénise 45, fos. 9-9^v).

[58]D'Aligre to Châteauneuf, Vénise, 2 déc. 1626 (A.A.E., C.P.: Vénise 44, f. 423).

D'Aligre protested that as a member of his staff the servant enjoyed diplomatic immunity; the city authorities insisted that he be punished according to the law. As well as reporting the case to Herbault Etienne appealed directly to Richelieu.[59]

There was involved, of course, the question of who was covered by diplomatic immunity, but prestige was at stake too. In March d'Aligre objected that while his servant was still in detention over a peccadillo, by contrast a servant of the Spanish ambassador, guilty of a far more serious misdemeanour, had been released.[60] In Paris Richelieu, even the king, demanded of the Venetian ambassador that the *valet* be released; but although the Venetians made conciliatory noises, still they detained the servant while failing to act on the large numbers of their own citizens who openly carried arms.[61] The dispute turned acrimonious. D'Aligre was forbidden by the Venetians to visit other embassies.[62] He in turn boycotted all official functions. His duties as ambassador therefore were seriously disrupted.[63] By summer he lamented: 'Il nous reste dans cet estat fort peu de gens affectionnés au nom françois, de sorte que j'essaye à les conserver par les moyens qui me sont possibles.'[64] The first indication of a break in a deadlock which embarrassed the *collegio* as much as it exasperated d'Aligre, derived from the death of 'Madame', Marie de Bourbon, wife of Gaston d'Orléans the king's brother, in June 1627. The embassy in Venice went into mourning; the *collegio* expressed its condolences, hinting that as a gesture of goodwill it might release the *valet*.[65] Such a move would leave honour intact on both sides. By the middle of July d'Aligre was reporting that his relations with the Venetians had undergone remarkable improvement and that he was resuming attendance at official functions.[66] Does this mean that his servant had been freed? Probably, although the few letters of his remaining correspondence do not explicitly say so. But he was now approaching the termination of his period as ambassador, and there was little

---

[59] D'Aligre to Herbault, Vénise, 30 jan. 1627 (A.A.E., C.P.: Vénise 45. fos. 21-3); d'Aligre to Richelieu, Vénise, 30 jan. 1727 (A.A.E., M.D.: France 246, f. 191^v).

[60] D'Aligre to Herbault, Vénise, 5 mars 1627 (A.A.E., C.P.: Vénise 45, fos. 36-6^v).

[61] The same, 7 avril 1627 (*Ibid.*, fos. 47-7^v).

[62] D'Aligre to Richelieu, Vénise, 9 mars 1627 (A.A.E., M.D.: France 246, f. 191^v).

[63] For instance, he was instructed by Richelieu to prepare a report on Venetian commerce, but never completed it because of the ban and the boycott (A.A.E., C.P.: Vénise 45, f. 16).

[64] D'Aligre to Herbault, Vénise, 2 juin 1627 (*Ibid.*, f. 68).

[65] The same, 1 juillet 1627 (*Ibid.*, fos. 76-6^v).

[66] The same, 13 juillet 1627 and 17 juillet 1627 (*Ibid.*, fos. 83-4^v, 81-2^v).

constructive that he could do except to prepare the way for his replacement, d'Avaux. His last year was thus empty of real achievement or satisfaction, and it is probable that he looked forward with relief to his return to France. He made several requests that since his wife now had two more infants, he be allowed to remain in Venice until easter so as to avoid the dangers of winter travel through the alps.[67] He was refused and left Venice at the end of September 1627.[68]

The Significance of the Embassy

A discussion of the importance to d'Aligre of the years in Venice must acknowledge how extraneous they were to his career before 1625 and to its course after 1627. Under different circumstances — that is if his father had remained active in office — he might now have aspired to high political appointment involving a knowledge of international relations; but his newly-acquired diplomatic skills were not exploited further by Louis XIII. His career instead was diverted into more prosaic channels within France. Yet his professional competence had profited enormously from his experiences in a Venice which occupied a pivotal position in the international situation of the mid-1620s. In every sense the d'Aligre of 1627 was a shrewder, more accomplished figure than in 1625. The political and diplomatic manoeuvres of the Venetians, the intrigues of the Spanish, those of the nuncio, the English, the Danes, the Dutch, not to mention Etienne III himself, engendered in him a versatility, a sardonic worldly wisdom, that life in Paris alone could not have supplied. Read in their entirety his letters to Herbault, Béthune, Châteauneuf and others, bear witness to an evolving maturity. From early sober reports of events and discussions, they develop into sensitive assessments often accompanied by astute recommendations concerning the Republic and its relations with France. That the freshly-refined prowess and up-to-date experience of somebody like d'Aligre were not further put to use in international affairs by the regime, is a comment upon its tendency to waste talent that was ready to hand.

In a more general sense Venice taught d'Aligre to think subtly about international relations, the forces influencing them, and their interaction with domestic policy. He came to appreciate the role of geography, climate, communications, finance, personalities, military

[67] D'Aligre to Richelieu, Vénise, 4 mai 1627 and 26 juin 1627 (*Ibid.*, fos. 56-6^v, 73-4).

[68] D'Aligre to Béthune, Vénise, 4 sept. 1627 (B.N. Collection Cinq Cents de Colbert 371, pièce 10).

strengths and weaknesses, in international affairs. Above all did he learn to despise that simplistic notion, so beloved of many *dévots* in his own country, that the major divisions in Europe were of a religious nature. How could he have adhered to such a fallacy having observed at first hand the confusions and struggles of catholic Italians wrestling with catholic Spanish hegemony, or the efforts of protestant Dutch and German emissaries to achieve harmony with the catholic Venetians, just as they were with the catholic French? Instead d'Aligre perceived that an excessive proportion of Europe's problems emanated from the dynastic and territorial ambitions of the Habsburgs, ambitions all the more sinister and difficult to combat in that they were justified in alluring religious phraseology. The Valtelline was a classic case, for under the guise of restoring catholicism the Spanish were intent upon forging more links in the Habsburg chain. To d'Aligre it followed, therefore, that Habsburg policy must be impeded on every front. Equally, he considered, his fellow countrymen must learn not to suspend their critical faculties when confronted by spurious Spanish claims that service to the church was the abiding concern of their foreign policy. Frenchmen must distinguish between the language in which Spanish policy was expressed and the realities disguised by that language. By extension d'Aligre envisaged international relations, not as the search for a 'just' and static order of European states, but as the dynamic interplay of states pursuing their interests in an impermanent international environment. That meant short or long-term associations between states, irrespective of their constitutional traditions or religious dispositions. The realisation of interests, he considered, must transcend the methods employed. And how were interests to be defined? Not by a single, all-embracing imperative such as the defence of catholicism at all costs, but by many changing criteria, secular and material as well as spiritual. Priorities would have to be determined, and the spiritual from time to time subordinated to the secular.

Such views, which are reflected in d'Aligre's Venetian correspondence, were close to those of Richelieu himself.[69] When Etienne described himself as the cardinal's *créature* he was implying not merely adherence to his 'clan', but also to Richelieu's outlook on public affairs. It should be emphasised that the association with Richelieu required no drastic alteration of attitudes on d'Aligre's part. The practicalities of diplomacy persuaded him that the cardinal truly comprehended the necessary course of French policy. Although by

---

[69] For a discussion of Richelieu's views especially on the Valtelline see, W.F. Church, *Richelieu and Reason of State* (Princeton, 1972), 103-72.

1627 self-interest bound d'Aligre to Richelieu, at the same time they saw eye to eye on the great questions of the day. He easily adapted to the role of *créature* of the cardinal, who in turn was to find in d'Aligre a valuable activist in the king's service. When Etienne III returned to France in the autumn of 1627 it was with high hopes of an appointment suited to an ex-ambassador; but it was to be several years before they were realised.

5

ETIENNE D'ALIGRE III IN NORMANDIE AND LANGUEDOC, 1634-1646

Interlude, 1627-34

For the time being Etienne received no new charge, although he was still in favour and a member of the royal court. For instance, he was part of the entourage that accompanied Louis XIII on the king's visit to the south of France in the summer of 1629.[1] There is also ample evidence that d'Aligre was well off financially. One sign is that he began to loan money through *rentes constituées*. He made his first loan when he was in Venice: through his cousin Jean Turpin who represented his interests in France during his absence, he loaned 3,000 livres on a *rente* of 187 livres 10 sous.[2] After his return he loaned on average twice a year: one contract in 1627, two each year from 1628 to 1632, one in 1633 and three in 1634.[3] Including that of 1626 these contracts meant an outlay of 117,900 livres for a *rente* of 7,362 livres 10 sous (6.25 per cent). In 1631 he loaned 12,000 livres for one year;[4] he also sold a surplus office, of *lieutenant du grenier à sel* at Saulieu in Bourgogne, for 2,550 livres.[5] By 1634 some of the *rentes* just listed had been redeemed, but the remainder returned him 6,025 livres on a principal of 96,400. Most of the *rentes* were paid to him by *officiers,* but his debtors included two aristocrats: Charles de Lorraine, duc de Guise, and François de Béthune, comte d'Orval. Two families from Pontgouin borrowed small sums.

It was during these years that Etienne's wife Jeanne made substantial contributions to their joint resources. Two uncles left her

---

[1] See above p. 74.

[2] A.N., M.C., LI-84: Constitution, 11 juillet 1626.

[3] A.N., M.C., LI-87: Constitution, 26 oct. 1627; XXIV-323; Constitution, 14 août 1628, 18 août 1628; XXIV-327: Constitution, 13 sept. 1629; XXIV-334: Quittance, 5 fév, 1632 on *rente* constituted 25 nov. 1629; XXIV-328: Constitution, 28 jan. 1630; LXXXVI-295: Transport, 23 juillet of *rente* constituted 5 juillet 1630; XXIV-333: Constitution, 9 oct. 1631, 26 oct. 1631; XXIV-334: Constitution, 21 avril 1632; XXIV-348: Partage, 9 mars 1638 refers to Constitution of 6 déc. 1632; XXIV-348: Constitution, 24 juillet 1633; XXIV-340: Constitution, 7 fév. 1634; LI-103: Constitution, 25 fév. 1634; XXIV-340: Constitution, 11 avril 1634.

[4] A.N., M.C., LI-96: Obligation, 18 jan, 1631.

[5] A.N., M.C., XXIV-331: Traité d'office, 6 mars 1631.

legacies totalling 1,400 livres[6] and her sister Hélène, who was a nun, transferred to her a promissory note of 6,500 livres.[7] But it was on the death of her father on 21 April 1641 that she came into her principal bequest.[8] It was of impressive proportions. There were state *rentes* bringing in 2,479 livres; if we assume that sum to represent 8 per cent of the capital invested, then some 31,000 livres are indicated. In addition there were *rentes constituées* of 1,900 livres; if they had been constituted at 5 per cent then their principal was some 38,000 livres, or if at 6.25 per cent then 30,400 livres. *Rentes* together thus came to 4,379 livres per annum on a principal of between 61,400 and 69,000 livres. Jeanne also inherited shares in offices. There was a 25 per cent share in the offices of *regrature de sel* and *revendeur à petites mesures* in the *grenier à sel* of Meaux; the share was worth 22,300 livres, although its annual return is not known.[9] Then there was a half share in the offices of *contrôleur* and *marqueur de cuires* at Falaise; its value was 6,700 livres, but again its annual return is unknown. Jeanne inherited property: a house in Vaugirard which she and Etienne sold in 1632 for 10,500 livres, and another in the rue de la Haute Vénerie in Paris which they sold in 1631 for 7,000 livres. Finally there was a small sum in cash; 1,038 livres 6 sous. The joint value of the houses, the offices, the principals of the *rentes* was well over 100,000 livres: a healthy injection of capital into the resources of Jeanne and her husband.

Preceding passages have testified to Etienne III's prosperity, but they do not explain how he came to enjoy cash surpluses which he was able to put into *rentes constituées*. To that query available documentation provides no answer. He may been receiving a pension from the king; his father may have been transferring funds to him; but speculation is all that is permissible, and it does not take us very far.

Six years had passed since his return from Venice and still he was without office. As Etienne II grew older (he was now in his seventies) and no charge came his son's way, Etienne III must seriously have wondered whether in fact he had been cast aside like his father. Was he destined to devote the rest of his life to an agreeable *vie noble,* but

---

[6]A N, M C, LXXXVI-319: Inventaire, . . de Jeanne l'Huillier, 22 oct. 1641 ('Papiers de la famille', nos. 5,6).

[7]*Ibid.,* ('Papiers de la famille', no. 4).

[8]*Ibid.,* ('Papiers de la famille', nos. 9-28); Jeanne shared the inheritance with two brothers and three sisters ('Papiers de la famille', no. 7).

[9]The office of *regrature* was later suppressed and redeemed by the government; Etienne III used the resultant capital in 1635 to purchase state *rentes* of 1,604 livres 13 sous (on a principal of about 20,000 livres).

one in which public service to the king would play no part? At times he must have concluded that Etienne II's disgrace had indeed left an indelible stain-by-association on his own prospects. Such apprehensions were at least dispelled in 1634. He was chosen for a commission which, if much inferior to the embassy in Venice, at least showed that he had not been consigned to oblivion. He was appointed head of a *recherche de la noblesse* in the *généralité* of Caen.

The 'Recherche', 1634-5

The charge arose out of Richelieu's financial preoccupations. For several years he had been multiplying devices for extracting money from the public at an alarming rate, chiefly to help to finance the Swedes and others in their war against Spain. Moreover, by 1634 it was generally considered only a matter of time before France too went to war with Spain. The resulting exigencies and strains would inevitably compel Richelieu to demand ever-increasing financial sacrifices of the country. Paradoxically, at the same time Richelieu was aspiring to scale down the *taille* which, for all it was the fundamental direct tax, was widely admitted to exert debilitating effects on those who paid it. Plans to diminish the *taille* were announced at a *lit de justice* in the *parlement* of Paris on 18 January 1634,[10] after which an important edict was forthcoming which decreed a reduction of the tax by 25 per cent.[11]

The reconciliation of two apparently conflicting propositions — that the government must further plan to supplement its revenue, but that the *taille* should be pared — was envisaged by Richelieu as deriving in part from a third consideration. Large numbers of wealthy people, he considered, were evading *taille*, often by assuming false titles of nobility and enjoying illegally the noble right not to pay direct taxation. If *faux nobles* could be detected and forced to pay *taille*, indeed if tax-avoidance as a whole could be cured, then funds hitherto lost to the government would accrue sufficiently to permit the rate of *taille* to be lowered. Accordingly the edict of January 1634 prescribed:

> [Clause 2] Défendons à tous nos Subjects d'usurper le tiltre de Noblesse, prendre la qualité d'Escuyer, et de porter

---

[10]*Harangue de Monsieur le Cardinal, par luy faite en Parlement le Roy y scéant, le dix-huictiesme de Janvier mil six cents trente quatre* (Paris, 1634) [B.N., Imprimés, Lb^{36}2981].

[11]*Edict du Roy sur le Règlement Général des Tailles. . . du dix-huictiesme Janvier dernier, mil six cens trente quatre* (Paris, 1634) [B.N., Imprimés, F46978].

armoiries timbrées, à peine de deux mil livres d'amende, s'ils ne sont de maison et extraction noble.

[Clause 3] Seront taxez et imposez aux Tailles, tous ceux lesquels n'estans nobles de race, usurpent ledit tiltre, sous prétexte de quelques Sentences et Jugemens par eux ou leurs prédécesseurs obtenus, si elles ne sont confirmées par Arrests contradictoirement donez, avec parties valables et intéressés.

So bold a programme required an all-out attack on the problem of *fausse noblesse*, which had foiled successive regimes.[12] In May 1634 Richelieu established commissions to investigate the distribution and collection of *taille* in seventeen of the country's twenty-one *généralités*.[13] D'Aligre was head of that to Caen; his chief assistant was to be Jean Cardinet, sieur de Loigny, *trésorier général des finances* at Orléans. The instructions issued to the commissions[14] laid most stress upon the identification and exposure of abuses in the collection of *taille*. Commissioners were to visit the main towns of a *généralité*, to meet the *trésoriers* and discuss problems in their particular areas, searching for solutions where possible. The commissioners were to tour the *élections*, calling together local financial and legal officers for the purpose of inspecting the *taille* rolls. Particular attention was to be paid to the equity with which *taille* was distributed. In each parish the clergy were to post details of when the commissioners would be in the area so that people could present any grievances. After examining the *taille* rolls the commissioners were to meet the *marguilliers* (church wardens often also serving as magistrates) of the parishes to enquire about the inhabitants there, especially the wealthy ones, to verify that they were not being underassessed. Commissioners were to keep an especially vigilant eye open for abuses at which local *officiers* connived. If a *faux exempt* were discovered he was to be inscribed on the *taille* roll at a rate fixed by the commissioners after taking statements from five people (including a priest) as to the means and possessions of the person in question. When nobles presented documentary proof of their titles, the commissioners were to accept only the originals, 'prenant bien garde que les roturiers ne supposent des noms et armes de familles vrayement nobles'.

---

[12]For a discussion of the problem and attempts to remedy it see, D.J. Sturdy, 'Tax evasion, the *faux nobles*, and state fiscalism: the example of the *généralité* of Caen, 1634-35', *French Historical Studies*, ix, no. 4 (1976), 550-1.

[13]Bonney, *Political Change in France*, 41.

[14]They are printed in L. du Crot, *Le Nouveau Traité des Aydes, Tailles, et Gabelles* (Paris, 1636), 475-88.

Richelieu was taking on a problem whose final solution had evaded his predecessors, and was indeed to elude him too. In the *généralité* of Caen, for instance, there had been *recherches de la noblesse* in 1463-4 and 1598-9,[15] and commissions to the whole province of Normandie, including Caen, for the purpose of reviewing the distribution of *taille* in 1578, 1593, 1598, 1617 and 1623-4.[16] D'Aligre's selection as head of this, the latest in a series of commissions, exhibited the strengths and weaknesses of this particular method of bringing central authority to bear directly on a province. D'Aligre personally was equipped with a fine mind, he was thoroughly trustworthy, and he was anxious to re-establish himself in the king's service. Yet in the Cotentin peninsula he was almost as much abroad as when in Venice. He had no family connections there, and so far as is known, had never visited that part of France. While such considerations guaranteed his exclusive fidelity to the interests of the king during the enquiry, he suffered the drawbacks of the stranger with an unpopular mission, who was forced to rely heavily upon assistance and advice drawn locally.

The 'Généralité' of Caen

What of the region to which he was sent?[17] It comprised nine *élections* and 1,426 parishes; in 1634 it was assessed to pay *taille* at 1,434,202 livres 8 sous 8 deniers,[18] which made it eighth out of the twenty-one *généralités*. The neighbouring *généralité* of Rouen was top of the list at 2,612,620 livres 16 sous 9 deniers; together the two *généralités* made Normandie the most heavily-taxed province in France. D'Aligre's commission, in other words, was to a region which formed part of the financial backbone of the country.

In the *généralité, taille personnelle* was paid, but it was assessed only on property owned in the parish where the taxpayer resided. Therein was the source of much injustice, for property

---

[15]The report of the 1598 commission is in B.N., MS Français 32574, 32576.

[16]E. Esmonin, *La Taille en Normandie au Temps de Colbert (1661-1683)* (Paris, 1913), 43-4.

[17]Works of relevance include M. Caillard *et al.*, *A Travers la Normandie des XVIIe et XVIIIe Siècles* (Caen, 1963); M. Foisil, *La Révolte des Nu-pieds et les Révoltes Normandes de 1639* (Paris, 1970); P. Logié, *La Fronde en Normandie* (Amiens, 1951-2); Esmonin, *La Taille en Normandie* contains much of value on the early seventeenth century.

[18]Du Crot, *Le Nouveau Traité*, 431-3; du Crot divides this figure into its component parts per *élection*, which in fact total 1,434,252 livres 8 sous.

owners with land in another parish were not liable for *taille* upon it. In such cases the tax was borne by local peasants.[19] The edict of January 1634 terminated this state of affairs by rendering landowners liable for all their property. It further restricted the exemption from *taille* enjoyed by clergy and nobility to one house and its estate.[20] Such reforms, commendable as they might appear to modern eyes, provoked resentment among those affected, who were now faced with yet more prying into their affairs by the d'Aligre commission. Moreover, such chagrin was a dangerous sentiment to provoke in a part of France which had displayed much social unrest over the preceding fifteen years. In Normandie as a whole there had been numerous outbursts of rioting; in the *généralité* of Caen the most serious had been at Coutances in 1623, Saint-Lô in 1628, and in Caen in 1630 and 1631.[21] The factors underlying social turmoil have been closely examined by historians[22] who emphasise the diseases that afflicted crops, livestock and humans in the 1620s, the *misère* common to wide ranges of Normandie, and the commercial and industrial depression of the 1620s and early 1630s which damaged textiles, metallurgical and leather enterprises. Economic grievances were exacerbated by the financial exploitation of the whole of Normandie by the government, whose endless fiscal impositions more than any other single factor united disparate communities into violent resistance. The incident to ignite a rising was usually the arrival of royal agents to collect the most recent and burdensome demand. There was bound to be popular suspicion of d'Aligre and his team in a *généralité* which had developed a rancorous suspicion of central government. The estates of Normandie, guardian of the financial privileges of the *généralité*, protested at the *recherche* and at least attempted to win the concession that nobles might be allowed to prove their titles by copies, not necessarily the originals of the relevant documentation.[23] It met with refusal. D'Aligre duly travelled to the *généralité* to open his enquiries in the *élection* of Carentan on 27 September 1624. Throughout the autumn and

---

[19]Esmonin, *La Taille en Normandie*, 280; Caillard et. al., *A Travers la Normandie*, 86.

[20]Caillard et al., *A Travers la Normandie*, 51, 95; Foisil, *La Révolte des Nu-pieds*, 63.

[21]Caillard, et al., *A Travers la Normandie*, 37-8; Logié, *La Fronde en Normandie*, i, 91-3.

[22]Caillard et al., *A Travers la Normandie*, 86-119; Logié, *La Fronde en Normandie*, i, 21, 91-3; Foisil, *La Révolte des Nu pieds*, 117-60; G. Vanel, *Une Grande Ville (Caen) aux XVIIIe et XVIIIe Siècles* (Caen, 1910-13), i, chap. 7.

[23]C. de Robillard de Beaurepaire (ed.), *Cahiers des Etats de Normandie sous les Règnes de Louis XIII et de Louis XIV* (Rouen, 1876-8), iii, 8.

winter he moved steadily around the Cotentin to the other *élections* of Valognes, Coutances, Avranches and Mortain, and finally to the *bailliage* of Caen-et-Vire where he completed the *recherche* in May 1635.

The Findings of the Commission[24]

The *recherche* was aimed exclusively at the lowest of noble ranks, the *écuyers*. As the edict of January 1634 recognised,[25] it was at that level that the problem of *fausse noblesse* was concentrated. Holders of *fiefs de dignité* (barons and other titles upwards) were not required to present themselves to the commission. It was at that blurred junction of the social structure where small nobility and land-owning commoners met, that confusion existed and *faux nobles* were to be found. As d'Aligre toured the *généralité* the procedure was for families claiming to be *écuyers* to report to the commission on appointed days, bringing documentary proof of their titles. On the basis of such evidence the commission took its decision to confirm or to deny a title.

During the eight months of its duration the mission examined 994 families: 211 in Carentan, 253 in Valognes, 188 in Coutances, 124 in Avranches, 101 in Mortain, and 117 in Caen-et-Vire. Of that number 880 were able to satisfy d'Aligre as to the authenticity of their titles. They brought a mass of documentation on the principle that an excess of proof was preferable to the bare minimum. But some categories of documentation tended to predominate. Of the 'successful' families 157 (17.8 per cent) rested their claims principally on *lettres de noblesse,* 89 (10.1 per cent) on recognition by the *cour des aides* of Paris, 11 (1.2 per cent) on recognition by the *cour des aides* of Rouen, 57 (6.4 per cent) on favourable decisions by the *recherche* of 1598 and 130 (14.7 per cent) on that of 1624. As regards the remaining 436 families, the report of the commission does not define the nature of the proof given; it generally enters each case thus: 'Vû les titres présentés par X de la paroisse de Y'; then follows a brief genealogy usually of three generations, followed by the decision, 'Jouira'. It was here that the commissioners were called on to exercise their judgement

[24]They are contained in, 'Regitre des Jugemens rendus par nous Etienne d'Aligre, sr. de la Rivière, conr. du Roi en ses conls. et Jean Cardinet, sr. de Loigni, Trésorier gnal. de ses Finances à Orléans;comme députés par Sa Majesté pour le Régalement des Tailles en la généralité de Caen sur les exemptions prétendues par les Gentilhommes et autres privilégiés de lad. gnalité...' (B.N., MS Français 32577; another copy is in MS Français 32574).

[25]Its text refers exclusively to *écuyers*.

most assiduously as people doubtless brought a bewildering variety of papers to impress them. Marriage contracts, bills of sale, other legal documents drafted by notaries, letters from other nobles addressing the recipient as 'sieur de', and a host of disparate records, transactions and dossiers would be pressed on the commissioners by nobles anxious to put their quality beyond question. As almost half the families confirmed in their nobility fell into this amorphous category, d'Aligre evidently had been obliged to exercise his judgement a great deal during the course of the *recherche*. He was even prepared to endorse titles lacking sufficient documentation, provided the 'feel' of a case was right. This happened, for instance, to the advantage of Jean and Charles de la Mariouse at Caen-et-Vire: 'Enfans de Jean, fils Robert, fils Jean, fils autre Jean de la Mariouse, tous sieurs de Lassi; manquent preuve sufisante pour la descente de Robert fils Jean; il y a néantmoins aparence de vérité. Jouiront.'[26] Leadership of a *recherche* was no task for a pedant; it required an ability to treat each case on merit and to exercise intelligent discrimination in that large proportion of instances where impressions were as telling as formal evidence.

The dilemma in which commissioners often found themselves is further illustrated when we turn our attention to those deemed *faux nobles*. A clear decision to this effect was taken in sixty-six cases. The majority, forty-five, were straightforward usurpers, the culprits simply assuming a title illegally. A typical example can be cited:

> Vû les titres de noblesse à nous représentés par Jean de Mari, Ecuyer, de la paroisse de Carentan y demeurant; fils Nicolas, fils Jacques; après qu'il ne nous a pu justifier de sa noblesse demeurera imposé à la taille dans la paroisse de Carentan à la somme de 5 livres et à la restitution de la somme de 12 livres pour avoir usurpé ladite qualité.[27]

After usurpation the next most common misdemeanour was *dérogeance:* the practice of occupations irreconcilable with nobility, even though a title otherwise was valid. There were fifteen cases, six in the *élection* of Carentan and nine in Valognes. Almost all were so judged because the people concerned were exercising minor offices.[28] For instance:

> Vû les titres de noblesse de Julien et Robert de Chaumontel, lesdits frères fils François, fils Michel, fils Jacques, fils Guillaume,

[26]B.N., MS Français 32577, p. 373.

[27]*Ibid.*, 11.

[28]Esmonin, *La Taille en Normandie,* 246-56, discusses which offices rendered the holder immune from *taille.*

> fils Geffroy de Chaumontel, sieur d'Andrieu. Julien jouira et pour le regard de Robert, attendu qu'il a dérogé pour être exerçant l'ofice d'huissier et sergent à Carentan, ordonné qu'il sera imposé l'année prochaine à la somme de vingt sols au Rôle de ladite paroisse de Carentan.[29]

Or again:

> Vû les Titres présentés par Nicolas Michel, Ecuyer, de la paroisse de Saint Pierre Eglise; fils Antoine, fils Jean, fils autre Jean, fils Thomas Michel, Ecuyer; Contrats passés, lesdits Nicolas et Antoine son père en qualité de Tabelions au siège du Val de Saire des 2e novembre 1576, 3e février 1585 et 25e janvier audit an. Avons ordonné que ledit Michel comme dérogeant sera imposé à la somme de trois livres.[30]

One nobleman sacrificed his title having become a tailor,[31] while two brothers from La Haie du Puis were penalised, not because they themselves pursued derogatory occupations but because their father had done so. He had been a *fermier du greffe*. Since his sons had not restored their status by acquiring *lettres de relief de dérogeance* (by which nobility was restored after a period of loss through *dérogeance*) they suffered the consequences.[32] The remaining six families of the sixty-six at present under consideration were classified as *faux* for a variety of other reasons such as failure to have *lettres de noblesse* registered in the *cour des aides* or the *chambre des comptes*.

Beyond the sixty-six families on which the commission passed decisive adverse judgement came another forty-eight which for the time being were left in abeyance. They comprised those who had failed to convince d'Aligre of their status but were sufficiently marginal to warrant a second opportunity. The procedure was to specify a concessionary period in which to vindicate themselves.

For instance:

> Vû les titres présentés par René le Cesne, sieur de Pontrilli et Nègreville, Bailli de Cotentin, de la paroisse de Nègreville; fils Richard le Cesne. Arrest de la Cour de Parlement de Rouen du 8e février 1577 par lequel sans avoir regard à plusieurs oppositions formées par plusieurs Gentilshommes du Cotentin soutenant ledit Richard n'être Gentilhomme, est ordonné que ledit Richard sera reçu en

---

[29] B.N., MS Français 32577, p. 9.
[30] *Ibid.*, 179.
[31] *Ibid.*, 37.
[32] *Ibid.*, 76-7.

ladite charge et office de Bailli de Cotentin; avons ordonné que ledit le Cesne justifiera plus amplement de sa noblesse dans huitaine autrement sera imposé en ladite paroisse de Nègreville.³³

Difficulty arises in that the commission report does not indicate any subsequent measures to ascertain that its instructions were followed. There is a strong suspicion that in many such instances 'nobles' themselves doubted whether they could corroborate their titles even having received a stay of execution, and therefore hoped that when the commission moved on, and as time passed, they might be forgotten. By avoiding the authorities, with luck old habits would reappear leaving them to continue their questionable exemption from the *taille*.³⁴ Here was one of the murkiest aspects of the *recherche*, exemplifying admirably the complexities of a society wherein the legalistic divisions between one stratum and another could be obscured by social realities. Perhaps what is remarkable is that only forty-eight, or 4.8 per cent, of the 994 families scrutinised, fell into this dubious category. The commission succeeded in passing definitive judgement in just over 95 per cent of the cases it examined, a proportion that probably explains the popular grumbles that d'Aligre was excessively zealous.³⁵

To return to the sixty-five families condemned as *faux nobles*, that too is a surprisingly small figure given Richelieu's supposition that *fausse noblesse* was rampant. Even if the worst is assumed, namely that all the forty-eight 'ambiguous' families proved to be frauds, that unlikely circumstance gives a total of only 104 examples of *fausse noblesse*, or just over 10 per cent of the *écuyers* (not, it should be repeated, of the nobility as a whole). In practice the real figure would have been less, say between 5 per cent and 10 per cent. There is a further consideration. To Richelieu, putative nobility was also a stratagem whereby wealthy commoners shirked heavy taxes. The d'Aligre commission demonstrated the reverse: that in the *généralité* of Caen it was poverty, not wealth, that drove people to assume titles. There was, for instance, the widow Guillemine Osmont, 'veuve de Jean Blondel, soi disant Ecuyer', who made representations for herself and her son: 'attendu que ladite Osmont n'a justifié, ordonné qu'elle demeurera imposé à 5 sous... sans restitution vu sa pauvreté.'³⁶ Of the sixty-five families

---

³³*Ibid.*, 145.
³⁴I owe this suggestion to Prof. R. Pillorget.
³⁵Caillard *et al.*, *A Travers la Normandie*, 54.
³⁶B.N., MS Français 32577, p. 90.

newly inscribed on the *taille* roll, forty-six were assessed at under 10 livres a year, sixteen at between 10 and 14 livres, three at between 20 and 24 livres, while the highest was at 26 livres. When it is considered that peasants in Normandie at this time on average paid *taille* at between 10 and 20 livres,[37] these figures testify to a deadening weight of poverty. Almost two-thirds of the *faux nobles* were deemed harder up than most peasants, with most of the remainder on the same level as peasants. The *taille* for which the sixty-six families were now liable was the paltry sum of 449 livres; hardly a significant proportion of the 1,434,202 livres which the *généralité* was obliged to raise! Even if that figure is augmented by a notional amount for the forty-eight families required to furnish more evidence (and proportionally they would have been assessed at about 330 livres), then the 114 families between them would have paid from 775 to 800 livres in *taille*. Even this is an exaggerated figure. Far from being well-moneyed social climbers, the *faux nobles* of Caen were for the most part miserable wretches struggling to make ends meet.

Although the fines that d'Aligre imposed fell well short of the 2,000 livres which the edict of Janurary 1634 threatened, in view of the poverty of most of the offenders they were punitive. Nine families in fact were absolved because of their impecuniosity, ten paid up to fifty livres, sixteen up to 99 livres, seven paid a fine of 100 livres, three of 150 livres, five of 200 livres, and seven paid a fine over 300 livres (the highest being 600 livres).[38] If these penalties were not exemplary in absolute terms, they were if expressed as numbers of years' *taille*. In the *élection* of Carentan the Fortécu brothers were fined 100 livres, or ten years' *taille*.[39] The Tardif family was punished by seventeen years' *taille*.[40] In the *élection* of Valognes the François, Marchant and Dancel families were all fined thirty-three to thirty-four years' *taille*.[41] On all but the poorest families, d'Aligre brought a heavy hand to bear. Herein may lie the essential clue to the small percentage of *faux nobles* discovered by the commission. The imposition of stiff penalties in a *généralité* which had been the subject of several investigations in recent decades was a reasonably effective antidote to this particular social malady.[42] The fines realised the sum

---

[37] Caillard *et al.*, *A Travers la Normandie*, 107.

[38] B.N., MS Français 32577, p. 273.

[39] *Ibid.*, 67.

[40] *Ibid.*, 64.

[41] *Ibid.*, 90, 114, 174.

[42] For suggestions as to why people still risked *fausse noblesse* see, Sturdy, 'Tax evasion', 569-71.

of 6,201 livres; if to that we add a notional sum for the other forty-eight families (about 4,840 livres), then such conjecture indicates that at the outside, the d'Aligre commission could have raised some 11,000 livres in fines as well as the 800 livres or so in *taille*. As a fiscal device the *recherche* was a failure, mainly because the assumptions on which it rested were faulty.

The hard months spent perambulating the Cotentin brought Etienne III face to face with some of the harshest of realities. Through his contacts with Chartres and Le Perche he was already familiar with the tenor of provincial life, but a concentrated and systematic visitation like that of 1634 to 1635 was bound to leave a vivid impression of its sombre side. To the present-day observer it is evident that in the mid-1630s Norman society was highly unstable, and was soon to explode into the rebellion of the *nu-pieds* in 1639. That revolt was exceedingly ominous from the viewpoint of the government, for it speedily developed into a general rising of the province, backed by all social groups. None of d'Aligre's correspondence during the *recherche* has been traced and so it is impossible to assess how far d'Aligre was conscious of a gestating crisis; but it is hard to believe that someone of Etienne's experience and maturity was incapable of recognising warning signs. Indeed, the rates of *taille* at which he assessed *faux nobles* suggest that he was alert to the *misère* that overlaid much of the province. When he had completed his inquiries, drawn up his report and returned to Paris, it must have been with a sense of relief.

Intendant, 1636-9

Throughout summer and autumn of 1635 and into spring 1636 d'Aligre remained in or near Paris. This enabled him to be with his father at La Rivière when he died in December 1635. But it was not long before he was off on his travels again, although not in the way that he first expected. Richelieu was clearly impressed by d'Aligre's performance as head of the *recherche,* and in the autumn of 1635 the cardinal revealed his intention of sending him as *intendant* to Provence; instructions to that effect were duly prepared.[43] However, circumstances led Richelieu to change his mind, and to despatch d'Aligre back to the Cotentin peninsula instead.

In 1635, of course, Richelieu committed France to open war with Spain. In order to meet the sharp acceleration in military expenditure

---

[43] A[rchives de la] G[uerre], A^{1}26, no. 198.

he was driven to devise and impose yet more financial exactions on the country. Naturally, Normandie was alloted its due share of loans, taxes and other impositions. Richelieu rightly anticipated an upsurge of resistance in the province that would have to be circumvented or, if necessary, overcome. During the early, and as it transpired very difficult, phase of the war he needed *intendants* whom he could trust and whose talents were up to the mark. He therefore decided not to send d'Aligre to Provence, but straight back to the *généralité* of Caen where his recently acquired knowledge of the region was an invaluable asset. Thus it was that in 1636 Etienne III found himself in the Cotentin once again; this time, however, he was concerned with far more than an investigation of one section of society: principally, he was charged with managing the application of the government's fiscal policy.

His task was made all the more difficult by two governmental decisions which affected the *généralité*. Firstly, in May 1636 there was created a new *généralité*, that of Alençon. It comprised eight *élections* taken from Rouen and one from Caen.[44] Now reduced in size Caen was nevertheless assessed at heavier rates of *taille* than in the days when it contained nine *élections:* 2,175,737 livres in 1636, 1,395,067 in 1637, 2,442,444 in 1638 and 2,101,986 livres in 1639.[45] Secondly, in December 1636 a new forced loan was announced, to which the *généralité* of Caen was to contribute 885,000 livres.[46] It fell to d'Aligre to allocate and collect this sum. Predictably he would face protests from every side, pleas of grinding poverty and inability to pay; each protest would have to be heard and judged. From towns and villages all over the *généralité* would come demands for a reduction of their assessment; they would have to be visited and adjudications made. D'Aligre and his assistants would have to be prepared to spend months riding around the Cotentin haggling with a stubborn and resistant population. Nor should it be forgotten that such peregrinations would take a place in an area that was riddled with plague.[47] An outbreak hit the province in 1637 and 1638, when Coutances, Mortain and Vire suffered the worst ravages of a general epidemic. It is no exaggeration to say that he must have met hundreds if not thousands of people who were potential plague-carriers capable of transmitting disease to him.

---

[44]Caillard, *A Travers la Normandie*, 116.

[45]Foisil, *La Révolte des Nu-pieds*, 69.

[46]*Ibid.*, 62-3; the loan explains why the *taille* was lowered for 1637.

[47]*Ibid.*, 117-26.

The two and a half years that d'Aligre spent there, apart from intermittent visits to Paris, were among the toughest of his career. As was to be anticipated, the forced loan met with resistance. For a time the towns of Avranches, Valognes, Coutances and Carentan flatly refused their portions; it was only after months of discussion that they agreed to pay about 50 per cent less than their original assessments.[48] Numerous individuals or groups whose excuses had been overriden by d'Aligre appealed to the king, often with success. Such was the experience of two *officiers,* Louis de Rauend, *lieutenant du bailli de Cotentin,* and Thomas Alexandre, *procureur du roi en l'élection de Carentan;* wealthier *officiers* than they had been exempted from the loan, but between them they had been assessed by d'Aligre at 3,330 livres. They appealed on the grounds of poverty; the king concurred, instructing that the sum be charged to the *taillables* of Carentan.[49] Again, d'Aligre assessed the *élus* of Mortain jointly at 2,330 livres, refusing to permit them to draw the income from their offices until they paid up. They petitioned the king, arguing that their offices gave them exemption; he agreed.[50] The town of Caen was instructed to contribute 150,000 livres to the loan. In 1636 it had already agreed to a special gift of 40,000 livres to the king and submitted that another 150,000 livres were too much. After discussions with d'Aligre the figure was adjusted to 112,500 livres, but it was now up to d'Aligre to reallocate the surplus of 37,500 livres and furthermore establish the local taxes through which the 112,500 livres would be realised.[51] Such examples could be multiplied, but they illustrate something of the complexities involved in raising the loan, and testify to the resources of physical hardiness and mental tenacity that were required of an *intendant.*

More than that, by 1637 there was a malevolence in the air which made d'Aligre and his assistants vulnerable to violence. Wherever they went they were subjected to verbal abuse, especially from, '[des] peuples rendus nécessiteux par le misère du siècle'.[52] They were even menaced with assault. One of his *collecteurs,* Jacques d'Avoys, sieur de l'Aigle, reported that after d'Aligre had lodged with him in the village of Guibre, not only were he and his family reviled by villagers but a gang of local malcontents actually made more than one attempt on their lives. D'Avoys insisted that without the help given by some

[48]*Ibid.,* 64.
[49]A.N. E 140B, fos. 103-3ᵛ.
[50]*Ibid.,* fos. 105-6.
[51]*Ibid.,* fos. 86-7.
[52]Mousnier, *Lettres. . . au Chancelier Séguier,* i, 412.

'notables bourgeois' he and his family would have been murdered.[53] D'Aligre and his men appeared to the populace as so many predators who spelt financial exploitation wherever they went. No doubt the regime's predicament was palpable as mounting debts, soaring rates of interest and fearful military expenditure meant that it could only sustain its policies through the kind of treatment meted out to the *généralité* of Caen.[54] Yet in 1637 and 1638 d'Aligre was encountering a nascent violence which portended serious consequences. The hostility that confronted him on his tour of the *généralité* can have left him in little doubt that even the king's most compliant subjects were close to the limits of obedience.

In 1638 it fell to him to implement yet another controversial measure. In July there was created a *cour des aides* at Caen.[55] It was to be staffed by ninety-three officers whose posts in the short run had been purchased by a Parisian *traitant* Charles Cappon, who had also bought the offices of the newly-formed *élection* of Saint-Lô; for both sets of offices he had paid 315,000 livres.[56] The offices of the four *présidents* of the new *cour* were to be sold at 21,000 livres each, but the rest were simply to be auctioned, the profits of the sale going to Cappon. The *cour* encountered opposition from the *trésoriers* of the *bureau des finances* in Caen, for inevitably it would divert many of their functions and responsibilities to itself, thereby diminishing their income. Likewise the *cour des aides* at Rouen under whose authority the Cotentin hitherto had fallen, objected to the new institution.[57] Even so its establishment proceeded. As *intendant* it was d'Aligre's role to oversee the sale of the necessary offices, to negotiate premises, to help in initiating the proceedings of the *cour,* and to answer the protests of the *trésoriers*.

While he was thus occupied the task of provisioning troops loomed large among his responsibilities. Since the outbreak of war Normandie not only had been obliged to raise forces, but also to provide quarters for regiments near the war zone.[58] There was a long tradition everywhere in Europe of troops and civilians living in a state of mutual hostility. As the number of soldiers in Normandie ebbed and flowed there were the usual outbreaks of violence as well as

[53] A.N. E 140B, fos. 410-11.

[54] A full account of fiscal policy as it affected Caen is in Foisil, *La Révolte des Nu-pieds,* 62-83.

[55] *Ibid.,* m 98-9.

[56] A.N., E 149B, fos. 13-16.

[57] *Ibid.,* fos. 59-60; Foisil, *La Révolte des Nu-pieds,* 99.

[58] Foisil, *La Révolte des Nu-pieds,* 102-14.

lamentations from the estates of Normandie that the cost to the province of provisioning the troops was crippling. The government could cope with sporadic clashes between the military and civilians, and with the protests of the estates. What did agitate Richelieu, however, was the possibility of mutiny by soldiers because of long delays in receiving pay and provisions. European history, indeed the European war since 1618, provided too many horror stories of the destruction and atrocities perpetrated by rampaging troops, for him to take the risk lightly. D'Aligre consequently was subjected to a steady stream of instructions from Paris impressing upon him the necessity to verify that military supplies were delivered punctually. It was in November 1638 with the arrival of a Scottish regiment that the pressure on him began:

> Ayant envoyé le régiment d'infanterie Escossoise de Douglas pour tenir garnison, scavoir dix campagnies à Avranches avec l'estat major, six à Granville et quatre à Ganvey, j'ay bien voulu vous en donner advis par cette lettre, et vous dire que vous ayez à pourvoir à ce que la subsistance soit ponctuellement fournie.[59]

Throughout the winter and spring of 1638 and 1639 much similar correspondence was addressed to him, for the government could not rid itself of the fear of military indiscipline. On 1 January 1639 for instance, he was commanded immediately to pay a company of light horse, 'en sorte que les compagnies ne puissent prendre aucun prétexte de vivre à discretion aux lieux où elles sont'.[60] Military officers readily exploited such fears. Douglas on one occasion refused to obey orders to move until his regiment's pay was brought up to date.[61] Another difficulty arose from deceptions practised by officers. In theory each company of horse contained eighty men, and each regiment 1,500 men (considered the equivalent of twenty companies). The rates of pay per quarter were 6,000 livres to each company of light horse, 4,000 livres to each company of mounted musketeers, and 22,000 livres to each regiment. In practice many regiments and companies were undermanned, their officers nevertheless drawing subsistence for a full complement; alternatively, officers would haul in the dregs of society to make up numbers, but themselves pocket the pay and provisions of the unfortunate *gens de néant* who were often then discarded when the regiment moved on.[62] As well as supervising

---

[59]The king to d'Aligre, [S. Germain], 18 nov. 1638 (A.G., A^{1}47, f. 376 bis).

[60]The king to d'Aligre & Croismare, [S. Germain], 1 jan 1639 (A.G., A^{1}50, 1ère. partie, f.16).

[61]The king to d'Aligre, [S. Germain], 29 mars 1639 (A.G., A^{1}51, f. 293).

[62]The same, 4 jan. 1639 (A.G., A^{1}50, 1ère. partie, fos. 30-30^v).

supplies to the troops, d'Aligre was therefore also instructed to expose chicanery and verify that the companies were up to strength, an exercise requiring miracles of detective work.[63] Then there were numerous individual snags to be overcome, such as settling quarrels between military and civil leaders,[64] or resolving disputes over billets.[65] Such laborious toil supplemented his other duties considerably, and the modern observer can only wonder at the array of responsibilities facing an *intendant,* who required remarkable powers of omnicompetence if he were to function efficiently. D'Aligre was called on to execute several programmes of great complexity and much controversy in an environment that was anything but agreeable. Even his extensive gifts at times must have been extended to the limits. There can only be sympathy at any exasperation he felt when, in February 1639, at a time when he was beleagured by problems which were arising on every side, he received a letter from Paris reprimanding him for delegating responsibilities![66]

In her study of the revolt of the *nu-pieds* Mlle. Foisil has demonstrated convincingly that by early summer 1639 the cumulative effects of *misère,* economic depression, and fiscal exploitation by the government, had made insurrection in the province a probability. The fragility of the social order by that date is indicated by the fact that it was a rumour, not concrete action by the government, that initiated the rising of 16 July. The Cotentin was a major centre for the production of sea salt. Thousands of peasants found employment in the industry, while others were involved in associated enterprises, especially the production of timber which was the main fuel used in the salt industry.[67] The region enjoyed the privilege of paying no *gabelle;* instead it was a *pays de quart bouillon* which meant that the producers delivered one quarter of their yield to the king and were free to sell the rest at profit. In July the rumour spread that the privilege was to be abrogated and the hated *gabelle* introduced. It provoked anger throughout the Cotentin, for if it were true then it meant widespread ruin.[68] In fact, although the government was contemplating such a move it wisely held its hand; but it was too late to forestall rebellion. On 16 July a *lieutenant particulier* from the *présidial* in Coutances arrived in Avranches. The local grapevine immediately

[63] The same, 16 jan. 1639 (*Ibid.,* f. 140).
[64] The same, 12 avril 1639 (A.G., A^{1}51, f. 434).
[65] The same, 28 mars 1639 (*Ibid.,* f. 263).
[66] The same, 24 fév. 1639 (A.G., A^{1}50, 2e. partie, f. 267).
[67] Foisil, *La Révolte des Nu-pieds,* 152-6.
[68] *Ibid.,* 156-60.

transmitted the news that he had come bearing the anticipated edict proclaiming the *gabelle*. Within a matter of hours a crowd had gathered; an ugly mood developed; violence broke out, and the wretched *lieutenant,* whose business had nothing to do with the salt tax, was beaten to death. From this incident sprang the revolt.[69]

D'Aligre's movements during these and subsequent weeks are something of a mystery, for clear evidence all but disappears.[70] Certain clues are to be found among the records of the Minutier Central in Paris where, by tracing notarial contracts bearing his signature, it is at least possible to establish roughly when he was in the capital rather than in the Cotentin. He was in Paris, for instance, during January, February, and part of March 1638 in connection with the disposal of the family estate after his mother's death. He next reappears in Paris on the significant date of 19 July 1639;[71] in other words he had left the Cotentin just as rebellion was about to erupt. The next contract to carry his signature is dated 4 August 1639.[72] Fortunately for his personal safety he was therefore absent from the *généralité* during the opening weeks of the rebellion, for as *intendant* he would have been a target for popular loathing. Beyond early August his whereabouts are again difficult to trace. No official correspondence refers to him later that month or in September; the next notarial contract in Paris in which he was involved does not emerge until 12 June 1640.[73] On the other hand, in October 1639 there was appointed a new *intendant* to the *généralité* of Caen: Charles le Roy de la Potherie.[74] If d'Aligre did return to the Cotentin in mid-August 1639 it was only for the remaining weeks of his mission.

Back in Paris, 1639-43

At the end of 1639 he resumed his functions as *conseiller d'état*. After his hectic exploits in Caen even a raucous city like Paris must have appeared tranquil as he pursued the routine of his office undisturbed.

---

[69]Mousnier, *Peasant Uprisings,* 87-113, 305-48 sets the revolt in its national and international contexts.

[70]'Nous n'avons pas trace de sa présence dans la généralité de Caen au moment de la révolte et d'une action quelconque de sa part' (Foisil, *La Révolte des Nu-pieds,* 58).

[71]A.N., M.C., LXXXVI-262. Quittance, 19 juillet 1639.

[72]A.N., M.C., LXXXVI-262: Constitution, 4 août 1639.

[73]A.N., M.C., XXIV-416: Vente, 12 juin 1640.

[74]Foisil, *La Révolte des Nu-pieds,* 287.

Ruptures occurred in his personal and family life. Between 1637 and 1643 there occurred the deaths of his mother and two brothers. But the heaviest blow came in October 1641 when his wife Jeanne also died; she was in her thirty-eighth year and had just given birth to their fifteenth child, Marguerite. At the age of forty-nine Etienne III was left a widower with a large family, some of the children being in their teens and requiring close guidance. It was imperative that he marry again if the household and many children were to be managed competently, and aid given in supervising the estates in the provinces. Expressed in the most businesslike terms, what Etienne III needed was a wife of maturity who could bring an experienced hand to the running of a large and wealthy family unit.

In government change was in the air. Richelieu and Louis XIII died within a few months of each other, leaving the highly undesirable situation of a minority regime. The history of minorities in France was far from reassuring, for traditionally they had afforded opportunities for aggrieved and aggressive factions to revive their ambitions. If they ran true to form the first few years of Louis XIV's reign would in all likelihood be troubled; the more so since the war against Spain laboured on indecisively, but continued to exacerbate tensions within the country. D'Aligre played a minor role in terminating the affairs of the old regime. He and Bignon, another *conseiller d'état*, were commissioned to verify all the claims made on Richelieu's estate in order to protect it from wasting away through long disputes and litigation.[75] As he reflected on the achievements of the cardinal and contemplated the immediate future, he may well have sensed that nevertheless great trials lay ahead not dissimilar to those of the minority of Louis XIII. The new regime which he hoped to serve as he had its predecessor, would have to fight hard to prevent the reversal of the programme of that highly effective team of Louis XIII and Richelieu.

The Mission to Languedoc, 1645-6

It was not long before he was called on to perform a mission for Louis XIV. At the end of 1645 he was sent by Mazarin to Languedoc. By 1640 the French had found themselves fighting on three fronts: Flanders, the Moselle and Rhine, and Roussillon. The last of these was a dependancy of Catalonia and so in Spanish hands. The French

---

[75]*Lettres de commission aux sieurs d'Aligre et Bignon, pour procéder à la vérification et liquidation des dettes, dont est chargée la succession du cardinal de Richielieu* (s.l.n.d.) [B.N., Imprimés, F 5001 (113)].

cause in Roussillon was aided by the revolts in Portugal and Catalonia at the end of 1640, that distracted the Spanish government. In 1641 the Catalans 'deposed' Philip IV and elected Louis XIII 'count of Barcelona'. French forces exploited the situation and conquered Roussillon in 1642, while much of Catalonia was then occupied by 1646.

Military progress was made at heavy social and financial cost. The government sank ever more deeply into debt. In many parts of the country there was an upsurge of popular revolts, as in Normandie and Provence.[76] Languedoc too experienced rebellion. Social tensions there had been exacerbated both by the fiscal impositions of the government, and by the passage and presence of large numbers of troops involved in the campaigns in Catalonia and Roussillon. Underpaid, mutinous, they were a source of violence and hatred in the community. Peasant uprisings occurred in the early 1640s, but there were urban disturbances too, notably at Montpellier in July 1645.[77] The *parlement* in Toulouse and estates of Languedoc, which in the spring and early summer of 1645 met in Narbonne, protested to the king at the atrocities committed by soldiers and refused to vote the extraordinary loans which he had requested. After the governor of the province, Schomberg, had suppressed the risings the estates were ordered to reassemble. They were to meet in November 1645, only this time at Pézenas where there was a royal fortress and the king's authority was paramount. Etienne III was sent as royal commissioner with the specific task of persuading the estates to raise an extraordinary loan; but also with the more general purpose of restoring royal prestige in this important frontier province. This particular session of the estates lasted until March 1646, when d'Aligre returned to Paris. Throughout the winter he and Schomberg worked hard to win over the assembly, but with only moderate success.

The debates in which they participated bear eloquent testimony to the difficulties surrounding their charge.[78] They also illustrate time and again that ambivalent relationship between the crown and provincial assemblies whereby loyalty and resistance, threats and appeals, coexisted. In the debates Schomberg generally adopted a blunt, almost peremptory tone; d'Aligre appeared as the prudent mollifier of touchy provincial sensibilities. Proceedings opened with a speech by

[76]Pillorget, *Les Mouvements Insurrectionnels*, 471-564, deals with Provence.

[77]B. Porchnev, *Les Soulèvements Populaires en France au XVIIe Siècle* (Paris, 1972), 123-7, 245-67.

[78]They are printed in C. Devic et J. Vaissète, *Histoire Générale de Languedoc* xiv (Toulouse, 1872-92) 97-130.

Schomberg on 28 November. His message was clear from the start: 'il faut que je vous représente combien vous avez travaillé à votre ruine et ce que j'ay essayé de faire pour vous en garantir, je suis forcé de mêler les reproches et les plaintes avec les preuves que je vous donne de ma sincère affection.'[79] Recalling the revolts and *émotions populaires* of the preceding summer he placed much of the blame on the estates, and especially on the 'faux zèle pour la patrie' (i.e. Languedoc) which the third estate adopted by denying 'les sommes extraordinaires' to the king. Almost the entire assembly was infected by this mentality, and even preferred to see the province plunged into the horrors of rebellion and its suppression than to accede to the king's demand. The result was to 'faire de votre patrie un spectacle de misère, de confusion et d'horreur'.[80] Now, however, France was enjoying a favourable military balance. How tragic if a dissident mentality were to persist forcing Schomberg again to 'punir un peuple repentant et humilié'. Let the estates instead acquiesce in the royal request for money. That the king and queen mother held the estates of Languedoc in high esteem,

> vous en jugerez assez par le choix que la Reyne a fait de Monsieur d'Aligre, l'un des principaux du Conseil, qui n'est pas moins considérable par son extraction, étant fils d'un chancelier de France, que par sa vertu et par les eminentes qualités si généralement reconnues et estimées en sa personne.[81]

D'Aligre rose to address the assembly. After expressing his sense of honour to be in their presence, he reminded the estates that of all the forms of government, 'le monarchique est le plus naturel, et conforme à l'ordre du monde et à celui de la première puissance du Ciel'. Furthermore it is a hierarchical system which leads to a single head. This is why the Romans were wise to compare their state to the human body whose members obey and are controlled by the head. If the human body suffers convulsions it is because of sickness; so it is with states when subjects do not obey those who govern. Turning to Languedoc in particular d'Aligre assured the estates that the province was regarded with special affection by the crown, for it had long served as an ally against internal and external enemies of the kings of France. In recent years great efforts have been made to protect the security of Languedoc against Spanish aggression; thus he confessed he was astonished that, 'après tant de grâces de nos Roys... vous avez non seulement pensé, mais résolu de dénier au Roy les secours nécessaires au bien de son Etat'.[82] He appealed:

[79]*Ibid.*, 99.
[80]*Ibid.*, 99-100.
[81]*Ibid.*, 105.
[82]*Ibid.*, 107-8.

> Considérez Messieurs, que, sans efforts extraordinaires de Sa Majesté, l'armée espagnole ne seroit point à Leucate ni à Narbonne, mais au milieu de votre Province, contre laquelle le Roy d'Espagne destinoit ses forces et projetoit par la conquête du Languedoc et de la Provence, l'union des Espagnes avec ses Etats d'Italie; et vous gémiriez peut-être à present sous le rude joug de cette nation étrangere.

God has confounded Spanish ambition and given many signs of favour to France. He has raised up a queen mother who, 'par un esprit et courage tout françois, perdant le mémoire de sa nation, élève la grandeur de son fils au-dessus des autres souverains de l'Europe';[83] He has raised up military leaders whose armies take fury and fire into enemy provinces: he has infused the French nation with a Roman genius for government and administration.[84] Should such blessings be thoughtlessly cast aside? 'Non, non! Il faut ensemble contribuer à la conservation de notre bonne fortune par les moyens qui dépendent de nous'. The king intends to follow the example of the Romans by wintering his troops on the frontier or even in enemy territory; but they will have to be paid and supplied. Other provinces have voted ordinary and extraordinary funds to the king. Being so close to the frontier Languedoc surely has a special interest in seeing the armies well maintained. Can it be that Languedoc wishes other provinces to pay for its defence? The earlier refusal of the estates to respond to the king's appeal must have resulted from the influence of some malign planet; come, aid the king and erase the unhappy memory of recent events.

The response to Schomberg and d'Aligre was given by Rebé, archbishop of Narbonne. 'Messieurs, il ne sera jamais nécessaire d'employer les forces de l'éloquence ni du raisonnement pour persuader l'obéissance à cette Province.'[85] In these hard times it has been Languedoc which has driven back the enemy and joined Schomberg in the attacks on Roussillon and Catalonia. As scripture instructs, we are faithful subjects of the king. But we also know that scripture places obligations on the monarch: they are justice and the protection which sovereigns owe to their subjects. As regards protection, there are two forms: firstly against internal oppression and wrongdoing, for which the remedy is royal justice; secondly against foreign invaders by the appropriate deployment of the king's armies. In recent years the king has concentrated on the second, but war has

---

[83] The point was, of course, that Anne the queen mother was Spanish by birth.
[84] Devic, *Histoire Générale de Languedoc,* xiv, 108.
[85] *Ibid.,* 112.

prevented him from guaranteeing justice to his people. Therefore certain elements, 's'avantagent au préjudice de leurs concitoyens; ... par une voye téméraire et scandaleuse, les veulent opprimer sous prétexte du service du prince'.[86] These elements are tax farmers and their agents who persecute the province and resort to unscrupulous and ruthless methods of seizing money and property.

> Après avoir humilié les plus florissantes familles, après avoir mis la plus belle et plus opulente province dans la nécessité, après avoir rendu incultes nos champs et nos vignes, apres avoir enlevé le meilleur et le plus liquide de nos héritages. . . . ils ont levé les armes, attaqué le veuve, le pupil et l'orphelin, et en un mot, ennemis du genre humain et désolateurs des provinces, deviennent les parricides de leur patrie. . . [87]

The estates implore Schomberg and d'Aligre to procure justice for a province which once flourished but is now 'dans une désolation extrême'. They deeply regret having to refuse aid to the king, but have no alternative. If justice is forthcoming then Languedoc will be restored and be able to provide subventions.

This first set of speeches introduced all the ingredients of a classic deadlock. The crown appealed to honour, loyalty, duty, divine purpose, and even excused rebellion on the grounds of astrological phenomena. The estates protested their loyalty, but blamed inability to obey the king on the transgressions of his fiscal agents. The language of the debate with its appeals to history, to ancient Rome, to the scriptures, was again of the age, as was the imagery of the state as a human body, and rebellion as a form of sickness. Using such traditional language and modes of argument, which eschewed any possibility of revolution, provincial assemblies drove hard bargains with royal commissioners. Language indeed played a crucial role in such debates, for it permitted assemblies to defy royal appeals without raising dangerous constitutional issues; equally it saved the crown from the humiliation of being bettered by its subjects, who could claim that circumstances, not disobedience, explained their behaviour. On this particular occasion d'Aligre was operating from an exceedingly weak base. Louis XIV was still only seven years old; the authority of the queen mother, as was usual under a regency, was but spasmodically effective; more notably, in this part of France d'Aligre had to stress that her Spanish birth did not interfere with her conduct as a French queen; Mazarin's prestige and power were as yet a pale shadow of

---
[86]*Ibid.*, 117.
[87]*Ibid.*, 118.

those of Richelieu. A more unfavourable set of circumstances in which to extract funds from the estates would be hard to imagine.

Thoughout the winter d'Aligre stuck assiduously to his brief. He addressed the full assembly on two more occasions. In December, in a speech blending threats with appeals, he called for an extraordinary sum of 1,500,000 livres to be paid in 1646.[88] The estates offered only 600,000. In March he transmitted concessions by the crown whereby over 3,000,000 livres would be removed from the taxes to be imposed on the provinces, provided an extraordinary sum of 1,500,000 livres were voted immediately.[89] Even payment over two years would be acceptable. But d'Aligre got nowhere. When the estates disbanded in March 1646 he returned to Paris with the issue unresolved.

A Comment

For several years after his return from Venice Etienne III had been kept in the background by Richelieu. From 1634 onwards d'Aligre was thrust into the front line of the government's financial assault on the provinces. It was the war against Spain more than anything which produced this transformation. From about 1630 the government had been stationing *intendants* and other agents in the provinces in increasing numbers,[90] and the outbreak of war in 1635 meant there could be no reversal of this trend. Ever more royal commissioners were required; the government's need supplied d'Aligre's chance to rehabilitate himself.

His experiences suggest certain observations on the role of royal commissioners and *intendants* in the late 1630s. Apart from his individual skills, d'Aligre's great attraction to Richelieu was his dependability. D'Aligre was anxious to restore his flagging career, but was under no illusions as to the consequences of an indifferent performance in Normandie. When he went to the Cotentin he was in a sense being put to the test: a well-conducted *recherche de la noblesse* followed by a successful period as *intendant* could lead to other appointments. He was hungry for success, and in this sense was a shrewd choice by Richelieu. Indeed, it was generally recognised that an outstanding tour of duty as *intendant* could be a prelude to great

---

[88]*Ibid.*, 122-5.
[89]*Ibid.*, 125-9.
[90]Bonney, *Political Change in France,* 30.

things;[91] hence it was in the *intendant's* self-interest to serve as conscientiously as possible. To the government, the good *intendant* was one who obeyed instructions to the letter and gave his loyalty exclusively to his political masters in Paris. Such qualities could best be encouraged by selecting people seeking further promotion, and by rewarding them with higher appointments if they performed their duties satisfactorily.

Once in the field the *intendant* faced an immensity of problems and pressures. D'Aligre's years in Normandie show that the charge of *intendant* could be the toughest of assignments. He needed to be robust physically to stand up to the travelling that was involved (in d'Aligre's case, through some extremely rugged country). The *intendant* was under constant double pressure, from the government on one side, and on the other from regional institutions and pressure groups which could go behind his back and appeal directly to the king. Wherever he went in the 1630s the *intendant* was associated with bad financial news and accordingly was the object of popular hostility. He personified 'Paris', the power of a distant government which heaped one imposition on another. This particular characteristic happily was to change. During the personal reign of Louis XIV the *intendant* came to be seen in other ways, for as often as not he was to become a source of governmental investment in, say, local communications or industry; or he might be a channel through which provincial grievances or difficulties could be transmitted to the king. Colbert was to push as hard as he could the idea that the *intendant* was a link between monarch and subjects, an agent through whom the king could *soulager le peuple.* In the 1630s, however, the *intendant's* function was far less equivocal: he was a prime instrument of royal fiscal policy, who inevitably helped to create a climate of provincial hostility to central government.

D'Aligre's experiences in Normandie and Languedoc further suggest that the *intendant* or royal commissioner was far from omnipotent. His long negotiations with pressure-groups, his frequent attempts to catch out crooked army officers who were robbing the public purse, the existence of successful appeals against his decisions by many individuals, indicate that a high level of frustration could accompany the charge of royal representative. The forces of regional resistance to royal policy were often well organised and experienced in the arts of procrastination and obfuscation. This emerged most clearly in d'Aligre's encounter with the estates of Languedoc, the most powerful of all provincial institutions. Admittedly it was a

[91]*Ibid.,* 40, 90-111.

different prospect from some small town council in the Cotentin, but both used similar tactics to deal with the royal representative. Appeals to local traditions and rights, claims of extremes poverty, accusations against tax farmers, protests at the misconduct of troops or at the king's failure to rectify grievances, formed the stock-in-trade arguments of great and small provincial assemblies alike. For every reason that the crown could advance as to why an extraordinary sum should be raised, provincial assemblies could supply a counter. The *intendant* or commissioner could not lightly brush aside provincial protest; he relied heavily on skills of debate and persuasion. Whatever meaning is attached to the 'absolutism' of Louis XIII and Richelieu, that phenomenon relied to an amazing extent upon negotiation and argumentation.

6

ETIENNE D'ALIGRE III AND THE 'FRONDES': PROBLEMS OF A ROYALIST

Given the advantage of hindsight we now know that in the 1640s France was heading for its most prodigious upheaval of the century. The difficulties that d'Aligre had encountered in the estates of Languedoc, as in Normandie, were symptomatic of the frustration which royal policies were producing throughout the country. This is not the occasion for a digression on the reasons for the Fronde rebellions, which have been analysed in detail by many scholars,[1] yet one comment is appropriate: the Frondes cannot be dismissed simply as a series of aimless outbursts by mischievous *parlementaires,* anarchic mobs, or anachronistic aristocrats. Profound issues were at stake the resolution of which was to have immense long-term political significance. Our purpose here is to assess the importance of these years in d'Aligre's life and career, but the exercise is not without implications for a more general understanding of the Frondes. One of the many lines of inquiry still to be followed in connection with the risings concerns the conduct of people like d'Aligre who maintained a royalist position even through the most turbulent periods. The Frondeurs are comparatively well known by modern scholars; the royalists less so. Of course, everybody including the Frondeurs claimed to be royalist, but in the present context the word is taken to mean those who actively supported the regent and Mazarin, and never joined a Frondeur movement.

Events in Paris

On his return from Languedoc d'Aligre resumed his duties as *conseiller d'état*. In 1647 he was one of a team negotiating a contract for a marsh-drainage scheme in Blaye.[2] In the following year he and Omer Talon[3] were arbitrators in a dispute between the duc de Savoie and the sieur de Nevestan concerning certain ecclesiastical dues.[4] In

---

[1] A full bibliography is in A.L. Moote, *The Revolt of the Judges: the Parlement of Paris and the Fronde, 1643-1652* (Princeton U.P., 1971).

[2] A.N., E 1692, fos. 421-9.

[3] Omer Talon (1595-1652), a leading magistrate and *avocat général.*

[4] A.N., E 1692, fos. 52-52^v.

April 1648 he was given the task of investigating alleged corruption by the *trésoriers de la marine de Levant*.[5] However, the critical turn of public affairs swept such immediate issues to one side. Of all the short term triggers that fired rebellion in the summer of 1648 the conduct of the *parlement* of Paris is the most notable. Already hostile to much royal policy[6] it was involved in a clash with the regime over the renewal of the *paulette,* whose most recent nine-year cycle had ended on 31 December 1647. After the usual bargaining the government sought both to fix the new rate and to save money by its edict of 30 April 1648: the *paulette* was granted, but the *officiers* of the *grand conseil,* the *cour des aides,* and the *chambre des comptes,* were to lose four years' *gages* (payments attached to an office). In a crude attempt to forestall united opposition to this provision the government exempted the *parlement.* Ignoring such a tendentious manoeuvre, the *parlement* joined the other sovereign courts in organising resistance. There followed the *arrêt d'union* of 13 May whereby the four sovereign courts elected deputies to assemble in the Chambre Saint Louis to discuss reform of the state. The deputies met, issuing in June a text of twenty-seven articles listing their demands, which included suppression of the *intendants* and all special commissioners, prohibition on the creation of new *offices*, and cessation of royal intervention in the proceedings of law courts. Further, in July the *parlement* itself issued demands relating to public finance: revocation of all contracts between the government and tax farmers, reduction of the *taille* by 25 per cent, no taxes other than those registered in the sovereign courts.

In the face of such an ambitious and resolute programme the regent made one concession after another, for Mazarin's energies were concentrated on the war against Spain and the negotiations that were to result in the peace of Westphalia. This was no time to become embroiled in internal strife. But miscalculations by the regency were to augment rather than diminish tension during the summer months. For the time being Anne and Mazarin yielded to the *chambre Saint Louis* and the *parlement.* All extraordinary commissions including those of the *intendants* were revoked (save those of *intendants* in frontier provinces); the *taille* was reduced by 12 per cent, a concession registered by the *parlement* which nevertheless continued to press for 25 per cent; the *paulette* was settled on the terms of 1604, the most advantageous ever to the *officiers;* and on 9 July the hated

---

[5] A.N., E 229ᶜ, fos. 275-6.

[6] On the growth of *parlementaire* opposition to the crown see the relevant articles in R. Mousnier, *La Plume, la Faucille et le Marteau.*

Michel Particelli d'Emery,[7] *surintendant des finances,* was dismissed. This particular decision was to have grave financial consequences. With all his faults (his financial deals were dubious even by seventeenth-century standards) d'Emery had at least been an expert who spoke the same language as the *traitants.* He kept their loans flowing into the government, albeit at exorbitant rates of interest. Sacrificed as yet another act of appeasement by the regency, he was replaced by the *maréchal* de la Meilleraye, an old soldier of little if any financial acumen, but of known honesty.[8] In fact he was a front man. Most of the work in practice was undertaken by two newly-appointed assistants with the ranks of *directeurs des finances:* d'Aligre and Antoine Barillon, sieur de Morangis, another *conseiller d'état.*[9] Etienne III found himself at the topmost level of state financial machinery, and one of a triumvirate inexperienced when it came to handling the incredibly complex difficulties of 1640. Many observers must have shared the sentiments of Madame de Motteville:

> On lui [la Meilleraye] donna Morangis et d'Aligre, qui sous lui devoient signer toutes les expéditions, gens de probité qui ne pouvoient être soupçonnés de péculat, ni même capables de le souffrir en la personne des autres, et qui apparement haisseront autant les partisans que les plus zelés du parlement, mais gens en effet qui avoient plus de vertu que de capacité: je veux dire de cette capacité qui trouve les moyens d'enrichir les rois sans appauvrir leurs sujets.[10]

The 'Fronde' to the peace of Rueil

The new financial directors could hope to do little more than stave off disaster. Even this modest aspiration proved unattainable in the short term, for d'Aligre and de Morangis were confronted by intolerable

---

[7]Michel Particelli d'Emery (c. 1596-1650); *intendant* in Languedoc 1631-2; *contrôleur général* 1643-7; *surintendant* 1647-8, 1649-50.

[8]Charles de la Porte, duc de la Meilleraye (1602-64); *maréchal de France* 1639; *surintendant des finances* 1648-9; he continued a military career to his death.

[9]B.N., MS Français 4178, fos. 51-3; MS Français 4222, fos. 177-9^v; A.G., A^1 108, fos. 3^v-4, 29^v-51.

[10]Madame de Motteville: J.F. Michaud et J-J. F. Poujoulat [eds.], *Mémoires de Madame de Motteville (*Nouvelle Collection des Mémoires Rélatifs à l'Histoire de la France, xxiv 1881), 172; Mazarin wrote to Longueville: 'La reyne ayant résolu d'ôter M. Emery des affaires. . . Sa Majesté a déclaré M. le maréchal de la Meilleraye surintendant, et lui a adjoint deux de MM. les conseillers d'Etat en qualité de directeurs, qui sont MM. d'Aligre et de Morangis, dont vous connaissez sans doute la suffisance [i.e. la capacité] et la probité' (Quoted in A. Chéruel, *Histoire de France Pendant la Minorité de Louis XIV,* iii [Paris, 1880], 13-14).

conditions. The crown's concessions to the *chambre* and *parlement* drastically diminished its income. The loss of the *intendants* deprived the *directeurs* of badly-needed agents in the country.[11] The *traitants*, reacting both to d'Emery's dismissal and to rumours that the king was about to abolish all taxes, withheld further loans. There was therefore an air of inevitability about the governmental bankruptcy that occurred in July 1648.[12] Not satisfied with its gains the *parlement* pressed more demands, including legal proceedings against some of the *traitants*. But at last the retreat of the regency ceased. On 21 August news reached Paris of the victory of the duc de Condé over the Spanish at Lens. His forces would now be at the disposal of queen Anne. Confident at last of military strength the king's council – Anne, Mazarin, Gaston d'Orléans, Séguier, la Meilleraye, Bouthillier – judged the time ripe for retribution: the arrest of leading radical *parlementaires*, of whom the most outspoken and prestigious was Broussel. The appointed time was the *Te Deum* to be sung in Notre Dame on 26 August as a thanksgiving for Lens. As they left the cathedral, selected *parlementaires* would be seized. What followed is well known. The plan was effected. Popular outcry and rioting began; barricades were erected (one line ran through the rue de l'Arbre Sec and the rue Saint Honoré, passing within a few yards of Etienne III's residence in the rue d'Avron);[13] the Parisian Fronde had begun.

The melodrama and tumult of 26 and 28 August were assuaged by the release of Broussel on the latter date, but it was only a matter of time before the regency again attempted to redress the reversals and humiliations of 1648. Throughout the autumn relations between court and *parlement* scarcely concealed the underlying acrimony. The day of 24 October was one of rejoicing and of further despondency for the regency: the treaty of Westphalia was signed (although the war against Spain continued), but the *parlement* registered a royal decree conceding and confirming the propositions of the *chambre Saint Louis*. During the remainder of the year the *parlement* sustained opposition to the regency, much of its animadversion being directed specifically at Mazarin, now being censured for having failed to protect France's best interests at Westphalia. Nevertheless, those *parlementaires* who supposed that such conduct would be tolerated

---

[11] But notice d'Aligre's revealing words to le Tellier in his letter of 22 mai 1649: *maîtres de requêtes* would be sent into the provinces, and, 'soubs le prétexte de faire leurs chevauchées reprendront l'auctorité d'intendants ainsy que par le passé' (MS Français 6881, f. 282).

[12] Bonney, *Political Change,* 55; R. Bonney, *The King's Debts: Finance and Politics in France, 1589-1661* (Oxford, 1981), ch. 5

[13] R. Mousnier, 'Quelques raisons de la Fronde', *La Plume,* 275.

much longer, or that the Parisian excesses of August 1648 would go unpunished, embraced a profound fallacy. On the night of 5-6 January 1649 Anne, Louis XIV, his brother Philippe, Mazarin, Mademoiselle (daughter of Gaston d'Orléans) and other courtiers slipped away from Paris to take up residence at Saint Germain. Attempts at reconciliation by the *parlement* failed. Paris was placed under a siege by Condé that lasted until early March.

In spite of winter weather the siege did not produce the miseries of, say, that of 1590. As shocked as the court at the news from England of the execution of Charles I on 30 January, the *parlement* carefully refrained from any action that could be interpreted as rebellion. Its members, like all property owners in the city, kept a wary eye on armed gangs roaming the streets: they needed no instruction as to the unpredictability of the Parisian masses, especially if food shortages became excessive. At the other social extreme too many of *les Grands* like Madame de Longueville, the duc de Bouillon, Turenne, not to mention Paul Gondi, archbishop-coadjutor of Paris who preached a series of inflammatory sermons in the city during the month of January, indulged in dangerous talk of spreading armed resistance to the crown and of inviting foreign armies into France. Aristocratic anarchy was as much anathema to *parlementaires* as popular. The siege hit their personal interests. Taxes had to be raised to pay for the defence of Paris. More *bourgeois* had to join the city militia to the prejudice of their professional activities. Psychologically, therefore, most *parlementaires* were agreeable to attempts by the *premier président*, Molé, to seek accommodation with the regency. On its side the regency too favoured a settlement. It feared the plotting of *les Grands*, and as spring approached so did a new season of campaigns against the Spanish who were mustering forces in the Netherlands. Neither *parlement* nor regency was prepared for a fight to the finish. It proved surprisingly easy to arrive at the terms of the peace of Rueil.[14]

The Return to 'Normality'.

The peace, registered by the *parlement* on 1 April, afforded limited respite to the government on the financial front. It provided for advances on the *taille,* albeit only up to the end of 1650; but it also prescribed that taxes should be collected only through the regular machinery of the state, not by paid officials of the *traitants* or *fermiers*.[15] During the siege d'Aligre had been trapped in the city,

[14] Moote, *Revolt of the Judges,* 212-14.
[15] *Ibid.,* 212-13.

going in fear of his life and property because of his position as *directeur des finances* and his known royalist sympathies. On more than one occasion he appealed to Michel le Tellier, secretary of state for war and his cousin by marriage, for help in leaving Paris, but he could never find an escort willing to risk accompanying him. He lay low as much as possible, rarely appearing on the streets, and able to do little as regards his direction of state finance. After the peace he and de Morangis were able to resume their duties, although as they picked their way through the financial ruins the prospects must have appeared chilling. Neither was an acknowledged financial expert, but they did endeavour to introduce a minimum degree of order. They may have originated no novel fiscal methods, but they devoted an inordinate amount of time and energy to negotiations with *receveurs généraux* and senior *parlementaires,* whose concurrence in royal fiscal policy had effectively been made necessary by the peace of Rueil. The *directeurs* had two broad aims: a clear assessment of the state's financial position after the disarray of recent years, and agreement with the *receveurs* and *parlementaires* in restoring time-honoured procedures for raising money. The peace of Rueil reinforced what was temperamentally a natural trend of d'Aligre and de Morangis towards conservative, orthodox fiscal policies.

For a time d'Aligre considered that they were making commendable progress, and was able to submit moderately encouraging reports to Mazarin.[16] But he was soon cavilling that the incessant and exhausting work in which he was involved (and which may have contributed to a serious affliction of the eyes which he suffered in May[17]) was rendered almost pointless by the widespread social disorder and troop violence which infested the country, almost ruling out the collection of taxes.[18] In the worst-afflicted areas such as Touraine, Maine and Anjou, people were simply unable to pay taxes, 'nonobstant touttes les décharges qu'on leur accorde'.[19] Risings in Bordeaux cut off the flow of taxes from the city and region.[20] Mutinous soldiers were the cause of much disorder. D'Aligre urged le Tellier to remove a particularly vicious German regiment 'resting' in the *généralité* of Soissons, because of the atrocities and depredations

---

[16] Mazarin to d'Aligre, [S. Germain], 16 mai 1649 (A.A.E., M.D.: France 264, f. 322); Mazarin expressed his pleasure that, 'vous ayez réglé les fonds de diverses dépenses importantes'.

[17] He was half-blind and had to dictate his correspondence: d'Aligre to le Tellier, Paris, 4 mai 1649 (B.N., MS Français 4231, fos. 166^v-7).

[18] Mousnier, *Lettres... au Chancelier Séguier,* ii, 912-13.

[19] D'Aligre to le Tellier, Paris, 9 mai 1649 (B.N., MS Français 6881, f. 244^v).

[20] The same, 27 mai, 3 juin 1649 (*Ibid.,* fos. 290, 302-3).

for which it was responsible.[21] He tried to ease the general problem of French troops stationed in the country by paying a portion of their arrears at the rate of 2 sous 6 deniers in the *livre*,[22] but he and de Morangis were so perturbed at the unrest stemming from military indiscipline that they put a joint warning to le Tellier, 'pour vous dire que je veoy toutes nos provinces en désordre et que vous debvez instamment retirer les trouppes, aultrement on ne payera rien et serons plus mal que jamais'.[23] So long as much of the country verged on anarchy there was no prospect of the government's financial exigencies being met. There was a twist to the problem. Even in provinces escaping the worst *désordres, receveurs* were collecting fewer taxes than they ought, excusing the deficits by inventing local unrest.[24] When they did collect revenue they frequently first repaid loans to their friends who, afraid that in the uncertain climate of 1649 taxes would not be collected, called in their debts; *receveurs* then delivered to the government only what remained.[25] One of the messages that d'Aligre tried to drive home to his masters was that the future financial condition of the government was closely related to social stability. The days were gone when the government could decide upon its fiscal requirements and then meet them at no matter what social cost.[26]

An obstacle to progress was the readiness with which *traitants* and *fermiers,* like the *receveurs généraux*, capitalised on the regime's predicament. Those in frontier provinces, pleading both *désordre* and vulnerability to invasion, would sign contracts only at excess profit to themselves.[27] In the case of *fermiers des aides* from Tours, Poitiers and Alençon, agreement was reached only on terms highly advantageous to them.[28] A *traitant* from Poitiers demanded a *lettre de cachet* before he would agree to a contract, 'affin de contenir les peuples dans l'obéissance et ayder à payer les droits du Roy'.[29] The *traitant* from Dauphiné insisted on a revision of his existing contract, otherwise he would simply renege upon his commitments.

---

[21] The same, 23 juin 1649 (*Ibid.,* f. 347).

[22] The same, 9 mai 1649 (*Ibid.,* f. 244^v).

[23] The same, 23 juin 1649 (*Ibid.,* f. 350).

[24] The same, 9 mai 1649 (*Ibid.,* f. 244).

[25] The same, 22 mai 1649 (*Ibid.,* f. 282).

[26] See the points made by Guéry, 'Les finances de la monarchie française'.

[27] D'Aligre to le Tellier, Paris, – juin 1649 (B.N., MS Français 6881, f. 383).

[28] The same, 3 juin 1649 (*Ibid.,* fos. 302-2^v).

[29] The same, 27 mai 1649 (*Ibid.,* f. 290).

127

As for the province of Languedoc, the *receveurs* and *traitants* were so obstructive that, 'si son Altesse Royale n'y employe son authorité je tiens cette province demy perdue et ne recevrons rien des deniers ordinaires des tailles'.[30] The *directeurs* met such obstacles on every side, but the difficulties were, 'un mal sans remède et vault mieux souffrir ces dûretés pour un temps que de veoir périr l'estat devant nos yeux'.[31]

Relations with the *parlement* were still delicate. D'Aligre recognised that its cooperation was fundamental to any significant amelioration of the crown's financial condition. He was fortunate in that Molé, the *premier président*, was a personal friend and a sympathiser with the cause of 'legitimate' royal authority.[32] On more than one occasion d'Aligre paid tribute to Molé's sagacious handling of debates in the *parlement* concerning *aides, gabelles, gages* amd *rentes*.[33] Again, there was a group of *parlementaires* whose views were close to those of Molé.[34] But royal fortunes required more systematic representation if they were to undergo transformation. D'Aligre and de Morangis urged that they be appointed by the crown as *conseillers honéraires* in the *parlement*; they would have right of entry and be able to defend royal interests in a regular and coordinated manner.[35] For all the weight of the argument and the evident advantages that such a manoeuvre would produce, the crown procrastinated. It was not until February 1652 that the charges were forthcoming.[36]

Meanwhile the relentless pressure of expenditure continued. The armies in Germany, Piedmont and Catalonia had to be supplied.[37] D'Aligre was told to pay the Swiss Guards. Willing as he was in principle there were chronic problems:

> Je ne vous puis exprimer la difficulté que nous avons de trouver de l'argent. La dûreté de tous nos fermiers et les traverses continuelles que nous donne la Cour des Aides tant par les Arrests que par la longueur qu'elle apporte à l'expédition des affaires du Roy, nous remettant de jour à aultre, en sorte que de

[30] The same, 6 juin 1649 (*Ibid.*, f. 306).

[31] The same, 27 mai 1649 (*Ibid.*, f. 290).

[32] Moote, *Revolt of the Judges*, 109-110.

[33] E.g. d'Aligre's letters to le Tellier of 5 & 9 mai 1649 (MS Français 6881, fos. 238-9, 244-6).

[34] The same, 9 mai 1649 (*Ibid.*, f. 245).

[35] The same, 9 mai 1649 (*Ibid.*, fos. 250-50^v).

[36] *Gazette de France*, 24 fév. 1652 (the appointment was made on 20 fev.).

[37] D'Aligre to le Tellier, Paris, 5 mai 1649 (B.N., MS Français 6881, fos. 238-9).

lundy dernier qu'ils nous donnoient espérance de finir ils nous renvoyentà l'aultre lundy, et jusques à ce que cette affaire soit terminée je ne veoy pas que nous puissions rien espérer des fermiers des Aides, sans des violentes exécutions soit contre eux, soit contre leurs sous-fermiers, et fault chercher quelque aultre moien de satisfaire vos Suisses...[38]

It was not until June that he managed to scrape together some 300,000 livres for the Guards;[39] payment of their full arrears would have meant withholding pay from French troops, and perhaps even from the royal household itself.[40] Crises sometimes reached the ludicrous: on one occasion there was not even enough cash available to take d'Aligre and an assistant from Paris to the suburb of Villejuif![41] On occasion he tried to borrow money in his own name, but potential lenders demanded the impossible condition of receiving detailed accounts as to how their money would be employed by the government.[42] Then there were items of expenditure which, usually for reasons of national prestige, simply had to be met and which taxed d'Aligre's ingenuity to the limits. The ambassador to Piedmont had not been paid for over a year; so desperate was his plight that he was requesting recall.[43] Mazarin issued an injunction that no matter what the cost, something at least must be sent to preserve French honour.[44] De Brégy, the ambassador to Poland, was about to go to Constantinople but could not move because of a chronic lack of funds. This was 'au grand préjudice, et de la dignité, et des affaires du Roy'.[45] Once again Mazarin insisted that money somehow be found and sent.[46] There were foreign subsidies to be paid. The cardinal was insistent that the Assembly of the Swiss Cantons be advanced 200,000 livres to prevent it taking decisions inimical to French interests. He gave d'Aligre only three days in which to raise the money, a condition which provoked indignant protest from the *directeur*.[47] Henriette, ex-

---

[38] The same, 15 mai 1649 (*Ibid.*, f. 269).

[39] The same, 4 juin 1649 (*Ibid.*, f. 304).

[40] The same, 3 août 1649 (*Ibid.*, f. 413).

[41] The same, 4 mai 1649 (*Ibid.*, f. 168).

[42] The same, 6 juin 1649 (*Ibid.*, f. 306^v).

[43] Mazarin to d'Aligre, Saint Germain, 13 juillet 1649 (A.A.E., M.D.: France 264, fos. 385-5).

[44] The same, 18 juillet 1649 (*Ibid.*, fos. 394-4^v).

[45] The same, 6 juillet 1649 (*Ibid.*, fos. 373-3^v).

[46] The same, 15 juillet 1649 (*Ibid.*, f. 390).

[47] D'Aligre to le Tellier, Paris, 10 juin 1649 (B.N., MS Français 6881, f. 320).

queen of England had to be provided with a suitable residence, an entourage, and appropriate funds.[48] Again, Mazarin demanded payments to various individuals who had exhibited loyalty to his or the royal cause. During the siege of Paris a Monsieur de la Valette, who had remained faithful to the king, had his residence pillaged by a mob; he was to be rewarded with a payment of 12,000 livres and a promise of more to come.[49] D'Argenson, who had served the king conspicuously in Guienne, was to be paid all his dues immediately.[50] A royalist sea-captain had brought two prizes into Toulon; d'Aligre was to ensure that he received the most generous prize money possible.[51]

Such were some of the pressures upon the *directeurs des finances* at a time when financially as well as in other respects the French crown reached the nadir of its fortunes. More than once Mazarin expressed his gratitude at the diligence and tenacity with which d'Aligre and de Morangis struggled with one wretched task after another.[52] They received a vote of his confidence in them at the end of 1649 when there was a change of personnel at the head of the administration of state finance. D'Emery was reintroduced as *surintendant des finances* along with d'Avaux;[53] d'Aligre and de Morangis were retained as *directeurs* and were confirmed in their posts on 17 March 1650.[54]

The General Assembly of the Clergy

While the attention of the crown was occupied in domestic affairs, chiefly in the problems posed by the Frondes, the time came round for the Assembly of the Clergy which met in Paris from 25 May 1650 until 13 April 1651. By custom the crown nominated a royal representative whose principal function was to persuade the Assembly to vote a sum of money, a *don gratuit*, to the king; he then had to negotiate the size of the gift. In 1650 it was Etienne III who was appointed by Mazarin. d'Aligre's role in state finance and his

---

[48] Mazarin to d'Aligre, Saint Germain, 20 mai 1649 (A.A.E., M.D.: France 264, f. 322^v).

[49] The same, 24 mai 1649 (*Ibid.*, fos. 323-3v).

[50] The same, 15 juillet 1649 (*Ibid.*, f. 389^v).

[51] The same, 14 juillet 1649 (*Ibid.*, fos. 386^v-7).

[52] E.g. The same, 16 mai, 23 juillet 1649 (*Ibid.*, fos. 322, 403^v-4).

[53] Bonney, *Political Change*, 61-2.

[54] A.G., A^{1}120, fos. 166-6; B.N. MS Français 4181, fos. 165-6.

experience of dealing with a large assembly in Languedoc doubtless counted in his favour. But his selection equally was a mark of the trust that Mazarin placed in him; it showed to the world that he was the cardinal's man. The appointment was to be significant in other ways too. D'Aligre was reselected for the assemblies of 1655-7, 1660-1 and 1665-6. For fifteen years he was the main royal representative to the clergy, and it was largely through his endeavours and skill that a change in the nature of the *don gratuit* occurred: when he first met the Assembly in 1650 the *don* was extraordinary, but by the end of his last session in 1666 it had become a custom.[55] In 1650, however, the task was to cajole the clergy into making a gift to the crown. The task proved far from easy.

Although the Assembly opened in April 1650 it was not until August that d'Aligre was admitted to present the royal proposal for a *don gratuit*. He met a mood of deep opposition. The king was requesting funds to help, 'dissiper les troubles de mon Royaume, et y rétablir la paix et la tranquillité',[56] a general purpose for which the clergy showed little sympathy. The president of the Assembly, the archbishop of Rouen, outlined the objections: church property was being violated by French troops and the immunity of the church to billeting was being flouted; clerical exemption from *taille* and *gabelle* was being over-ruled; *parlements* encroached on the rights of the church and had not yet registered the statement of grievances that the Assembly of 1635 had drawn up; the government approached the church for aid yet readily entered into associations and alliances with protestant powers, meanwhile tolerating heresy within the kingdom. Between 1636 and 1641 the church had given some sixteen million livres to the crown, an outflow that left the church exhausted and unable to respond affirmatively on this occasion.[57] Such assertions by the archbishop might have contained nothing new but they did range ominously wide, their censure of foreign policy recalling the objurgation directed at Richelieu in earlier decades. It was this independent frame of mind that prevailed in the debate on the *don gratuit* that was held in September. By a majority the Assembly voted to make no gift. When d'Aligre met a deputation at his residence he protested that the clergy traditionally made a gift to the king. The bishop of Agen stressed that here was one reason for the refusal: the *don* must not become a tradition but remain an extraordinary sum granted according to the

---

[55] Blet, *Le Clergé de France*, ii, 287.

[56] *Collection des Procès-Verbaux des Assemblées-Générales du Clergé de France* (Paris, 1769), iii, 525.

[57] *Ibid.*, 527-9.

merits of the case presented by the king.⁵⁸ Further efforts by d'Aligre failed to budge the Assembly. On 29 November he again addressed the clergy, this time bearing a specific command from the king that they must debate the *don*. He also brought concessions: *lettres de cachet* instructing the *parlement* of Paris to register the clerical statement of grievances of 1635, and *arrêts* dealing with other aspects of church grievances. A debate was fixed for 3 December. Delays occurred. It was put off until 7 December. On that day the Assembly confirmed the decision to make no gift.⁵⁹ In the following weeks d'Aligre held numerous meetings and discussions with members of the Assembly, as did others from the king's council. The queen personally appealed for a third debate. At last a way through the deadlock was devised. The crown changed the purpose for which it sought a gift. The general aim of internal order was replaced by a request for financial help with a particular item of expenditure: the coronation of Louis XIV. The Assembly thus adhered to its original decision not to grant funds for the first request of the crown. This was a new topic for negotiation, and on 25 Janary 1651 the Assembly agreed to a contribution of 600,000 livres. The court accepted the figure within a few days.⁶⁰

D'Aligre had driven himself hard to reach this sum, unspectacular as it was (in 1657 the *don* was to be 2,700,000 livres, in 1661 two million, and in 1666 2,400,000). Even so the crown had come close to defeat. The Assembly had defended its contention that the gift was extraordinary, not traditional, for everybody acknowledged that a coronation was an exceptional event. The coronation in fact did not occur until June 1654, by which time the 600,000 livres had filtered through into other branches of expenditure. But on paper and in theory the Assembly had successfully asserted its view of the *don gratuit*; the hard-pressed crown was in no position to prolong the dispute and took what it could.

The Resurgence of Violence

D'Aligre's negotiations with the Assembly, a time-consuming adjunct to his regular financial duties, were conducted against a background of accelerating violence as the *Fronde des princes* of 1650 formed an alliance with the *Fronde parlementaire* in 1651. The arrest of Condé,

⁵⁸*Ibid.*, 531.
⁵⁹*Ibid.*, 537.
⁶⁰*Ibid.*, 538.

Longueville and Gondi in 1650 had provoked rebellion in provinces where they were governors: Bourgogne for Condé and Normandie for Longueville. Violence erupted elsewhere, as in Provence.[61] Condé's wife had fled to Bordeaux where she received strong support from the *parlement* and the populace. A royal army, accompanied by Anne and Mazarin, besieged Bordeaux which held out from August until October. The archduke Leopold, governor of the Spanish Netherlands, exploited the opportunity to invade northern France with the help of Turenne. The fortunes of the regency revived. Bordeaux surrendered, Normandie, Bourgogne and Provence were pacified, while on 15 December 1650 Mazarin commanded the royal army that defeated Turenne at Rethel. At the beginning of 1651 the government looked to have the advantage. Within a few weeks, however, Mazarin was forced out of the country. Since November 1650 Gondi had been organising an alliance with Gaston d'Orléans, his daughter Mademoiselle, Madame de Chevreuse, Broussel and a large portion of the *parlement* of Paris. The *parlement* resumed its agitation, concentrating its attacks on the cardinal. On 2 February Orléans broke with Mazarin, whose exile was demanded by the *parlement*. The union between hostile princes and *parlementaires* was too dangerous for Mazarin who fled from Paris on the night of 6-7 February. This was no master-stroke designed to split his enemies. It was the retreat of one who recognised when he was beaten.

With Mazarin in exile fissiparous tendencies soon reasserted themselves among the Frondeurs. Gaston's plans for an estates general (a date was fixed, some provinces even drawing up *cahiers de doléances*) were offensive to the *parlement* of Paris which could envisage such a gathering superseding itself as the chief spokesman of the 'rights' of the nation. Condé and Gondi fell out. Then a coalition of Gondi, Beaufort, Mademoiselle de Chevreuse and others formed against Condé, who in September 1651 took up arms in defence of his interests. Civil war began again. The context was changed on 7 September when Louis XIV declared his majority: the former pretence that resistance to the regent did not imply disloyalty to the king was no longer credible. Anarchy afflicted the region around Paris as the Frondes entered their most destructive period. Royal and aristocratic forces fought each other indecisively, but the divided Frondeurs were driven together again by the return of Mazarin to France with a small force in January 1652. The *parlement* put a price on his head, while Gaston and Condé suspended their differences, allied, and swore to fight on until Mazarin was again driven from France.

[61] Pillorget, *Mouvements Insurrectionnels,* 641-56.

Etienne d'Aligre in 1652

Once again trapped in Paris when mass violence became endemic in the city, d'Aligre was to find this the hardest year of all during the Frondes. His fidelity to the crown was to be questioned, his health was to decline, family problems arose, while unrest within the city, which magnified as refugees poured in from the countryside, placed him and his family in danger. Yet he not only survived; he was to end the year honourably by performing more exemplary service to the king.

For a time his chief predicament was his relations with the new *surintendant des finances*, la Vieuville, who had been appointed on 8 September 1651. Now in his seventieth year la Vieuville briefly had been *surintendant* from 1623-4; Anne hoped that he would be able to convince the *parlement* and the *chambre des comptes* of the regime's ability to handle its finances competently.[62] But la Vieuville shared the widespread aversion towards Mazarin;[63] moreover, he and le Tellier were rivals in the king's council.[64] D'Aligre, on the other hand, was known to be a sympathiser with the cardinal[65] and was, of course, a kinsman of le Tellier. La Vieuville and d'Aligre inevitably found themselves at odds. Soon d'Aligre was expressing fears to le Tellier that the *surintendant* was moving to have him, d'Aligre, disgraced by spreading rumours that politically he was unsound. At the end of 1651 la Vieuville took the staff of the finance ministry to join the court at Poitiers; only the two *directeurs* remained in Paris.[66] Etienne III felt ominously isolated, calling upon his cousin to defend him at court. He protested that la Vieuville was deliberately holding up the king's instructions so as to make it appear that he, d'Aligre, was tardy in obeying.[67] Confessing that; 'Je ne scaurois pénétrer les intentions de M. de la Vieuville... je puis dire qu'il souffle le chaud et le froid d'une mesme bouche',[68] he appealed to le Tellier to protect him against the *surintendant*.

La Vieuville's central allegation was that even after the court returned to Saint Germain, as it had by April 1652, d'Aligre failed to

---

[62]Moote, *Revolt of the Judges*, 318-19.

[63]Comte de Cosnac, *Mazarin et Colbert* (Paris, 1892), i, 210.

[64]I. Murat, *Colbert* (Paris, 1980), 26-32.

[65]'[D'Aligre] est une personne dont j'estime infiniment le mérite et que je tiens tout-à-fait de mes amis' (Mazarin to l'Abbé Fouquet, Saumur, 15 fév. 1652 [A. Chéruel (éd.), *Lettres du Cardinal Mazarin Pendant son Ministè*re (Paris, 1889), v, 49]).

[66]Moote, *Revolt of the Judges*, 27.

[67]D'Aligre to le Tellier, Paris, 4 jan., 3 mars, 30 avril, 1 mai 1652 (B.N., MS Français 6889, fos. 13, 108, 151-2).

[68]The same, 21 jan. 1652 (*Ibid.*, f. 69^v).

escape from Paris so as to join the king. The imputation was clear: like his father, Etienne III was unreliable in a crisis; he preferred to stay in Paris flirting with Frondeur elements. D'Aligre defended himself. He earnestly wished to leave the city, but on at least one occasion la Vieuville did not inform him of an escort to take royalists out of Paris until it had departed.[69] If he were to attempt to leave without a pass from Condé (who had refused him one) his residence would be pillaged and in all probability he himself molested.[70] Furthermore his health was bad, frequently consigning him to a sick-bed from which it would be foolish to rise prematurely; he was subject to recurring eye trouble, and was being treated by his doctors with purges that left him weak for several days at a stretch.[71] He looked for other arguments to justify his presence in Paris. Was it not to the court's advantage to have two such ingenious agents as de Morangis and himself in the capital to keep the court informed of the situation there?[72] Accordingly, throughout 1652 d'Aligre supplied le Tellier with his observations on the shifting tenor of events, both to aid the court in forming its policy towards Paris and to protect his own threatened reputation. Following Condé's arrival in Paris in April, d'Aligre perceived a marked heightening of tension as radical groups in the *parlement* and on the streets of Paris again gained the initiative. Even citizens whose deeper aspirations were for peace and who had little in common either with *les Grands* or *la canaille* subscribed to a sense of impending crisis. Known royalists were harried and, he warned: 'On parle librement de république du gouvernement Anglais.'[73] By summer he was urging the court to handle the city with utmost caution. Heavy-handed actions, provocative words, could easily let loose the old Frondeur spirit. The focal point of animosity was the cardinal himself. The presence in France of Mazarin was sufficient to unite otherwise disparate groups and to fuel the tensions and violence that were pushing Paris to the verge of anarchy by the summer of 1652.[74] D'Aligre's apprehensions were realised. On 4 July a rioting crowd burned down the *hôtel de*

[69] The same, 30 avril 1652 (*Ibid.,* f. 151).

[70] The same, 12 mai 1652 (*Ibid.,* f. 161).

[71] The same, 30 avril, 14 juin, 20 sept., 23 sept., 1652 (*Ibid.,* fos. 151-2, 168-8^v; MS Français 6890, fos. 201-2, 250-1); there remains the possibility that some of these periods of illness were invented; at least one other royalist, Omer Talon, lay low during the dangerous month of August 1652, claming a 'convenient' sickness that prevented him from leaving Paris or appearing on the streets (Omer Talon, *Mémoires* [Michaud & Pougoulat (eds.), *Nouvelle Collection,* xxx], 504-7).

[72] D'Aligre to le Tellier, Paris, 24 juin, 21 juillet 1652 (B.N., MS Français 6889, fos. 176-7, 195-5^v).

[73] The same, 12 mai 1652 (*Ibid.,* fos. 161-1^v).

[74] Moote, *Revolt of the Judges,* 342-3.

ville, killing and beating many of its members. On 20 July a rump of the *parlement* (most having fled) effectively handed over control of the city to Condé who appointed his own administration. Such spectacles d'Aligre observed with repugnance, but he found the whole sorry episode explicable by one great fact: Mazarin. There were, he advised, certain measures open to the court, such as the withdrawal of troops from the environs of Paris so as to ease the dread of the populace whose hostility then would turn on the unruly forces of the princes,[75] but there was only one decision that would subvert the hold of the princes on Paris: 'Si Son Excellence [Mazarin] eust voulu s'éloigner pour deux mois il changeoit la face des affaires, et eust retrouvé son establishment avec plus de satisfaction.'[76] He reiterated his message with telling force: 'Les levées d'argent dans Paris, le pillage des trouppes des Princes, et la prison des bourgeois dans la closture dégoustent fort les peuples et encore plus les honnestes gens, et si M. le Cardinal s'éloignait pour quelque temps sans conditions et sans traitté, je croy que tout reviendrait aisement nonobstant l'opposition des princes. . ..'[77] Mazarin was already under pressure from the sovereign courts to withdraw again from the country,[78] but it is of the greatest significance that somebody of d'Aligre's views and temperament – royalist, conservative – likewise should urge departure.

Mazarin left on 19 August. Immediately d'Aligre detected a transformation in the mood of the city. Paris was like a patient approaching 'la crise d'une maladie'. Talk of peace was heard in the streets. The sovereign courts were rumoured to be contemplating peace proposals. People were recalling the promise of the princes to fight on until Mazarin was gone; did not his departure mean that the time for peace therefore had come? The entry of Henri IV into Paris in 1594 and the generosity with which he treated the city were being spoken of; would Louis XIV be equally merciful?[79] As the princes' soldiers continued their rapacious ways a popular craving for peace swelled up in Paris. By early September d'Aligre was asserting that the city was almost ready for submission to the king.[80] Such prognostications appeared well-founded when, on 23 September, *échevins* met d'Aligre requesting that he arrange an interview between them and le Tellier so that they could 'porter les obéissances de la

---

[75] D'Aligre to le Tellier, Paris, 15 juillet 1652 (B.N., MS Français 6889, fos. 193 3ᵛ).
[76] The same, 21 juillet 1652 (*Ibid.,* f. 195).
[77] The same, 2 août 1652 (*Ibid.,* f. 201).
[78] Moote, *Revolt of the Judges,* 348-9.
[79] D'Aligre to le Tellier, 21 août 1652 (B.N., MS Français 6889, fos. 211-11ᵛ).
[80] The same, 5 sept. 1652 (B.N., MS Français 6890, fos. 44-4ᵛ).

ville'. D'Aligre urged his cousin to agree, for the prestige of the princes was ebbing fast. The king must return to Paris soon so as to ride the favourable tide.[81]

La Vieuville's attempts to cast aspersions on d'Aligre's loyalty failed. Proof came in October when Etienne III was called on to perform a highly secret and delicate task. One precondition of the restoration of royal authority in Paris was an armistice involving the two key princes, Condé and Gaston d'Orléans. Once they were pacified other Frondeur aristocrats would follow and the king could safely return to the capital. At the beginning of October d'Aligre was informed that he had been chosen to conduct secret negotiations with Orléans (installed in his residence in Paris, the Luxembourg) via Léonard Goulas, the duke's *secrétaire des commandements*. For three weeks Etienne's days and nights were monopolised by these talks. He secured agreement just in time for Louis XIV's entry into Paris on 21 October. A treaty with Orléans was signed on 28 October. D'Aligre's correspondence with le Tellier during the negotiations reveals that the court, albeit with more hesitation than contemporary observers like de Retz or Madame de Motteville realised,[82] had established three chief priorities: to separate Condé and Orléans, at the same time detaching Beaufort, Lorraine, Sully and Rohan from Condé;[83] to sign peace with both dukes; to ensure that Gaston left Paris before the entry of the king.[84] In a secret *mémoire* to d'Aligre, le Tellier expressed a personal opinion that, 'on penche absolument à faire l'accommodement général. C'est à dire avec M. le prince [Condé] aussy bien qu'avec M. [Orléans], par ce qu'on espère que celuy-là nous pourroit bien tost procurer la paix générale'. A settlement with Orléans alone would diminish trouble but not end it, another consequence being to delay peace with Spain even longer. Such considerations, le Tellier confessed, had created in the queen a state of mind ready to pay a heavy price to the princes.[85] Far from suggesting that the court was confidently sensing victory in October 1652, le Tellier's letters and *mémoires* testify to suspicion, hesitancy, an instinct that even at this late stage all could be lost.

---

[81] The same, 23 sept. 1652 (*Ibid.*, f. 250^v).

[82] Relevant passages in their *Mémoires* suggest a clarity of purpose on the part of the court that is not indicated by the sources used by the present writer.

[83] 'Mémoire envoyé à M. d'Haligre', 4 oct. 1652 (B.N., MS Français 4212, fos. 300-2^v).

[84] This emerges from two other *mémoires* sent to d'Aligre by le Tellier on 9 and 10 oct. 1652 (*Ibid.*, fos. 302^v-8, 311-12^v).

[85] 'Mémoire envoyé à M. d'Haligre', 9 oct. 1652 (*Ibid.*, fos. 304^v-5).

As negotiations between d'Aligre and Gaston proceeded, Etienne III was far more confident than was the court that Condé and Orléans were being prised apart. Gaston's preference was for an armistice involving Condé as well as himself,[86] but the extremity of Condé's demands and his threats to join the Spanish, threats ultimately to be realised, were irksome to Orléans. Condé's terms of settlement included two which the crown, even in its mood of generous compromise, would not concede. During the troubles one of Condé's lieutenants in the west, Louis Foucault, comte de Daugnon, had seized the towers of La Rochelle,[87] committing atrocities against royalists. Condé demanded that command of the towers be restored to Daugnon. The crown refused. For military reasons it could not contemplate the surrender of this strategic stronghold, but equally, honour forbade any betrayal of the memory of those loyal subjects who had suffered at Daugnon's hands.[88] Condé also insisted on the suppression of the *cour des aides* of Guienne.[89] It had sought to curtail his activities in the region and was a powerful obstacle to his influence in the province. This too was inadmissible to the crown. Its abolition would drive the other *cours des aides* into the arms of provincial governors; moreover, the *cours* were indispensable counters to the pretensions of the *parlements*, 'qui sembloient n'avoir aultre dessein que de se rendre arbitres de toutes choses'; and if it were legitimate for Condé to call for the suppression of the *cour des aides* of Guienne simply because it had frustrated his plans, how much more would the crown be justified in similarly punishing that errant assembly, the *parlement* of Paris[90]! On 8 October d'Aligre had a personal interview with Gaston on these and related questions. The duke was clearly impatient with Condé's intransigence, but even more so with his evident readiness to join the Spanish. He promised to do all in his power to prevent Condé's apostasy; he sent Rohan to plead with Condé to come to terms. It would not be long, judged d'Aligre, before Gaston and Condé parted company.[91]

If Condé as yet could not be coaxed into an armistice, at least the prospect of division between the two dukes was welcome to the court. There were signs that other aristocrats could be lured away from the

---

[86] D'Aligre to le Tellier, Paris, 7 oct. 1652 (B.N., MS Français 6891, f. 85).

[87] D. Parker, *La Rochelle and the French Monarchy: Conflict and Order in Seventeenth-Century France* (London, 1980), 54, 121.

[88] D'Aligre to le Tellier, Paris, 7 oct. 1652 (B.N., MS Français 6891, f 85^v).

[89] The same (*Ibid.*, fos. 85^v-6).

[90] The same (*Ibid.*, fos. 85^v-6).

[91] The same, 8 oct. 1652 (*Ibid.*, fos. 105-5^v).

princes. Rohan and Beaufort dropped hints to d'Aligre that they were amenable to a settlement,[92] and while it was no part of his brief to deal with them directly, he had been authorised to encourage this trend by intimating that as long as they remained with Condé they would receive no concessions from the crown. Should they recant, however, then Rohan's governorship of Anjou, for instance, could be restored.[93] In the event Orléans acted as 'agent' for these and other aristocratic Frondeurs. The peace that he signed on 28 October involved several of his associates: Rohan was restored to Anjou, Beaufort was paid the sum of 100,000 livres (he had sought 200,000), Brienne and Langeron were reinstated respectively in the governships of Carcassonne and La Charité, Sully was restored to Nantes, and so on.[94]

We have moved ahead of events. In the middle of October the court was acutely suspicious of Gaston's talk of peace. It questioned his trustworthiness. Was his apparent abandonment of Condé a mutually agreed ruse to secure a generous settlement which would allow them to recoup their resources? D'Aligre thought not. Having met Gaston he was convinced that, 'Il désire passionnement son accommodement ou je suis la plus aveugle personne de la terre'.[95] Orléans personally had pledged that as soon as an armistice was promulgated he would quit Paris. Some hot-headed followers were urging him to retire to Languedoc, of which he was governor, to continue the struggle from there; but, d'Aligre estimated, the duke was wisely turning a deaf ear.[96] A more serious proposition that might carry weight with Gaston, was that retreat from Paris would be derogatory to his honour. D'Aligre urged the court to reach agreement with him before this particular argument sank in.[97] But the court still would not shed its doubts. Orléans had consistently acted in concert with Condé and Lorraine. What reason was there to suppose that he was now pursuing an independent line?[98] On 14 October Orléans transmitted a *mémoire* to the court via d'Aligre suggesting terms of an armistice. The document merely reinforced royal suspicion, for it included clauses repeating Condé's demands on the towers of La

[92]The same, 13 oct. 1652 (*Ibid.*, fos. 146-6ᵛ).

[93]'Mémoire envoyé à M. d'Haligre', 4 oct. 1652 (B.N., MS Français 4212, fos. 302-2ᵛ).

[94]'Traicté faict par S.A.R. avec le Roy le 28 oct. 1652' (*Ibid.*, fos. 332-7ᵛ); the terms are printed in De Retz, *Mémoires* (Michaud & Poujoulat, Nouvelle Collection, xxv), 408-9.

[95]D'Aligre to le Tellier, Paris, 11 oct. 1652 (B.N., MS Français 4232, f. 208).

[96]The same, 12 oct. 1652 (B.N., MS Français 6891, f. 140).

[97]The same, 13 oct. 1652 (B.N., MS Français 4232, fos. 218-18ᵛ).

[98]Le Tellier to d'Aligre, Mantes, 15 oct. 1652 (B.N., MS Français 4212, f. 313).

Rochelle and the *cours des aides* of Guienne. Furthermore, it proposed a two weeks delay in which to allow Condé to be persuaded of the merits of an armistice. What was this but a crude attempt to hamper royal moves against Condé in the *parlement* and on the battlefield?[99] To surmount what threatened to be another deadlock d'Aligre secured evidence of Gaston's good faith: the duke would provide a copy of a letter he had sent to Condé, in which he explained that although he had done his best over the *cours des aides*, and la Rochelle, he would still accept an armistice if the court proved immovable on those matters.[100] Again, Goulas had continually stressed in his discussions with d'Aligre that his master's desire for peace was authentic, while he, Goulas, would never be, 'instrument d'aucune tromperie contre le service du roy'.[101] To d'Aligre the chief difficulty was not the genuineness of Gaston's peace talks but his insistence that an armistice must be registered by the *parlement*, for Condé, 'ayant des créatures dans le Parlement qui formeront touttes les difficultés possibles pour rompre l'accommodement s'il se fait sans loy'[102] would still prove a stumbling-block.

D'Aligre's assurances concerning Orléans's motives must have carried weight. The court proceeded with its plans for the royal entry into Paris on 21 October. Orléans was to be instructed by Etienne III to leave the Luxembourg and retire to Blois.[103] At first Gaston resisted the order, but yielded under the threat of arrest by royal troops.[104] He went as far as Limours. Louis XIV's triumphal entry into Paris went ahead. D'Aligre and Goulas spent a few days tidying up various loose ends of an armistice, the agreed document of peace between Anne and Orléans being signed on 28 October.

D'Aligre and the Frondes: a Perspective

The Frondes did not end in October 1652 (Bordeaux was to remain in a state of rebellion well into 1653), but at least Paris and its region were pacified. For d'Aligre, like all Parisians, the immediate prospects were hopeful as life returned to normal. He had passed through a

---

[99]'Mémoire envoyé á M d'Haligre', 16 oct. 1652 (*Ibid.*, fos. 320ᵛ-3).

[100]D'Aligre to le Tellier, Paris, 17 oct. 1652 (B.N., MS Français 6891, f. 199).

[101]The same, 17 oct. 1652 (*Ibid.*, f. 202).

[102]The same, 17 oct. 1652 (*Ibid.*, fos. 202ᵛ-3).

[103]'Instruction donné à M. d'Aligre', 20 oct. 1652 (B.N., MS Français 4232, fos. 244-4ᵛ).

[104]De Retz, *Mémoires* (Michaud & Poujoulat [eds.], *Nouvelle Collection*, xxv), 403.

testing and chastening period, Paris having been an uncomfortable place for supporters of Mazarin. He appears to have borne his professsional tribulations and psychological strains reasonably well, although his health was far from sound. One direct consequence of the Frondes was a shift in his relationship with le Tellier. Le Tellier owed the first important step in his career to Etienne d'Aligre II.[105] As a young man he had felt indebted to the d'Aligres. Now it was a d'Aligre who was indebted to him. Le Tellier's support at court, his presence as an influential voice in favour of the beleagured Etienne III, had been crucial in warding off la Vieuville's attacks. The *surintendant* died in January 1653, but henceforth the d'Aligres continued to look to the le Telliers as protectors. It was a reversal of the position earlier in the century.

Was there any substance to la Vieuville's contention that Etienne III's continued residence in Paris implied political vacillation? The evidence strongly indicates that there was not. No such allegation came from any other quarter, while Mazarin, ever sensitive to treachery, never lost faith in d'Aligre. It is also inconceivable that the secret negotiations with Gaston would have been entrusted to one who was less than totally trusted. The inescapable conclusion is that la Vieuville was motivated by political scheming against the Mazarin-le Tellier circle when he impugned d'Aligre's reliability. Even so, Etienne III was embarrassed by his prolonged absence from court. He was aware that by remaining in Paris he was exposing himself to hostile rumour. As Frondeurs moved from clique to clique, and when yesterday's friend could be today's enemy, a climate existed wherein constancy was among the rarest of virtues. Without somebody at court to champion him, it was inevitable that his absence would be interpreted maliciously; hence his frequent letters to le Tellier explaining his activities, offering his observations on current events, stressing his desire but his inability to leave the city. In the atmosphere of the Frondes d'Aligre's fidelity would not be taken for granted; it had to be demonstrated. D'Aligre may not have performed actions of conspicuous bravery during the Frondes, but by his conduct he sought to emphasise as unequivacally as he could just wehre his sympathies lay.

His periodic expressions of alarm over the safety of his family and property deserve serious consideration. His position was complicated in that some members of his family and much of his property were situated in the war zone around Paris, where they were vulnerable to depredations committed during the fighting in 1652. D'Aligre was emphasise as unequivocaily as he could just where his sympathies lay.

[105] See above pp. 26-7.

abbess of Saint Cyr although only in her early twenties. On more than one occasion the convent was raided by marauding troops, even those of the king. Elisabeth herself fell dangerously ill in 1652. D'Aligre pleaded with le Tellier to persuade the queen to send aid to the convent, but in the circumstances of 1652 nothing could be done. Saint Cyr was left to fend for itself; Etienne's anxieties were unassuaged.[106] In May 1652 his *seigneurie* of La Chapelle d'Aunainville, half way between Chartres and Etampes, was looted by royal troops: 'plusieurs quevalliers de l'armée du Roy, contre l'ordre de la milice se seroient transportez audict lieu de la Chappelle, ou ilz auroient pillé, desrobé et emporté, emmené, les bestiaux dudict sieur.' The *fermier*, Alexandre David, was molested. The soldiers, 'l'auroient battu et exeddé, despouillé de ses vestemens mesme de sa chemise, rompu les portes de sa maison, faict un grand dégat, emporté sa vesselle d'argent, quantité de linge. . . aussy pris son argent monnoye'. Then on 12 June a second attack came, this time from troops of the princes: 'lesquelz ont achevé de briser les portes et pillé le reste de la maison, mesme rompu son carosse, rompu son moulin à vant, emporté les toilles et grains qui estoient en iceluy, faict paistre et gaster la pluspart de ses bledz qui estoient aux champs, où il y a perte de plus de dix mille livres.'[107] In August Etienne III had cause to fear even for La Rivière when he heard that royal troops *en route* to Maine and Touraine would be passing through the region. He wrote to le Tellier: 'Je vous supplie de vous souvenir d'envoyer un garde à ma maison de la Rivière proche Pontgoint. Elle est en estat de se défendre sans canon pourveu que l'authorité des généraux ne s'y mesle point.'[108] Back in Paris there were recurrent threats against himself, his residence, and the life of his son Michel.[109]

In their detail the experiences of d'Aligre and his family during the Frondes were personal and so unique, yet they may be taken as typical of the kinds of trials that royalists had to endure in Paris. There were periods, such as in the wilder weeks of summer 1652, when the wise royalist kept his head down and avoided the public eye. Equally, there were times when life proceeded with a relative degree of normality. D'Aligre managed to keep reasonably up to date with his duties as *directeur des finances,* he fulfilled his obligations at the Assembly of the Clergy, and also kept his personal financial activities

---

[106] D'Aligre to le Tellier, 2 jan., 21 jan., 30 avril, 8 oct. 1652 (B.N., MS Français 6889, fos. 7-9, 69-70, 151-2, MS Français 6891, f. 101).

[107] A.D., Eure-et-Loir, MS G 3205, fos. 155-6.

[108] D'Aligre to le Tellier, Paris, 2 août 1652 (B.N., MS Français, 6889, f. 201^v).

[109] E.g. The same, 5 juillet 1652 (*Ibid.,* fos. 189-9^v).

going.[110] It would be wrong, therefore, to suggest that the life of a royalist in Paris during the Frondes was one of permanent dread of arrest or worse. Nevertheless, the basic fact remains that d'Aligre, like other royalists, felt that danger was never far away, and he remained in effect a prisoner in the city. His loyalty to the royal cause was to be rewarded richly in future years, for Louis XIV was to display generosity to those who stuck to Mazarin and the regent. In the short term Etienne III was reappointed *directeur des finances* in 1653 and again in 1654;[111] he moved on to higher things in the later 1650s and 1660s.

---

[110] See below, pp. 184-6.
[111] *Gazette de France,* 25 fév. 1653; A.G., A^{1}142, no. 381.

7

ETIENNE D'ALIGRE III: HIS CAREER TO THE CHANCELLORSHIP

The Treaty with the Hanse

Between 1653 and 1659 there were joint *surintendants des finances,* Servien and Foucquet, who assumed close control of central finances. D'Aligre found the charge of *directeur des finances* far less demanding than during the Frondes, most of his work consisting of routine correspondence and administration. There were various additional tasks to be performed.[1] One stood out. In 1654 he was instructed to negotiate a treaty with the Hanseatic League (represented by two senators from Hambourg) aimed at updating earlier agreements, the most important being those of 1464, 1483, 1489, 1536, 1552 and 1604.[2] The central issue concerned ships of the League trading with enemies of France: should those ships be intercepted by the French? Since the talks were designed to reinterpret well-established principles of the earlier treaties, they were completed within a matter of months, a new treaty being signed in May 1655.[3] It was agreed that vessels of the Hanse falling into this category would not be molested provided they were not carrying contraband (defined as weapons, munitions, food); they were to secure from the authorities of the port of departure a written statement as to the cargo, this statement being acceptable to French captains in lieu of right of search; procedures were agreed should a French ship capture one belonging to the League that was carrying contraband.

The General Assembly of the Clergy, 1655-7

Later in 1655 d'Aligre was again appointed royal representative to the quinquennial General Assembly of the Clergy; one of his assistants was his son-in-law, Michel de Verthamon.[4] He was

---

[1]He was involved in several commissions to investigate a variety of financial problems; e.g. see A.N., E 1701, fos. 13-14; E 1702, fos. 9-9^v; E 1705, fos. 54-5; E 1710, fos. 54-5^v.

[2]'Pouvoir donné à Mrs. de Brienne, d'Haligre et Bignon pour traiter d'alliance avec les villes Hanséatiques, sept. 1654' (A.A.E., C.P.: Hambourg 2, fos. 327-7^v).

[3]*Ibid.,* fos. 402-5^v.

[4]The following passage is based on *Collection des Procès-Verbaux,* iv, 116-40.

conscious of the 'defeat' that the crown had suffered at the hands of the Assembly of 1650-1. He saw more at stake in the new Assembly than simply the negotiation of a *don gratuit:* there was the question of the balance of royal authority among the clergy. It is significant that Mazarin himself gave all the support that he could to d'Aligre, joining in discussions with small groups of clergy at d'Aligre's home, and meeting members of the Assembly separately to press the royal case. The crown brought great weight to bear upon this particular Assembly in order to reassert royal influence.

A reading of the debates on the *don gratuit* recalls much that is familiar from the Assembly of 1651, although new features do emerge. D'Aligre adopted a different strategy from that of five years before: instead of casting the royal request for funds in general terms for the purpose of *soulager le pays,* he expressed it in specific terms for the purpose of paying troops at this crucial phase of the war against Spain. He employed many well-known arguments: great sacrifices have been made, a few more are all that are necessary; everybody's security is defended by the king's war, therefore everybody should contribute to its costs; the clergy are among the wealthiest sections of society and so should give more generously than most. He also introduced new forms of reasoning, employing a contract theory of government on one occasion: 'C'est dans le droit des gens, qui a fait dire, que dans l'établissement des monarchies, il se passoit un contrat synallagmatique entre les Rois et leurs sujets, qui obligeoit les sujets de les assister dans la nécessité sans distinction des qualités ni des conditions.'[5]

The clergy repeated old objections: grievances have not been redressed; the finances of the church are in disarray and the Assembly cannot offer very much, if anything at all. The Assembly devoted several sessions to the theory underlying the *don,* its history, the forms it had taken in the past. As a result it decided to apply two conditions: firstly, 'aucune Assemblée ne pourra faire ou accorder aucune imposition. . . si ce n'est que les Députés en aient nommément le pouvoir par leurs procurations'; secondly, 'en matière de don et gratification, il n'y aura aucune conclusion, s'il ne passe de plus des deux tiers des Provinces'.[6] Curiously the Assembly paid little attention to the principles enunciated with such vigour in 1650-1, namely that the *don* was in no sense a custom. Perhaps it felt that the point had been settled! D'Aligre was careful not to reopen this particular issue, concentrating instead on the immediate question of

[5]*Ibid.,* 118.
[6]*Ibid.,* 126.

the war, the king's resolve to end it as quickly as possible, and the need for the clergy to agree to a *don* on as generous a scale as possible. This proved the wisest approach. D'Aligre was saved the interminable debates on matters of principle that had occupied the Assembly of 1650-1, although it was not until January 1657 that the clergy agreed to a gift. At first they proposed one million livres; the crown suggested three millions. There followed many weeks of bargaining behind the scenes as well as in the debating chamber (this was the period when Mazarin's support was invaluable to Etienne), which terminated in a figure much closer to that of the crown than of the clergy: 2,7000,000 livres. A contract was signed in May 1657.[7] In financial terms d'Aligre had improved dramatically upon the *don* of 1651. He was, of course, working under vastly improved conditions: the regency was over, the Frondes had subsided, and he was backed by an all-powerful Mazarin. Both sides had refrained from debate as to the rationale behind a *don* (debates on this question were between the clergy alone, not between them and the king's representative). Altogether d'Aligre could feel well satisfied with what he had achieved.

The Death of Mazarin

As regards his career, the year 1657 ended well for d'Aligre. There occurred one of the first moves in what was to become a programme of comprehensive administrative reform during the first years of the personal reign of Louis XIV. In recent years the number of *conseillers d'état* had risen to over 120. In 1657 there was a drastic reduction, first to thirty-two, then to thirty.[8] The thirty comprised twenty-four drawn from the *robe,* three from the clergy and three from the *épée.* Twelve of those drawn from the *robe* were designated '*ordinaires*'; that is, their commissions were full-time like those of the clergy and the *épée.* The others were '*semestres*' serving only six months at a time. The reform reinforced the elite character of the *conseillers d'état,* confirming them as the apex of the central administrative system. Etienne III was included among the *ordinaires* by the decree of 1657. It was another recognition of his talents by the regime. He was charged with various commissions. One investigated alleged malpractices by the agent handling claims on the succession of Marie de Médicis,[9] and another supervised the restoration of alienated royal

---
[7]*Ibid.,* 142.
[8]B.N., MS Français, 7654, fos. 19-20.
[9]A.N., E 1712, fos. 140-140ᵛ; she had died in 1642.

domains.[10] At one stage Colbert, suspecting that trouble was again brewing among the nobles of Normandie and elsewhere, expressed the opinion that d'Aligre was exactly the kind of investigator to be sent to root out any plots; he only regretted that Etienne was now too senior for such a mission.[11]

In public affairs two great events predominated, of course, at the end of the 1650s and the start of the 1660s: the peace with Spain (with the ensuing marriage of Louis XIV and Maria Teresa), and the death of Mazarin followed by the assumption of government by the king. They did much to subdue social and political tensions within the country, while Louis inherited from the cardinal a team of ministers and advisers who displayed loyalty and dependability as well as high powers of statesmanship. The one possible exception, Foucquet, was soon removed; incidentally, after Foucquet's arrest it was Etienne III who was sent to Vaux-le-Vicomte to seize and examine the *surintendant's* papers.[12] The ministers and others inherited by Louis XIV were backed by 'clans' of followers associated by bonds of marriage, of family, of fidelity, who were placed in central and provincial administration. The ranks of those who served Louis XIV were no place for young intellectuals of independent views; obedience and an assiduous sense of duty were qualities required in abundance by those who would serve Louis XIV. Etienne d'Aligre was among those servants bequeathed by Mazarin to Louis. The king appreciated his qualities and talents, for not only did he escape the fate of his superior in central financial administration, Foucquet, but when the *surintendance des finances* was suppressed to be replaced by a *conseil des finances,* d'Aligre was named a member of the council and so continued his duties in finance.

The General Assembly of the Clergy, 1660-1

The death of Mazarin occurred as the Assembly of the Clergy, attended again by d'Aligre on behalf of the crown, was in session. It had first met at Pontoise from 25 May 1660 until 24 September, when it moved to Paris where it remained until it disbanded on 22 June 1661.[13] D'Aligre found the Assembly in resistant mood when it

[10]A.N., E 1710, fos. 54-5.

[11]Colbert to Mazarin, Paris, 8 août 1658 (P. Clément [éd.], *Lettres, Instructions et Mémoires de Colbert,* i [Paris, 1661], 308-9).

[12]Colbert to the king, [Paris, 1661] (*Ibid.,* vii, 191).

[13]The following passage is based on *Collection des Procès-Verbaux,* iv, 457, 537-65, and on A.M. Boislisle (éd.), *Mémoriaux du Conseil de 1661,* i, (Paris, 1905), 13-14, 142-3, 146.

turned to the *don gratuit;* sessions were reminiscent of the tough days of 1650-1 rather than of the more easy-going ones of 1655-7. The chief reason was the peace of 1659. Why, queried many speakers, should the clergy be expected to make an extraordinary gift to the king now that extraordinary circumstances were no more? They could understand that during the war the king required exceptional financial aid, but surely in time of peace his regular sources of income should be sufficient for his needs. Another explanation for the resistance of the clergy is the decision of the crown to cast its request for a gift in very general terms. The Assembly of 1650 had been suspicious of this strategy; that of 1660-1 was equally so.

D'Aligre first addressed the clergy on 1 September 1660. In the aftermath of war, he proclaimed, heavy debts remained to be settled. Peace did not suddenly dispel the chaos created by war. Indeed, did they but appreciate the full complexity of the problems facing the king, they would doubtless regard even the 2,700,000 livres voted in 1657 as inadequate. He made a promise: 'Ce sera un dernier effort du Clergé de France, pour faciliter l'affermissement de la paix, après lequel vous n'entendrez plus parler des pressantes nécessités de l'Etat, ni de nos instances pressantes pour le soulager.'[14] How much credence the more worldly-wise of the clergy gave to these words is open to question, but here was the offer: meet this request and there will be no more. The clergy proved sceptical. Some questioned the right of the king to expect a gift. Others insisted that a gift must be linked to the prior redress of grievances. When d'Aligre refuted such propositions in his second speech on 4 October, the clergy appealed directly to Mazarin against the, 'maximes qui ont été avancées par lesdits Sieurs Commissaires, comme étant contraires à la piété du Roi'.[15] There followed a series of meetings at the hôtel d'Aligre between representatives of the clergy, d'Aligre and Mazarin. The upshot was that on 31 January 1661 the Assembly repeated its manoeuvre of 1650: it refused a gift for the general purpose that d'Aligre originally had outlined, but did agree to contribute to an item of expenditure which it, not the crown, specified: the cost of recent peace negotiations and resultant marriage of the king.

What was the crown to do? D'Aligre protested at the decision, but the Assembly proceeded to drive home its advantage. In February 1661 it appointed a committee to investigate methods of raising money although a sum had not yet been agreed. On 26 March the

[14]*Collection des Procès-Verbaux,* iv, 540.
[15]*Ibid.,* 544-5.

Assembly made an offer of one million livres, which fell far short of royal aspirations. At this juncture d'Aligre proved the value of his long experience. To the surprise of the Assembly he accepted the figure, but only for the royal wedding. He then reintroduced his general request for aid, adding that the king, 'attend de plus grands efforts de votre bonne volonté, par la considération de sa propre personne et de son Etat'; he proposed four millions as an appropriate sum. By this sleight of hand he intended both increasing the *don* and circumventing any notion that the clergy alone might dictate royal expenditure.

D'Aligre had tipped the balance, forcing the clergy onto the defensive. Then came the death of Mazarin on 9 March, which immediately affected the negotiations. The cardinal's judicious support had been essential to d'Aligre's handling of the Assembly. As an air of uncertainty for a time surrounded the government, the clergy won back the initiative. When a deputation met the king on 4 April Louis lowered his request to three million livres. After another debate the Assembly offered 1,800,000. On 6 and 7 April a deputation again met the king to explain the reasoning behind this figure; Louis again lowered his proposal, this time to two millions. On 11 April d'Aligre spoke in the Assembly for the last time. He attempted a bluff: the king had raised his demand back to four millions. The clergy hastily agreed on two millions and appealed to the king to accept. He did. D'Aligre signed the contract on 17 June.

It had been a difficult Assembly from d'Aligre's point of view, Mazarin's death coming at a particularly sensitive stage. Financially the crown had done less well than in 1657, while on the matter of principle the contest may be judged a draw: one million livres went towards the marriage as the clergy desired, and one million towards royal debts as the king required. Peace had revived many of the defensive attitudes of the clergy towards the *don*. It gave them an opportunity to emphasise their independence as an Order of society; especially did it allow them to refute any suggestion that they were liable to taxation under another name, in the form of an automatic *don gratuit.*

Etienne III and Colbert

Meanwhile, in affairs of government Louis XIV had assumed personal control. Within his inner council, of which Etienne III was a member, three men predominated: le Tellier, Colbert and Lionne. D'Aligre's relations with le Tellier have already emerged, but those with Colbert deserve examination, for in the new political order

Etienne III was to work closely with the great minister. Although their links in the 1650s had been only sporadic, d'Aligre and Colbert appreciated each other's qualities. Etienne admired the talents of Colbert, who in return recognised the value of one who had experience of so many aspects of government and administration. Accordingly d'Aligre was brought into the *conseil des finances* after Foucquet's fall[16] and into the *conseil de commerce* that was established in 1664.[17] These were bodies in which Colbert placed great hopes as he planned the financial and economic rejuvenation of government and country. D'Aligre was one of Colbert's right-hand men as the minister sought to engineer the great transformation. The work of the two councils naturally overlapped, a conjunction assisted by having d'Aligre on both bodies. He was able to ensure that they worked in harmony and avoided unnecessary rivalries. His special responsibilities within them also reflected the close association between questions of finance and of commerce. In the *conseil de commerce* he was charged with collating commercial information that was supplied by merchants.[18] In the *conseil des finances* he was instructed to review all the royal properties, a long and complex task.[19] He investigated alleged misconduct by financial *officiers,* an undertaking for which he was an excellent choice after his years as *directeur des finances*.[20] He was responsible for adjudicating disputes over the distribution of prize money after the capture of enemy ships.[21] As in the 1650s, so in the 1660s he led a busy, demanding life. He was part of a team headed by a statesman of exceptional will-power and decisiveness, who in turn was supported by a king who displayed an immense capacity to inspire adulation and obedience. In the 1660s an air of optimism, of creation, a sense that at last the crown was shaping events not responding to them, attached to the monarchy. D'Aligre, who for so long had served a king who was on the defensive, must have found these years a satisfactory, even exhilerating experience.

In addition to his regular duties deriving from the *conseil des finances* and the *conseil de commerce,* he was to be involved in two other major enterprises which in retrospect can be seen to have been the last before the chancellorship: one was Colbert's *recherche de la*

---

[16]B.N., MS Français 7654, f. 37; Boislisle (éd.), *Mémoriaux du Conseil,* iii, 138-9, has details on membership of the *conseil.*

[17]*Gazette de France,* 23 août 1664.

[18]Boislisle (éd.), *Mémoriaux du Conseil,* iii, 164.

[19]D'Aligre to Colbert, Paris, 10 mai 1662 (B.N., Mélanges de Colbert 108, f. 503).

[20]The same, 20 juin 1662 (B.N., Mélanges de Colbert 109, f. 503).

[21]The same, - juin 1660 (B.N., Mélanges de Colbert 138, fos. 26-7).

noblesse, the other was the General Assembly of the Clergy of 1665-6.

The 'Recherche de la Noblesse'

Colbert was alert to the fact that his elaborate plans for the kingdom must depend too much on inspired guesswork until reliable statistical information on the extent of the country and its resources, and on the size and distribution of the population could be gathered.[22] In 1664 he instituted the first great *enquête* whereby the *intendants* were ordered to amass information on the population according to elaborately drafted instructions.[23] One section of the instructions covered the nobility. But who were the nobles? Colbert faced an old, debateable question.[24] It had never been resolved satisfactorily, and still there existed an extensive twilight zone between genuine nobility and commonalty. He therefore proposed a national *recherche de la noblesse* to clarify the issue once and for all; thereafter his *enquête* begun in 1664 would return more accurate information, while the treasury too would profit from the increased taxes resulting from *faux nobles* being inscribed on the *taille* rolls (Colbert shared the common belief that the *faux nobles* harboured large numbers of wealthy social climbers.).[25] Again, it was consistent with the authoritarian tendencies within the regime that an opportunity should be exploited to drive home to the nobles of France, many of whom had participated in the Frondes, that a king now reigned whose will would brook no opposition; a *recherche de la noblesse* had great disciplinary potential.[26]

Accordingly the *recherche* was organised and activated, being directed from Paris by two committees, one of which included Etienne d'Aligre.[27] But of all Colbert's projects this one soon proved to be among the least productive. D'Aligre's personal experience of the *recherche* in Normandie in the 1630s had taught him, at least, just how profound was noble resentment and obstructionism at the appearance of royal commissioners querying the validity of titles; the chances of a national inquiry succeeding were slight. The *recherche*

[22] A. Corvisier, *La France de Louis XIV, 1643-1715* (Paris, 1979). 220-2, 224-5.

[23] B. Gille, *Les Sources Statistiques de l'Histoire de France: les Enquêtes du XVIIe Siècle à 1870* (Paris, 1964), 24-7.

[24] See above, pp. 18-19, 96-8.

[25] Clement (éd.), *Lettres. . . de Colbert,* iv, 38.

[26] Lavisse, *Histoire de France,* 7(i), 372-5.

[27] Clément (éd.), *Lettres. . . de Colbert,* ii, 760, n. 1; see also, G. Chamillart, *Recherche de la Noblesse faite par Ordre du Roi en 1666 et Années Suivantes* (Caen, 1887).

lacked the manpower necessary to so ambitious a scheme, while it was not long before allegations of inefficiency and corruption among its agents began to pour into Paris from aggrieved nobles. Indeed, so unsatisfactory was the entire enterprise that it was suspended in 1670.[28] D'Aligre's precise role in the *recherche* is hard to determine. He helped to receive and collate reports from the *chercheurs;* he was also active in the *recherche* of the nobles around Compiègne.[29] In Paris he was used by the king to settle appeals, usually in favour of the appellant. There was the sieur de Vaudenil, a *lieutenant* in a regiment of light horse, who protested to the king that although the *intendant* of Picardie had judged his title valid, he was still being pestered by agents of the *recherche.* D'Aligre was ordered to interview de Vaudenil and settle the matter in his favour.[30] A *gentilhomme* from Guienne, Monluc de Rochebrune, doubted his ability to prove the authenticity of his title. He persuaded friends whose own nobility was beyond question to write to the king on his behalf; Louis in turn handed the correspondence on to d'Aligre with instructions to concede the title.[31] The sieur de Chasteaumal petitioned the king to be confirmed in his nobility; the papers once more were sent to d'Aligre with the recommendation that he look on the case favourably.[32] The *recherche* cannot be considered one of Colbert's more inspired exercises, and it was probably a wise move to abandon it after about three years. It was beyond the capacity even of a Louis XIV to purge the ranks of the nobility, while the pressures of war in the 1670s were to compel him to resort to the 'nefarious' practice of once more selling titles. To modern observers it might appear unrealistic for the regime of Louis XIV to have supposed that it could succeed in purifying the nobility where its predecessors had failed. But the attempt was symptomatic of the spirit of would-be achievement that fired much royal policy in the 1660s. That it failed is not necessarily an indictment of the original aspiration.

The General Assembly of the Clergy, 1665-6

This, the last Assembly to be attended by d'Aligre on behalf of the king, contrasts markedly with others in which he had participated.

[28] Lavisse, *Histoire de France,* 7 (i), 373-4.

[29] D'Aligre to Colbert, Compiègne, 28 juin 1667 (B.N., Mélanges de Colbert 144, f. 449).

[30] The king to d'Aligre, (Saint Germain), 12 jan. 1667 (A.G., A^{1}206, f. 22).

[31] The same, 20 avril 1667 (*Ibid.,* f. 135).

[32] The same, 26 mars 1668 (A.G., A^{1}213, f. 337).

Opening in Pontoise on 6 June 1665, transferring to Paris on 17 August where it remained until its dissolution on 14 May 1666, it proved unprecedentedly tractable over the *don gratuit*. If we refer back to the Assemblies since 1650, it is evident that the *don* had always been subjected to long, searching debate, not only in full assembly but behind the scenes and in private discussions between the king's *commissaires* and groups of clergy. The clergy had consistently repudiated any suggestion that the *don* was a tradition or an obligation; indeed, so anxious were they to preserve its 'extraordinary' character that in 1650 they had refused it. Even when they had agreed to a *don,* they had stated themselves the purpose for which it was given, generally setting aside the broad terms in which the king's request was couched; this too served to stress that it was the will of the Assembly that was being exercised, not that of the king. Another tactic was to procrastinate, to relegate the *don* to a lowly point on the agenda, to let weeks pass between debates on the *don,* forcing the royal representatives or even the king himself to urge the Assembly to proceed more quickly. Such impedient measures should not necessarily be intepreted as expressions of disloyalty, although the Assembly's conduct in 1650 and 1651 unquestionably made the most of the king's disabilities. The First Estate was genuinely committed to its independence, and could point to a lengthy list of its own grievances which had gone unattended by the crown. No institution or assemblage in the seventeenth century responded to royal demands for money without first scrutinising the request, and if the clergy made the royal representative to the Assembly work hard for their rewards, it was no more or less than d'Aligre and his colleagues expected.

It follows that as chief royal representative to the Assembly d'Aligre required skill in negotiation, a knowledge and understanding of the leading personalities in the Assembly, and sensitivity towards the shifting moods of the clergy. It made sense that the crown retained him through successive Assemblies, for although his subordinates changed on each occasion, he thereby acquired an experience of dealing with the clergy which allowed him to pursue a long-term policy on behalf of the crown. Throughout his many discussions with members of the Assembly in the 1650s and 1660s two issues predominated: for what purpose should the *don* be voted and how large should it be? By 1661 he had made considerable progress on both these matters. On one occasion he explained his strategy to Colbert:[33] at his first appearance before a particular Assembly he

---

[33] D'Aligre to Colbert, Paris, 22 juillet 1665 (B.N., Mélanges de Colbert 130 bis, f. 879).

would normally begin by sticking to the tradition of couching the request for a gift in general terms, and of refraining from being the first to suggest a figure for the *don*. This was intended to convey to the Assembly the message that the crown too regarded the *don* as a gift, not as a tax by another name. Behind the scenes in private discussions with groups of clergy, however, he had sought to undermine this principle, and in public debate he had endeavoured to cast doubt up it. In 1661 he had succeeded in securing from the clergy an admission that they were not competent alone to designate those items of governmental expenditure to which a *don* should be devoted (half the *don* of that year was reserved to general purposes, to be decided by the crown). In addition, d'Aligre had managed to drive up the *don* from 600,000 livres in 1651 to between two and three millions; this in itself was no mean accomplishment when the church, like every institution, was feeling the financial effects of almost two decades of warfare. A reading of the Assembly debates conveys a vivid impression of how hard it was for d'Aligre to shift the clergy on these matters. They fought hard to defend the proposition that because the *don* was extraordinary they should be informed in detail as to its use; also that it should be kept as small as possible.

The new Assembly met in Pontoise on 6 June 1665. It disbanded only ten and a half months later. Etienne first presented the request for a *don* on 27 July. He did so in broad terms. Money was needed by the king, 'lui faciliter les moyens de continuer ce qu'il a si prudemment commencé, pour remédier aux désordres de son Royaume; le rétablir en sa splendeur, et élever sa Monarchie au plus haut point de grandeur qu'elle ait jamais été'.[34] But the speech bore many hallmarks of the new political order, especially of the influence of Colbert. The king, continued d'Aligre, was resolved to reorganise his finances so that regular expenditure would be met from regular income; he was even aiming at a surplus to finance the defence of the country and the support of his allies. He had created trading companies[35] to keep bullion in France, and was improving communications dramatically. This was a vast programme, 'que toute personne qui en fait part est obligée d'aider. . . , et encore plus le Clergé de France, qui possédent la plus grande partie des fonds de terre', for the clergy 'recevra le plus d'avantage et le plus d'utilité'.[36] Such sentiments are so reminiscent of

---

[34]*Collection des Procès-Verbaux,* iv, 888.

[35]The companies founded by Colbert were the Compagnie des Indes Orientales 1664, the Compagnie des Indes Occidentales 1664, the Compagnie du Nord 1669, and the Compagnie du Levant 1670.

[36]*Collection des Procès-Verbaux,* iv, 889.

Colbert[37] that it seems likely that d'Aligre had shown the speech to him. At the very least he had based the demand for a *don* upon the minister's policies. He employed another argument especially appropriate to his audience, namely religion. The king was defending catholicism by waging war against Islam in the Mediterranean, but also by campaigning against protestantism abroad and at home. In view of such considerations, surely the clergy would rise to the occasion by voting a *don gratuit*.

The response of the Assembly to this call was astonishing, especially when its past performances are recalled: it proved completely tractable, even timorous, putting up hardly any struggle at all. It discussed the *don* on 4 August and agreed immediately to the request. This was unprecedented in d'Aligre's experience. Two provisos were appended to the agreement of 4 August: there must be no hint that the *don* was 'un tribut d'obligation auquel l'Eglise fut assujettie', and the king must take steps to defend the rights and privileges of the church.[38] These ritual statements could not disguise the fact that as never before the Assembly had conceded the *don* on the very first occasion of its request. The ascendancy of the crown was emphasised when d'Aligre made his next speech on 24 August: he broke with tradition by proposing that the *don* should be of four million livres. He thus repudiated the 'right' of the clergy to initiate discussion of a figure. Significantly, the Assembly did not protest at this breach with custom. It proclaimed the sum too high, then resorted to inertia. It put off further debate until 14 October, notwithstanding d'Aligre's many appeals. On that date it appointed a committee to investigate the size of the *don*, but in spite of more promptings from the royal commissioners there was no more progress until the following year. On 19 March 1666 d'Aligre again spoke in debate, urging the Assembly to agree to four millions, especially since the king was now at war.[39] The clergy debated the figure and on 26 March offered 2,400,000 livres. The archbishop of Toulon transmitted the decision to the king advising him to accept, for this was the first occasion in the entire history of Assemblies of the Clergy that the *don* had been fixed in one session by unanimous vote. Faced with escalating costs of war Louis agreed. D'Aligre signed the contract on 16 April.[40]

[37] See Colbert's famous *mémoire* on commerce of 1664 in Clément (éd.), *Lettres. . . de Colbert*, ii (1), cclxiii-cclxxii.

[38] *Collection des Procès-Verbaux*, iv, 890-1.

[39] On the motives behind the French invasion of the Spanish Netherlands see, J. Wolf, *Louis XIV* (London, 1968), ch. 15.

[40] *Collection des Procès-Verbaux*, iv, 899.

In almost every essential respect the Assembly must be judged a success for the crown. It faced little opposition and no intricate harangues over questions of principle. The only weapon that the clergy used was delay. They even swallowed the abrogation of their right to initiate discussion on a figure for the *don*. It would be too much to pretend that the submission of the clergy was achieved by d'Aligre alone, for unquestionably a new climate had been created by Louis XIV and his ministers; but equally it would be erroneous to suppose that d'Aligre's contribution was negligible. That the crown gained the initiative over the Assembly was in no small part the outcome of his endeavours over the years, and if any individual could claim credit for this outcome it was he. Indeed, within his immensely variegated career spanning almost five decades, the transformation of the obstructive spirit of the Assembly of 1650 into the compliance of 1665, was his main contribuiton as an individual to the cause of royal absolutism in France. His role in other aspects of government was distinguished by any measure, but in none did he make his personal mark as he did in his dealings with the Assembly. If any strand of his professional career deserves special mention it is surely this. He could well have regarded the outcome of the Assembly of 1665-6, the last which he was to attend, with a sense of considerable satisfaction.

The Chancellorship

By the late 1660s Etienne III, now a septuagenarian, was slowing down. The crown, generous to its respected officers, handled him with admirable attention to propriety even though his days of usefulness clearly were coming to an end. Prestigious but undemanding titles were conferred on him. In 1668 he was designated *doyen du conseil du roi*[41] by which he was recognised as senior *conseiller d'état* responsible, for example, for informing members of the main *conseils,* such as the *conseil des parties,* as to the times and places of meetings.[42] He would also chair such meetings if necessary.[43] In 1672 came d'Aligre's next promotion, to the keepership of the seals, the chancellorship following two years later.

These two stages opened up with the death of Séguier on 28 January 1672. He had succeeded Etienne II as chancellor in 1635,

---

[41]B.N., MS Français 17396, f. 178.

[42]See for instance A.N., V²16, 4 fév. 1672; B.N., MS Français, 4583, f. 254; Mélanges de Colbert 158, fos. 205, 223.

[43]Clément (éd.), *Lettres. . . de Colbert,* vi, 285.

and for long periods had been *garde des sceaux* as well.[44] In his later years he had been but a pale shadow of his former, vigorous self, proving no match for Colbert in the 1660s, when Colbert deprived the chancellorship of most of its powers.[45] Séguier left the chancellorship as an exceedingly remunerative sinecure, which Louis XIV was to use thereafter as a form of recognition conferred on outstanding, and usually elderly, servants of the crown. Etienne III was to be the first to fall into this category; his successors confirmed the principle. He was to be followed in 1677 by Michel le Tellier, then seventy-four; after his death in 1685 came Boucherat, aged sixty-nine; finally there was Pontchartrain, a comparative stripling of fifty-six when he became chancellor! By then, however, time had confirmed the nature of the charge, and there was no prospect of it returning to its former glory as one of the most prestigious royal appointments.

For a few weeks in February and March 1672 Louis XIV exercised the functions of chancellor himself, personally directing the ceremony of affixing the seal to royal acts and decrees.[46] The experiment was soon suspended as foreign policy, particularly the opening of the Dutch war, came to occupy most of his attention. Louis's decision to accompany his army to the Netherlands meant that arrangements had to be made for his absence. A top priority was the appointment of a *garde des sceaux*, for without the appropriate seal no royal act had legal force. Who should be chosen? D'Aligre was the obvious choice. He was already *doyen du conseil* and an acknowledged legal expert. Louis departed on the Dutch campaign on 6 April; on 23 April came the announcement that Etienne III was *garde des sceaux:*

> Tant à cause de son mérite particulier, et de la grande expérience qu'il s'est acquise dans tous les emplois considérables qu'il a exercés, que pour les grands et recommendables services qu'il a rendu au feu roy nostre très-honoré seigneur et père, et à nous depuis nostre avènement à la couronne, et qu'il continue journellement de nous rendre à la tête de nostre conseil.[47]

It was a fitting, condign step for d'Aligre. Financially, too, it brought rich returns: 10,000 livres a year in *gages*[48] and another 80,000 or so

---

[44] 28 Feb. 1633 – 1 March 1650; 15 April – 6 Sept. 1651; 11 Jan. 1656 – 28 Jan. 1672.

[45] Antoine, *Le Conseil du Roi*, 46-53.

[46] Etienne III attended as *doyen du conseil;* see B.N., MS Français 7654, f. 3.

[47] 'Provisions de garde des sceaux pour M. d'Aligre: Donné à S. Germain-en-Laye, avril 1672' (A.N., 0^{1}16. fos. 252^v-254^v).

[48] Clément (éd.), *Lettres. . . de Colbert*, vi, 297.

in rights attaching to the charge.[49] Etienne's advancement in a sense did not stop there, for as his replacement as *conseiller d'état* was nominated his son Charles, who entered the ranks of the *ordinaires,* by-passing the normal stage of *'semestre'*.[50] In 1673 Charles also succeeded to his father's office of *conseiller d'honneur* in the *parlement* which Etienne III had held since 1652.[51]

Louis was away for three months. On his return in July he did not resume responsibility for the seals, preferring to leave d'Aligre in the post. But still there was no chancellor, and there seemed every possibility that this charge too would follow into oblivion those other *grands offices de la couronne* which were abolished in the 1660s, those of constable and admiral general. Etienne III naturally coveted the chancellorship, and there may well have been quiet manoeuvres by, say, le Tellier, on his behalf. Whatever the truth, by the end of 1672 rumours were circulating that the king was inclining in d'Aligre's favour.[52] Hints and suggestions continued throughout 1673. At last in January 1674 the announcement came from Saint Germain: Etienne d'Aligre was to be chancellor of France.[53] The citation spoke of:

> Les rares et recommandables qualités que nous avons toujours reconnues en la personne de nostre très-cher et féal messire Estienne d'Aligre, chevalier, garde des sceaux de France, et le zéle et la fidélité qu'il a fait parroistre dans tous les emplois que nous lui avons confiés, etc., etc.; pour ces causes nous avons résolu de lui donner les titre et dignité de chancelier de France, estant bien aise de mettre dans sa famille une marque particulière et extraordinaire de nos bienfaits, en lui donnant cette première dignité et charge de nostre couronne, dont le feu sieur d'Aligre, son père, fut pourvu par le feu roy, nostre très-honoré seigneur et père de glorieuse mémoire...

So, like his father he reached 'le solstice des honneurs'. The circumstances surrounding the appointments of father and son could

---

[49]B.N., MS Français 7655, f. 15.

[50]B.N., MS Français 7654, f. 32; MS Français 7666, fos. 15ᵛ-16.

[51]A.N., X8659, f. 122; Bibliothèque de la Chambre des Députés, MS 352, f. 47.

[52]'Je n'oserois me resjouir du bruit qui s'est respandu que Mr Daligre... estoit regardé pour luy estre substitué dans la charge qu'il possède présentement en le faisant chancelier pour enterrer la sinagogue avec honneur [i.e. pour bien finir]. Je ne l'oserois de peur que ce ne fust qu'un bruit sans effet, mais je le souhaitte pour le bien de l'Estat et pour l'avantage de sa maison' (Chapelain à M. de Paillerois, Paris, 5 oct. 1672 [P. de Tamizey de Larroque (éd.), *Lettres de Jean Chapelain,* ii (Paris, 1883), 792-3]).

[53]'Provisions de Chancelier de France pour M. d'Aligre, à S. Germain-en-Laye, jan. 1674' (A.N., 0¹274, fos. 16-17).

scarcely have been more different. Etienne II had been carried to the top amidst political uncertainty and at a time when Louis XIII, on the defensive against a formidable array of problems, was casting around for trustworthy officers; Etienne III was exalted by a master omnipotent at home and assured of the loyalty of all his great servants.

Etienne was in his eighty-second year, and that he could be other than chancellor in name only, manifestly was an impossibility. A decline in his mental faculties was observed, one person writing: 'J'ai vu M. le chancelier, ... son corps est plus vigoureux que son esprit, car il marche fort droit et lit sans lunettes, mais il ne sait guère ce qu'il dit.'[54] His son François, *abbé* of Saint Jacques, was brought to court ostensibly to assist him in his duties, but in fact to do his work for him and to see to his needs.[55] For almost four years Etienne accompanied the court from one *château* to another, although most of his time was spent at Saint Germain and Versailles. The chancellery was a reasonably efficient department capable of operating without the personal intervention of the chancellor.[56] That he was decreasingly effective as his physical decline continued was without consequence for the functioning of the chancellery. Etienne III was working in the chancellor's chambers at Versailles when he collapsed and died on 25 October 1677. He was aged eighty-five.

Observations on d'Aligre's Career

An assessment of Etienne's career cannot avoid stressing its sheer length. For over fifty unbroken years he had served the crown in one guise or another; no other major seventeenth-century figure in France matches this record, excepting 'le roi soleil' himself. Certainly by 1677 he was the oldest member of central government. Given the vicissitudes of political fortunes in the seventeenth century (amply illustrated by the fate of his father) it was no mean accomplishment to survive for so long near or at the top. It required a broad range of capacities: to spot winners and to join them; to avoid too many

---

[54]M. de Saint Maurice au marquis de Saint Thomas, Paris, 20 juin 1675 (F. Ravaisson-Mollieu, *Archives de la Bastille*, iv [Paris, 1870], 110).

[55]M. Lecomte, 'Une grande figure Provinoise: François d'Aligre, abbé de Saint-Jacques de Provins (1643-1712)', *La Semaine Religieuse du Diocèse de Meaux*, no. 25 (1909), 392; L. Michelin, *Essais Historiques, Statistiques, Chronologiques, Administratifs, etc., sur le Départment de Seine et Marne*, i (1829), 275-6.

[56]Schwob, *Un Formulaire de Chancellerie*, 42-50, deals with its operations under Etienne III.

enemies in high places; conversely, to incur the gratitude and indebtedness (in a literal sense if necessary) of great aristocratic families. Above all did it depend on a spotless reputation for total loyalty to the king, for assiduous attention to the minutest detail in the execution of duty. Such qualities d'Aligre exhibited from the outset of his career. From the occasion of his father's disgrace when, from Venice, he speedily despatched affirmations of fidelity to Richelieu, he ingratiated himself first with the cardinal and subsequently with Mazarin. Thereafter he resisted all temptations to equivocate in his role as their agent. It was a stance easier to preserve in the lifetime of the former than of the latter, as Mazarin became embroiled in feuds and conflicts with such an array of powerful enemies as all but subjugated him. Indeed, if any series of episodes belied any suggestion that d'Aligre's adherence to the chief ministers was not an expression of conviction as much as of self-interest, it was the Frondes. In the highly unsettled mood of those years many erstwhile servants of the crown were caught up in conspiracies or uprisings if only for a time, and even if for the most undefiled of motives. That d'Aligre did not, but persisted in linking his destiny to that of the king and of Mazarin, even at risk to his own and his family's safety, testifies to a constancy and integrity far from common at the time. Such unswerving royalism can be ascribed in part to his 'uprootedness'. For all that his origins were in Chartrain and Le Perche where the bulk of his estates and many of his relations were to be found, Etienne III himself was a Parisian by upbringing, education and temperament. The only periods of any length that he spent away from Paris were on royal commissions. Throughout his life, but especially after his father's death in 1635, his visits to his estates were few and far between. He showed no desire to intersperse life in Paris with sojourns in the country; he was an absentee landlord whose active interest in his estates was limited. He was therefore relatively free from the provincial loyalties and sentiments that complicated the response of large numbers of nobles to royal policy. It would be an exaggeration to pretend that he felt no affinity with provincial opinion, but it appears to have exerted no appreciable influence on his royalist sympathies. His resolve was aided by the le Telliers whose own political advancement was a buttress to the position of the d'Aligres. Michel le Tellier defended Etienne III against the calumny of critics during the Frondes, and as le Tellier went on to attain political powers far in excess of those of his kinsman he remained a potential protector of the first order. If d'Aligre anticipated generous treatment by Louis XIV after the Frondes he was not disappointed. More responsibilities came his way during the personal reign of the king, he in turn making a notable contribution to the achievements of the regime.

So much can be argued for the cohesion of a long and varied career. At the same time it is evident that for all its success, certain of the high expectations of his youth went unrewarded, at least in part. As ambassador to Venice he had assimilated skills and experience appropriate to a career in international relations. Further, he must have considered that a timely blend of circumstances conceivably might raise him to one of the great state offices in the forseeable future. It was not to be, for although he saved his political skin in 1626 by entering the ranks of Richelieu's *créatures,* his father's exile to La Rivière and Richelieu's impregnability, directed his career into somewhat less exalted channels than looked possible before 1626. He was never to be a star performer in the French government, always a step or two from the spotlight. He was sufficiently realistic to make the necessary mental readjustments, wisely eschewing an excessive sense of grievance, but accommodating himself to the realities of his position.

Whatever its setbacks and disappointments his career emphatically enabled him to acquire immense material wealth. A description and analysis of that wealth is still to come. Nevertheless, even at this juncture it has to be emphasised that throughout his career he was to organise and manage his deals in land and in finance with exceptional care and success. He acquired more and more *seigneuries* as well as land *en roture,* much of it from hard-pressed nobles in the region of Chartres who were struggling to keep family territories intact, albeit to no avail. Since Etienne III held various posts in royal service, almost in unbroken succession between 1624 and 1677, he was always in receipt of the cash returns that accompanied those posts. He was never dependent on his own property as a sole source of income. His career provided him with a constant supply of money from the state, which he was able to employ to great personal advantage as he built up his material possessions.

A necessary but difficult task is to attempt an assessment of the personality of Etienne d'Aligre. None of his private correspondence has survived, while most of the documents relating to his private affairs are notarial records whose legalistic vocabulary hides the man himself. Nevertheless, scattered throughout d'Aligre's official papers and other sources are sufficient clues to warrant at least an attempt to reconstruct his mind and character.

Already one prominent trait has emerged: the consistency of his royalist political views. This should not be taken to imply that strict orthodoxy was uniformly typical of his mental outlook. As a young man he had travelled widely in the south of France, developed close links with Peiresc, spent almost three years in Venice from where only the most vapid of spirits could have returned unstimulated, and in Paris moved in 'advanced' *salon* circles. Such facts do not indicate an unadventurous mind. A particularly knotty problem concerns the extensive library that he gathered. The story can be taken up in 1676. In that year he bequeathed to his son François, *abbé* of Saint Jacques, all his books and manuscripts at La Rivière and in the chancellor's chambers at Versailles and Saint Germain.[57] François later arranged for the transfer of the stock to Provins where, with the addition of his own books and the few others that were in the monastery, it formed the library of the abbey. Difficulties now arise. The bequest did not include the books in the hôtel d'Aligre. No affirmative record of what they included exists; thus the reading material that Etienne III normally had to hand cannot be assessed. Again, there are two sources which include lists of the books donated to François: the 'Catalogue des livres de la bibliothèque de M. François d'Aligre, abbé de S. Jacques de Provins, donnée par lui aux religieux de cette abbaye et au public le 30 août 1681...'[58] and the 'Catalogue de la bibliothèque de St. Jacques de Provins, de la main du p. le Pelletier'.[59] Neither distinguishes between the books given by Etienne III and those already in the monastery, nor does it discriminate between those from La Rivière, which Etienne probably never read, and those from Versailles and Saint Germain. But our counsel is not entirely one of despair. It is known that Etienne's donation far outnumbered the existing meagre resources of Saint Jacques, and that without suggesting proportions, it is certain that most titles in the 'Catalogues' came from him.[60] Further, it is self-evident that most books already in the monastery would be religious in subject-matter; the non-religious categories in the 'Catalogues' may therefore be assumed to have come from d'Aligre. It is also possible that in the division of his property that occurred after his death[61] some of the books in the hôtel d'Aligre were given to François informally so as to keep the collection relatively intact. With such reservations in mind, what do the 'Catalogues' indicate regarding Etienne III's collection? Firstly, he was a sedulous collector, for well over 10,000 volumes came into François's possession. In seventeenth-century terms this represents a

---

[57] A.N., Y231, fos. 342ᵛ-343; M.C., LXXXVI-420: Donation, 2 mai 1676.

[58] Bibliothèque de Provins, MS 239.

[59] Bibliothèque Sainte Geneviève, MS 2156.

[60] A. Braichotte, 'L'Abbé d'Aligre (d. 1712)', *Bulletin de la Société d'Histoire et d'Archéologie de l'Arrondissement de Provins,* iii, no. 2 (1898), 26.

[61] See below, pp. 203-4.

collection of major importance and places Etienne III among the leading bibliophiles of his day.[62] Predictably titles concerned with different aspects of law bulk large in the 'Catalogues': Roman and canon law, different *coutumes,* histories of law, collections of *ordonnances* and *arrêts.* But in addition, almost every subject is solidly represented: political thought, patristics, theology, devotional aids, classical and modern literature, the sciences, architecture, travel, history, geography (including atlases of Mercator and the Sansons); there was a section on the history and topography of Venice which presumably he had bought when ambassador. It was a truly catholic collection, a creation of sustained, judicious accretion. Again, the 'Catalogues' confront us with a library that does not eschew 'dangerous' or controversial works and authors. Machiavelli, Calvin, Melancthon (though not Luther), Jansen, Descartes, Rabelais are but some of the heterodox, or 'dubious' authors that appear. Their presence indicates an open-mindedness, or at least a fascination for provocative, even egregious ideas, that no pedant or dogmatist could have sustained. A certain degree of caution is necessary, of course, Possession of books does not necessarily imply that they were read. Still less does the presence of particular volumes on an owner's shelves mean that he agreed with their content. Yet in the case of Etienne d'Aligre there are sufficient suggestions from other quarters to indicate that for most of his life his was an enquiring, self-reliant mind, fully at home in the company of authors over a wide range of disciplines. Even though the library inherited by François may not represent the whole of Etienne III's collection, even though it is beyond the bounds of possibility to identify his favourite books, it supplies further evidence that he valued ideas and did read widely. We might see in d'Aligre a type becoming more familiar as the seventeenth century progressed: the educated nobleman of the *robe,* trained chiefly in law and with a strong distaste for social upheaval, yet intellectually sophisticated, *au fait* with trends and shifts in the world of ideas. How far d'Aligre perceived any contradiction here is impossible to ascertain. Did he consider that social order and intellectual ferment in France were compatible? Or did he suspect causative links between the social and political *désordres* of his times, and the spirit of doubt and questioning that increasingly characterised French intellectual endeavour? It is hard to believe that a figure of his intelligence and experience in public life never posed such questions. If we suppose that he did, then his royalism again

---

[62]H.J. Martin, *Livre, Pouvoirs et Société à Paris au XVII*[e] *Siècle (1598-1701)* (Paris, 1969), i, 475-84; ii, 922-52.

begins to look the result of mature, considered reflection. If these speculations are sound, it follows that d'Aligre saw the crown as the sole institution either capable of maintaining social order in a world whose traditional intellectual foundations were crumbling, or of reshaping French society effectively. Either way a powerful king was indispensable to the future of France if that future were to avoid the hideous anarchy that too often had been the country's fate. This study has attempted to evince reasons for d'Aligre's loyalty to the crown; some connected with self-concern unquestionably played their part, yet there is an 'ideological' dimension which we would be ill-advised to ignore.

As for his views on religion, they remained conventional, the least 'adventurous' part of his intellectual formation, although he remained a devout catholic. He was a member of the congregation at Saint Germain l'Auxerrois, one of the most patrician churches in Paris. It was there that he was buried. He had given strong backing to his sons François and Charles when they introduced reform into their respective monasteries, and likewise had encouraged the charitable works of his wives Geneviève Guynet and Elisabeth l'Huillier. There is no trace of his will, making it impossible to say what charitable bequests he left or to what extent the church was a beneficiary of its provisions. His library was well stocked with books of a religious nature, including at least thirty-one bibles in Latin or French (the earliest published in Basle in 1491) and a polyglot in five volumes printed in London in 1657. However, since he also owned several copies of the Koran as well as the works of protestant theologians, it would be injudicious to estimate his religious fervour by these particular statistics! Several of his children entered holy orders, François in particular showing real spiritual distinction. Of course, Etienne's many years of experience in the Assembly of the Clergy gave him an insight into the structure and operations of the French catholic church which few other laymen could have matched. He was exceptionally well placed to gauge the temper of catholicism in the fifteen years following 1650. As royal representative to the Assembly he had striven to canalize its energies into the service of the crown, frequently employing debates on the *don gratuit* as the occasions for hard-hitting lectures on the obligation of the church to serve the broader interests of the state. It would be an exaggeration to describe d'Aligre as an Erastian, but emphatically he was of the opinion that in secular matters the church must be subordinated to the purposes of the king.

Viewed in the context of the age, Etienne d'Aligre emerges as one fully in harmony with the development of Bourbon absolute monarchy. Possessing intellectual gifts and administrative talents of no mean order, he was attuned to the requirements of the monarchy and ready to place himself at its disposal. Knowing at first hand the dangers that beset France at home and abroad, he repudiated any illusion that the alternative to royal absolutism was some form of neo-feudal Utopia. His own lifetime as well as that of his father had supplied sufficient evidence that civil war, invasion, *la misère,* social upheaval, were the true alternatives to the absolutist state painfully constructed under Henri IV, Louis XIII and Louis XIV. No viable third way offered itself. Whatever the defects of Bourbon absolutism, it alone held the key to national unity.

8
THE FAMILY AND FORTUNE OF ETIENNE D'ALIGRE III BEFORE AND AFTER THE 'FRONDES'

We turn to the domestic affairs of the d'Aligres during the 1640s and 1650s. These were decades when significant changes occurred, stemming in part from the effects of the Frondes.

The Household

When his wife Jeanne died, she and Etienne III had been living in style in the rue d'Avron.[1] Some of the rooms including the library were leased by Louis d'Aligre, but they used most of the residence themselves. They had two ground floor rooms, eight bedrooms, a large study or *cabinet* where Etienne worked with a small *cabinet* adjoining, a private chapel, the main reception room on the second floor with a store room leading off, a kitchen with larder and cellar, a wine store and stables. There was plenty of every-day furniture and utensils, and the house was well stocked with luxury goods as befitted a family of substance. In the large *salle basse* hung a tapestry from Bruxelles as well as several paintings. Etienne's bedroom contained a Hungarian tapestry and Venetian mirror. In his *cabinet* were more paintings and a tapestry from Bourges. The smaller *cabinet* was adorned with a Turkish carpet. The principal room was on the top storey. It held a large bed where Madame could recline when receiving guests; there were between ten and fifteen tapestries, six Turkish rugs, eight or ten tables, numerous chairs and cabinets. There were ornaments throughout the house: busts, statuettes, vases, chandeliers, bowls, bronze and ivory figurines. Then there was silver plate whose importance was more than decorative: it formed part of the accumulated wealth of the family, to be bequeathed to the next generation. The silver was valued at 12, 927 livres and the jewelry at 18,832 livres. The outstanding item in this latter category was a pair of ear-rings containing four large pearls and forty-two diamonds valued at 9,000 livres. There was a necklace of Scottish pearls worth 3,000 livres, a small box studded with twenty diamonds and estimated at 2,300 livres, and a diamond necklace of 151 stones worth 1,600 livres.

---

[1] The following information is based on A.N., M.C., LXXXVI-319: Inventaire... de Jeanne l'Huillier, 22 oct. 1641.

Other pieces were valued at under 1,000 livres each and included gold chains and necklaces, diamond rings and bracelets.

Despite lacunae in the inventory it is possible to establish an approximate value of the contents of the d'Aligre household in the rue d'Avron.

Table 6

Jewels	18,832 livres	37.2%
Silver	12,927	25.5
Principal room	8,129	16
Statues & ornaments	4,917	9.7
Linen, blankets etc.	2,423	4.7
Eight bedrooms	1,465	3
Stables	1,000	2
Other rooms	670	1.3
Kitchen etc.	350	0.6
Chapel	?	
	50,713	

In spite of its limitations this does emphasise that the jewelry, silver, ornamentation and furnishings of the principal room or *grand grenier,* accounted for the overwhelming bulk of the value of the contents of the residence: some 44,805 livres or 88 per cent of the total. The figure for the stables includes four horses whose joint value was 700 livres, and two carriages, one estimated at 200 livres and the other at 100. If the luxury categories and stables are extracted from the list above, then it means a large residence like that of the d'Aligres could be stocked with furniture, bedding, kitchen implements and so on, for about 5,000 to 6,000 livres. That does not include the running costs of food, wine, clothing, animal fodder, the salaries of the servants. No household accounts of the family have survived, but evidence shortly will be presented to suggest that some 6,000 livres a year may be a reasonable estimate of running costs.

One thing is clear: it was a large and busy household. In addition to Etienne and Jeanne, there was a growing number of children (twelve by 1641), Etienne's mother after Etienne II's death, and the servants. Moreover, the residence being so close to the Louvre, and belonging to a prominent public figure, it is to expected that it received a constant stream of visitors; scholars, courtiers, *officiers,* friends, ladies of high society on their rounds, must have come and gone in large numbers.

By 1641 the birth-pattern of the children was established. Of the fifteen born, twelve grew to maturity. The first four were sons. Louis (1619-54) followed a military career; François (1620-1712) was to be the most revered of all the *abbés* of Saint Jacques de Provins; Michel (1623-61) was the only son to marry; Etienne (1624-44) was a Knight of Malta killed in a sea battle against a Turkish ship. Then came two daughters both of whom were nuns: Elisabeth (b. 1625) and Anne (1628-69). They were followed by two more sons: Charles (1630-95) later *abbé* of Saint Riquier near Amiens, and Jean (1632-1710) another Knight of Malta. The remaining children were daughters. Françoise (1637-1719) entered a convent, while the others married: Hélène (1636-1712), Marie (1640-1724) and Marguerite (1641-1722) (See Appendix 2).

Several of these children will reappear in greater or lesser detail, but as a group their significance for the family was considerable. Etienne III and Jeanne had married in 1617; the first child was born eighteenth months or so later. Thereafter births came at roughly annual intervals, and while there is no proof the supposition is strong that Jeanne's death was linked to the birth of Marguerite one month previously. By any standards it was a large family, with almost a generation between the eldest and youngest. The daughters who married were all at the junior end of the scale. Their marriages occurred in the mid-1650s, which is to say that Etienne did not have to provide dowries until he was in his sixties and had long since amassed his fortune. Had he been responsible for three marriageable daughters as a younger man of lesser means, the relative burden of their dowries would have much heavier. As it was, he was in a position to provide generous settlements enabling them to marry into the highest social echelons. The other daughters chose the conventual life. Questions of vocation aside, it was of course to Etienne's financial advantage that they did not require marriage dowries. As regards the sons, the most striking and potentially most dangerous feature in the context of the future of the family, was that only one married. Two were priests, two took vows of celibacy as Knights of Malta, while Louis, the eldest, whose relations with his father were usually strained chose first the religious life, then the military, but never married. Such diversity of activities among the sons may have exemplified a family of great wealth capable of fulfilling the aspirations of its sons, that only one married may have saved the d'Aligre estates from chronic subdivision; but such features threatened the family name with extinction should the one son who married meet with premature death.

Etienne III's Second and Third Marriages

Given his domestic circumstances after 1641 Etienne III desired another wife. He remarried in 1645, his new spouse being a widow, Geneviève Guynet, whose first husband had been Jean de Gué, sieur de Villetaneuse, a *maître ordinaire* in the *chambre des comptes* who had died in 1640.[2] Her background was similar to that of Etienne in that her father had been a *conseiller* and ultimately *doyen* of the *grand conseil*. Her age is not known, but she had married de Gué in 1611 and so cannot have been very much younger than Etienne.[3] She was a lady of means and property. Since 1640 she had been residing in her house in the rue Michel le Conte in the parish of Saint Nicholas des Champs. She owned two more houses in the rue Vieille du Temple, another in the rue Saint Thomas du Louvre, and held half shares in two properties in the faubourg Saint Germain. From her father she had inherited 1,743 livres a year in *rentes* on the state (which suggests a capital investment of about 21,800 livres) and 1,502 livres in *rentes constituées* (on a principal roughly of 30,000 livres). She herself had invested in both types of *rentes*, which gave an annual return of 2,508 livres (on about 43,200 livres). From her deceased husband she had inherited 228 livres in *rentes constituées* (on a principal of some 4,560 livres). She thus had an annual income of just below 6,000 livres in *rentes*, plus whatever she charged through renting her property.[4] In their marriage contract she and Etienne agreed to hold nothing in common, but to retain individual ownership of their possessions. Instead, Geneviève was to contribute 2,000 livres a year to to their joint expenses and Etienne 4,000 livres. From this arrangement it may be inferred that 6,000 livres per annum were thought adequate for the running of a large household. The marriage served their respective purposes admirably. There was an element of affection and companionship; Etienne had a wife of maturity capable of administering the *maison* and supervising the children, a wife who for many years had moved in his own circles and was well known in Paris. In her turn Geneviève had reinforced her status and enjoyed the protection of a wealthy and esteemed husband. This was a union based on different

---

[2] A.N., Y184, fos. 305-5ᵛ: Contrat de mariage, 14 mai 1645.

[3] A.N., M.C., LXXXVI-281: Inventaire de Geneviève Guynet, 15 mai 1645; this document is the source for the discussion of her property.

[4] If all the property were leased it could have realised about 3,000 livres a year; this is suggested by three *contrats de bail* that have survived, all in A.N., M.C., LXXXVI-295, dated 15 mai, 2 juin, 25 sept. 1655, which gave three-year leases at 400 livres per annum (a house in the rue de Petit Brune, faubourg Saint Germain), 500 livres (her house in the rue Michel le Conte), and 350 livres (a house in the rue Vielle du Temple).

assumptions from their first marriages and intended to fulfil different purposes. The surviving evidence concerning Geneviève indicates a lady of at least conventional piety who made donations to convents,[5] and who assisted the career of at least one of her servants: in 1656 she apprenticed him to a shoemaker for four years, meeting the charge of 90 livres herself.[6] She died in September 1657; there were no children by this marriage.

In 1658 Etienne married again. His third wife was Elisabeth l'Huillier (1607-85), widow of a *lieutenant civil* in the Châtelet; she was a cousin of Etienne's first wife Jeanne l'Huillier. By their marriage contract Etienne and Elisabeth retained separate property rights.[7] She was of a deeply religious temperament, and was heavily committed to lay charitable work in Paris. In the post-Fronde years the city badly needed the ministrations of people like Elisabeth, for it abounded in social problems in the aftermath of civil war. She was active in supporting the work of the Hôpital des Enfants Trouvés.[8]

Louis d'Aligre (1619-54)

During the 1640s some of Etienne's children reached maturity and decided on careers. His eldest son Louis would normally have been regarded as chief heir to his father's property, but relations with his father were poor and he was to bring shame to the family. For some years he was *abbé commendataire* of Saint Jacques de Provins, but in 1640 he resigned in favour of his brother Michel. In 1643 he purchased a captaincy in a prestigious regiment, that of Normandie.[9] After several years on campaigns in Italy he resigned in 1648.[10] Shortly afterwards he was promoted to *maréchal de champ* in the Piedmont army; then in 1650 he transferred to the Italy army.[11] His final promotion came in 1651 when he became commander of cavalry in the Italy army.[12] In that year his army was sent to Catalonia where

---

[5] A.N., Y189, fos. 113^v-4: Donation, 27 mai 1652; A.N., M.C., LXXXVI-389: Donation, 2 oct. 1657.

[6] A.N., M.C., LXXXVI-297: Apprentissage, 31 juillet 1656.

[7] A.N., M.C., LXXXVI-300: Contrat de mariage, 30 juin 1658.

[8] P. Coste, *Le Grand Saint du Grand Siècle: Monsieur Vincent,* i (Paris, 1932), 269, n.4.

[9] A. Corvisier, *La France de Louis XIV, 1643-1715* (Paris, 1979), 181.

[10] A.G., A^{1}123, no. 134.

[11] A.G., A^{1}116, no. 221: A^{1}122, no. 66.

[12] A.G., A^{1}125, no. 181; B.N., MS Français 4182, fos. 374-5.

the French position was parlous. Since the invasion of Catalonia in 1642 the French and their Catalan rebel allies had experienced mixed fortunes. The French were badly affected by the Frondes: pay fell into even worse arrears, food and munitions failed to arrive, mutiny began to rumble. The Spanish renewed their assault upon the province, besieging Barcelona late in 1651. The Italy army was sent to break the siege and relieve the city.

At first Louis d'Aligre covered himself with glory. He led a successful attack on the town of Terrasa, near Barcelona, one of the Spanish strong-points.[13] But he found French troops in an appalling condition. To le Tellier he wrote: 'Si vous voulez Monsieur nous secourir, nous manquons de tout, point de munitionnaire, point de Canon, point d'armée navale, et point d'argent, et ne sommes pas payés du payement de 1,200 pistoles que nous devons rècevoir en janvier'; mutiny could erupt at any time, for there was much talk, especially in the Normandie regiment, of simply marching home.[14] By April 1652 shortages of food and money were so chronic that Louis was beginning to advise abandoning the campaign, for: 'Il vaudrait mieux sauver les Trouppes en perdant le Pays, que de perdre les Trouppes et le Pays;'[15] by May talk of retreat was common among the officers.[16] With summer came plague, more indiscipline, a rising rate of desertion,[17] and danger to the lives of officers from embittered and mutinous soldiers: 'L'armée est devenue si insolente par la nécessité qu'elle a, qu'il n'y a plus de seureté de ma vie, n'estant plus résolu de me tenir dans le corps d'armée. Et quoy qu'il soit mort de peste quatre domestiques depuis le dernier ordre, je ne quitterois pas sans le péril d'estre assassiné.'[18]

Even allowing for exaggeration, Louis d'Aligre's letters to le Tellier in the summer of 1652 testify to a French army that was demoralised, sick, weak, denuded of supplies, and utterly incapable of resisting even the second-rate Spanish army that was in the field. The attempt to relieve Barcelona proved a fiasco, the city surrendering to the Spanish royal forces on 13 October 1652. Shortly before that Louis was caught up in the malaise afflicting the French, and was

[13]A.G., A^{1}137 bis, no. 6; *Gazette de France,* 28 jan. 1652.
[14]Louis d'Aligre to le Tellier, Camp de Saint Boy, 15 mars 1652 (A.G., A^{1}137, no. 57).
[15]The same, 30 avril 1652 (*Ibid.,* no. 112).
[16]The same, 6 mai 1652 (*Ibid.,* no. 135).
[17]The same, 9 juillet 1652 (A.G., A^{1}137 bis, no. 258).
[18]The same, Cordedeau, 15 juillet 1652 (*Ibid.,* no. 281).

involved in an incident that ruined his career. The precise sequence of events is difficult to establish, but the essence of his 'crime' can be established: a royal *ordonnance* of 20 October ordered his arrest and that of other officers on the grounds that he led a premature retreat of the cavalry of the Italy army from Catalonia, having failed to relieve Barcelona; Louis 's'est mis à leur Teste, abandonnant le Service de Sa Majesté ainsy que ses fidelles sujets en la bonne ville de Barcelonne'.[19] The cavalry regiment was to be disbanded, and Louis and the other officers reduced to the ranks pending further punishment. Louis's correspondence during the weeks preceding the mutiny include many warnings that trouble was afoot; indeed, he was to protest at his arrest, claiming that his chief obligation was to hold his troops together in reasonable discipline, and not allow them to decline into anarchy.[20] But retreat was deemed mutiny; the arrest was carried out.

The mutiny occurred some time in September, for at the end of the month, Etienne III, having received the news, wrote a pathetic and despairing letter to the secretary of state for war, hoping to salvage something from the ruins of his son's career:

> Vous scavez la peine que mon fils aisné m'a donné toute sa vie et combien j'ay désaprouvé sa conduitte. Il fault maintenant que j'en recoive un si signal desplaisir que je ne scay si cela ne me fera point mourir, mon saissement estant tel que je n'ay pas la force d'écrire sur ce subjet. Je vous envoie la lettre qui m'a donné ce coup par laquelle vous verrez le narré de cette action que je condanne si fort que s'il estoit entre mes mains je le mettrois dans la Bastille. Aussy n'entreprene je pas de l'excuser si ce n'est que la chose ne soit pas telle que la lettre l'a représenté... Mais si la chose s'est passée en la forme qu'elle est écrite, tout ce qu'il pourra ne le mettra point à couvert. Je vous suplie seulement Monsieur de faire en sorte que l'on attende de ses nouvelles avant que de le condanner. Je pense pas qu'il manque de vous rendre compte de cette action, quand mesme il ne me le manderoit pas n'ayant aucune lettre de luy depuis longtemps. Je remets le tout soubs vostre conduitte pour en ordonner comme il vous plaira.[21]

Shocked and humiliated as Etienne III was, he still acknowledged a paternal duty to Louis, 'puisque Dieu me l'a voulu donner il fault que j'en ai soing'; he continued to plead for him, although: 'Il serait plus

---

[19]B.N. Collection Châtre de Cangé 28, fos. 159-9ᵛ.

[20]Louis d'Aligre to le Tellier, –, 26 nov. 1652 (A.G., A¹134, no. 392).

[21]Etienne d'Aligre to le Tellier, Paris, 30 sept. 1652 (B.N., MS Français 6890, fos. 304-4ᵛ).

heureux mort en l'attaque des lignes de Barcelonne et en servant l'estat'.[22] Perhaps his son had not been the ringleader of the mutiny?[23] At last Etienne had news from his son, who asked him to pass on to le Tellier an enclosed letter.[24] The contents of this missive are not known, but it is probable that Louis argued that indiscipline was so rife that retreat had been the only way to avert full-scale mutiny. Le Tellier, who had promised Etienne III such help as he could give over Louis's case, wrote to Louis on 15 October calling on him to take steps to restore order before fresh troops arrived;[25] doubtless he was trying to give his kinsman a chance to redeem himself. It was too late, for the order for Louis's arrest was issued five days later. The affair disappears from the records until June 1653 when the crown was considering a suitable punishment for Louis.[26] The outcome is unknown, but in any event Louis did not live much longer. He died in 1654, his reputation ruined.

Here, then, is a dark side to d'Aligre family affairs at the beginning of the 1650s. It could be argued that Louis was a casualty of the last, miserable day of the Catalonian campaign, whose chances of success had been severely damaged by the interruption of supplies caused by the Frondes. His disgrace stained the family name, and brought grief to his father. The long letter from Etienne III to le Tellier that has just been cited, indicates that relations between father and son had been poor for many years, and that this last episode was but one of many which Etienne regarded as reprehensible in the career of his son. The death of Louis in some respects was almost welcomed by Etienne. It meant that another son must now be considered principal heir to the d'Aligre estates and fortune.

Michel d'Aligre (1623-61)

The son on whom the mantle fell was Michel, and Etienne III had to adjust his thinking and strategy on family affairs accordingly. The need to do so became more urgent as the years went by, for the careers of Etienne's other sons in the church or as Knights of Malta meant that Michel was the only son who married. On him, therefore, fell the

---

[22]The same, 6 oct. 1652 (B.N., MS Français 6891, f.76^v).

[23]The same, 9 oct. 1652 (*Ibid.,* f. 113).

[24]The same, 12 oct. 1652 (*Ibid.,* f. 140^v).

[25]Le Tellier to Louis d'Aligre, Pontoise, 15 oct. 1652 (B.N., MS Français 4185, f. 264).

[26]B.N., Collection Châtre de Cangé 28, f. 160.

responsibility for perpetuating the family name. Born in 1623 he succeeded his brother Louis as *abbé* of Saint Jacques de Provins; but he too resigned and followed a secular career. In 1647 his father bought for him the office of *conseiller* in the *conseil des parties*.[27] In 1651 Michel married a niece of his stepmother, Geneviève Guynet: Cathérine de Machault, whose father was a *correcteur* in the *chambre des comptes*.[28] In the marriage contract Etienne III transferred the *seigneurie* of Boislandry to his son; Cathérine's dowry was 150,000 livres. But the marriage proved to be tragically brief, for Cathérine died later in the year on 20 July.[29] For self-evident family reasons Michel had to marry again. Indeed, so sensitive was Etienne III to the danger that the male line might die out during the uncertain years of the Frondes, that in 1652 he admitted privately to le Tellier that one of the reasons why he stayed in Paris, even at the height of civil disorder, was to find a second wife for Michel.[30] He succeeded, although the choice might look strange to modern eyes. She was Marie Arragonet, daughter of a *trésorier des gardes françaises;* but she was extremely young, for the day selected for the wedding, 23 October 1652, was also her twelfth birthday.[31] One possible explanation as to why Michel was willing to marry somebody so much younger than he, is the size of her dowry: 300,000 livres.[32] Yet this marriage like the first was brief. Marie died in 1657, the child that she had borne lasting only a little longer.[33] The d'Aligres therefore were again confronted by the threat of extinction; the search for yet another wife had to be resumed.

Michel's career, meanwhile, had proved prosaic. In 1653 he had purchased the office of *maître des requêtes*,[34] but advanced no further. Moderate promotion came in 1659 when he was sent as *intendant* to Caen where his father had served some twenty years before, but there

---

[27] A.N., M.C., LXXXVI-377: Traité, 26 juillet 1647; the office cost 124,000 livres.

[28] A.N., M.C., LXXXVI-286: Contrat de mariage, 29 jan. 1651.

[29] A.N., M.C., LXXXVI-287: Retrocession, 10 août 1651; Michel returned to Geneviève Guynet 27,000 livres out of the 30,000 that she contributed to Cathérine's dowry; he retained 3,000 livres; by a second document of the same date he returned to Cathérine's father 100,000 livres out of the 120,000 that he had contributed, Michel retaining 20,000 livres.

[30] D'Aligre to le Tellier, Paris, 20 sept. 1652 (B.N., MS Français 6890, fos. 201-2^v).

[31] The same, 20 sept. 1652 (*Ibid.*, f. 202).

[32] A.N., M.C., LXXXVI 325: Inventaire après-décès de Marie Arragonet, 4 avril 1657 ('Papiers privés', no. 2: contrat de mariage, 17 mars 1652).

[33] The child was named Etienne; he is mentioned in Marie's 'inventaire après décès'.

[34] A.N., M.C., LXXXVI-325: Inventaire après-décès de Marie Arragonet, 4 avril 1657 ('Papiers privés', no. 5); the office cost 189,000 livres and was resold in 1661 for 325,000 livres (A.N., M.C., LXXXVI-392: Délaissement et traité d'office, 4 sept. 1661).

were no signs of higher office. Happier omens came with his third marriage; it was to Madeleine Blondeau, daughter of a *président* in the *chambre des comptes*.[35] Fears as to the survival of the family name receded as two sons were born to Michel and Madeleine: Etienne IV (1660-1725) and Gilles (1661-1711). But as before, premature death struck again, this time Michel himself being the victim. In 1661 at the age of thirty-eight he died; perhaps he succumbed to the plague that swept France that year.[36] It was a hard blow to the family, for even if Saint Simon's opinion that he was, 'plus imbécile que le père'[37] is to be trusted, his was the responsibility for sustaining the family interest in the next generation as his father and grandfather had done in theirs. His death posed many questions. How should Etienne III's succession now be divided in the event of his decease? What proportion should devolve on Etienne IV and Gilles? What were the implications for Etienne III's other children, especially his daughters who had married and might produce children of their own? Worst of all, what would happen if Etienne IV and Gilles, both infants in 1661, should die? The family prospects in that year were far from encouraging. Meanwhile, Madeleine Blondeau and her sons moved in with Etienne III who for the time being oversaw their education, handled their financial interests, and managed the affairs of the *seigneurie* of Boislandry on their behalf.

Etienne III's Daughters

In the 1650s Etienne III's daughters began to come of marriageable age. Three went to the altar in quick succession as the troubles of the Frondes died down. Firstly there was Marie who, in 1654 at the age of seventeen, married Michel de Verthamon, baron de Bréau, a *maître des requêtes* and later *conseiller d'état*.[38] In the following year Hélène, aged nineteen, married Claude de l'Aubespine, marquis de Verderonne and *capitaine d'un régiment des gardes du roi*.[39] Then in 1658 Marguerite, aged seventeen, married François Bonaventure, marquis de Manneville, whose father was *gentilhomme de la*

---

[35] A.N., Y196, fos. 275ᵛ-7; her dowry was 240,000 livres.

[36] E. Labrousse *et al.*, *Histoire Economique et Sociale de la France*, ii (Paris, 1970), 38.

[37] Boislisle (éd.), *Mémoires de Saint Simon*, xxii, 257.

[38] The contract is in the possession of M. Georges Fessard of Courville-sur-Eure, who kindly supplied the writer with a copy.

[39] The contract is missing from the Minutier Central, but its details are in A.N., M.C., LXXXVI-294: Donation, 5 fév. 1655.

Table 7

Marie's dowry[40]

Principal	Rente	Constituted
20,000	500	20 oct. 1648 by Jacques Tubeuf
24,000	1,333	4 juillet 1633 by Charles de Schomberg
12,000	666-13-0	20 août 1653 by Anne du Roure
84,000	4,620	15 déc. 1653 by Charles de Schomberg (part of a *rente* of 7,694-16-0 on a principal of 153,896-16-0)
140,000	7,119-13-0	
Cash 16,000		
156,000 livres		

Hélène's dowry[41]

Principal	Rente	Constituted
38,000	1,900	29 oct. 1623 by Anne du Roure
20,000	1,000	15 déc. 1653 by Charles de Schomberg (part of the *rente* of 7,964-15-9 above)
28,000	1,400	10 mars 1654 by Charles de Schomberg
20,000	1,000	2 sept. 1653 by François du Foit
106,000	5,300	
Cash 50,000		
156,000 livres		

Marguerite's dowry[42]

Principal	Rente	Constituted
24,000	1,200	31 juillet 1633 by Charles de Schomberg
27,000	1,500	5 juin 1656 by Emmanuel d'Amerton
35,000	1,750	17 déc. 1653 by Louis Brûlart de Sillery (part of *rente* of 2,850 on 57,000 livres)
10,000	500	2 juin 1657 by Michel Particelli
10,000	500	2 avril 1657 by Claude Gallard
106,000	5,450	
Cash 50,000		
156,000 livres		

[40] A.N., M.C., LXXXVI-292: Transport, 26 mars 1654.
[41] A.N., M.C., LXXXVI-294: Donation, 5 fév. 1655.
[42] A.N., M.C., LXXVI-300: Quittance, 20 mai 1658.

chambre du roi.⁴³ Each daughter received the same sized dowry: 156,000 livres. Such were d'Aligre's resources that each dowry was conveyed in full in a single contract, not spread over a number of years to ease the burden. Hélène and Marguerite received one third of their settlements in cash, the remainder in *rentes;* Marie received only 10 per cent in cash. Etienne used twelve *rentes constituées* in composing the dowries, most contracted in recent years: one in 1623, two in 1633, one in 1648, but eight between 1653 and 1657. When it is considered that between 1654 and 1657 he contracted seventeen *rentes constituées*, thus using about half for the dowries, it is again clear that he was well able to cope with the provision of 468,000 livres in a few years. In terms of social status his daughters married exceptionally well. Hélène and Marguerite entered the *noblesse d'épée*, Marie's husband being of the *noblesse de robe* like herself. It would be erroneous to suppose that d'Aligre had 'bought' his daughters into the *épée* for generous as the dowries were, they do not merit the epithet 'spectacular'; compare, for instance, the 156,000 livres that Hélène and Marguerite brought to their marriages, with the 300,000 livres that Michel d'Aligre's second wife brought, and the 240,000 livres of his third wife. There is no hint of *mésalliance* about the marriages of Hélène and Marguerite; their husbands appear to have considered them suitable matches in every respect.

Marguerite's husband, de Manneville, used her dowry to ease his debts, and in so doing persuaded Etienne III to change the nature of the dowry. He owed money to Michel d'Aligre, which he paid off in the form of 1,600 livres in cash and a herring boat based at Dieppe.⁴⁴ He also redeemed a *rente* of 1,500 livres on a principal of 24,000, contracted by his father in 1653. To do so, he persuaded Etienne III to exchange the *rente* of 31 July 1633 in Marguerite's dowry for a lump sum of 24,866 livres (the equivalent of the principal of that *rente*); with this money he redeemed his own *rente*.⁴⁵ He paid off three more debts in this manner: in 1659 he exchanged the *rente* of 2 June 1657 in Marguerite's dowry for 10,722 livres cash, and then redeemed a *rente* that he had been paying;⁴⁶ in 1660 he exchanged the *rente* of 2 April 1657 in the dowry for 10,135 livres to pay off a debt to his uncle, and to redeem yet another *rente* on 6,000 livres which his father had

---

⁴³A.N., Y195, fos. 279-82.
⁴⁴A.N., M.C., LXXXVI-302: Transport, 17 jan. 1659.
⁴⁵A.N., M.C., LXXXVI-302: Retrocession, 1 fév. 1659.
⁴⁶A.N., M.C., LXXXVI-303; Retrocession, 22 oct. 1659.

borrowed in 1634.[47] Marguerite's dowry thus brought considerable financial aid to her husband, but only because her father was willing to alter its provisions.

The Move to the Hôtel Schomberg

Since the earliest years of the century the d'Aligres had resided in the rue d'Avron, whose chief advantage was its closeness to the Louvre. But it was a narrow, unprepossessing street; moreover, the quarter had lost some of its lustre since the great days of Richelieu, for during the Frondes many of its noble residents withdrew for long periods. When Louis XIV succeeded as king, he tended to absent himself from the Louvre in favour of his country seats. Reference will be made in due course to Etienne III's practice of leasing property in and around the rue d'Avron; it is significant that his clients included a glass merchant, a baker, a gunsmith, a wine merchant: solid but unpretentious people.

The opportunity to move into more ostentatious quarters came in August 1656 when Etienne III acquired the Hôtel Schomberg in the rue Saint Honoré, just around the corner from the rue d'Avron.[48] Constructed in the late 1500s or early 1600s, it had been bought in 1609 by Henri de Schomberg, comte de Nanteuil, *surintendant des finances* and *maréchal de France;* he paid 80,000 livres. On his death in 1632 it passed in the proportions of one third to his son Charles and two thirds to his daughter Jeanne; Charles borrowed large amounts of money from Etienne III.[49] Charles died in 1656 leaving both crippling debts of his own, and others inherited from his father. Jeanne was now sole owner of the *hôtel*, but she lived in the rue des Saints Pères with her husband Charles de Rohan, duc de Montbazon. She therefore sold the property to Etienne III for 100,000 livres, using the sum to pay off her brother's debts.[50] D'Aligre moved into the *hôtel* which was nevertheless too large for his own requirements; he thus leased two sections at 1,550 livres and 650 livres respectively;[51] he leased his

---

[47]A.N., M.C., LXXXVI-304: Retrocession, 20 août 1660.

[48]A.N., M260 dossier 6; M.C., LXXXVI-298: Inventaire, 4 jan. 1657.

[49]See Table 7.

[50]The procedure was that Rohan gave d'Aligre details of the debts; Etienne III paid the debts to the amount of 100,000 livres; he did not actually transfer money to Rohan.

[51]A.N., M.C., LXXXVI-300: Bail, 23 mars 1658; LXXXVI-297: Bail, 27 nov. 1656.

Plan of area surrounding the Rue d'Avron

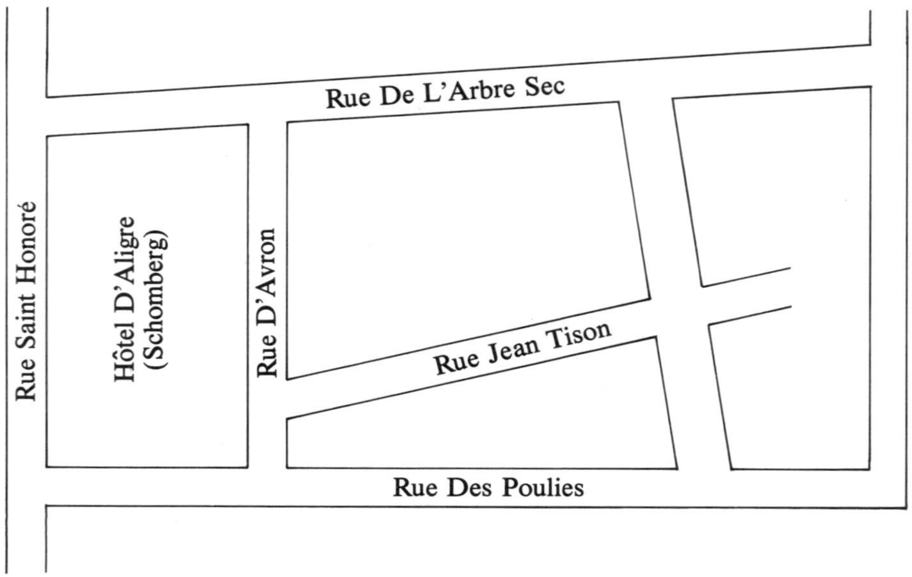

former residence in the rue d'Avron at 3,000 livres.[52] Over recent years he had acquired other property: two more houses in the rue d'Avron leased at 600 and 700 livres,[53] and two in the rue des Poulies leased at 800 and 400 livres.[54] In 1660 he built a third house in the rue des Poulies which he rented out at 900 livres[55] and by 1664 had bought a house in the rue Saint Honoré close to his *hôtel*, which he let at 450 livres.[56] By this date d'Aligre owned seven properties in addition to the *hôtel*, which together brought a return of 6,850 livres a year. If this sum represented about five per cent of their value they were worth about 137,000 livres. They made him one of the main property-owners in that area of Paris.[57]

Etienne III's Land

As we turn from family affairs to questions of property, the most notable feature of d'Aligre's land deals is that, in contrast to the 1630s when lengthy absences from Paris had prevented him from devoting much attention to his land, by the mid-1640s he had made substantial additions mainly near La Rivière. Between 1636 and 1644 in eight transactions he bought the rest of the *seigneurie* of La Fôret near Pontgouin, where he already had a few parcels of land.[58] Held in fief to Maximilien de Béthune, duc de Sully, it included a *château* in five arpents of land, five lakes of 5, 6, 8, 12 and 15 arpents, a watermill and windmill, 3,500 arpents of forest, over 300 arpents of arable land, hunting and fishing rights, and rights of justice.[59] Part he had acquired from Claude de Gruel, sieur de Digny, by transferring to him *rentes constituées* of 444 livres 7 sous 10 deniers; the rest was bought for cash from several people for 20,550 livres. Although La Fôret included a fair portion of arable land, it was the extensive forest that

---

[52] A.N., M.C., LXXXVI-297: Bail, 25 août 1656; LXXXVI-393: Bail, 20 avril 1662.

[53] A.N., M.C., LXXXVI-300: Bail, 21 mars 1658; Bail, 10 mai 1656.

[54] A.N., M.C., LXXXVI-304: Bail, 5 juillet 1660; Bail, 6 août 1660.

[55] A.N., M.C., LXXXVI-304: Bail, 2 juillet 1660.

[56] A.N., M.C., LXXXVI-396: Bail, 30 avril 1664.

[57] The diagram on p. 178 is based on the *Plan de Paris... par Sr. Builet* (Paris, 1710).

[58] The contracts are: A.N., M.C., XXIV-345: Echange, 6 sept. 1636; XXIV-346: Vente, 6 mars 1637; XXIV-347: Retrocession, 15 nov. 1637, XXIV-348: Vente, 1 fév. 1638; XXIV-416: Vente, 12 juin 1640; XXIV-417: Vente, 30 juillet 1640; LXXXVI-273: Quittance, 23 mai 1642; LXXXVI-278: Vente, 6 avril 1644.

[59] A.N., M.C., XXIV-417: Dénombrement, 12 juillet 1640; LXXXVI-378: Dénombrement, 6 fév. 1648.

conferred its character. Most d'Aligre land around La Rivière was arable; a large tract of forest helped to correct the balance, giving the estate a more 'noble' aspect. In 1641 Etienne purchased the tiny *seigneurie* of Clamart in the village of Le Favil; it included just under 64 arpents of land, all of which he bought from a nearby monastery for 2,500 livres.[60] Another substantial acquisition in the parish of Pontgouin came in 1645 when for 15,000 livres he bought the *métairie* of Les Vallées de Boissard: as well the farm house and outbuildings there were 135 arpents of land, of which 97 were arable, 26.6 meadow and pasture, 9 woodland and 2.4 fruit trees.[61]

Away from La Rivière another small *seigneurie* passed into his possession in 1640: La Chapelle d'Aunainville some fifteen miles east of Chartres on the road to Etampes. It was donated to him in return for a life pension of 300 livres a year by a cousin also named Etienne d'Aligre (in honour of the chancellor), a student at the university of Orléans. His education had been paid for by Etienne II; he wanted to continue his studies and proposed the arrangement in order to finance himself.[62]

The final addition to his land in the 1640s by Etienne III came with the death of his brother Louis in 1643. By Louis's will he inherited the immensely wealthy and prestigious *seigneurie* of Boislandry (which, as we have already seen, Etienne transferred to his son Michel in 1651);[63] also land at Uscouan and Neuilly, and various *rentes* whose combined value was 15,000 livres.[64] By the mid-1640s, therefore, Etienne had extended his land holdings considerably. He had done so by acquiring property from local landowners, a monastery, a dependant relation, and his brother. He is an example of a large landowner profiting at the expense of lesser ones. His two brothers had failed to marry, so that the family estates around La Rivière continued to expand, escaping the subdivision that threatened the prosperity of so many families in the seventeenth century.

This process of expansion came to a halt during the Frondes. The anarchy of those years of rebellion created a climate which discouraged land speculation on his part. In any case, his personal and professional preoccupations were such as to divert his attention from the land market. He did, however, make minor adjustments to his holdings. He

[60] A.N., M.C., LXXXVI-270; Vente, 17 juillet 1641.
[61] A.N., M.C., LXXXVI-280: Vente, 6 fév. 1645.
[62] A.N., M.C., LXXXVI-267: Donation, 3 oct. 1640.
[63] See above, p. 173.
[64] A.N., M.C., LXXXVI-277: Accord, 1 déc. 1643.

sold a tiny vineyard at Auteuil just west of Paris, and bought another one.[65] He sold a house at Chartres.[66] He leased out a *seigneurie* at Chenincourt,[67] farmed out his *droits* at Falaise,[68] and let rooms in his residence in the rue d'Avron.[69] Apart from such small-scale arrangements he ceased dealing in property during the Frondes. He judged it wiser to stay his hand, at least for the time being.

Etienne III's Finances up to the Frondes

A survey of d'Aligre's financial position in the mid-1640s shows that he possessed immense resources which, apart from the purchase of land that has just been described, he invested predominantly in *rentes*. There is only one exception to this rule, and it speaks volumes on the values and outlook of a nobleman like d'Aligre: it occurred in 1642 when for 600 livres he bought a one-sixteenth share in a ship operating from Rouen.[70] Otherwise his money went into *rentes*, some of which were on the state. If the year 1647 is taken as an example, just before the Frondes broke out, it emerges that he had investments in state *rentes* totalling about 241,070 livres giving a theoretical annual return of 12,558 livres.[71] He had inherited a small proportion of these sums:

Table 8

1628:	4,740 livres	1636:	2,055
1631:	5,050	1638:	14,836
1632:	11,514	1646:	6,820
1633:	29,175	?	14,545
1634:	44,708		
1635:	91,897	Total	225,340

---

[65] A.N., M.C., LXXXVI-287: Vente, 24 nov. 1651; LXXXVI-288: Vente, 20 avril 1652.

[66] A.N., M.C., LXXXVI-292: Vente, 25 avril 1653.

[67] For seven years at 2,300 livres per annum: A.N., M.C., LXXXVI-292: Bail, 31 août 1654; in fact the *seigneurie* belonged to Charles d'Aligre as *abbé* of Saint Riquier; Etienne probably was acting on his son's behalf.

[68] A.N., M.C., LXXXVI-286: Compte, 16 fév. 1651.

[69] A.N., M.C., LXXXVI-286: Transport, 28 fév. 1651.

[70] A.N., M.C., LXXXVI-272: Transport, 15 mars 1642.

[71] The figures given here are collated from A.N., M.C., LXXXVI-326, 328, which contain details on investments in state *rentes* by the clients of this notary, Parque, and from B.N., Pièces Originales 36, nos. 140-68.

15,315 livres capital giving a *rente* of 1,147 livres. The rest comprised personal investments through sixteen transactions between 1628 and 1646. The sums invested by year were as set out in Table 8. It must be emphasised that the 12,558 livres which by 1647 his state investments generated was a notional figure only, since the state was usually tardy in its payments. *Rentes* due in March 1638 were not forthcoming until August 1639;[72] others due in March 1639 were paid in May 1641;[73] those for March 1641 appeared in February 1643.[74] Some of the sixteenth-century *rentes* he had inherited were hopelessly delayed. He possessed one that had been purchased in 1579; in December 1643 he received the payment due in March 1614![75] With another *rente* of 1588 he did not receive the sum due in June 1638 until March 1645.[76] The 1640s were a particularly bad decade because of the chaos in government finances exacerbated by the strains of war; delays of between three and seven years were common. Nevertheless Etienne III did his financial duty by the crown through investing well over 200,000 livres in state *rentes,* even though considerable risk and delay was attached to them. Nobility might have conferred certain financial privileges, but prosperous nobles were still expected to supply money to the crown in times of crisis, albeit in ways other than taxation.

Even more of Etienne's investment went into *rentes constituées.* Between 1635 and 1647 he entered into thirty-seven contracts, eight of which had been redeemed by 1647. If that year is again taken as an example, he had almost 373,700 livres at loan creating an annual *rente* of 21,400 livres. A glance at the graph illustrates the 'rhythm' of his loans policy. Peaks occurred at roughly three-yearly intervals: 1628, 1630-1, 1634, 1637-8, 1641-3, 1646, 1648. In other words, he would nurse his resources for a couple of years then invest fairly heavily. On balance the levels of his loans were higher after 1636 than before. This is explained by the fact that before 1636 he was regularly purchasing state bonds; with one or two exceptions he invested thereafter only in *rentes constituées.* Within the post-1636 period the years 1641 and 1642 stand out dramatically. Instead of the one or two loans a year which was his usual practice, he signed eleven contracts in 1641 and six in 1642 which together involved an outlay of 174,000 livres on a *rente* of 9,672 livres. Three possibilities may account for

[72] B.N., Pièces Originales 36, no. 144.
[73] *Ibid.,* no. 148.
[74] *Ibid.,* no. 157.
[75] *Ibid.,* no. 161.
[76] *Ibid.,* no. 163.

Fig 1: ETIENNE D'ALIGRE III: INVESTMENT IN 'RENTES', 1626-49

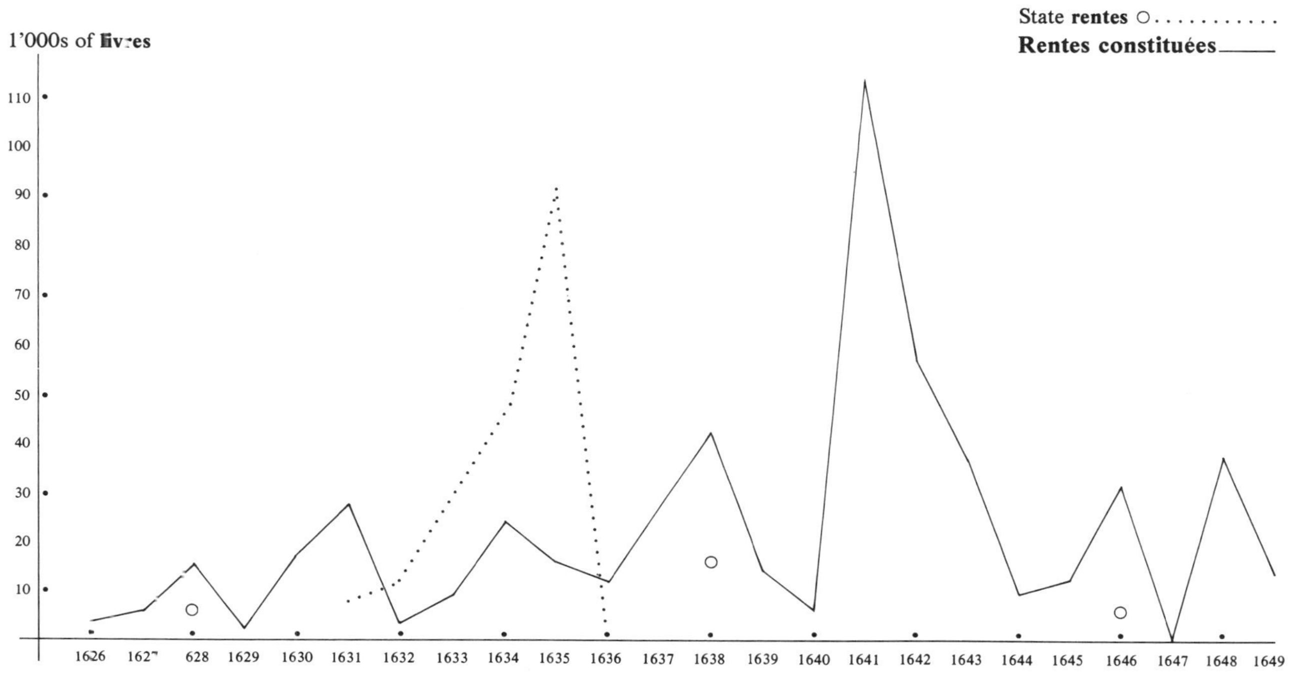

State rentes ○ ········
Rentes constituées ─────

such abundance of funds: he had just completed seven years' service in Normandie for which he would have been rewarded by the crown; his father had recently bequeathed him money; and, as has just been remarked, he was now concentrating his resources on *rentes constituées*.

Another of their features that requires comment is the sudden change in the rate of interest that he charged. From 1626 to the end of 1634 his loans were all at 6.25 per cent interest; at the beginning of 1636 the figure dropped to 5.5 per cent and remained constant, apart from a few loans at 5 per cent, until the mid-1650s. An explanation of this phenomenon must be speculative, but may be found in the state of the Parisian money market around 1635. Government finances were already in a state of confusion when war was declared against Spain, and were to become worse as the war dragged on.[77] Louis XIII resorted to many manipulations of the currency, the most drastic being the 21 per cent devaluation of the *livre tournois* in June 1636.[78] A paradoxical situation developed. On the one hand the exigencies of the government multiplied and had the effect of attracting large amounts of money from abroad; on the other, there emerged a marked reluctance by French investors to put their money into the schemes of a regime at war.[79] Thus a glut of money could have existed in Paris around 1635 and 1636, with investors looking for safe enterprises. If that were the case it could account for d'Aligre's having to lower his rate of interest even when the *livre tournois* had been devalued. Throughout the long war period he received a smaller return on his *rentes constituées* than before 1635. Even so, he concentrated on this form of investment. Family considerations doubtless influenced his thinking. As the father of several daughters, one day he would have to provide marriage dowries. It was a matter of prudence to anticipate the future by setting aside sums which could later be employed to that end.

Etienne III's finances during the Frondes

In contrast to his land deals, which almost ceased during the Frondes, d'Aligre's financial activities continued unabated. In particular he continued to invest in *rentes constituées*. To those listed in Table 9

[77] A valuable discussion is in A. Guéry, 'Les finances de la monarchie française sous l'ancien régime', *Annales E.S.C.,* no. 2 (1978), 216-39.

[78] This and other monetary devices are discussed in R. Pillorget, 'Les problèmes monétaires français de 1602 à 1689', *XVIIe Siècle,* nos. 70-1 (1966), 109-30.

[79] P. Chaunu et R. Gascon, *Histoire Economique et Sociale de la France,* i (Paris, 1977), 188-9.

Table 9

Year	Contracts	Rente	Principal	Year	Cont	Rente	Principal
1648	3	2,100	39,000	1653	4	6,000	228,895
1649	1	606-17-4	13,000	1654	2	1,900	37,000
1650	2	1,066-13-4	19,200	1655	1	500	10,000
1651	3	1,400	25,200	1656	4	3,700	71,000
1652	0	0	0	1657	5	2,500	49,000

should be added a contract of 1649 in which his brother-in-law, François de Courseulles, sieur du Rouvray, transferred to him a *rente* of 1,125 livres in return for 20,000 livres, which du Rouvray needed in order to buy a *lieutenance au régiment des gardes du roi* for one of his sons.[80] There should also be appended another of 1654 when a *conseiller* in the *parlement* of Paris borrowed 20,000 livres in order to buy the same rank for his son.[81] The pre-Fronde strategy that Etienne III followed, whereby every three or four years he loaned heavily, moderating his investments in the intervening years thus continued. The exception is 1652, the most violent year of the Parisian Fronde, when he made no loans. That apart, the social and political turmoil of those years did not interrupt his financial proceedings.

Who borrowed? The 13,000 livres in 1649 went to a monastery at Senlis; the monks redeemed the loan in 1651.[82] Two borrowers were *parlementaires*[83] and three were widows. They included Marie Camus, widow of Particelli d'Emery (who had died in 1650),[84] and Anne du Rour, widow of Charles de Créqui, comte de Canaples.[85] There was one of Etienne's nephews, Louis de Courseulles, sieur de Joudraye-en-Thimerais,[86] and also members of two families prominent in recent history: Louis Brûlart, sieur de Sillery[87] and Armand Léon le Bouthillier.[88] Charles Descoubleau, marquis de Sourdis and

[80] A.N., M.C., LXXXVI-380: Retrocession, 6 mai 1649.

[81] A.N., M.C., LXXXVI-293: Vente, 8 oct. 1654.

[82] A.N., M.C., LXXXVI-381: Constitution, 30 sept. 1649.

[83] A.N., M.C., LXXXVI-382: Constitution, 12 fév. 1650; LXXXVI-388: Constitution, 29 mai 1656.

[84] A.N., M.C., LXXXVI-382: Constitution, 12 fév. 1650; LXXXVI-388: Constitution, 29 mai 1656.

[85] A.N., M.C., LXXXVI-292: Transport, 26 mars 1654 ('Constitution, 20 août 1653').

[86] A.N., M.C., LXXXVI-300: Transport, 8 avril 1658 ('Constitution, 10 juillet 1653').

[87] A.N., M.C., LXXXVI-300: Quittance, 20 mai 1658 ('Constitution, 17 déc. 1653').

[88] A.N., M.C., LXXXVI-387: Constitution, 23 déc. 1655.

governor of Orléans, Blaisois and Chartrain, borrowed from him; most significantly there was Charles de Schomberg, duc d'Halluin and *marechal de France,* who borrowed 153,895 livres from d'Aligre in 1653[89] and other 28,000 soon afterwards.[90] This was the Charles whose *hôtel* passed into d'Aligre's possession in 1656.

---

[89] A.N., M.C., LXXXVI-292: Transport, 26 mars 1654 ('Constitution, 15 déc. 1653').

[90] A.N., M.C., LXXXVI-294: Donation, 6 fév. 1655 ('Constitution, 10 mars 1654').

9

THE FAMILY AND FORTUNE OF ETIENNE D'ALIGRE III IN THE LAST PHASE OF HIS LIFE

The Outlook in the 1660s

The death of Michel d'Aligre in 1661 dealt a hard blow to family prospects. Had he survived, then his would have been the responsibility for overseeing family affairs in the generation following Etienne III; he would have been the natural focal point of the d'Aligres since none of his surviving brothers married and had children. Who now would assume this role? His death also meant that the d'Aligre presence in central government and administration was under threat: Etienne III was approaching his seventieth year, while his grandsons Etienne IV and Gilles as yet were infants. There existed every possibility that after the death of Etienne III a whole generation could pass with no d'Aligre prominent in the service of the king. After such a long absence, was there any realistic prospect that the family would re-emerge in royal service? Although he had produced six sons Etienne III had only three left in 1661, and each was vowed to celibacy. He faced a situation that a few years before looked impossible: the potential disappearance of the male line.

As regards the dual problem of providing a leader during the next generation and safeguarding a d'Aligre presence in government, Etienne III sought a partial answer by advancing one of his remaining sons Charles. Although *abbé* of Saint Riquier, Charles was introduced into central administration so as to preserve a family presence until Etienne IV and Gilles grew to maturity. In addition, his father gradually transferred to him various responsibilities in connection with general family affairs.

Charles d'Aligre (1630-95); the period to 1677

It was while Charles was a student at the Collège de Clermont in Paris that his father acquired for him in 1643 the Benedictine abbey of Saint Riquier; it had been one of Richelieu's benefices until his death that year.[1] The cardinal left it in a lamentable condition. The spiritual

---

[1] Charles was nominated 5 Feb. 1643: see A.N., M.C., LXXXVI-298: Inventaire de titres, 12 mars 1657; A.P.M. Gilbert, *Description Historique de l'Eglise de l'Ancienne Abbaye Royale de Saint-Riquier et Ponthieu* (Amiens, 1836), 173-4.

qualities of the monks left much to be desired, while the buildings were in a state of disrepair after too many years of neglect. Nevertheless, it was a wealthy foundation with potential revenues of some 20,000 livres a year.[2] Charles adopted the usual practice of farming out the revenues. In 1647 a *fermier* contracted to pay him 16,400 livres a year for twelve years, the *fermier* then collecting the abbey dues himself.[3] Charles also leased the *seigneurie* of Chenincourt, a dependancy of the abbey, for 2,300 livres.[4] He thus derived an income of 18,700 livres a year from the abbey. Being so close to the Spanish Netherlands Saint Riquier was vulnerable to attack during the war against Spain. Fortunately it was never assaulted and Etienne III secured its immunity from the billeting of troops;[5] but its security was always in question, and it is highly likely that as long as war continued it produced fewer cash returns than in times of peace.

Reform was in the offing. Charles's brother François, *abbé* of Saint Jacques at Provins, was reinvigorating his own abbey, and was anxious that discipline should be restored at Saint Riquier. He had a powerful ally in his father, for Etienne III was equally keen to see Saint Riquier restored to its former eminence. Charles himself, although only in his teens, fully acquiesced in the lead given by his father and brother, personally accepting the need to transform the abbey. Another and vital source of support was the Benedictine order itself. In 1621 the Congrégation de Saint Maur, had been founded which sought to revitalise the order by strict adherence to monastic rule and renewed devotion to scholarship. The Mauristes were one of the richest seams of the French counter-reformation and deserve much credit for Benedictine renaissance in that country. In 1659 Charles d'Aligre asked the Congregation to undertake reform of Saint Riquier now that the war was over. Dom Harel, superior-general of the Congregation, and Dom Brachet his assistant, visited Saint Riquier to assess its condition. In 1660 they transferred ten Mauristes there, who proceeded to subject the monks to a classic Mauriste programme: absolute observance of monastic discipline and application to scholarship. This latter aspect was assisted by the purchase of books and manuscripts, in particular by the acquisition in 1665 of one of the most extensive private libraries in Abbeville.[6] Physically, much had

[2]*Illustrations Nobiliaires*, 16.

[3] A.N., M.C., LXXXVI-376: Bail, 17 mars 1647.

[4] A.N., M.C., LXXXVI-374: Bail, 15 mai 1646; LXXXVI-293: Bail, 31 août 1654; the leases were for seven years.

[5] A.G., A^{1}142, f. 277.

[6] J. Hénocque, *Histoire de l'Abbaye et de la Ville de Saint-Riquier*, ii (Amiens, 1883), 247-8.

to be done to restore the abbey. To this end Charles revised its finances in 1657. New leases on the revenues were negotiated and the income redistributed: one-third to the monks for their upkeep, two-thirds to Charles for use exclusively in the interests of the abbey.[7] His portion went mainly into a scheme of rebuilding which lasted several decades, the heaviest expenditure coming in the 1680s when Charles's private resources, augmented by his share of Etienne III's succession, were devoted to that end.[8] For the time being, however, a start had been made, the spiritual and physical recovery of Saint Riquier proceeding together.

Meanwhile there occurred in Charles's career a move which in the longer term can be seen to have introduced a new theme into d'Aligre history: in 1660 his father bought for him the office of *conseiller clerc* in the *parlement* of Paris.[9] Etienne II and Etienne III had spent almost all their careers in direct royal service; an exception is the period that Etienne II spent in the *grand conseil*. No member of the family had ever held an office in the *parlement*. From Charles onwards, however, the d'Aligres were to remain *officiers* of the *parlement*, and they were to acquire a sense of obligation to that institution that did not always coexist easily with their loyalty to the king. This is a topic to be discussed later.[10] For the time being it is sufficient to note Charles's acquisition of the office in the greatest of the sovereign courts.

After the death of Michel, Etienne III thought it essential to the family interest that Charles somehow be introduced into central administration, so as to continue the d'Aligre tradition there after his own, Etienne's, decease. The opportunity to advance him arose in 1665. Colbert, conscious that one outstanding obstacle to royal authority was the diversity of legal systems in the country, not to mention the corruption and inefficiency with which much law was administered, in 1665 appointed working parties to study judicial reform.[11] Members, mostly *conseillers d'état*, submitted written proposals and met in groups for discussion. Agreed papers were submitted to a higher committee of some of the most powerful figures in the country: Colbert, la Reynie, Séguier, Boucherat, le Pelletier, le

---

[7] A.N., M.C., LXXXVI-298: Bail, 6 mai 1657 (3 contracts), Hénocque, *Histoire... de Saint-Riquier*, ii, 341.

[8] See below, pp. 206-7.

[9] A.N., M.C., LXXXVI-304: Accord, 12 jan. 1660; the office cost 145,250 livres.

[10] See below, pp. 215-16.

[11] Lavisse, *Histoire de France*, 7 (i), 296-302.

Tellier, were all involved. This committee met the king to produce a policy of judicial reform.[12] Charles d'Aligre was selected to work both with the working parties and as a member of the higher committee, even though he was not yet a *conseiller d'état*. The hand of Etienne III and perhaps even of le Tellier may be seen in this appointment.

Apart from a share in technical discussions, Charles's main contribution to judicial reform was a *mémoire* outlining his own proposals.[13] It dealt in part with the activities of notaries. Since much litigation derived from ambiguous wording in contracts and wills, Charles urged that notaries be obliged to use clear, precise language and to keep copies of all their contracts. He further pressed the government to apply all existing legislation on notaries, especially that which required them to pay to the government a charge of five sous per contract. To forestall disputes over wills which involved land, copies of a will with a sizeable entailment of land should, on the death of the testator, be lodged with the *présidial* nearest to the testator and with the *présidial* nearest to the land in question. The *mémoire* also included suggestions designed to speed up the process of appeals. Instead of appeals going from one court to its immediate superior and so on through the hierarchy, they should go immediately from a lower court to a *présidial*. *Procureurs* should be authorised to pass judgement on behalf of the *présidiaux* in cases involving less than 500 livres, and provisional judgement (simply requiring ratification by a *présidial*) in cases involving up to 1,000 livres. The *droit de committimus* (the right of many *officiers* to have a case heard before a certain high court) should be disallowed where less than 100 livres were at stake. Finally, the *mémoire* turned to the higher courts. Since the *présidiaux* and *parlements* followed such different and individual procedures that no individual could know them all in detail, and considering that there were many judges and other officers in these courts who were well-disposed towards reform, judges and others should be invited to submit views on the weaknesses of their particular courts along with any ideas on reform; in other words, reform should proceed in cooperation with the courts rather than be imposed from outside. Within the courts, work should be distributed among officials as evenly as possible so as to minimise delays; judges should moderate their costs; individual families should not monopolise offices in individual courts; the king's council should refuse to accept appeals from lower courts when the judges of those courts were competent to rule.

[12] Clément (éd.), *Lettres... de Colbert*, vi, 18-19, 369.
[13] *Ibid.*, 18-19; an early draft is in B.N., Collection Clairambault 613, fos. 3-16.

Charles presumably discussed the *mémoire* with his father before submitting it. It was overwhelmingly practical and moderate in character; it eschewed abstractions or radical propositions. It included no criticism of the overall structure of judicial practice in France, no assessment of the courts in their relationship to the crown and its subjects. Its constant stress was upon the more efficient exercise of existing powers by the courts. If it contained nothing that would spark off a new train of thought in Colbert's fertile mind, it equally contained little that would displease him. There is one possible exception. The last clause of the *mémoire* suggested that the chancellor, as 'chef et protecteur de la justice', was the most appropriate figure to head a programme of reform. This contradicted Colbert's views on the chancellorship. Since 1661 he had steadily deprived the tired and aged Séguier of many of his functions: Séguier no longer attended the king's inner council, he had lost his financial responsibilities, the administration of waterways and forests had passed into Colbert's hands.[14] Colbert's 'revolution of government' involved reducing the chancellorship to a formal position of no real power; he was therefore bound to object to any notion that the chancellor should head an important reform of the judiciary. Yet Charles's proposal was consistent with the conservative tone of the rest of the document; the orthodox reasoning of the *mémoire* leads naturally to the orthodox contention that the official head of the judiciary should be responsible for implementing reform.

The precise nature of Charles's role in Colbert's search for ideas on the judiciary may have cast him as a small cog; but the machine was unquestionably exceedingly powerful. He had at last operated at the very core of government and in association with one of the two or three most influential men in the kingdom. His aspirations in this direction were encouraged within a few years: in 1672 he was promoted to the much-sought ranks of the *conseillers d'état*, being made immediately an *ordinaire*, without having to follow the more conventional route of *maître des requêtes* and *conseiller d'état semestre*.[15]

At this stage of Charles's life there is one other development that should be noted. His father, wishing to relinquish the day-to-day management of his extensive financial interests, chose not to employ an *intendant*, but Charles. In 1661 he handed over to his son the supervision of his finances and the tutorship of Etienne IV and

---

[14]Antoine, *Le Conseil du Roi*, 46-53.
[15]B.N., MS Français, 7654, fos. 3, 32, 133; A.N., X8659, f. 122.

Gilles;[16] in 1667 he added the management of his property.[17] Although Etienne continued to deal in property and cash transactions to the day of his death, the administration of the resulting contracts was left to Charles. Etienne's transfer of responsibilities to Charles no doubt owed something to his recognition of his own declining powers: at the age of eighty years or so, he could not be expected to attend to his personal affairs with the same acumen as in the past. At the same time, he was grooming Charles to assume charge of general family interests when Etienne was gone. Charles acquired a close and detailed knowledge of his father's affairs, so that when Etienne eventually died, there would be somebody capable of assuming direction of his interests in property and finance, and of bringing a comprehensive view of those interests to the affairs of the family as a whole.

Etienne III's Property in the 1660s

The Frondes had forced Etienne III to suspend activities on the property market, but the social and political stability of the late 1650s and 1660s enabled him to make a fresh start. One feature has already emerged: his purchase of property in Paris whereby he developed substantial holdings adjacent to his *hôtel* in the rue Saint Honoré. It bears the marks of a conscious policy. Evidently he had decided that property in post-Fronde Paris was something into which he should sink capital. In the 1660s he bought other houses, this time for his own use when in attendance at the royal court; they were at Fontainebleau, Versailles and Saint Germain.[18] One of Louis XIV's highest priorities was the creation of the most spectacular court in Europe. His movement from one royal *château* to another with his enormous entourage stimulated the property market in adjoining towns; Versailles in particular, but Fontainebleau and Saint Germain too profited as courtiers and others sought residences. Being in a stronger financial position than most d'Aligre was able to purchase three houses outright.[19] They testified to his closeness to the king, that he was one

---

[16] A.N., M.C., LXXXVI-305: Procuration, 6 juillet 1661.

[17] A.N., M.C., LXXXVI-401: Procuration, 1 juin 1667.

[18] The house in Fontainebleau was bought in 1661, that in Saint Germain in 1668; the house in Versailles was bought for about 31,800 livres (A.N., M.C., LXXV-408: Inventaire de Charles d'Aligre, 7 juin 1695 [Papiers privés, nos. 25, 37, 262]).

[19] By contrast Charles Descoubleau, marquis d'Aluys, in 1670 borrowed 8,000 livres from Etienne III, to buy a house at Versailles (A.N., M.C., LXXXVI-408: Constitution, 19 juin 1670).

of that elite body, 'the court'. One other house came into his possession as part of the sorry tale of the financial plight of the du Rouvrays.[20] It was in Rouen and was bought from his nephew in 1665 for 17,000 livres as a means of easing du Rouvray debt.[21]

At the same time as he was investing in urban property after the Frondes, d'Aligre resumed his acquisition of land. In 1656 he bought the *seigneurie* of Gambaiseul about half way between Dreux and Versailles;[22] five years later he purchased a house attached to the *seigneurie*, for 2,100 livres.[23] He kept this estate until 1677 when he sold it for 15,000 livres.[24] Again in 1656 he added to his land near Chartres by purchasing the small *seigneurie* of Les Bois Auneau just outside the city, for 7,400 livres.[25] In neither instance is the area of the *seigneurie* known, but it cannot have been very extensive. The following year he made his last land purchase of the 1650s: a *métairie*, 'vulgairement appelée l'Etangcheau' near Champrond; he paid 4,000 livres for the buildings and ninety arpents.[26] In the 1660s two more *seigneuries* passed into his ownership. They were well to the west of anything he possessed so far, deep in Le Perche and on the banks of the Eure. One, which he bought in 1667, was La Lande, about five miles north-east of Longny-au-Perche. It must have been a large estate, for he leased it for eight years at 4,500 livres per annum during the first four years, and at 5,000 livres per annum during the remainder; that suggests a value of between 90,000 and 100,000 livres.[27] The other, Manou, he acquired in 1668;[28] nothing can be said as to the value or size of this *seigneurie*.[29] Closer to Paris he acquired property in the village of Auteuil through a series of transactions beginning in 1651 when he bought a house and parcel of land. He added to the land, which backed onto the Bois de Boulogne,

[20] A.N., M.C., LXXXVI-418: Constitution, 19 mars 1675.

[21] See below, p. 208.

[22] A.N., M.C., LXXXVI-388: Procuration, 6 mai 1656; B.N., MS Français 20567, f. 49; it was leased on 13 juin 1656 at 700 livres (5.4% if we evaluate the land minus the house at 13,000 livres).

[23] A.N., M.C., LXXVI-305: Vente, 18 juin 1661.

[24] A.N., M.C., LXXXVI-422: Vente, 28 mars 1677.

[25] A.N., M.C., LXXXVI 297: Transport, 25 nov. 1656.

[26] A.N., M.C., LXXXVI-298; Accord, 18 juin 1657.

[27] A.N., M.C., LXXXVI-403: Procuration, 5 sept. 1667; LXXXVI-403: Bail, 23 déc. 1667.

[28] A.N., M.C., LXXXVI-405: Procuration, 18 juillet 1668.

[29] A description of the *château* is in P. Siguret, *Manoirs et Châteaux des Cantons de Courville et de la Loupe* (Cahiers Percherons, xvi, 1960), 30-1.

in 1652, 1653, 1654, 1668 and 1676; in 1652 and 1660 the king also made him gifts of land there.[30] The whole – the house and land (mostly vineyards) – covered about eight arpents and was worth 40,000 livres.[31] It would have been leased at about 3,200 livres.

Etienne III's Finances in the 1660s

The late 1650s and 1660s were a period of exceedingly heavy expenditure by d'Aligre on property of various types, and on the marriage settlements which he bestowed on his daughters. What effect did this have on his *rentes constituées*? Firstly can be shown the number of *rentes* which he contracted at this period.

Table 10

Year	Contracts	Rente	Principal
1658	0	0	0
1659	4	2,891-13-4	52,650
1660	1	300	5,400
1661	0	0	0
1662	2	2,000	38,000
1663	4	2,450	47,800
1664	0	0	0
1665	4	3,100	62,000
1666	2	500	11,000
1667	2	300	6,000
1668	0	0	0
1669	1	600	12,000
1670	3	600	12,000

The figures given in Table 10, which can also be expressed on a graph to be compared with that for the years 1626-49,[32] afford answers to the question. The same general practice as before emerges, of d'Aligre making heavy loans every three or four years, but easing off in the intervening period; there is the difference, however, in that after the Frondes the contrasts between the peak years (1653, 1656, 1659, 1665) and those in between, are more pronounced than for the period 1626-49. This is because the 'peaks' in the latter years not only

---

[30] A.N., M.C., LXXXVI-424: Décharge, 24 juin 1678.
[31] A.N., M.C., LXXXVI-424: Vente, 24 juin 1678.
[32] See above, p. 183.

Fig 2: ETIENNE D'ALIGRE III: RENTES CONSTITUÉES, 1648-70

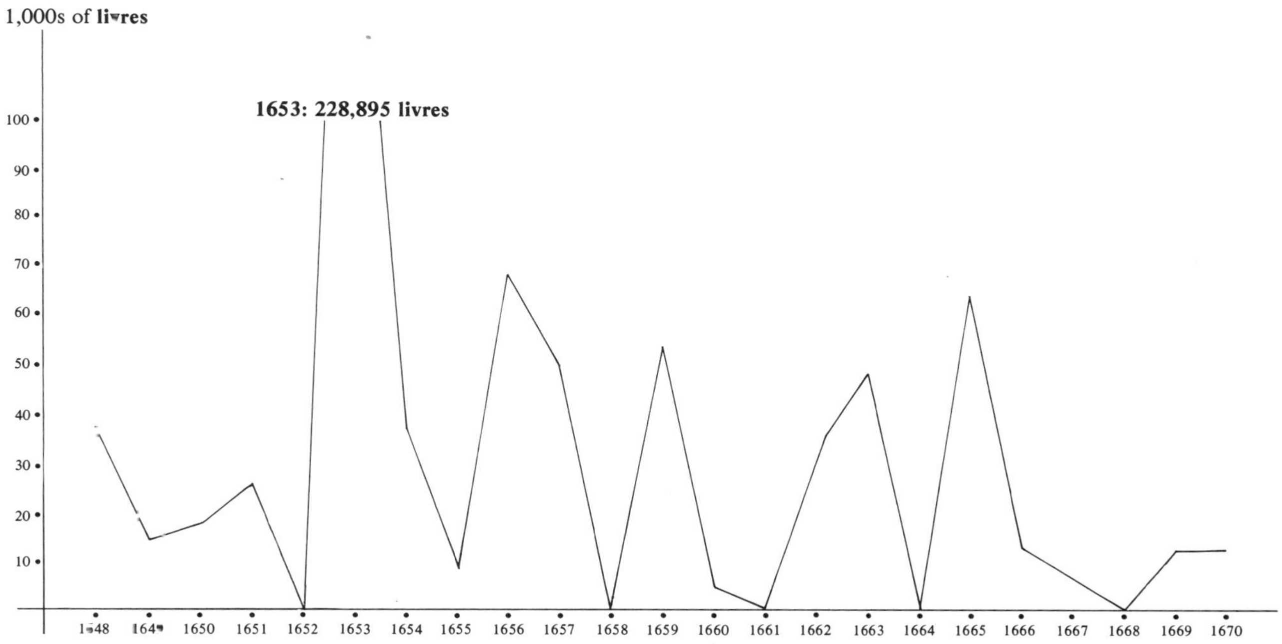

1,000s of livres

1653: 228,895 livres

were higher on the whole than between 1626 and 1649, but also the 'valleys' too were more pronounced; before and during the Frondes (that is between 1626 and 1653) there were only two years, 1647 and 1652, when he made no loans, whereas after the Frondes he suspended investment in *rentes constituées* in 1658, 1661, 1664 and 1668. So, although the broad features of d'Aligre's loans through the medium of the *rente constituée* were unaffected by his alternative investments in the late 1650s and 1660s, there were more 'fallow' years in the latter decade than in those which preceded it.

In other respects the traditions associated with his *rentes constituées* in the 1620s, 1630s and 1640s continued. He still loaned on average three to four times a year, and still to the kinds of people who had been his 'clients' in those earlier decades. Between 1659 and 1670 inclusive, he was involved in twenty-three contracts: five concerned his relations, mostly the du Rouvrays, now deeply in debt to him; six provided loans to nobles and five to aristocrats (Armand-Léon le Bouthillier, comte de Chavigny; Guy du Bar, governor of Amiens; Léon Potier, marquis de Bosuret, governor of Maine; François de Boullainvilliers, comte de Saint Sair; Paul Descoubleau, marquis d'Aluys, governor of Orléans); two involved *conseillers* in the *parlements* of Paris and Metz, two more concerned widows, another a musketeer and one a *maître ferrurier*. D'Aligre, in short, remained a source of funds to people from the upper reaches of society, his family, and members of the *robe*. He was an important channel through which funds flowed to nobles and aristocrats in a society in which such people did not always have ready access to large amounts of cash. If only in a restricted sense he provided certain banking services to nobles and aristocrats who could borrow from him while keeping their reputations intact.

D'Aligre's Financial Provisions for his Family

As he approached and then entered his eighties Etienne III began to make certain financial arrangements affecting different members of his family; this was in addition to handing over to Charles d'Aligre much of the administration of his personal affairs. Some decisions took immediate effect, while others were to be held in abeyance until after his death. One move concerned Charles himself. On 30 April 1675 Etienne transferred to him 44,000 livres. It was given in the form of a *rente constituée*, Charles contracting to pay his father 2,000 livres a year, having received an immediate payment of the sum by his father. By a family compact of July 1680 – that is after the death of

Etienne III – the *rente* was annulled, the 44,000 livres thus being converted into a straightforward gift.³³ In February 1677 Charles was also the beneficiary of yet another gift theoretically of 182,666 livres; but there were subtracted the 120,000 livres which Etienne paid in 1661 when he purchased for his son the office of *conseiller clerc* in the *parlement*; the remaining 62,666 livres would come to Charles after his father's death.³⁴ On 24 July 1677 the chancellor transferred to Charles the income from the *seigneurie* of one of his debtors, Charles Desguez, sieur de la Potinière.³⁵ Finally, Charles assumed receipt of a *rente constituée* of 400 livres on a principal of 7,204 livres that had been paid to his father since 1641.³⁶ Thus, either immediately or in the form of promises Charles received fixed sums or principals amounting to 113,870 livres. Much of this he devoted to the rebuilding of Saint Riquier, but he also employed 23,000 livres to buy out Charles Desguez.³⁷

Marguerite, Hélène and Marie d'Aligre each received 40,000 livres in the form of *rentes constituées* converted into gifts by the agreement of July 1680,³⁸ plus other payments. Marguerite and her husband were donated a state *rente* of 6,000 livres which Etienne III had purchased in January 1677.³⁹ Marie, now a widow, was provided with 27,500 livres to buy the charge of *maître des reqûetes* for her son Michel; once again this was as a *rente constituée* annulled in July 1680, Marie retaining the principal.⁴⁰ Between them, Charles and his sisters profited by over 336,000 livres.

Other of Etienne's children were given pensions. Jean, a Knight of Malta, was to receive 2,300 livres a year after Etienne's death,⁴¹ plus the *seigneurie* of Manou.⁴² Elisabeth, abbess of Saint Cyr, had been paid a pension of 400 livres since 1654;⁴³ to this would be added

---

[33] A.N., M.C., LXXXVI-418: Constitution, 30 avril 1675.
[34] A.N., M.C., LXXXVI-422: Consentement, 16 fév. 1677.
[35] A.N., M.C., LXXXVI-423: Transport, 24 juillet 1677; the income is unknown.
[36] A.N., M.C., LXXXVI-423: Transport, 10 août 1677.
[37] A.N., M.C., LXXXVI-423: Vente, 4 oct. 1677.
[38] A.N., M.C., LXXXVI-422: Constitution, 5 juin 1677, 23 juin 1677.
[39] A.N., M.C., LXXXVI-422: Donation, 23 juin 1677.
[40] A.N., M.C., LXXXVI-423: Constitution, 15 sept. 1677.
[41] A.N., Y190, f. 148 (1653), Y193, fos. 81ᵛ-82 (1656): M.C., LXXXVI-296: Donation, 8 jan. 1661.
[42] A.N., M.C., LXXXVI-416: Donation, 18 mars 1674.
[43] A.N., M.C., LXXXVI-293: Transport, 4 août 1654.

1,000 livres a year after Etienne's decease, the same sum also going to her sister Françoise, who was likewise a nun at Saint Cyr.[44] It has already been noted that François, *abbé* of Saint Jacques, was bequeathed much of Etienne's library.

The provisions that have just been outlined represent the first phase of the division of d'Aligre's possessions. Most of the contracts in which they were embodied were drawn up in 1677, a few months before his death, the money and property involved being worth over a third of a million livres. Accepting that he was approaching the end of his life, he began the process of distributing his wealth within the family, leaving his children to continue the division as indeed they did in the months following 25 October 1677.

His Estate in 1677

This is an appropriate stage at which to attempt a summary of d'Aligre's land and other possessions in 1677. It must be admitted that a certain degree of speculation is inevitable, for there have survived none of the documents listing property that conventionally are employed in such an exercise. There is no *inventaire après-décès*, no *acte de partage* for Etienne III.

a) Urban property

The chief features of his urban possessions have already been noted: the acquisition of houses in Paris and elsewhere, notably near the royal palaces. The value of the *hôtel* and other properties in Paris will be taken as 237,000 livres, plus an estimated 30,000 livres for the contents of the *hôtel*.[45] That gives a grand total of 267,000 livres; the annual return on the leased property will be taken as 9,050 livres.

The houses at Versailles, Saint Germain and Fontainebleau will be assumed to have had a joint value of 90,000 livres,[46] and their contents one of 30,000 livres. The house at Rouen was worth 17,000 livres, and was leased at 430 livres. That at Auteuil with its land has been assessed at 40,000 livres, with an annual return of some 3,200 livres. In the total picture of d'Aligre's property, his houses in Paris

---

[44] A.N., M.C., LXXXVI-416: Donation, 18 mars 1674.

[45] The 30,000 livres are based on the same assumption as when Etienne II's property was evaluated i.e. that the contents of a house are about one-third of its value.

[46] That at Versailles was worth 31,800 livres; the other two have been ascribed a similar but smaller value.

and elsewhere will be calculated on the basis of a total value of 444,000 livres and an annual return of 12,680 livres.

b) **'Seigneuries' and other land**

Firstly, what land did he own? This is listed in Table 11.

Table 11

Title[47]	Estimated Value	Title	Estimated Value
La Rivière (with Pontgouin & Le Favril	165,213	La Forêt	30,000
		La Chapelle d'Aunainville	6,000
Clamart	2,500		
Manou	?	Néron	140,500
La Lande	100,000	Les Bois Auneau	7,400
Chartres	14,000	Neuilly	3,000
Champrond	4,000		

The known or estimated values of this land in round figures come to 472,600 livres, which on a 5 per cent annual return (which will be taken as an average) would have raised the equivalent of some 23,000 livres a year. This is a conjectural figure, but as far as the writer can ascertain, it does not exaggerate d'Aligre's income from land. La Rivière, of course, remained the principal *seigneurie* from which he took his title. After his father's death in 1635 he rarely went there. Yet through his wives and children he maintained links with the area and its people. D'Aligres frequently appear in local baptismal records as godfathers or godmothers to the children of tenants or minor *officiers*.[48] That Etienne III personally was an absentee landowner should not be taken to imply that he and his family were virtually unknown in the area.

c) **Offices**

In the strictest sense Etienne III was no longer an *officier* by the time he died; he had long since moved beyond that status. The posts of

[47] In this list the values for La Fôret, La Chapelle and La Lande are estimates based on the rates of leases; the value of La Rivière is the 1684 rate, Clamart is the 1641 rate, Néron the 1681 rate, and Les Bois Auneau the 1656 rate; these are the dates for which hard evidence is available.

[48] A.D., Eure-et-Loir, Commune du Favril, GG1, 2, 7; Commune de Pontgouin GG1-3, 5, 6, 9, contain many examples.

conseiller d'état, directeur des finances, garde des sceaux and *chancelier de France* were all *charges* to which he was appointable and removable by the king (excepting the chancellorship, from which he could not be dismissed). None was in any sense 'property' as were *offices*. Yet he did own the titles to some minor provincial offices which he leased out. Some were attached to the administration of the *cinq grosses fermes* which he leased at 3,300 livres a year;[49] in 1671 he purchased for 1,082 livres a share in the office of *greffier civil et criminel* in the *bailliage* of Meaux, on which he presumably drew a few hundred livres each year.[50] In the same category, although not as an office, may be listed the 3,100 livres he drew each year on the *droits de cuir* of Falaise and other towns in Normandie, which he had inherited from Jeanne l'Huillier.[51] The income from his *charges* is impossible to calculate with certainty. As chancellor he received at least 110,000 livres a year in *gages* and *droits*,[52] but his income as *directeur des finances*, for instance, is not known. As *conseiller d'état* his *appointements* had been 5,600 livres and 10,800 when *doyen*;[53] in addition he would have received extra payments for extraordinary missions, such as to the General Assembly of the Clergy. A key question that is unanswerable yet which should be posed, concerns his years as *directeur des finances*: did any of the money that passed through his hands, stick? In his defence it must be admitted that he had a reputation for honesty that was never queried,[54] and that he was retained in the *conseil des finances* after Foucquet's arrest, not being implicated in the *surintendant's* peculation. During the 1650s in particular, d'Aligre's correspondence indicates such a shortage of money in the royal coffers, that it is hard to see how very much could have ben filched; if anything he was having to place some of his private funds at the disposal of the king.[55] On the other hand, seventeenth-century notions on the management of public finance were not those of the twentieth century. It is by no means inconceivable that funds were directed into his personal resources in a fashion that was irregular but tolerable. Certainly the scale of his loans in the 1650s and 1660s indicates that he had large surplus funds at his disposal. If

---

[49] A.N., M.C., LXXXVI-402: Bail, 3 juin 1667; the offices would be worth about 66,000 livres.

[50] A.N., M.C., LXXXVI-410: Vente, 26 mai 1671.

[51] e.g. A.N., M.C., LXXXVI-396: Bail, 17 mai 1664.

[52] B.N., MS Français 7654, fos. 1-2.

[53] *Ibid.*, f. 19.

[54] See above, p. 122.

[55] Dent, *Crisis in Finance*, 149.

he did practise financial legerdemain from time to time, it was within accepted limits, and in accordance with current standards.

d) **'Rentes'**

In 1677 d'Aligre was being paid *rentes constituées* on seventy-six contracts: one of 1627, one of 1628, fifteen between 1630 and 1639 inclusive, twelve between 1640 and 1649, twenty between 1650 and 1659, seventeen between 1660 and 1669, and ten between 1670 and 1677. These exclude the 'gifts' to his children temporarily cast as *rentes constituées*. They represent an annual return of 42,927 livres on a capital of 789,693 livres; since the sums made over to his family in the 1670s totalled some 336,000 livres, it means that he had on loan to other people about 1,125,700 livres. The types of people who borrowed have emerged frequently in this study: aristocrats, members of the *robe*, nobles and others from the neighbourhood of La Rivière, and people related by marriage. It was these two latter groups who were most vulnerable to the burden of debt and could find themselves having to surrender land. This happened to Charles Desguez, sieur de la Potinière, a *gentilhomme de la chambre du roi*. His *seigneuries* of La Potinière, La Lande et Marsolières, were close to La Rivière. Not only had he personal difficulties over the volume of his debt to d'Aligre, he also inherited from his father obligations amounting to 41,850 livres which he managed to pay off in 1656.[56] Parisian notarial records tell only part of the story of how indebted to Etienne III he became, but clearly it led to a crisis, for in 1667 some of his *seigneuries* – La Lande et Marsolières – passed into d'Aligre's possession;[57] there had been a court case (perhaps over debt) with the tribunal granting the land to d'Aligre. In 1672 Desguez is found redeeming another debt of 24,381 livres,[58] and in 1676 his wife one of 26,575 livres.[59] By 1677 he had transferred to Etienne III the income from his remaining *seigneurie* of La Potinière.[60] Still his predicament continued. Shortly before Etienne III's death he paid off another 8,997 livres,[61] but the heaviest blow came when he was forced to sell his last *seigneurie* to Charles d'Aligre for 23,000 livres.[62]

---

[56] A.N., M.C., LXXXVI-296: Rachat, 24 juin 1656.

[57] A.N., M.C., LXXXVI-403: Procuration, 5 sept. 1667.

[58] A.N., M.C., LXXXVI-412: Transport, 13 avril 1672.

[59] A.N., M.C., LXXXVI-421: Constitution, 18 août 1676.

[60] Etienne in turn transferred it to Charles: A.N., M.C., LXXXVI-423: Transport, 24 juillet 1677.

[61] A.N., M.C., LXXXVI-423: Transport, 4 oct. 1677.

[62] A.N., M.C., LXXXVI-423: Vente, 4 oct. 1677.

As regards state *rentes*, Etienne III remained circumspect in later years as in earlier. He did invest, but at a rate lower than in *rentes constituées*. In the mid-1640s he had been drawing a theoretical sum of 12,558 livres a year on his state bonds, in which he had invested 225,340 livres.[63] In later decades he made only two adjustments to these figures: in 1659 he purchased another *rente* of 2,000 livres, which suggests an investment of 25,000 livres;[64] In 1669 he bought from his nephew and great-nephew, François and Louis de Courseulles, their state *rentes* of 1,726 livres, whose principal would have been about 21,500 livres.[65] In round figures that leaves a total state *rente* of 16,284 livres on 271,840 livres.

Summary

The sums in the foregoing pages are summarised in Table 12.

Table 12

Source	Value	%	Annual Return	%
Urban property	444,000	21.7	12,680	5.2
Seigneuries & land	472,600	23.1	23,000	9.4
Offices and charges	66,000	3.3	150,000	61.2
Rentes constituées	789,693	38.6	42,927	17.5
State rentes	271,840	13.3	16,284	6.7
	2,044,133		244,891	

Just as when Etienne II's fortune was estimated, the policy here has been to underestimate Etienne III's assets. It may be asserted with confidence, therefore, that altogether he was worth well in excess of two million livres. The figures for his income are far less reliable. For one thing, the 150,000 livres on *charges* is applicable only to the years from 1672 when he was *garde des sceaux* and chancellor; in the years before 1672 something of the order of 50,000 livres might have been the case. Again, the income from state *rentes* is theoretical rather than actual, for the state continued to be tardy in its payments.[66] His income in any one year could further be affected by creditors redeeming large *rentes constituées*. The extraordinary duties that he performed for the crown would also be remunerated, although not

---

[63] See above, p. 181.
[64] B.N., Pièces Originales 36, no. 198.
[65] A.N., M.C., LXXXVI-406: Vente, 12 avril 1669.
[66] See above, p. 182.

necessarily straight away. In short, d'Aligre's annual income probably fluctuated considerably, so that no year or group of years could be depicted as 'typical'. In overall terms Etienne III in 1677 was worth roughly twice what his father had been in 1635. He died an exceedingly wealthy man, proof if any were needed, that those who flourished in the service of the king would not go unrewarded.

The Division of his Property

Although documentary references speak of a will and the preparation of an inventory of his possessions,[67] these are not extant; it is also doubtful whether the inventory was ever completed. Yet it is possible to outline at least the principles which governed the division of his property by the family, even if most of the details are lost. It has already been seen that those daughters who were nuns were guaranteed life pensions, and that Jean d'Aligre, a Knight of Malta, was to inherit the *seigneurie* of Manou. François, in addition to the library, was later provided with a life pension of 3,000 livres by his brothers and sisters.[68] Otherwise Etienne III's property and fortune were apportioned between Charles, Marie (widow of de Verthamon), Hélène and her husband de l'Aubespine, Marguerite and her husband de Manneville, and Etienne III's grandsons Etienne IV and Gilles, represented by their mother Madeleine Blondeau.[69] The principle they adopted was to divide the inheritance into six equal portions.[70] Each would therefore receive property, *rentes* and so forth, of a capital value of over 340,000 livres. Some of the property they converted into cash by selling it off: the house and land at Auteuil went for 40,000 livres[71] and the *seigneurie* of Néron for 140,000 livres.[72] The principal *seigneurie* of La Rivière went in the first instance to Charles,[73] who later transferred it to his sister Marguerite;[74] she in turn sold it to her nephew Etienne IV for 165,213 livres.[75] The hôtel d'Aligre was

[67] A.N., M.C., LXXXVI-424: Procuration, 28 jan. 1678; LXXXVI-425: Extrait d'inventaire, 25 août 1678.

[68] A.N., M.C., LXXXVI-425: Extrait d'inventaire, 25 août 1678.

[69] S.N., M.C., LXXXVI-424: Procuration, 8 jan. 1678.

[70] A.N., M.C., LXXXVI-425: Extrait d'inventaire, 25 août 1678.

[71] A.N., M.C., LXXXVI-424: Vente, 24 juin 1678.

[72] A.N., M.C., LXXXVI-431: Quittance, 10 fév. 1681.

[73] A.N., M.C., LXXXVI-426: Procuration, 27 fév. 1679.

[74] A.N., Y239, fos. 399-401.

[75] A.N., M.C., LXXV-408: Inventaire de Charles d'Aligre, 7 juin 1695 ('Papiers privés', no. 70).

settled on Etienne IV and Gilles to the proportion of four-fifths; the remaining fifth belonged to Charles, who in 1680 conferred it upon his nephews.[76] In that year Charles moved his residence to the rue des Saints Pères,[77] and the *hôtel* appears to have been used very little until the *grand conseil* leased it in 1686; the *conseil* stayed there until 1754 when the poor condition of the neglected building forced it to leave.[78] The inheritors to Etienne III's estate engaged in a series of subsequent arrangements whereby, for instance, Charles acquired the house in Fontainebleau and two in the rue des Poulies,[79] Marguerite acquired one in the rue d'Avron[80] and another adjoining the hôtel d'Aligre.[81] At this remove it is impossible to say further to what extent the settlement was refined, but the chief strategy is clear: a straightforward division into six equal shares.

---

[76] A.N., M.C., LXXXVI-426: Bail, 1 avril 1679: LXXV-408: Inventaire de Charles d'Aligre, 7 juin 1695 ('papiers privés', no. 24).

[77] A.N., M.C., LXXXVI-429: Transport, 31 juillet 1680.

[78] Antoine, *Guide des Recherches,* 42.

[79] A.N., M.C., LXXXVI-425: Bail, 28 août 1678; LXXXVI-426: Bail, 6 mai 1679; LXXV-408: Inventaire de Charles d'Aligre, 7 juin 1695 ('Papiers privés', nos. 24, 25, 27).

[80] A.N., M.C., LXXXVI-425: Bail, 30 nov. 1678.

[81] A.N., M.C., LXXXVI-427: Bail, 23 nov. 1679.

10

THE FAMILY AFTER ETIENNE D'ALIGRE III

The death of Etienne III by no means exhausts the themes to be explored in this study. Others remain, even if their treatment must be relatively sketchy. Before they are attempted, however, some final words on his children are required. An early beneficiary of the wealth distributed after 1677 was his daughter Marie, now a widow in her mid-forties, with a son. The receipt of one-sixth of her father's fortune favoured her in her search for another husband. Noted equally for her asperity as for her ambition, she selected her 'victim', as Bussy Rabutin dubbed him,[1] in the ageing (he was seventy-one) but immensely prestigious Godefroi, comte d'Estrades, *maréchal de France, chevalier des ordres du roi,* governor of Dunkerque and duc de Chartres. D'Estrades at the time stood at the centre of international affairs as *premier ambassadeur extraordinaire et plénipotentière* of the king at the negotiations being conducted at Nimegen, a charge which effectively placed him at the head of the French delegation.[2] It is easy to appreciate his appeal to Marie: he was close to the king and would confer great prestige on his wife. Her chief attraction to him can be described in one word: money. D'Estrades was plagued by incessant financial crises, exacerbated by the extravagances of his son Louis, and by the heavy cost of maintaining himself and his entourage in suitable style at Nimegen. So desperate was his situation that he was contemplating the sale of his governorship of Dunkerque.[3] Marie d'Aligre, disagreeable as was her character, represented nothing less than financial salvation. Throughout marriage discussions with Marie he remained in Nimegen, his son Louis acting on his behalf. Marie agreed to the match, a contract being signed on 8 June 1678. It is a remarkable document, not in its clauses which are of a routine nature, but in the list of witnesses who signed it. They included the king himself, the queen, the dauphin, the duc d'Orléans and his wife Elisabeth Charlotte, Michel le Tellier, now chancellor of France, and his son Louvois.[4] This was the most illustrious gathering ever to grace

---

[1] Bussy Rabutin wrote of d'Estrades: 'Pour cent mille francs il avait bien vendu sa vieille peau'; see A. de Saint Léger et L. Lemaire (éds.), *Correspondance Authentique de Godefroi, Comte d'Estrades de 1637 à 1660,* i (Paris, 1924), xi-xii.

[2] See G. Livet, 'Colbert de Croissy et la diplomatie française à Nimègue (1675-1679)', *The Peace of Nijmegen, 1676-1678/79* (International Congress of the Tricentennial, Amsterdam, 1980), 181-223.

[3] Saint Léger (éd.), *Correspondence. . . de Godefroi, Comte d'Estrades,* i, xi-xii.

[4] A.N., M.C., CII-94: Contrat de mariage, 8 juin 1678.

an event in the private history of the d'Aligres, and it was sufficient even to satisfy Marie's sense of self-importance! The clauses of the contract, which specify separation of possessions in the marriage, disguised the true and understood purpose of the match, which was that Marie would help to extricate d'Estrades from the financial morass into which he had sunk. In return she would be, and indeed was in future, a lady of the highest society in regular attendance at the royal court. Her inheritance from her father, in short, raised her even higher in the social hierarchy. In similar fashion the fortune inherited by her sister Marguerite enabled Marguerite to move up the social ranks after the death of her first husband de Manneville in 1684. She did not remain unmarried for long. In 1685 she accepted the proposal of Louis-Charles d'Albert, duc de Luynes, *pair de France* and *chevalier des ordres du roi*. This too was a brilliant match facilitated by the financial resources at her disposal.

Charles d'Aligre, from 1677 to 1695

His brother François having returned to Provins at the end of 1677, Charles was *de facto* head of the family, implementing such adjustments to the disposition of Etienne III's property as the inheritors agreed over the next few years.[5] His own share of the legacy allowed him to press ahead with his building plans at Saint Riquier. Their principal features involved the decoration of the interior of the church (some of the outstanding artists of the day were employed: Girardon, Coypel, Guy), the addition of a magnificent altar in Florentine marble, the restoration of side-chapels and, outside, the construction of gardens and an abbot's residence.[6] Charles was in a position to make generous contributions to the cost. In 1688 he turned over to the abbey an annual sum of 18,000 livres which hitherto he had drawn from its revenues;[7] he subsequently made a loan of 32,000 livres,[8] and to the building charges of 16,069 livres he contributed three years of his portion of the abbey revenues.[9] Saint Riquier was beautified

---

[5]Details are in his private papers listed in A.N., M.C., LXXV-408: Inventaire de Charles d'Aligre, 7 juin 1695.

[6]Hénocque, *Histoire. . . de Saint Riquier,* ii, 258-9; E. Martène et U. Durand, *Voyage Littéraire de Deux Religieux Bénédictins de la Congrégation de Saint Maur* (Paris, 1717), 174-5.

[7]A.N., M.C., LXXV-408: Inventaire de Charles d'Aligre, 7 juin 1695 ('Papiers privés', no. 154).

[8]*Ibid.*, no. 166.

[9]*Ibid.*, no. 264.

and given a splendour it had never known. Although he was a frequent visitor to the abbey, Charles regarded Paris as his home. For a time he continued in his rooms in the hôtel d'Aligre, but after its transfer to his nephews he moved first to the rue des Saints Pères,[10] then in 1687 to the hotel de Luynes which he leased from his brother-in-law, Marguerite's new husband, at 2,350 livres a year.[11] This remained his residence until his death in 1695. He was still officially a *conseiller d'état* and *conseiller* in the *parlement*, although how active he was is open to question.

Like most d'Aligres, Charles had a shrewd head for finance, for not all his resources went into Saint Riquier. Some went into state *rentes*: in 1681 he invested 200,000 livres on *rentes* of 9,000 livres, and in 1682 purchased another six bonds for 99,500 livres on a return of 4,975 livres.[12] He also put funds into commerce on the Rhône and the Seine.[13] He entered into partnership with two others, le Comte and Bellemont, whereby they first built two boats and bought trading rights between Lyon and Arles. In 1690 they purchased two more boats to sail between Rouen and Poissy, and in 1691 another salt boat on the Rhône. It was a highly profitable enterprise. In 1692 Charles's share of the year's profits was 11,000 livres;[14] two years later he bought out le Comte and Bellemont for 50,000 livres. If it is assumed that each partner owned roughly one-third of the business, then it was worth about 75,000 livres. An annual profit of 11,000 livres on their total trading was exceptionally good. Charles was the only member of his family to invest in commerce. In this respect he is the odd-man-out in a family which shared current noble prejudice against such activity.

As acting head of the family Charles assumed appropriate financial responsibilities. When his nephew Etienne IV married in 1684, Charles transferred to him *rentes* of 15,000 livres.[15] Likewise, when another nephew, de Manneville (Marguerite's son) married in 1686, he presented a *rente* of 7,500 livres.[16] To a few individuals, usually related by marriage, he made loans: Louis d'Estrades, Marie d'Aligre's step-son, borrowed 69,650 livres from Charles between

---

[10] See above, pp. 204.

[11] A.N., M.C., LXXV-408: Inventaire de Charles d'Aligre, 7 juin 1695 ('Papiers privés', no. 45).

[12] *Ibid.*, nos. 73-87.

[13] *Ibid.*, nos. 59-67.

[14] *Ibid.*, no. 66.

[15] *Ibid.*, no. 71.

[16] *Ibid.*, no. 44.

1690 and 1694;[17] Louis's sister Marguerite de Rambouillet also approached him for money, and when she died she owed him 32,870 livres.[18] One set of relations sank so deeply into his debt that, much as happened to Desguez de la Potinière, their estates were broken up to meet their commitments: the de Courseulles, sieurs du Rouvray, who were first cousins to the d'Aligres. Etienne III's sister Elisabeth had married François de Courseulles, sieur du Rouvray; among their children were François II, a *lieutenant au régiment des gardes du roi*; he in turn had a son Louis, sieur de Joudraye who also pursued a military career in a cavalry regiment. During the 1650s, 1660s and 1670s François II and Louis borrowed spasmodically from Etienne III and his sons Michel and Charles. For instance, in 1669 they received 34,400 livres from Etienne III[19] and in 1672 another 36,681 livres from Charles.[20] They occasionally redeemed part of their debt but it is clear from a perusal of Charles's private papers[21] that the approaches of the de Courseulles to the d'Aligres became increasingly frequent and that their indebtedness (to others too) rose dangerously. By the early 1690s their credit was exhausted and they had fallen badly behind in their repawments. Charles took François II to court, obtaining a judgement in 1694 ordering the seizure of his property in order to meet debt, both to Charles and to others.[22] Financial mismanagement by the de Courseulles drove them to the same fate as the de la Potinières, namely the loss of their estates, principally to their wealthy kinsmen the d'Aligres. Charles was not a financial operator on anything like the scale of his father or grandfather, yet he handled his affairs skilfully, profitably. Like most members of his family, he died in prosperity.

At his residence, the hôtel de Luynes in the rue Saint Dominique, he lived in a certain style, although not opulently. He maintained a staff of eleven: an *homme d'affaires,* a *maître d'hôtel, cuisinier, sommeiller, servante de cuisine, cocher, postillon, portier,* and three *lacquais*.[23] The possessions listed in his *inventaire après-décès* are unremarkable. No mention of silver, jewellery or tapestries is made; only six paintings are listed (one of himself, two of his father, two of

[17] *Ibid.,* nos. 181, 216.
[18] *Ibid.,* nos. 208, 210, 213.
[19] *Ibid.,* no. 10.
[20] *Ibid.,* no. 72.
[21] See *ibid.,* nos. 72, 94, 96, 98, 100-14, 202, 203.
[22] *Ibid.,* nos. 96, 100-4, 108.
[23] A.N., M.C., LXXV-408: Testament de M. d'Aligre, déposé, 18 juin 1695 [the will is dated 26 déc. 1686].

his sister Marguerite and her daughter, and one of Sainte Cécile); the furnishings, draperies and so forth were functional, not of luxury quality. He did own two coaches. But as far as the inventory indicates, Charles's lifestyle was straightforward. His library was undistinguished and indicates a mind that rarely strained itself. It comprised only 100 titles (416 volumes), almost all falling into the categories of law, religion, and the classics. There was no modern literature (Plutarch was the most up-to-date author!), no science, no philosophy. It compared poorly with the great collection built up by his father. Indeed, it is conceivable that it contained some of the books left at the hôtel d'Aligre after Etienne III's death, and that Charles himself rarely used it.

As we look back over Charles's life and career, he emerges as a worthy, solid citizen, unlikely to accomplish anything exceptional. Unquestionably the outstanding achievement of his life was the doggedness with which he pushed ahead with the rebuilding and extensions at Saint Riquier. In spite of his father's support he never proceeded beyond *conseiller d'état*, nor was he ever chosen for special mission to the provinces; it is highly significant that when Etienne III was appointed chancellor it was François who was invited to assist him, not Charles. Nevertheless, within his limitations his life was a success. Certainly his memory at Saint Riquier was revered. In his will he bequeathed 62,750 livres for charitable work: 30,000 livres for the poor of the parish of Saint Gervais in Paris, 3,300 livres for those of Saint Germain l'Auxerrois, another 5,000 livres for those of Mitoy near Dammartin, and 23,500 livres for the poor of Marizy near Châteauthierry.

François d'Aligre (1620-1712)

In François we encounter a very different kind of person. Of Etienne III's sons he was undoubtedly the most endowed with talents. He is the only member of the family about whom scholars have written.[24] He has made an appearance in this study from time to time, and already the outstanding fact of his life has manifested itself: his sense of religious vocation. Several d'Aligres devoted all or part of their lives to the service of the church, yet none equalled the religious

[24]Barrault, 'Les d'Aligre, abbés de Saint-Jacques de Provins'; A. Braichotte, 'L'Abbé d'Aligre'; M. Lecomte, 'Une grande figure Provinoise: François d'Aligre'; Le R.P. Lenet, *Oraison Funèbre de. . . François d'Aligre, Abbé de Saint Jacques de Provins* (Paris, 1712); *Lettre Ecrite de Provins du 22 Janvier 1712 sur la Vie et Mort de Monsieur d'Aligre. . . Abbé Régulier de l'Abbaye de S. Jacques. . .* (Paris, 1712); Michelin, *Essais Historiques;* the following passages on François are based on these works.

greatness which contemporaries as much as later observers perceived in him. François was a counter-reformation figure par excellence: utterly obedient to the church, he personally embraced the harshest forms of austerity, insisted upon strict observance of monastic discipline during his many years as *abbé* of Saint Jacques, devoted long periods to spiritual exercises and devotions, ruthlessly scrutinising his own conduct to stamp out traces of sin. Yet the exacting standards to which he conformed never enticed him into either of those two extremes, spiritual passivity or contempt towards the things and people of this world. Like all the outstanding churchmen and women of his day he maintained a healthy balance between the demands of the secular and the divine; his vocation drove him to serve the physical as well as the spiritual needs of his fellow men. Throughout his life he displayed gifts of leadership, organisation, financial acumen, of the highest order. During the years when he assisted his father while Etienne III was chancellor, François more than held his own in the government and royal court; he was no simpleton of a priest to be manipulated by schemers.

He succeeded his brother Michel as *abbé* of Saint Jacques in 1643, being installed in 1644, after having entered as a novice in 1634 and taken vows in 1636. Under the leadership of the d'Aligres (Nicolas 1624-36, Louis 1637-40, Michel 1640-3) Saint Jacques had been steadily reformed, pressure being sustained by Etienne III working through his sons. When François succeeded as *abbé*, he stringently adhered to the path of reform. He was anxious to ameliorate the educational as well as the spiritual standing of the monks, he himself being well read in theology, philosophy, history and law. The creation of a good library naturally was a matter of high priority. He did not succeed in creating one until his father's bequest of 1677; thereafter Saint Jacques possessed one of the most important collections in the archdiocese of Sens. He introduced into Saint Jacques public lectures (available to townspeople as well as to the monks) on theology and philosophy, some given by visiting speakers, others by members of the monastery. Such stress upon spiritual and intellectual advance by no means diminished François's concern for the physical condition of the abbey. Like Charles at Saint Riquier he planned and executed the beautification of Saint Jacques. Using private financial resources he purchased Gobelins tapestries, religious paintings, statues, gold and silver vessels. The decades of François d'Aligre's leadership of Saint Jacques mark the peak of the abbey's history in every sense; it enjoyed a prestige never equalled before or after. He succeeded in transmitting to its communal life at least something of his own outstanding qualities.

His reputation derives too from the extent to which he placed the facilities and resources of the abbey at the service of the town of Provins. Earlier in the century the behaviour of the monks had scandalised the townspeople; under François d'Aligre Saint Jacques was respected as a source of aid and charity. François established a fund of 5,000 livres a year to provide for the education at any one time of twenty-four orphan girls from Provins and its neighbourhood. He bought and equipped a house in the town where indigent travellers or visitors could rest free of charge for a night and a day; it was financed by a *rente* of 250 livres. Such urban renewal as was attempted in the town in the second half of the century originated with François rather than with the town council. At personal cost he restored the town hospital in the 1660s, the walls of Provins and its gates were repaired, roads were paved, the charges all being borne by François. When food shortages hit the region, Saint Jacques was a chief line of defence. During the famines of 1693-4 and 1704-5, for example, François diverted the abbey's revenues into the purchase of grain in Paris, which he then distributed in Provins; alms were distributed to the poor with which they could then purchase grain.

At court and in the upper reaches of the ecclesiastical hierarchy he was regarded as an outstanding figure marked for promotion. Yet François consistently turned down offers of advancement, insisting that his vocation must be satisfied at Provins alone. As early as 1649 he was nominated *conseiller d'état*, but refused the charge. In 1668 he was offered the bishopric of Avranches; again he declined to accept. Thereafter hints occasionally were dropped that should he change his mind he had but to say so. He never did. This absence of ambition was a source of grievance to his father,[25] for while Etienne III was a devout catholic, he was also a man of the world desirous of furthering family interests. A son who was a bishop (and in view of François's ability, he doubtless would have been moved to a more prestigious see than Avranches in due course) potentially was of considerable help in this connection. François resisted all such allurements, much to his father's chagrin. He did, of course, spend almost four years at the court from 1674 to 1677, but his experiences appear to have reinforced his vocation.

He was no recluse after 1677. He periodically visited his sister Elisabeth, abbess of Saint Cyr. The convent buildings had suffered damage during the Frondes; François paid for the repairs, and as long

---

[25] Having been offered advancement, 'il résista généreusement à la voix du peuple, qui l'en jugeoit digne: au choix du Roy qui les luy offrit: aux sollicitations de ses parens que son refus mortifioit' (Lenet, *Oraison Funèbre,* 9-10).

as his health lasted, visited his sister to encourage her in a reform programme similar to his own. Likewise he was a source of encouragement to his brother Charles. He sometimes spent as much as three months at a time working at Saint Riquier as a builder's labourer, in addition to advising Charles on the building programme. The other religious house which he visited regularly was La Trappe where his great friend Rancé was *abbé*. Indeed, after 1677 François adopted a Trappist discipline (although he did not insist upon it among the monks of Saint Jacques): his diet consisted only of bread, salads, fruit and water; he wore a hair shirt; his bed was three planks and a blanket, and his pillow a stone. This singularly austere style he maintained to his dying day.

Running through the history of the d'Aligres in the seventeenth century is a strong religious theme which finds its most striking expression in François. The three foundations with which the d'Aligres chiefly were associated (Saint Jacques, Saint Cyr and Saint Riquier) all flourished. The religious atmosphere of the age favoured monastic regeneration, yet the role of the d'Aligres in their respective houses should not be underestimated. Some members of the family took their religious vows more seriously than others, but taking the century as a whole, there is no question that the establishments with which they were associated were in a healthier state at the end of the century than at the beginning. Nevertheless, François marks not only the climax but also the virtual end of this religious theme. In the eighteenth century no male members of the family entered holy orders; among the females, two daughters of Etienne IV were nuns: Marie-Madeleine-Françoise (1690-1747) entered Saint Cyr where she was abbess from 1719 in succession to her great-aunt Françoise, and Marie-Madeleine-Geneviève (b.1693) entered the convent of Sainte Marie in Paris. Otherwise the d'Aligres devoted themselves to secular careers.

The d'Aligres in the Eighteenth Century

The purpose of this study has been to trace the affairs of the d'Aligre family during those many decades in the sixteenth and seventeenth centuries when they resided first in Chartres and then in Paris. The means and consequences of their advancement have supplied most of the themes and problems that have been investigated. Yet our enquiries would be incomplete without at least an indication of the principal trends in the history of the d'Aligres de la Rivière in the eighteenth century, now that they were firmly established in the topmost strata of French society. During the 1700s they were recognised throughout the country as an eminent family, and certainly one of the most wealthy. If they were studied in their eighteenth-century context with as much detail as in their seventeenth-century context, many pages would have to be devoted to the further expansion of their wealth in the later 1700s.

Demographic Patterns

The problem that was observed in connection with Etienne III whereby, although he produced a large number of children the male line came uncomfortably close to extinction, persisted in later generations. The thread can be taken up with Etienne IV and Gilles. The latter had only one daughter who lived but a few months. Etienne IV married three times.[26] By the first marriage there were five children: one died in infancy, two entered convents, a daughter married but died childless within three years; only his son Etienne-Claude (1694-1752) had a family. By the second marriage there was a daughter who survived only a few weeks. By the third there were three children, none of whom left issue. Thus, of Etienne IV's nine children, only Etienne-Claude later had children. The problem continued in that generation too. Etienne-Claude married twice, but only one child in turn produced heirs: he was Etienne-François, first marquis d'Aligre (1727-1798/1800), the eldest son of the first marriage (by which there was another son who died aged eleven, and a daughter who married but died childless). Etienne-Claude's second marriage produced a child that died in infancy. Etienne-François also married twice; by his first marriage there were no children, but by the second there were two: Etienne-Jean-François, second marquis d'Aligre (1770-1847), and Cathérine-Etienne-Claude who married a *pair de France*, the marquis de Boissy. The second marquis d'Aligre left only a daughter, Etienne-Marie, by the first of his two marriages. In 1810 she married Michel-Marie, marquis de Pomereau; her father saved the family name when, in 1825 he secured an *ordonnance* whereby his grandson, Etienne-Marie-Charles de Pomereau (1813-89), added the name 'd'Aligre' to his own and so became third marquis d'Aligre. He, however, died without issue and the family name passed into extinction.

Although in strictly human terms the high rate of mortality and low rate of reproduction by the d'Aligres indicates a family in some

[26] See Appendix 3.

difficulty, the economic consequences emphatically were to their advantage. The family estates remained safe from division in the eighteenth century, and indeed expanded considerably. There was no repetition after 1677 of the sexpartite partition of property such as occurred after Etienne III's death. Gilles d'Aligre died in 1711, whereupon his *seigneurie* of Boislandry reverted to Etienne IV and his heirs. Thereafter La Rivière, Boislandry, Le Favril and so on, usually remained with one owner. Interruptions in this pattern occurred from time to time in mid-century when, if more than one son was living, Boislandry would again be conferred on the younger; but the intervention of death always reunited d'Aligre estates.

Marriage continued as an instrument to uphold or enhance prestige, as well as to reproduce. The eighteenth-century d'Aligres found themselves in a strong position, being able to select husbands for their daughters from numerous suitors anxious to ally themselves to the family. If Etienne IV's daughters are taken as an example, Madeleine-Louise (1697-1714) in 1711 married Guillaume de Lamoignon; at the time he was *avocat général* in the Paris *parlement*, but he was to crown his career in 1750 with the chancellorship; her half-sister Jeanne-Madeleine-Cathérine (1712-38) in 1736 married into the *épée*, her husband being Henri-François, baron de Bretagne, comte de Vertus, a *chevalier de l'ordre royal et militaire de Saint Louis*. Etienne IV's youngest daughter Marie-Cathérine (b. 1713) entered one of the most prominent political families: in 1735 she married a son of Michel-Robert le Pelletier des Forts, *ministre d'état* and *contrôleur-général des finances*. In the next generation Etienne-Claude's daughter Marie-Madeleine (b. 1731) in 1748 married a *premier président* in the *parlement* of Aix. It has already been noted that Cathérine-Etienne-Claude d'Aligre married a peer of the realm. The ease with which eminent matches could be made for the d'Aligre females is nowhere more apparent than during the First Empire when Etienne-Jean-François, second marquis d'Aligre, reputedly one of the richest men in France, had only one daughter, Etienne-Marie (b. 1793). He was under pressure from many sources and young hopefuls, Napoleon himself intervening on behalf of general Arrighi. The marquis resisted all such blandishments, Etienne-Marie in 1810 marrying into the old and distinguished Pomereau family.

The male d'Aligres tended to choose wives among the *noblesse de robe*. The wife of Gilles was the daughter of a *maître des requêtes*, but Etienne IV went higher in the social hierarchy. His first wife was daughter of Claude le Pelletier, Louis XIV's *contrôleur-général des finances*; his second wife came from a noble family, the Fontaines des Montées; his third was the daughter of a *premier président* of the *chambre des comptes* and *cour des aides* of Normandie. Etienne IV's younger son, Etienne-Jean-François-Marie (1717-57) married the daughter of a *président des enquêtes,* while his brother Etienne-Claude married first the daughter of a *président* of the *grand conseil* and subsequently the daughter of a *conseiller* in the *parlement* of Paris. Etienne-Claude's son, the first marquis, married twice: his first wife came from a notable family, her father being Omer Talon, marquis du Boulay, *président à mortier* in the *parlement* of Paris: his second, already a widow, was the daughter of a *conseiller* in the *parlement.* The second marquis also married twice: first a member of the de Senneville family, and then the daughter of a *premier président* in the *parlement* of Rouen.

Careers

None of the eighteenth-century d'Aligres matched the achievements of Etienne II and Etienne III in their careers, partly because they tended to veer away from central government into the sovereign courts. It was a trend already noticeable in Gilles d'Aligre, who served as a *conseiller* in the *parlement* of Metz and later in that of Paris; he was never a *maître des requêtes* or *conseiller d'etat.* Etienne IV did spend five years (1683-8) as a *maître des requêtes*, but spent most of his career in the Paris *parlement* where he was *conseiller* and, from 1701, *président à mortier.* Etienne-Claude too spent the whole of his professional life in the *parlement* of Paris: as *conseiller* from 1716 and *président à mortier* from 1724. His brother Etienne-Jean-François spent a few years after 1743 as a *maître des requêtes*, but the larger part of his career was devoted to the *châtelet de Paris* (1737-40), the *parlement* (he became *conseiller* in 1740) and the *grand conseil* of which he was a *président* in 1745. He returned to direct royal service, passing the years 1749 to 1754 as *intendant* successively in Auch, Pau and Amiens.

As the d'Aligres served in sovereign courts a shift in their sense of obligation can be discerned, for they steadily acquired a sense of affinity with the traditions and 'liberties' of those assemblies, especially the *parlement.* During the 1700s a series of tensions developed between crown and *parlements,* the d'Aligres, like other *parlementaires*, finding themselves torn by conflicting loyalties. Such a dilemma is evident in the case of Etienne-François d'Aligre, in many ways the most fascinating and controversial member of the family in that century. He was noted as a lawyer of exceptional skills which led to rapid promotion. Equally he was known for his prodigious avarice as he ruthlessly amassed land and money, but gave nothing away. It was he, incidentally, who in 1777 secured letters patent elevating his title to that of 'marquis'. He entered the *parlement* as a *conseiller* in 1745 when he was only eighteen. His advance was rapid: *président à mortier* in 1752 and *premier président* in 1768. These were decades when relations between *parlement* and Louis XV reached their nadir.[27] A crisis occurred over the notorious *lit de justice* of 1766 whereby Louis XV reiterated the peremptory constitutional principle that *parlement* was the instrument of the king's will alone, possessing no independent attributes. Another occurred over the trial of d'Aiguillon, which resulted in the dissolution of the *parlement* in 1771. It was restored by Louis XVI, but there remained an array of disputes regarding the respective rights of crown and *parlement* which, if unresolved, portended acrimonious years ahead. As *premier président* Etienne-François was thrust to the forefront as a protagonist of the 'rights' of the *parlement*; he played a prominent part in organising resistance to the more controversial aspects of royal legislation. He was one of the leaders of the opposition to the fiscal schemes of Turgot, and subsequently to Necker's plans to 'reform' the *parlements*. Throughout the 1780s he adhered to a rigid parlementary line, resigning his office in 1788 over the Estates General. At first he had been favourable to the calling of that assembly, but on reflection judged that in the circumstances of the time it would cause irreparable damage to the interests of crown and *parlement* alike. In November 1788 he had a personal interview with Louis XVI and Necker, adjuring them not to open that particular Pandora's Box. The king and his minister heard out d'Aligre in silence, and remained silent. Securing not a word from them, Etienne-François left the interview and resigned his office. The d'Aligres had come a long way since the days of that other royal crisis, the Frondes, when Etienne III had stubbornly remained with the royal cause. The effect of several decades in the *parlement* and other courts, allied to the accretion of immense wealth and prestige, was to loosen the bonds between the d'Aligres and the crown. From being an ardently 'royalist' family they became 'parlementary'. They illustrate one of the quandaries of the French monarchy: it was all very well to take gifted provincial families into royal service and to reward them with material and social advancement, but how could their loyalty be sustained in the long term? As Louis XVI trod exceedingly dangerous ground in the 1780s he found aligned against him families like the d'Aligres, who had once been staunchly royalist.

[27] J.H. Shennan, *The Parlement of Paris* (London, 1968), 308-25.

Postscript

This outline of the d'Aligres in the eighteenth century would not be complete without at least a glance or two at their fortunes during the Revolution. Like many aristocrats and nobles Etienne-François had his share of adventures and near misses. He eluded arrest in 1789 and fled with his family to London where he had large financial deposits. In the 1780s he had been sufficiently prescient to anticipate the possibility of civil turmoil in France, and had transferred large sums of money (possibly as much as five million livres) to London banks. From London he invested funds in Danish and Venetian banks with his customary expertise, and, unlike many of his co-*émigrés*, had the satisfaction of seeing his fortune augment rather than diminish. He moved back to the continent, dying in Brunswick in either 1798 or 1800.[28] During the Revolution the family estates and property had been seized by the state.[29] His son, Etienne-Jean-François, second marquis d'Aligre, resolved to restore them. Favourable circumstances were created by the advent of Napoleon. Etienne-Jean-François returned to France and made his peace with Napoleon; more than that he secured promotion in Bonapartist circles, being nominated chamberlain to Caroline, queen of Naples, in 1804. She absolved him from the duties attaching to the charge, so that he was able to remain in France. He revived the former family interest in the region around Chartres. He managed to acquire again La Rivière, Boislandry and almost all the old estates. In 1806 he purchased another extensive property six or seven miles to the west of La Rivière: the *château* and estate of Les Vaux. Using his father's immense fortune, therefore, he succeeded not only in restoring the former possessions of the d'Aligres in Chartrain and Le Perche (now the *département* of Eure-et-Loir), but also in adding to them at the expense of less fortunate dispossessed nobles. He was anxious to enhance the family's reputation in the region. To that end he devoted resources to charitable works, the most notable being the foundation of the Hôpital d'Aligre at Bonneval and the Asile d'Aligre at Chartres. His involvement in the affairs of Eure-et-Loir was to continue after the Restoration. Wisely withdrawing from his Bonapartist acquaintances in the latter years of the First Empire, he was chosen by the city of Paris as one of the commissioners to welcome Louis XVIII at his entry. The king designated him *pair de France* in 1815. Again, in the

---

[28] The *Biographie Française* and Courcelles, 'Généalogie de la maison d'Aligre', say 1798: *Illustrations Nobiliaires* says 1800.

[29] Information on some of the d'Aligre property seized by the state is in A.N., M260, dossier 6; also S71 and S3765, dossier 1.

same year d'Aligre was appointed president of the electoral college of Eure-et-Loir, Louis XVIII estimating that somebody of d'Aligre's standing in the *département* would be an invaluable buttress to the regime in that part of France. Having accommodated himself to Bonapartism, Etienne-Jean-François just as easily reverted to Bourbonism.

During the 1790s and early 1800s the d'Aligres adapted to their environment and changed their alliances to great effect. It is no part of our present concern to moralise or pass judgement on them. Few who unswervingly pursued a certain political philosophy survived for long amidst the struggles and upheavals of Revolutionary and Bonapartist France. The governing strategy behind the movements and conduct of Etienne-François and more especially of his son, seems to have been the restoration of the family estates. This was accompanied by renewed activities to rehabilitate the reputation of the family in Eure-et-Loir. The general atmosphere of 'Restoration' required old noble families to resume their provincial roles, particularly if the country were to be stabilised. The d'Aligres duly revived their former territorial associations, rightly perceiving that if the nobility as a whole was to survive in the nineteenth century, it would have to perform socially useful functions.

CONCLUSION

By examining the affairs and fortunes of the d'Aligres de la Rivière over a period of some four hundred years, with an emphasis very firmly on the father and son Etienne II and Etienne III, this study has sought to trace the emergence of one of the leading families of the *noblesse de robe* in the France of the *ancien régime*. At each stage they have been treated as a 'nuclear' unit: the parents and children in each generation through the main line of descent. This has not been an exercise in 'extended family' history, which would have required a very different set of techniques and questions from those that have been employed. Yet some of the components of this study bear upon our understanding of aspects of family history in the old France. There is, for example, information of demographic significance. The number of births fluctuated strongly from generation to generation, 'peaks' being represented by Etienne II with seven children, Etienne III with fifteen, and Etienne IV with nine; for the rest, one or two were the norm. One feature that has emerged with striking force has been the problem of reproduction through the male line. Even when a large number of children were born, several could die in infancy: Etienne III lost three that way, his son Michel two, Etienne IV two, Etienne-Claude's son Etienne-Jean-Baptiste died aged eleven. Alternatively, the church, the army, and the Knights of Malta imposed celibacy on a high proportion of both male and female d'Aligres, while in the 1600s and 1700s several who married left no issue. At no stage in the seventeenth and eighteenth centuries was it self-evident that the family name would be perpetuated. The records of the male d'Aligres permit another observation, which is that the time between the celebration of a marriage and the birth of a first child varied considerably. Only in one or two cases did the pregnancy of a wife come within a few weeks of marriage. In some cases the time lapse can be explained by the youth of the bride at marriage, consummation being delayed until she reached the age of fifteen: this applies to the marriages of Etienne II, Etienne III and possibly of Michel.

Among the males of the family it was more common than not to marry twice or even thrice. Among the females this pattern was less pronounced. Etienne III's sister Elisabeth married once, his daughters Marie and Hélène each twice, and Marguerite once. Etienne IV's three daughters who married did so once only; so did Etienne-Claude's daughter Marie-Madeleine, and Etienne-Jean-François's daughter. Like most of their contemporaries the d'Aligres had to regard marriages as temporary, not lifetime arrangements. When

Table 13

Husband	Wife	Married	Birth of First Child
Etienne II	Elisabeth	1586/7	Etienne III, 1592
Etienne III	Jeanne	Feb. 1617	Louis, 1619
Michel	Madeleine (3rd wife)	Feb. 1659	Etienne IV, 3 Jan. 1660
Gilles	Cathérine	Aug. 1686	Jeanne-Elisabeth, 21 Sept. 1691 (d. 2 April 1692)
Etienne IV	i. Marie-Madeleine	April 1684	Etienne, 1686 (d. in infancy)
	ii. Marie-Anne	Aug. 1708	Marie-Anne, 1 June 1711 (d. 13 June)
	iii. Madeleine-Cathérine	Sept. 1711	Etienne-Jean-François, 19 Jan 1717
Etienne-Claude	i. Marie-Louise	Feb. 1726	Etienne-François, 17 July 1727
	ii. Henriette-Geneviève	May 1741	? (d. in infancy)
Etienne-François	i. Françoise-Madeleine	Jan 1748	No issue
	ii. Anne-Cathérine-Louise	Jan. 1769	Etienne-Jean-François, 20 Feb. 1770

remarriages occurred, they did so quickly, either within a few months or at the most within eighteen months of the death of the previous partner. The age at which a first marriage occurred was, for the males from Etienne II to Etienne-François, between 24 and 27 (the only exceptions were in the eighteenth century: Etienne-Jean-François was 40 and Etienne-François 21). Incidentally, in those cases where the ages of their wives are known, they were usually much lower: Etienne III's wife Elisabeth Chapellier was 13 or 14 when they married, Etienne III's wife Jeanne l'Huillier was 14, and although the age of Michel's first wife is unknown, his second was 12. Regarding the females of the family, Etienne III's daughters Marie, Hélène and Marguerite, married respectively at 14, 19 and 17; Etienne IV's daughters married at 14, 24 and 22; Etienne-Claude's daughter Marie-Madeleine was 17. In the sixteenth century spouses of the Aligres came from Chartres and its region, but in the seventeenth they derived usually from Paris and the royal court. This was a natural and inevitable development given that it was imperative to arrange marriages with a careful eye to prestige as well as to financial advantages. Parisian and court circles were where appropriate matches were to be made. The last d'Aligre to marry into a family from near Chartres was Etienne III's sister Elisabeth, whose husband was du Rouvray. The others in the seventeenth and eighteenth centuries found their husbands and wives in *robe* and *épée* families normally based in the capital or at court.

When we turn to deaths among the d'Aligres, certain characteristics have already been recognised: the persistence of infant mortality and the deaths of young wives in or following childbirth. Nevertheless a high proportion of d'Aligres in the seventeenth century lived to a ripe old age. Etienne II lived to be 75 and Etienne III to be 85, and if Etienne III's children are taken in 'ascending' order, Louis lived to 35, Michel to 38, Anne to 41, Charles to 65, Héléne to 76, Jean to 78, Marguerite to 81, Françoise to 82, Marie to 84, Elisabeth and François each to 92; Etienne was killed at the age of 20 while fighting Turks as a Knight of Malta. In the eighteenth century, by contrast, death tended to occur earlier. Gilles died at 50 and Etienne IV at 65; of Etienne IV's children (where details are available) Etienne-Claude died at 58, Marie-Madeleine-Françoise at 57, Madeleine-Louise at 17, Etienne-Jean-François at 40, Jeanne-Madeleine at 26. There was a 'revival' later in the century with Etienne-François living to 71 or 73 (although his brother Etienne-Jean-Baptiste died aged 11), and his son Etienne-Jean-François living to 77. The most dangerous period over the two centuries was that following the death of Michel in 1661. For several years his sons were very young, and there existed an uncomfortable age gap in the ranks of the family which lasted until the early decades of the eighteenth century.

A successful family, of course, needed not only to reproduce itself, not only to defend its social standing, but had to provide an appropriate standard of living for its members. The d'Aligres passed this latter test partly through the constant acquisition of wealth and partly through avoiding too many divisions of their property. On this question of inheritance patterns, the d'Aligres in the seventeenth century excluded those members of the family who were celibate by calling: at Etienne II's death his three daughters who were nuns received nothing by the *partage* of 1638; likewise in 1678, Elisabeth, Françoise and François who were in holy orders, and Jean a Knight of Malta, did not partake of the division of Etienne III's property. Nevertheless, the 'rule' was not applied dogmatically. Charles d'Aligre who, although he never took final vows, remained celibate, did participate in the division of his father's estate. Moreover, Etienne III had already made gifts of life pensions (and in the case of Jean, the *seigneurie* of Manou as well) to his 'excluded' children. Thus, although in 1677 and 1678 eight of Etienne III's children were extant, only four inherited. This leads on to the position of women and minors. Female members of the family succeeded to property if they were married and had children; alternatively their husbands might inherit. When Etienne II died the husband of his daughter Elisabeth, François de Courseulles, sieur du Rouvray, received a portion; after Etienne III's death Marie, Hélène and Marguerite all inherited, the last two jointly with their husbands (Marie was a widow). Minors were included in inheritances, their mothers or nominated guardians acting on their behalf until the age of majority. When Etienne II's son Louis died unmarried, he bequeathed some of his estate to Etienne III, but some to his nephews, the sons of his sister Elisabeth; again in 1678 Etienne IV and Gilles d'Aligre received one-sixth shares each in the division of Etienne III's property, their mother representing and acting for them. Although they did not insist upon a system of fixed proportions to inheritors, the d'Aligres did work a rough-and-ready rule: the *seigneurie* of La Rivière and its associated lands always went to the senior male, with Boislandry going to the second. These two impartible *seigneuries* excepted, property was shared on a broadly even basis.[1]

There was usually much to distribute. At every stage of this study the vigorous and effective measures taken by the d'Aligres to acquire land and other property have manifested themselves. While they rarely ceased acquiring and occasionally selling land, there were three periods when they made substantial additions to their holdings: the late 1400s in the aftermath of the Hundred Years war, the early 1600s after the Wars of Religion, and in the late 1650s and 1660s after the Frondes. Those great wars and conflicts disrupted economic and social order, especially in the Ile-de-France, to the extent that people like the d'Aligres who had cash resources could purchase land from hard-hit owners driven into sales by necessity. Having acquired land the usual practice of the d'Aligres was to lease it on a cash basis, usually for seven or eight years. La Rivière was not let, but almost every other portion, including Boislandry, was leased at one stage or another. Questions of estate management, such as leases to tenant farmers, collection of shares of crops, operation of the mills, were handed over to *fermiers*. The d'Aligres were concerned principally to secure a cash return on their lands. In the second half of the century they were active too in the Paris property market. As a form of investment this was a far-sighted move. The value of property in Paris consistently increased in the seventeenth and eighteenth centuries. It

---

[1] On French inheritance patterns in this period see: E. le Roy Ladurie, 'Family structures and inheritance customs in seventeenth-century France', in J. Goody, *et al.*, (eds.), *Family and Inheritance: Rural Society in Western Europe, 1200-1800* (Cambridge, 1976), 37-70.

was, too, more secure on the whole than land, where disease, flood, drought, rebellion, could wreak havoc. Urban property was vulnerable to civil violence, but by the time Etienne III bought up houses, the effective control of Paris by the crown was well advanced.

Of all the activities of the d'Aligres those relating to finance have proved to be among the more notable. Vast amounts of money were invested by them in *rentes,* either *constituées* or on the state. They may be termed *rentiers* if it is understood that they did not live off their *rentes.* Almost all male members of the family pursued active careers in government, church, armed forces. By contrast with the sums they invested in *rentes,* the amount they put into commerce was a pittance. There is no sign of their having bought shares in any of the great trading companies or in any industrial enterprises. They were redolent of that spirit which found it difficult to reconcile noble status and commercial enterprise. They restricted investment to areas which were comparatively safe and socially acceptable. We should reject any notion that they 'bought' their way up the social hierarchy, either through loans or by bestowing extravagant dowries on their daughters. Dowries suited their station in life, being ample but never excessive. Although they contracted *rentes constituées* with aristocrats as well as with *officiers* and nobility of the *robe,* it was always on the basis that the d'Aligres already belonged to such circles; they were not outsiders attempting to break in. The d'Aligres served as an important channel through which cash flowed. They had the resources to provide a large lump sum at relatively short notice. During the seventeenth century they made loans to several hundred people, and in those cases where a contract states the purpose of its *rente constituée,* it was normally to buy a civil or military office, or to acquire property. The d'Aligres and others like them were essential to the functioning of society at their level. If transactions such as the purchase of offices or property, the provision of dowries, the redemption of debts, in short anything that required a large sum of money, were to be effected in a pre-banking age, there had to be sources which people could approach. Yet the d'Aligres must be distinguished sharply from the *traitants* and other full-time financiers. They remained first and foremost active servants of the crown, financial manoeuvres being a highly profitable but secondary occupation.

Throughout this narrative an attempt has been made to place the d'Aligres in the context of their relationship to the crown. They were in every sense beneficiaries of Bourbon absolutism; indeed, the rise and fall of their fortunes after their arrival in Paris, the years of greatest peril or of greatest success, paralleled those of Henri IV, Louis XIII and Louis XIV. They well represent the type of people who were so prominent in the building of a state whose triumph over internal resistance looked much less inevitable to contemporaries than to many later observers. The central ingredient in their education was usually law, and it was as experts in law that the d'Aligres excelled. Once in royal service, however, they could find themselves performing a multiple array of duties. A perusal of the careers of the two Etiennes, Michel and Charles, illustrates the immense range of skills required by the successful *maître des requètes, conseiller d'état* or *intendant,* not to mention a chancellor. He needed to be lawyer, financier, administrator, able negotiator; to display a grasp of local traditions, customs, 'liberties', if he were sent on a provincial mission; to know something of military logistics, communications, commerce; in short, to possess an omnicompetence which was little short of staggering. If it is the case that in the seventeenth century there was a slow but sure trend in favour of specialisation in central government and administration, the careers of Etienne II and his descendants suggest that the process was not very far advanced even by the 1680s or 1690s, at least by comparison with what was to come later. Again, the personal element in government and administration remained paramount. Loyalties tended to be directed through human channels: to the king rather than to any abstract notion of 'state', or to a particular minister to whose 'clan' an individual belonged. As we seek to grasp the nature of government in seventeenth-century France, we should recognise that the d'Aligres and their like were brought in, not because they were 'bourgeois' (in whatever sense the term is understood), but because they had already served an aristocrat or a minister, and subsequently were advanced by their 'clan leader'. An ambitious individual could transfer from one 'clan' to another as Etienne III did in 1626 when he offered his services to Richelieu. Again, the leadership of a 'clan' could change; Michel le Tellier began as a *protégé* of Etienne II and his nascent 'clan', yet in the second half of the century the d'Aligres were seeking the protection of the le Tellier group. But whatever shifts, associations, rivalries transpired within and between 'clans', they remained as characteristic of French government as any tendency towards specialisation, or as any modification of the supposed sociological composition of the crown's chief servants.

Central as is the nexus between the ascension of the d'Aligres and their duties under the crown, the wealth and status which they thereby derived introduced new themes into the development of the family. One was military. Two of Etienne II's sons were Knights of Malta, and another fought in the king's armies. Contemporary social values may be discerned at work here. The d'Aligres were nobles of the *robe,* whereas the conviction persisted in France that 'true' nobility was military in nature, that the nobleman who wielded the sword in defence of his king exemplified nobility in its most exalted state. The establishment of three sons in the military life was intended to introduce *épée* influences into a firmly *robe* noble family. As Knights of Malta, two of the three belonged to an order that still adhered to the pretence that it was composed of the cream of European nobility devoted to the protection of Christendom. Unconvincing as the posture was by the seventeenth century, there still attached to the knights a mystique, a glamour, an esteem, which defied the passage of time and which accrued to their families too. At the risk of facetiousness it might even be admitted that when one of the two sons, Etienne, was killed in combat in 1644, he died in the best possible way and correspondingly enhanced the standing of his family. The other theme of which notice should be taken is, of course, the ecclesiastical. It is conceivable that had the d'Aligres remained in Chartres and lived out a wholly provincial existence, sons and daughters still would have entered holy orders. What is hard to envisage is that they would have headed important monasteries and convents and have been offered bishoprics. As it promoted its servants in the social hierarchy the crown indirectly affected great institutions like the church, which found leading figures coming from backgrounds which one or two generations before had been obscure or inconsiderable. The consequences for the d'Aligres of many of their sons and daughters entering military or ecclesiastical callings on the whole were economically advantageous, but involved other drawbacks. If the d'Aligres were to have succeeded in equalling the le Telliers, the Colberts and others in acquiring great offices of state, they would have needed more members of the family prominent in royal service. Simply and crudely too many d'Aligres, especially males, pursued careers away from Paris and in non-political occupations for an effective 'clan' to be organised. This is in no sense to judge them failures. A glimpse of their wealth and reputation in the eighteenth century is sufficient to dispel any such notions. By then they were in a sense 'independent' of the crown, no longer reliant upon the king for their existence as a prestigious family. They numbered among the great of the land, being prepared to adopt strikingly non-royalist views on the crises of that century.

The public careers of the d'Aligres touch on a question which is of central importance to the history of France under the Bourbons. It concerns the tendency for social and political stability to become inter-related, perhaps inter-dependent, in the seventeenth and eighteenth centuries. This was not necessarily the case everywhere in Europe; examples can be found in European history of regions where social and political stability owed relatively little to each other. The Holy Roman Empire maintained its imperial institutions and an unbroken succession of Habsburg emperors over many centuries, even amidst the most appalling social strife. In Gaelic Ireland before English conquest, social structures and the rule of traditional law were but minimally disturbed by the political anarchy created by warring chieftains struggling for contested rights and titles. It could even be argued that in the France of the sixteenth century, the crown with its political apparatus showed an impressive ability to ride out the storms of religious war. The Bourbons and their agents, however, took the subjugation of disruptive social forces in the country to be one of their major long-term tasks; 'réduction à l'obéissance', to borrow a phrase from Louis XIV's *Mémoires,* ranked high in their list of priorities. The thinking behind this objective reveals the conviction that monarchy could best fulfil its functions against a background of social stability; social stability was not necessary to the functioning of monarchy, but it did supply the most advantageous environment. The Bourbons employed a mixture of constraint and concession in their programme of social control. Richelieu, for one, was ready to use the mailed fist against disturbers of social stability, whoever they were. On the other hand, Colbert's tax reforms, wherein he shifted the emphasis from direct to indirect taxation, so distributing the burden as broadly as possible, were designed in part to abate popular fiscal grievances; the striking reduction in the incidence of tax revolts after 1661 testifies to his success. Again, the 'system' and ritual of Versailles have often been interpreted as one of Louis XIV's instruments for the disciplining of the great aristocracy; yet equally convincing is the contention that he was seeking to reconcile them to the regime, Versailles forging a powerful nexus between king and aristocracy. By a judicious blend of coercion and consensus the Bourbons did manage to stabilise French society to an extent that hardly looked likely during, say, the Frondes. But a heavy price was paid. In the eighteenth century the monarchy was to discover that it had so linked its political well-being to the control of social stability (and, it should be stressed, a stability in which the privileges of elite groups were confirmed), that when social disorder erupted in the 1780s and early 1790s there were immense political consequences. In short, one verdict of the French Revolution was that the Bourbons had gone dangerously far in associating their political fortunes with the maintenance of a certain type of social order. How far any style of monarchy could have adapted itself to meet the changing circumstances of the eighteenth century is far from clear; analogies drawn from elsewhere in Europe or even from the France of the nineteenth century, afford both positive and negative lessons. Either way, the

Bourbons created a state in which the social and political dimensions of national life became so interlocked that it was not possible for a crisis in the one to leave the other intact. The foregoing study, by concentrating on the experiences of the d'Aligre family, has enabled us to detect something of the character of this process, which has been integral to much of the history of France over the last three centuries.

Appendix 1: The Aligres before Etienne d'Aligre II

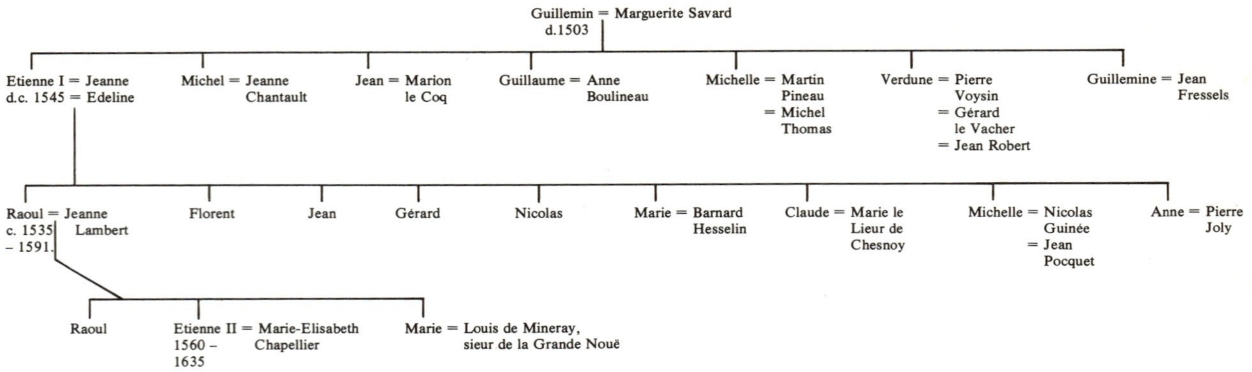

Guillemin = Marguerite Savard
d.1503

- Etienne I = Jeanne Edeline (d.c. 1545)
- Michel = Jeanne Chantault
- Jean = Marion le Coq
- Guillaume = Anne Boulineau
- Michelle = Martin Pineau = Michel Thomas
- Verdune = Pierre Voysin = Gérard le Vacher = Jean Robert
- Guillemine = Jean Fressels

- Raoul = Jeanne Lambert (c. 1535 – 1591)
- Florent
- Jean
- Gérard
- Nicolas
- Marie = Barnard Hesselin
- Claude = Marie le Lieur de Chesnoy
- Michelle = Nicolas Guinée = Jean Pocquet
- Anne = Pierre Joly

- Raoul
- Etienne II = Marie-Elisabeth Chapellier (1560 – 1635)
- Marie = Louis de Mineray, sieur de la Grande Noué

Appendix 2: The Three Generations after Etienne d'Aligre II

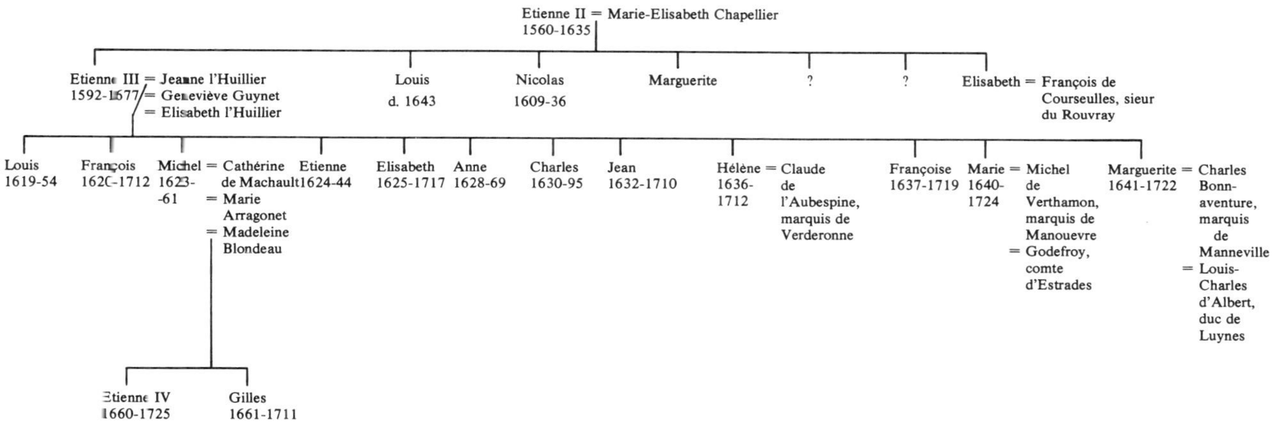

Etienne II = Marie-Elisabeth Chapellier
1560-1635

- Etienne III = Jeanne l'Huillier
  1592-1677 = Geneviève Guynet
           = Elisabeth l'Huillier
  - François Michel = Catherine   Etienne
    162C-1712 1623-   de Machault 1624-44
              -61   = Marie
                     Arragonet
                   = Madeleine
                     Blondeau
    - Louis
      1619-54
    - Etienne IV   Gilles
      1660-1725   1661-1711

- Louis
  d. 1643

- Elisabeth   Anne
  1625-1717 1628-69

- Nicolas
  1609-36
  - Charles
    1630-95

- Marguerite
  - Jean
    1632-1710

- ?
  - Hélène = Claude
    1636-   de
    1712   l'Aubespine,
             marquis de
             Verderonne

- ?
  - Françoise   Marie = Michel   Marguerite = Charles
    1637-1719   1640-   de   1641-1722   Bonn-
                1724   Verthamon,   aventure,
                         marquis de   marquis
                         Manoeuvre   de
                       = Godefroy,   Manneville
                         comte   = Louis-
                         d'Estrades   Charles
                                                   d'Albert,
                                                   duc de
                                                   Luynes

- Elisabeth = François de
             Courseulles, sieur
             du Rouvray

229

Appendix 3: The d'Aligres in the Eighteenth Century

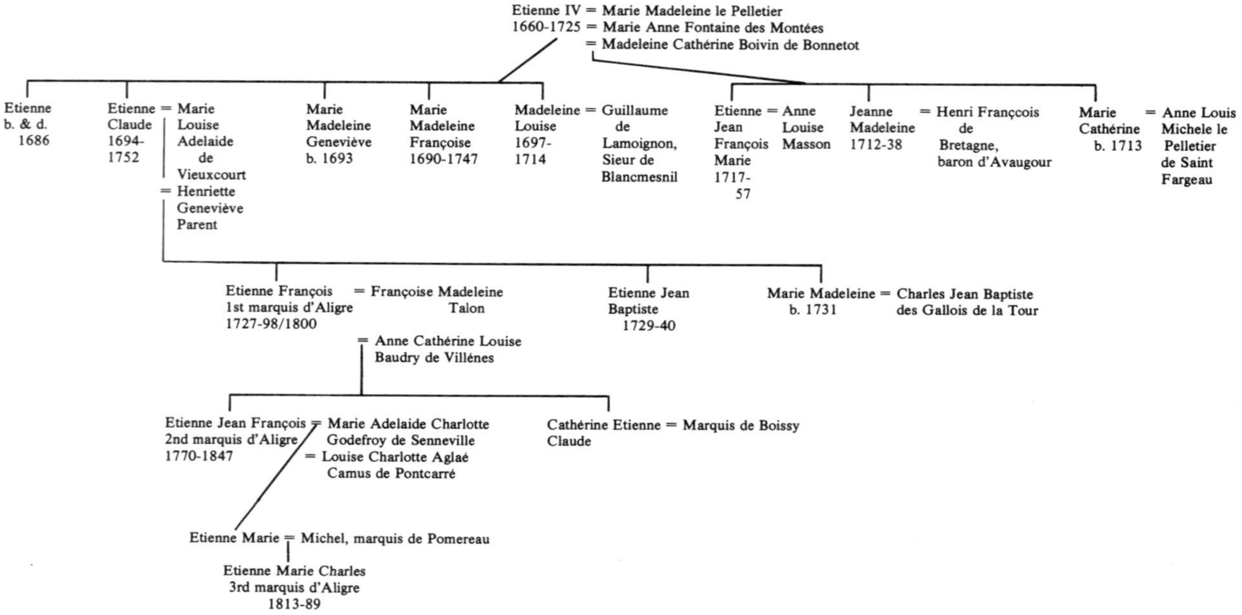

Etienne IV = Marie Madeleine le Pelletier
1660-1725 = Marie Anne Fontaine des Montées
= Madeleine Catherine Boivin de Bonnetot

```
Etienne      Marie           Marie              Madeleine   = Guillaume      Etienne    = Anne      Jeanne        = Henri François   Marie      = Anne Louis
Claude   =   Louise          Madeleine          Louise        de             Jean         Louise    Madeleine       de Bretagne,     Catherine    Michele le
1694-        Adelaide        Madeleine          1697-         Lamoignon,     François     Masson    1712-38         baron d'Avaugour b. 1713      Pelletier
1752         de              Geneviève          1714          Sieur de       Marie                                                                de Saint
             Vieuxcourt      Françoise                        Blancmesnil    1717-                                                                Fargeau
         =   Henriette       1690-1747                                       57
             Geneviève                              Marie Madeleine = Charles Jean Baptiste
             Parent                                 b. 1731           des Gallois de la Tour
```

Etienne
b. & d.
1686

Etienne François = Françoise Madeleine   Etienne Jean
1st marquis d'Aligre   Talon   Baptiste
1727-98/1800   1729-40
= Anne Cathérine Louise
  Baudry de Villenes

Catherine Etienne = Marquis de Boissy
Claude

Etienne Jean François = Marie Adelaide Charlotte
2nd marquis d'Aligre   Godefroy de Senneville
1770-1847   = Louise Charlotte Aglaé
                        Camus de Pontcarré

Etienne Marie = Michel, marquis de Pomereau

Etienne Marie Charles
3rd marquis d'Aligre
1813-89

BIBLIOGRAPHY

A. **Manuscript Sources**
   Archives Nationales
   Minutier Central
   Bibliothèque Nationale
   Archives du Ministère des Affaires Etrangères
   Archives Historiques du Ministère de la Guerre
   Bibliothèque de la Chambre des Députés
   Bibliothèque de Sainte Genevière
   Bibliothèque de l'Institut
   Archives Départementales d'Eure-et-Loir, Chartres
   Bibliothèque de Provins
   Bibliothèque de Carpentras
   Bibliothèque d'Aix
   Bibliothèque de Tours
   Bibliothèque de Rouen
   Archives Départementales de la Haute-Garonne

B. **Printed Sources**

C. **Secondary Sources**

BIBLIOGRAPHY

A. Manuscript Sources

Archives Nationales
Série E 140B, 141B, 149A, 149B, 229C, 231A, 1692, 1693, 1701, 1702, 1703, 1705, 1710-1713
Série K 121, 649
Série KK 626, 638
Série M 260
Série O^1 2, 5, 16, 274
Série S 71, 3765, 6160
Série U 622, 633, 948
Série V 147, 225, 262, 537, 942; V^1 29; V^2 16
Série X 8659, 8718, 8738, 8744, 8775, 17545, 17546; X^{1A} 8665, 8670
Série Y 158, 163, 171, 181, 184, 187-199, 214, 216, 222, 231, 237-239, 243, 245, 250, 269, 270, 274
Série Z^{1A}567

Minutier Central
Etude VIII Liasses 625, 626
Etude XXIV Liasses 222, 223, 226, 229, 232, 233, 236, 237, 249, 253, 322-325, 327, 328, 331-334, 327-348, 416-424
Etude XXV Liasses 435
Etude XXXVI Liasse 103
Etude LI Liasses 83, 84, 86, 87, 89, 94, 95 bis, 96, 98, 101, 103, 105, 106
Etude LXXV Liasses 408, 411
Etude LXXXVI Liasses 125, 223, 262, 266, 267, 270-275, 277-281, 283, 286-288, 291-306, 319, 320, 325, 374-383, 387-389, 392-416, 418, 420-435
Etude CII Liasse 94

Bibliothèque Nationale
Manuscrits Français 3668-3690, 4178, 4181, 4183, 4185, 4212, 4222, 4231, 4232, 4254, 4370, 4583, 6881, 6889-6892, 7545, 7654, 7655, 7736, 9542, 15582, 16218, 16827, 17396, 17414, 18274, 20567, 20652, 32138, 32577
Nouvelles Acquisitions 2770, 3645, 4814, 11643, 23419-23421, 23532-23535
Cinq Cents de Colbert 5, 136, 193, 256, 371, 403, 483
Mélanges de Colbert 108, 109, 130 bis, 138, 144, 156 bis, 158

Collection Dupuy 11, 17, 33, 463, 647, 672, 675, 844, 848, 851
Collection Clairambault 437, 613, 647, 1133
Collection Baluze 337
Collection Châtre de Cangé 28
Collection Morel de Thoisy 48, 85, 140, 203, 222
Pièces Originales 36, 37
Dossiers Bleus 11, 168, 378, 383
Cabinet d'Hozier 7:137
Carrès d'Hozier 16

Archives du Ministère des Affaires Etrangères
C.P. Hambourg 2
C.P. Vénise 43, 44, 45
M.D. France 134, 160, 246, 264, 278

Archives Historiques du Ministère de la Guerre
A[1] 25, 26, 41, 47, 50-53, 77-79, 82-84, 90, 101, 108, 112, 116, 117, 120-126, 132-134, 136-137 bis, 139, 142, 158, 161, 168-170, 206, 213, 215, 258, 375, 689

Bibliothèque de la Chambre des Députés
MSS 242, 351, 352, 353

Bibliothèque de Sainte Geneviève
MS 2156

Bibliothèque de l'Institut
MSS Godefroy 268, 269, 271, 519

Archives Départementales d'Eure-et-Loir, Chartres
a) Archives Départementales:
   B 2971, 4484
   E 13-16, 246
   G 116, 913, 1389, 1428, 3205
b) Archives Communales:
   Chartres E4, 13, 15; LdI2; Sa 3
   Le Favril GG 1, 2, 7
   Pontgouin GG 1 3, 5, 6, 9

Bibliothèque de Provins
MS 239

Bibliothèque de Carpentras
MSS 1780, 1781, 1804, 1871

Bibliothèque d'Aix
MS 1019

Bibliothèque de Tours
MS 1083

Bibliothèque de Rouen
MS 2987

Archives Départementales de la Haute Garonne
C 2304

B. Printed Sources

(Unless otherwise stated the place of publication is Paris)

Avenel, G. d'(éd.), *Lettres, Instructions Diplomatiques et Papiers d'Etat du Cardinal de Richelieu* (8 vols., 1853-77)
Boislisle, A.M. de (éd.), *Mémoires des Intendants sur l'Etat des Généralités, dressés pour l'Instruction du Duc de Bourgogne* (1881)
―――― *Mémoires de Saint Simon* (41 vols., 1879-1928)
―――― *Mémoriaux du Conseil de 1661* (3 vols., 1905-7)
Catalogue des Actes de François I (10 vols., 1887-1908)
Champollion-Figeac, A. (éd.), *Mémoires de Mathieu Molé* (4 vols., 1855-7)
Chantérac, A. de la C. de (éd.), *Journal de ma Vie: Mémoires du Maréchal de Bassompierre* (4 vols., 1870-7).
Chéruel, A. (éd.), *Lettres du Cardinal Mazarin pendant son Ministère* (6 vols., 1872-90)
Clément, P. (éd.), *Lettres, Instructions et Mémoires de Colbert* (10 vols., 1861-82)
Collection des Procès-Verbaux des Assemblées Générales du Clergé de France (8 vols., 1767-8)
Courcel, Baron de, *et. al., Mémoires du Cardinal de Richelieu* (10 vols., 1908-31)
Devic, C., et Vaissète, J., *Histoire Générale de Languedoc* (15 vols., Toulouse, 1872-92)
Edict du Roy sur le Réglement Général des Tailles... conformément à la Déclaration du dix-huictième Janvier dernier, mil six cens trente-quatre (1634)
Eloge de Messire Estienne Haligre, Chancelier de France, traduit du Latin par P. Greslet (s.l.n.d.).
Gassendi, P., *Lettres Familières à François Luillier, pendant l'Hiver 1632-1633*, éd. B. Rochet (1944)

Grillon, P. (éd.), *Les Papiers de Richelieu* (4 vols. to date, 1975-   )
Griselle, E. (éd.), *Lettres de la Main de Louis XIII* (2 vols., 1914)
Harangue de Monsieur le Cardinal, par luy faite en Parlement le Roy y scéant, le dix-huictiesme de Janvier mil six cens trente quatre (1634)
Lenet, le R.P., *Oraison Funèbre de... François d'Aligre, Abbé de Saint Jacques de Provins* (1712)
Lettre Ecrite de Provins du 22 Janvier 1712 sur la Vie et Mort de Monsieur d'Aligre... Abbé Régulier de l'Abbaye de S. Jacques... (1712)
Lettres Patentes de commission aux sieurs d'Aligre et Bignon, pour procéder à la vérification et liquidation des dettes, dont est chargée la succession du cardinal de Richelieu (s.l.n.d.)
Lettres Patentes de commission... à Messieurs d'Aligre, de Lezeau, Camus, Marin et Paget... pour l'entière exécution de l'edict du mois de May 1639, portant création des Offices héréditaires de Contrôleurs des Poids Royaux de ce Royaume... (1655)
Mauniaye Mahaut, Le sieur de la, *Discours sur l'Election de Monsieur D'Alligre à la Charge de Garde des Sceaux* (1624)
Michaud, J-F. et Poujoulat, J-J.F. (éds.), *Cardinal de Retz: Vie et Mémoires* (Nouvelle Collection des Mémoires pour servir à l'Histoire de France... xxv, 1837)
────── *Mémoires de Madame de Motteville* (ibid., xxiv, 1881)
────── *Mémoires du Cardinal de Richelieu* (ibid., xxi-xxii, 1837)
Pelletier [sic.], *Discours à Monsieur d'Haligre, Chancelier de France* (n.d. [1624])
────── *Discours sur la Promotion de Monseigneur le Chancelier et du Fruict que la France en doict espérer* (n.d. [1624])
Relazioni degli Stati Europei Lette al Senato degli Ambasciatori Veneti, Serie II Francia (2 vols., Venezia, 1859)
Robillard de Beaurepaire, C. de (éd.), *Cahiers des Etats de Normandie sous les Règnes de Louis XIII et de Louis XIV* (3 vols., Rouen, 1876-8)
Roussel, Le Sieur, *Discours Panégyrique pour M. le Chancelier* (1626)
Surirey de Saint-Rémy, H. de (éd.), *Registres des Déliberations du Bureau de la Ville de Paris* (xviii, 1953)
Tamizey de Larroque, P. de (éd.), *Lettres de Jean Chapelain* (2 vols., 1880-3)
────── *Lettres de Peiresc aux Frères Dupuy* (7 vols., 1888-98)
Traité sur le Fait de la Marine, fait entre Louis XIV, Roi de France et de Navarre, et les Villes et Cités de la Hanse Teutonique en l'Année 1655 (n.d.)

Valente, P., *Uniaversae Franciae ad Nobilissimum Virum Stephanum Haligraeum Illustriss. Galliarum et Navarrae Concellarium Gratulatio* (1625)

C. Secondary Sources

(Unless otherwise stated the place of publication is Paris)

Standard Biographies

Anselme de Sainte Marie, Le P., *Histoire Généalogique et Chronologique de la Maison Royale de France*. . . (9 vols., 1726-33)
Courcelles, J-B. P-J. de, 'Généalogie de la maison d'Aligre' (s.l.n.d.) (Extrait du t.iii de *L'Histoire Généalogique et Héraldique des Pairs de France)*
Dictionnaire de Biographie Française (1936-   )
Duchesne, F., *Histoire des Chanceliers et Gardes des Sceaux de France. . . depuis Clovis. . . jusques à Louis le Grand XIVe du Nom*. . . (1680)
Encyclopédie Biographique du Dix-Neuvième Siècle: Extrait de la Troisième Catégorie: Illustrations Nobiliaires (1844)
Jouglas de Morénas, H., *Grand Armorial de France* (1934)
Moréri, L., *Le Grand Dictionnaire Historique* (10 vols., 1759)
Nouvelle Biographie Générale (46 vols., 1857-66)

General

Actes du Congrés sur l'Ancienne Université d'Orléans, 6 et 7 mai 1961 (Orléans, 1962)
Adam, A., *Les Libertins au XVIIe Siècle* (1964)
André, L., *Michel le Tellier et l'Organisation de l'Armée Monarchique* (1906)
Antoine, M., et al., *Guide des Recherches dans les Fonds Judiciaires de l'Ancien Régime* (1958)
———   *Le Conseil du Roi sous le Règne de Louis XV* (1970)
Ardant, G., *Histoire de l'Impôt* (2 vols., 1971-2)
Avenel, G. d', *Histoire de la Fortune Française* (1927)
———   *Histoire Economique de la Propriété, des Salaires, des Denrées, et de Tous les Prix en général, 1200-1800* (6 vols., 1894-1912)
———   *La Noblesse Française sous Richelieu* (1901)
Barrault, A., 'Les d'Aligre, abbés de Saint-Jacques de Provins au XVIIe siècle: la réforme des chanoines réguliers (1623-1643)', *Bulletin de la Société d'Histoire et d'Archéologie de l'Arrondissement de Provins* (1958)

Baurit, M., *Saint-Germain l'Auxerrois, son Histoire, ses Oeuvres d'Art* (1952)
_____ et Hillairet, J., *Saint-Germain l'Auxerrois* (1955)
Bayard, F., 'Les chambres de justice de la première moitié du XVIIe siècle', *Cahiers d'Histoire*, xix, no. 2 (1974)
Benoist, L. et L'Huillier, T., *Notice Historique sur Mitry-Mory* (Meaux, 1895)
Berty, A. et Tisserand, L.M., *Topographie Historique du Vieux Paris* (6 vols., 1866-97)
Béthune, P. de, *Le Conseiller d'Estat, ou Recueil des Plus Générales Considérations Servant au Maniment des Affaires Publiques* (1633)
Billot, C., *Chartres aux XIVe et XVe Siècles, une Ville et son Plat Pays* (Thèse de Doctorat d'Etat, 1980)
Bitton, D., *The French Nobility in Crisis, 1560-1640* (Stanford, 1969)
Blet, P., *Le Clergé de France et la Monarchie: Etudes sur les Assemblées Générales du Clergé de 1615 à 1666* (2 vols., Rome, 1959)
Bloch, M., *French Rural History* (London, 1966)
Bluche, J.F., *L'Origine des Magistrats du Parlement de Paris au XVIIIe Siècle* (1956)
Blunt, A., *Art and Architecture in France: 1500-1700* (2nd. ed., London, 1970)
Bodin, J., *Six Livres de la République* (1579)
Bonney, R., *Political Change in France under Richelieu and Mazarin, 1624-1661* (Oxford, 1978)
_____ *The King's Debts: Finance and Politics in France, 1589-1661* (Oxford, 1981)
Bourgeon, J-L., *Les Colbert avant Colbert* (1973)
Braichotte, A., 'L'Abbé d'Aligre (d. 1712)', *Bulletin de la Société d'Histoire et d'Archéologie de l'Arrondissement de Provins*, iii, no. 2 (1898-9)
Braudel, F. et Labrousse, E. (éds.), *Histoire Economique et Sociale de la France* (4 vols., 1970-80)
Brown, H., *Scientific Organisations in Seventeenth Century France* (Baltimore, 1934)
Bry, G., *Histoire des Pays et Comté du Perche* (1620); 2e éd. revue et augmentée par P. Siguret (1970)
Caillard, M. et al., *A Travers la Normandie des XVIIe et XVIIIe Siècles* (Caen, 1963)
Caillet, J., *L'Administration en France sous le Ministère de Richelieu* (2e. éd., 2 vols., 1860)
Catinat, J., *C'est Arrivé à Croissy* (Chartres, 1970)

Chamillart, G., *Recherche de la Noblesse faite par Ordre du Roi en 1666 et Années Suivantes* (Caen, 1887)

Chasles, P., 'Mouvement social de Chartres au XVIe siècle', *Revue des Deux Mondes,* xxii (1848)

Chaunu, P. et Gascon, R., *Histoire Economique et Sociale de la France* (éd. Braudel, F. et Labrousse, E.), i; De 1450 à 1660, Ier volume, *L'Etat et la Ville* (1977)

Chéruel, A., *Histoire de France Pendant la Minorité de Louis XIV* (4 vols., 1879-80)

―――― *Histoire de France sous le Ministère de Mazarin (1651-1661)* (3 vols., 1882)

Church, W.F., *Richelieu and Reason of State* (Princeton, 1972)

Combaluzier, F. et Barrault, A., 'Témoignage de François d'Aligre, abbé de St. Jacques de Provins (de 1643 à 1712) sur Monsieur Vincent', *Annales de la Congrégation de la Mission,* cxxiv, nos. 491-2 (1959)

Corvisier, A., *La France de Louis XIV, 1643-1715* (1979)

―――― *Louvois* (1983)

Cosnac, Comte G-J. de, *Mazarin et Colbert* (2 vols., 1892)

Coste, P., *Le Grand Saint du Grand Siècle: Monsieur Vincent* (3 vols., 1932)

Crot, L. du, *Le Nouveau Traité des Aydes, Tailles et Gabelles* (1636)

Dent, J., *Crisis in Finance: Crown, Financiers and Society in Seventeenth-Century France* (Newton Abbot, 1973)

Dethan, G., *Mazarin et ses Amis* (1968)

―――― *Mazarin* (1981)

Doinel, J., 'Anne du Bourg à l'université d'Orléans', *Bulletin Historique et Littéraire* (Société de l'Histoire du Protestantisme Français), xxx (1881)

Dornic, F., *Une Ascension Sociale au XVIIe Siècle: Louis Berryer, Agent de Mazarin et de Colbert* (Caen, 1968)

Doucet, R., *Les Institutions de la France au XVIe Siècle* (2 vols., 1948)

Doyen, M., *Histoire de la Ville de Chartres, du Pays Chartrain, et de la Beauce* (2 vols., Chartres, 1786)

Dupont, G., *Histoire du Cotentin et de ses Iles* (4 vols., Caen, 1870-85)

Esmonin, E., *La Taille en Normandie au Temps de Colbert (1661-1683)* (1913)

Foisil, M., *La Révolte des Nu-Pieds et les Révoltes Normandes de 1639* (1970)

Fonteny, J. de, *Sommaire description de Tous les Chanceliers et Gardes des Sceaux de France, depuis le Règne de Mérovée jusques au Règne de Louis XIV* (1645)

Garçon, E., *Essai Historique sur le Grand Conseil* (Poitiers, 1876)
Gassendi, P., *The Mirror of True Nobility & Gentility, being the Life of the Renowned Nicolaus Claudius Fabricius, Lord of Peiresk, Senator in the Parliament of Aix,* Englished by W. Rand (London, 1657)
Gilbert, A.P.M., *Description Historique de l'Eglise de l'Ancienne Abbaye Royale de Saint Riquier et Ponthieu* (Amiens, 1836)
Gille, B., *Les Sources Statistiques de l'Histoire de France: Les Enquêtes du XVIIe Siècle à 1870* (1964)
Goody, J., Thirsk, J., and Thompson, E.P., (eds.), *Family and Inheritance: Rural Society in Western Europe, 1200-1800* (Cambridge, 1976)
Goubert, P., *Cent Mille Provinciaux au XVIIe Siècle: Beauvais et le Beauvaisis de 1600 à 1730* (1968)
Guéry, A., 'Les finances de la monarchie française sous l'ancien régime', *Annales E.S.C.,* no. 2 (1978)
Guyot, M., *Traité des Droits, Fonctions, Franchises, Exemptions, Prérogatives et Privilèges Annexés en France à chaque Dignité.* . (4 vols., 1786-8)
Hauser, H., *Recherches et Documents sur l'Histoire des Prix en France de 1500 à 1800* (1936)
Hayden, J.M., *France and the Estates General of 1614* (Cambridge, 1974)
Hénocque, J., *Histoire de l'Abbaye et de la Ville de Saint Riquier* (3 vols., Amiens, 1880-8)
Isambert, F.A. et Taillandier, A-H., *Recueil Général des Anciennes Lois Françaises* (29 vols., 1821-33)
Jacquart, J., *La Crise Rurale en l'Ile de France, 1550-1670* (1974)
Labrousse, E., Léon, P., Goubert, P., Bouvier, J., Carrière, C., Harsin, P., *Histoire Economique et Sociale de la France* (éd. Braudel, F. et Labrousse, E.), ii: *Des Derniers Temps de l'Age Seigneurial aux Préludes de l'Age Industriel (1660-1789)* (1970)
Ladurie, E. le Roy, 'Family structures and inheritance customs in sixteenth-century France' in Goody, J., Thirsk, J., Thompson, E.P., (eds.), *Family and Inheritance: Rural Society in Western Europe, 1200-1800* (Cambridge, 1976)
———— et Morineau, M., *Histoire Economique et Sociale de la France* (ed. Braudel, F. et Labrousse, E.), i; De 1450 a 1660, second vol: *Paysannerie et Croissance* (1977)
Lavisse, E., *Histoire de France depuis les Origines jusqu'à la Révolution* (9 vols., 1903-11)
Lebeurier, P.F., *Etat des Anoblis en Normandie de 1545 à 1661* (Evreux, 1866)

Lecomte, M., 'Une grande figure Provinoise: François d'Aligre, abbé de Saint-Jacques de Provins (1643-1712)', *La Semaine Religieuse du Diocèse de Meaux*, no. 25 (1909)
Lefèvre, E., *Documents Historiques et Statistiques sur les Communes du Canton de Courville* (2 vols., Chartres, 1870-5)
Legrelle, A., *La Normandie sous la Monarchie Absolue* (Rouen, 1903)
Lemarchand, G., 'A propos de la révolte des va nu-pieds', *Annales de Normandie* (1970)
Lemercier, P., *Les Justices Seigneuriales de la Région Parisienne de 1580 à 1789* (1933)
Lépinois, E. de, *Histoire de Chartres* (2 vols., Chartres, 1854-8)
Les Armoiries des Connétables... Chanceliers, Amiraux, Maréchaux de France... depuis leur Premier Etablissement jusques au très Chrétien Roi... Louis XIII (1628)
Lewis, P.S. (ed.), *The Recovery of France in the Fifteenth Century* (London, 1971)
Logié, P., *La Fronde en Normandie* (3 vols., Amiens, 1951-2)
Loyseau, C., *Cinq Livres du Droit des Offices* (1610)
Lublinskaya, A.D., *French Absolutism: the Crucial Phase, 1620-1629* (Cambridge, 1968)
L'Université d'Orléans du XIIIe au XIVe Siècle (Orléans, 1961)
Marion, M., *Dictionnaire des Institutions de la France aux XVIIe et XVIIIe Siècles* (1923)
Marténe, E., et Durand, U., *Voyage Littéraire de Deux Religieux Bénédictins de la Congrégation de Saint Maur* (1717)
Martin, H-J., *Livre, Pouvoirs et Société à Paris au XVIIe (1598-1701)* (2 vols., 1969)
Meurgey de Tupigny, J., *Guide des Recherches Généalogiques aux Archives Nationales* (1953)
Meuvret, J., *Etudes d'Histoire Economique* (1971)
Meyer, J., *Colbert* (1981)
Michaud, H., *La Grande Chancellerie et les Ecritures Royales au Seizième Siècles* (1967)
Michelin, L., *Essais Historiques, Statistiques, Chronologiques, Administratifs, etc., sur le Département de Seine et Marne* (3 vols., Melun, 1829)
Miraulmont, P. de, *Traicté de la Chancellerie, avec un Recueil des Chanceliers et Gardes des Sceaux de France* (1610)
Moote, A.L., *The Revolt of the Judges: The Parlement of Paris and the Fronde, 1643-1652* (Princeton, 1971)
Mousnier, R., *La Plume, la Faucille et le Marteau* (1970)
—— *Le Vénalité des Offices sous Henri IV et Louis XIII* (2e. éd., 1971)

_____ *Les Institutions de la France sous la Monarchie Absolue* (2 vols., 1974-80)
_____ *Lettres et Mémoires Adressés au Chancelier Séguier (1633-1649)* (2 vols., 1964)
_____ *Paris, Capitale au Temps de Richelieu et de Mazarin* (1978)
_____ *Peasant Uprisings in Seventeenth Century France, Russia and China* (London, 1960)
Murat, I., *Colbert* (1980)
Nani, B., *Histoire de Vénise* (4 vols., 1679-80)
Pagès, G. (éd.), *Etudes sur l'Histoire Administrative et Sociale de l'Ancien Régime* (1938)
Parker, D., *La Rochelle and the French Monarchy: Conflict and Order in Seventeenth-Century France* (London, 1980)
_____ 'The social foundation of French absolutism, 1610-1630', *Past & Present*, no. 53 (1971)
Pasquier, J., *L'Impôt des Gabelles en France aux XVIIe et XVIIIe Siècles* (1905)
Peace of Nijmegen, 1676-1678/9, The (International Congress of the Tricentennial; Amsterdam, 1980)
Peigue, M. J-B., *Histoire des Chanceliers de France et des Gardes-des-Sceaux de France depuis Clovis I jusqu'à Louis XVI* (Clermont-Ferrand, 1847)
Peléus, J., *Le Chancelier de France* (1611)
Peronnet, M., 'Généalogie et histoire: approches méthodiques', *Revue Historique*, ccxxxix (1968)
Picavet, C.G., *La Diplomatie Française au Temps de Louis XIV (1661-1715)* (1930)
Pillorget, R., 'Henri Pussort, oncle de Colbert, sa carrière, ses demeures parisiennes, son portefeuille', *Bulletin de Société de l'Histoire de Paris et de l'Ile-de-France* (1967-8)
_____ *Les Mouvements Insurrectionnels de Provence entre 1596 et 1715* (1975)
_____ 'Les problèmes monétaires français de 1602 à 1689', *XVIIe Siècle*, 70-1 (1966)
Pintard, R., *Le Libertinage Erudit dans la Première Moitié du XVIIe Siècle* (2 vols., 1943)
Pithon, R., 'La Suisse, théâtre de la guerre froide entre la France et l'Espagne pendant la crise de Valtelline (1621-1626)', *Schweizerische Zeitschrift für Geschichte*, xlii (1963)
_____ 'Les débuts difficiles du ministère de Richelieu et de la Valtelline (1621-1627)', *Revue d'Histoire Diplomatique*, lxxiv (1960)

Porchnev, B., *Les Soulèvements Populaires en France au XVIIe Siècle* (1972)
Prévost, G.A., *Notes du Premier Président Pellot sur la Normandie (1670-1683)* (Rouen, 1915)
Procès Verbaux de la Société Archéologique d'Eure-et-Loir, xiii-xiv (1914-24)
Ranum, O., *Richelieu and the Councillors of Louis XIII* (Oxford, 1963)
Ravaisson-Mollieu, F., *Archives de la Bastille* (19 vols., 1866-1904)
Ribier, J., *Mémoires et Avis concernant les Charges de MM les Chanceliers et Gardes des Sceaux de France, et autres Discours etc*. . . (1629)
Richet, D., 'La formation des grands serviteurs de l'Etat, fin XVIe-début XVIIe siècle', *L'Arc,* 65 (1976)
Roujon, J., *Louvois et son Maître* (1934)
Rouvier, L., *Les Sceaux de la Grande Chancellerie de France de 458 à nos Jours* (Marseille, 1935)
Saint-Léger, A. de et Lemaire, L. (éds.), *Correspondance Authentique de Godefroi, Comte d'Estrades de 1637 à 1660* (2 vols., 1924)
Salinis, A. de, *Madame de Villeneuve, née Marie l'Huillier d'Interville, Fondatrice et Institutrice de la Société de la Croix (1597-1650)* (2e. éd., 1918)
Salmon, J.H., *Society in Crisis: France in the Sixteenth Century* (London, 1975)
Schnapper, B., *Les Rentes au XVIe Siècle* (1957)
Schwob, E., *Un Formulaire de Chancellerie au XVIIIe Siècle* (1936)
Shennan, J.H., *The Parlement of Paris* (London, 1968)
Siguret, P., *Les Coutumes du Perche* (Cahiers Percherons, vii, 1958)
_____ *Manoirs et Châteaux des Cantons de Courville et de La Loupe* (Cahiers Percherons, xvi, 1960)
Souchet, J-B., *Histoire du Diocèse et de la Ville de Chartres* (4 vols., Chartres, 1866-73)
Sturdy, D.J., 'Tax evasion, the *faux nobles,* and state fiscalism: the example of the *généralité* of Caen, 1634-35', *French Historical Studies,* ix, no. 4 (1976)
_____ 'The formation of a "robe" dynasty: Etienne d'Aligre II (1560-1635), chancellor of France', *The English Historical Review,* xcv, no. ccclxxiv (1980)
Tapié, V-L., *France in the Age of Louis XIII and Richelieu* (London, 1964)
Tessereau, A., *Histoire Chronologique de la Grande Chancellerie de France* (1710)

Tessier, G., 'L'audience du sceau', *Bibliothèque de l'Ecole des Chartes,* cix (1951)
Valtat, M., *Les Contrats de Mariage dans la Famille Royale en France au XVIIe Siècle* (1953)
Vanel, G., *Une Grande Ville (Caen) aux XVIIe Siècles* (3 vols., Caen, 1910-13)
Visme, F.B. de, *La Science Parfaite des Notaires* (2 vols., 1771)
Wolf, J., *Louis XIV* (London, 1968)

INDEX

Abbeville, 188
Aix, 39, 74
Albert, Louis-Charles d', duc de Luynes (1620-90), 206, 207
Aleander, Hieronymus (1480-1542), 14
Alençon, 106, 126
Aligre family, 9-19, 61, 70-6, 212-27
Aligre, Anne d' (1628-69), 167, 221
Aligre, Charles d' (1630-95), 5, 157, 163, 167, 187-92, 196-7, 201, 203-4, 210, 212, 221, 224
Aligre, Claude, baron d'Arcueil, 16-17, 22
Aligre, Elisabeth d' (d. before 1635), 61, 70, 76, 219-20, 222
Aligre, Elisabeth d' (1625-1717), 140-1, 167, 197-8, 211, 221
Aligre, Etienne I (d.c. 1545), 12, 13-17, 19, 228
Aligre, Etienne d' (1624-44), 167, 221, 225
Aligre, Etienne d' II (1560-1635), 1, 5, 19, 20, 95, 166, 189, 215, 219-24; early years, 22-7; property and career to 1613, 27-9; steps to chancellorship, 29-33, 35-6; chancellorship and disgrace, 36-44, 77-8, 80, 88, 158; property, fortune and family, 46-60, 63-4, 69; death and achievements, 70-2
Aligre, Etienne d' III (1592-1677), 1, 5, 73, 77, 143, 145-6, 205, 210; career, 35, 78-93, 96-117, 120-42, 129-31, 143-55, 158-64; property, fortune and family, 18, 59-61, 67-8, 75-6, 165-77, 187-92, 213-24
Aligre, Etienne d' IV (1660-1725), 10, 174, 187, 191, 203-4, 207, 212-22
Aligre, François d' (1620-1712), 5, 9-10, 69, 158, 167, 198, 203, 206; and S. Jacques de Provins, 161, 163, 209-12
Aligre, Françoise d' (1637-1719), 167, 198, 212, 221
Aligre, Gilles d' (1661-1711), 174, 187, 192, 203-4, 213-15, 220-2
Aligre, Guillemin (d. 1503), 9, 12, 15, 18-19, 228
Aligre, Hélène d' (1636-1712), 167, 174-6, 197, 203, 219, 220-1, 222
Aligre, Jean d' (1632-1710), 18, 167, 197, 203, 221
Aligre, Louis d' (d. 1643), 2, 60-9, 71-6, 165, 180, 222
Aligre, Louis d' (1619-54), 77, 167, 169-72, 173, 210, 220-1
Aligre, Marguerite d' (1641-1722), 112, 167, 174-7, 197, 203-7, 209, 219-22
Aligre, Marie d' (1640-1724), 167, 174-6, 197, 203, 205-7, 219-22
Aligre, Michel d' (1623-61), 2, 141, 167, 172-6, 180, 187, 189, 210, 219-21, 224
Aligre, Nicolas d' (1609-36), 36, 61, 68-71, 73, 75-6, 210
Aligre, Raoul, (d. 1591), 17, 19, 21, 25, 26
Amboise, 14, 37
Amiens, 215
Angleberme, Pyrrhus d' (c.1470-1521), 13-14
Anjou, 125, 138
Anne of Austria (1601-66), queen of France, 121, 123-4, 139
Arles, 207
Arragonet, Marie (1640-57), 173

Arras, 13
Asile d'Aligre, 217
Aubespine, Charles de l', marquis de Châteauneuf (1580-1653), 87-8, 91
Aubespine, Claude de l', marquis de Verderonne, 174
Auch, 215
Augustinians, 72
Auteuil, 181, 193, 198, 203
Auvergne, 46
Avaux, Comte d', *see* Mesmes
Avranches, 100, 107, 110, 211
Avron, rue d': d'Aligre residence in, 28, 53, 67-9, 74, 77, 123, 165-6, 177-9, 181, 204
Azay-le-Rideau, 14

Balzac, Jean-Louis Guez de (1594-1654), 74
Bar, Guy du, 196
Barcelona, 170-2
Barillon, Antoine de, sr. de Morangis (1599-1672), 122, 125-7, 129, 134
Bassompierre, François de (1579-1646), 32, 80
Baudouin, Père Robert, 69
Beauce, La, 6, 21
Beaufort, duc de, *see* Vendôme
Belhomert, convent of, 61, 71, 72
Béthune, François de, comte d'Orval (1598-1678), 94
Béthune, Maximilien de, duc de Sully (1560-1641), 64-5, 179
Béthune, Maximilien-François de, duc de Sully (1614-61), 136
Béthune, Philippe de (1563-1649), 81, 91
Bignon, Jérôme (1589-1656), 112
Bigot, Emery (1626-89), 73
Blaye, 120
Blois, 14, 139
Blondeau, Madeleine, 174, 203, 220
Bois Auneau, Les, seigneurie of, 193, 199
Bois de Boulogne, 193
Boislandry, seigneurie of, 64-5, 67-8, 174, 180, 214, 217, 222
Bonaventure, François, marquis de Manneville (d. 1684), 174-6, 203, 206
Bordeaux, 125, 132, 139
Boucherat, Louis (1616-71), 156, 189
Bouillon, *see* Tour d'Auvergne
Boullainvilliers, François de, comte de S. Sair, 196
Bourbon, Anne-Geneviève de, duchesse de Longueville (1619-79), 124
Bourbon, Charles de, comte de Soissons (d. 1612), 20, 22, 27-8
Bourbon, François de, duc de Conti (d. 1614), 30
Bourbon, Henri II de, prince de Condé (1588-1646), 30, 32-3, 42-3, 58
Bourbon, Louis I de, prince de Condé (d. 1569), 20
Bourbon, Louis II de, prince de Condé (1621-86), 123-4, 131-2, 134-9

Bourbon, Louis de, comte de Soissons (1604-41), 28, 30, 42-3
Bourbon, Marie de, princesse de Dombes (d. 1627), 90
Bourges, 61-2
Bourgogne, 59, 132
Bouthillier, Armand-Léon le, comte de Chavigny, 185, 196
Bouthillier, Claude (1581-1652), 123
Brachet, Dom, 188
Brainville, 51-3, 60
Brégy, Nicolas de Flécelles, comte de (1615-89), 128
Bretagne, 29, 59
Brienne, Antoine de Loménie de, sr. de la Ville-aux-Clercs (1572-1638), 38
Broussel, Pierre (d. 1654), 123, 132
Brûlart faction, 31, 33, 37, 88
Brûlart, Louis, sr. de Sillery (1619-91), 185
Brûlart, Nicolas de, sr. de Sillery (1544-1624), 32-3, 35, 38
Budé, Guillaume (1467-1540), 33
Bury, 14

Caen, 99, 107-8
Caen, généralité of, 98-9, 103-4, 106, 108, 111, 173
Caen-et-Vire, 100-1, 106
Calvin, Jean (1509-64), 14, 162
Capuchins, 72
Carcassonne, 138
Cardinet, Jean, sr. de Loigny, 97
Carentan, 99, 101, 104, 107
Carlisle, *see* Hay
Catalonia, 112-13, 115, 127, 169-70, 172
Catholic League, 23-5
Challet, 52, 60
Chambord, 14
Chambre S. Louis, 121
Champrond-en-Gatiné, 64, 193, 199
chancellorship, 33-6, 55-6
Chapelain, Jean (1595-1674), 73-4
Chapelle d'Aunainville, La, seigneurie of, 141, 180, 199
Chapellier, Marie-Elisabeth (1573-1637), 26, 71-2, 220
Charles I of England (1600-49), 124
Charles IX (1550-74), 21-2
Chartainvilliers, 51-3, 60
Chartrain, 60, 159, 217
Chartres, 1, 3, 5, 30, 39, 44, 50, 55, 57, 60, 72, 75, 77, 105, 141, 160, 180, 212, 217, 220, 225; economy and society, 6-9, 10-2, 14-19; and wars of religion, 20-7; d'Aligre property in, 17, 51, 53, 67, 181, 193, 199
Chartres, bishop of, 49, 51

Châteauneuf, *see* Aubespine
Chaudebonne, Claude de, 42
Chaunay, 51-3, 60
Chenincourt, seigneurie of, 181, 188
Chenonceaux, 14
Chevreuse, Mme. de, *see* Rohan-Montbazon
Chonvilliers, seigneurie of, 15, 17, 27, 50-3, 60, 64-5, 67-8
Cinq Mars conspiracy, 74
Clamart, seigneurie of, 180, 199
Coeuvres, marquis de, *see* Estrées
Colbert family, 2, 44-5, 225
Colbert, Jean-Baptiste (1619-83), 118, 146, 148-54, 156, 189, 191
Collège de Clermont, 187
Compiègne, 151
Concini faction, 31
Condé, duc de, *see* Bourbon
Congrégation de S. Maur, 188
Congrégation de Ste. Marie, 69
conseillers d'état, 29
Conti, duc de, *see* Bourbon
Cordeliers, 72
Cotentin peninsula, 98, 100, 105-6, 108, 110-11, 117, 119
Courseulles du Rouvray family, 193, 196, 208, 220
Courseulles, François de, sr. du Rouvray, 60-1, 185, 202, 208, 222
Courseulles, Louis de, sr. de Joudraye-en-Thymerais, 185, 202, 208
Courville, 64
Coutances, 99, 100, 106-7, 110
Coypel, Antoine (1661-1722), 206

Daniel, François, 14
Dauphiné, 59, 126
Deloynes, François, 13
Descartes, René (1596-1650), 73, 162
Descoubleau, Charles, marquis de Sourdis, 185-6
Descoubleau, Paul, marquis d'Aluys, 196
Desguez, Charles, sr. de la Potinière, 197, 201, 208
Dieppe, 176
Dreux, 15-16, 193
Dunkerque, 205
Dupuy brothers, 44, 73-5
Dutch Republic, 38, 79-80, 82

Edeline, Jeanne, 15, 17, 228
Effiat, Antoine Coiffier de Ruze, marquis d' (1581-1632), 43

Elisabeth Charlotte, duchesse d'Orléans (1652-1722), 205
Emery, *see* Particelli
English marriage (1625), 37-8, 41-2, 82
Ensonville, 52, 60
Estrades, Godefroi, comte d' (1607-86), 205-6
Estrades, Louis d', 205, 207-8
Estrées, Annibal d', marquis de Coeuvres, 80
Etampes, 141, 180
Eure, river, 6, 50-1, 193

Falaise, 181, 200
Fargis, comte du, 85-6
Favières, 17
Favril, Le, 49, 50, 60, 180, 199, 214
Feria, Gómez Suarez de Figueroa, duke of (d. 1634), 80
Florence, 84
Fontainebleau, 62, 192, 198, 204
Fôret, La, seigneurie of, 27, 49, 179-80, 199
Foucault, Louis, comte de Daugnon, 137
Foucquet family, 44
Foucquet, Nicolas (1615-80), 143, 146, 149, 200
François I (1494-1547), 14, 16
Frétigny, 64, 65
Frondes, 120-43, 150, 159, 165, 170, 177, 180-1, 184-5, 192-6, 211, 216, 222, 226

Gambaiseul, seigneurie of, 193
Gassendi, Pierre (1592-1655), 73-4
Gaston d'Orléans, *see* Orléans
Gef, convent of, 61
Gellainville, 50-3, 60
General Assembly of the Clergy, 41, 129-31, 141, 143-5, 146-8, 151-5, 163, 200
Germany, 79, 84
Girardon, François (1628-1715), 206
Godefroy, Théodore (1580-1649), 73
Gondi, Jean-François-Paul, cardinal de Retz (1614-79), 124, 132, 136
Goulas, Léonard, 136, 139
Grand Conseil, 22, 23-4, 29, 204
Grisons, 79-81, 86-7
Grotius, Hugo (1583-1645), 72-3
Guienne, 137, 139
Guise brothers, 24
Guynet, Geneviève (d. 1657), 163, 168-9, 173

Hanseatic League, 143
Harel, Dom, 188
Hay, James, earl of Carlisle (d. 1638), 38
Hayes, Les, seigneurie of, 17, 27, 50-1, 53, 60-1, 65, 68
Henri III (1551-89), 7, 22-5
Henri IV (1553-1610), 3, 5-7, 23, 25-6, 28-9, 44, 47, 70, 135, 164, 223
Henriette (1609-69), queen of England, 37-8, 82, 87, 128-9
Herbault, *see* Phélypeaux
Hôpital d'Aligre, 217
Hôpital des Enfants Trouvés, 169
Hôtel d'Aligre, 177-9, 192, 203-4, 206
Huguenots, 8, 20-1, 25, 30-1, 62-3, 79, 82-3
Huillier, Elisabeth l' (1607-85), 163, 169
Huillier, François l', 73, 75, 77
Huillier, Jacques l', 39
Huillier, Jeanne l' (1603-41), 77, 94-5, 112, 165-7, 200, 220
Hundred years war, 15, 222

intendants, 117-19, 121

Jacobins, 72

Knights of Malta, 7, 18, 167, 172, 224-5
Knights Templar, 7-8

Lambert, Jeanne, 17
Lamoignon, Guillaume de, sr. de Blancmesnil (1683-1772), 214
Lande, La, seigneurie of, 193, 199, 201
Languedoc, 127, 138
Languedoc, Estates of, 112-17, 118, 130
Lefèvre, Louis, sr. de Caumartin (1552-1623), 32
Lens, battle of, 123
Limours, 139
Lionne, Hugues de, marquis de Berny (1611-71), 148
Loire, river, 6, 8, 14-15, 22
Longny-au-Perche, 193
Longueville, duc de, *see* Orléans
Longueville, Mme. de, *see* Bourbon
Lorraine, Charles de, duc de Guise (1571-1640), 94
Lorraine, Henri de, duc de Guise (1614-64), 136, 138
Loudun, peace of, 30
Louis XI (1423-83), 13, 18
Louis XIII (1601-43), 3, 28, 37, 40, 43-7, 70, 76, 78, 80, 82-7, 94, 112-13, 119, 158, 164, 223

Louis XIV (1638-1715), 3, 4, 35, 45, 112, 116, 118, 124, 131-2, 135-6, 139, 142, 145-8, 151, 155-7, 159, 164, 177, 192, 205, 223, 226
Louis XV (1710-74), 216
Louis XVI (1754-93), 216
Louis XVIII (1755-1824), 217-18
Louvre, 28, 166, 177
Luynes faction, 31
Lyon, 71, 207

Machault, Cathérine de (d. 1651), 173
Machiavelli, Niccolo di Bernardo dei (1469-1527), 162
Mademoiselle, *see* Orléans
Madrid, treaty of, 80
Maine, 125
Manneville, *see* Bonaventure
Manou, seigneurie of, 193, 197, 199, 221
Mansfeld, Ernst, count (1580-1626), 84, 89
Mantua, 79-81, 85, 89
Maria Teresa (1638-83), queen of France, 146, 205
Marillac, Michel de, sr. de Fayet (1563-1632), 35, 43
Marseille, 74
Marsolières, seigneurie of, 201
Mayenne, Charles, duc de (d. 1611), 25
Mazarin family, 2
Mazarin, Jules, cardinal (1602-61), 45, 112, 116, 120-42, 144-8, 159
Meaux, 95, 200
Médicis, Cathérine de (1519-89), queen of France, 21
Médicis, Marie de (1573-1642), queen of France, 30-1, 42, 145
Meilleraye, *see* Porte
Mercator, Gerhardus (1512-94), 162
Mesmes, Claude de, comte d'Avaux (1595-1650), 91, 129
Milan, 80, 82, 85
Milan, treaty of, 80
Minimes, 72
Molé, Mathieu, sr. de Lassy (1584-1656), 41, 124, 127
Montafié, Anne de, comtesse de Soissons, 28, 30-1
Montlandon, 64
Montpellier, 113
Monzón, treaty of, 86-7, 88
Morangis, *see* Barillon
Mortain, 100, 106, 107
Mothe, La, seigneurie of, 15, 17
Motteville, Françoise Bertaut de (c. 1621-89), 122, 136

Nantes, 138
Napoleon Bonaparte (1769-1821), 214, 217
Narbonne, 113
Necker, Jacques (1732-1804), 216
Neron, seigneurie of, 199, 203
Netherlands, 156
Neufville, Nicolas de, sr. de Villeroy (1542-1617), 30-1
Nimegen, peace of, 205
Neuilly, 52, 60, 64, 67, 180, 199
Nogent-le-Routrou, 64
Normandie, 6, 34, 46, 98-9, 104, 106, 108-9, 113, 117-18, 132, 146 150,184, 200

Olivares, Gaspar de Guzman, count of (1587-1645), 86
Orléans, 7, 11, 13-14, 24
Orléans, Anne-Marie-Louise d', duchesse de Montpensier (Mademoiselle) (1627-93), 124, 132
Orléans, Gaston, duc d' (1608-60), 42-3, 90, 123, 132, 136-40
Orléans, Henri d', duc de Longueville (1595-1663), 132
Orléans, Philippe, duc d' (1640-1701), 124, 205
Orléans, university of, 13-14, 22, 180
Ornano conspiracy, 42-3

Palatinate, 84
Papacy, 79-80, 84
Paris, 6-7, 12, 16, 19, 22-8, 39, 44-8, 53, 55, 60, 68, 72, 74, 88, 95, 100, 105, 107-11, 117-18, 139, 141, 146, 151-2, 159, 161, 173, 179, 184, 192-3, 198-9, 207, 209, 211-12, 220, 222-3, 225; and the Frondes, 120-42
Paris, parlement of, 23, 39-41, 121-38, 216
Particelli, Michel, sr. d'Emery (c.1596-1650), 122-3, 129, 175, 185
Pau, 215
Peiresc, Nicolas Claude Fabri de (1580-1637), 72-4, 81
Pelletier, Claude le (1630-1711), 189
Pelletier des Forts, Michel-Robert le (1675-1740), 214
Perche, Le, 6, 21, 59-60, 105, 159, 193, 217
Perpignan, 69-70
Pézenas, 113
Phélypeaux family, 44-5
Phélypeaux, Louis, comte de Pontchartrain (1643-1727), 156
Phélypeaux d'Herbault, Raymond (1560-1629), 84, 87, 90-1
Philip III of Spain (1578-1621), 80
Philip IV of Spain (1605-65), 85, 113
Piedmont, 127-8

Poissy, 207
Poitiers, 126, 133
Pomereau, Michel-Marie, marquis de, 213
Pontchartrain, *see* Phélypeaux
Pontgouin, 17, 27, 49, 58, 60, 72, 94, 179-80, 199
Pontoise, 146, 152-3
Porte, Charles de la, maréchal de la Meilleraye (1602-64), 122-3
Portugal, 113
Potier, Léon, marquis de Bosuret, 196
Potinière, La, seigneurie of, 201
présidiaux, 7-8
Provence, 59, 74, 106, 113, 132
Provins, 69, 161, 206, 211
Pussort family, 44

Rabelais, François (c.1494-c.1553), 162
Rabutin, Roger de, comte de Bussy (1618-93), 205
recherches de la noblesse, 96-105, 150-1
Réclainville, 25
Recollets, 72
Reims, 7
Renée, duchesse de Chartres, 21
Rethel, battle of, 132
Reynie, Nicolas Gabriel de la (1625-1709), 189
Rhône, river, 207
Rich, Henry, earl of Holland (1590-1649), 38
Richelieu, Armand-Jean du Plessis de, cardinal (1585-1642), 37-8, 41-5, 62-4, 71, 78, 80, 88-90, 92-3, 96-8, 103, 105-6, 109, 112, 117, 119, 159-60, 177, 187, 224, 226
Rivière, La, seigneurie of, 17, 27, 30, 43-4, 49-52, 60-1, 64, 71, 75, 105, 141, 160-1, 179-80, 199, 201, 203, 214, 217, 222
Rochefoucauld, François de la, cardinal (1558-1645), 38, 69
Rochelle, La, 137, 139
Rochelle, La, peace of, 83
Rohan, Charles de, duc de Montbazon (d. 1699), 177
Rohan, Louis de, duc de Montbazon (1599-1667), 136-8
Rohan-Montbazon, Marie de, duchesse de Chevreuse (1600-79), 132
Rouen, 6, 98, 100, 106, 108, 181, 193, 198, 207
Roussillon, 112-13, 115
Rouvray, *see* Courseulles
Rouvroy, Louis de, duc de Saint Simon (1675-1755), 1, 10, 174
Rueil, peace of, 124-5

Saint Baite, 52, 60, 64, 67

Saint Barthélemy, 52, 60
Saint Evroul, monastery of, 69, 70
Saint Germain, 158, 161, 192, 198
Saint Germain l'Auxerrois, 1, 23, 28, 163, 209
Saint Jacques de Provins, monastery of, 69, 71, 173
Saint-Lô, 99, 108
Saint Ménéhould, peace of, 30
Saint Prest, 52, 60
Saint Riquier, abbey of, 187-9, 206-7, 209-12
Saint Simon, duc de *see* Rouvroy
Sanson family, 162
Saumaise, Claude de (1588-1658), 72-3
Savard, Marguerite, 12, 228
Savoy, 79-81, 84-5
Schomberg, Charles de, comte de Nanteuil (1601-56), 113-17, 175, 177
Schomberg, Henri de, comte de Nanteuil, maréchal de France (1575-1632) 32-3, 37-8, 58, 177
Schomberg, Jeanne de, 177
Séguier, Nicolas, 69
Séguier, Pierre (1588-1672), 34-5, 69, 123, 155-6, 189, 191
Seine, river, 6, 15, 207
Sérèsville, 52, 60
Servien, Abel, marquis de Sablé (1593-1659), 143
Soissons, 125
Soissons, house of, 43-4, 70. *See also* Bourbon
Spain, 31, 62-3, 69-70, 80-92, 106, 112-15, 117, 121, 144, 146, 184, 188
Sully, *see* Béthune
Swiss Cantons, 79-80, 87, 89, 128
Swiss Guards, 127-8

Talon, Omer (1595-1652), 120
Tellier, le, family, 2, 225
Tellier, François-Michel le, marquis de Louvois (1639-91), 205
Tellier, Michel le (1603-85), 26-7, 71, 125-6, 133-4, 136, 139, 148, 156-7, 159, 170-3, 190, 205, 224
Thou, François-Auguste de (1607-42), 74
Thou, Jacques-Auguste de, 74
Toulouse, 113
Tour-d'Auvergne, Frédéric-Maurice de la, duc de Bouillon (1605-52), 124
Tour-d'Auvergne, Henri de la, duc de Bouillon (1555-1623), 30
Tour-d'Auvergne, Henri de la, vicomte de Turenne (1611-75), 124, 132
Touraine, 125
Tours, 23-4, 126

Turenne, *see* Tour-d'Auvergne
Turpin, Jean, 26, 94

Uscouan, 52, 60, 64, 67, 180

Vair, Guillaume du (1556-1621), 72
Valognes, 100-1, 104, 107
Valtelline question, 31, 37, 79-89
Vaux, Les, 217
Vaux-le-Vicomte, 146
Vendôme, François de, duc de Beaufort (1616-69), 132, 136, 138
Vendôme, César, duc de (1594-1665), 30
Venice, 78-93, 95, 117, 159-60
Versailles, 4, 158, 161, 192-3, 198, 226
Verthamon, Michel de, baron de Bréau, 143, 174, 203
Vertus, Henri-François, comte de, 214
Vic, Méry de, sr. d'Ermenonville (d. 1622), 32
Vieuville, Charles, marquis de la (1582-1653), 37-8, 43, 133-4, 136, 139
Villeroy, *see* Neufville
Vire, 106

wars of religion, 6-7, 20-6, 222
Westphalia, peace of, 121, 123